The Burdens of All
A Social History of American Tort Law

Joseph A. Ranney
Marquette University Law School

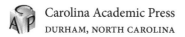

Carolina Academic Press
DURHAM, NORTH CAROLINA

Copyright © 2022
Joseph A. Ranney
All Rights Reserved

LIBRARY OF CONGRESS CATALOGING-IN-PUBLICATION DATA
Names: Ranney, Joseph A., 1952- author.
Title: The burdens of all : a social history of American tort law /
   by Joseph A. Ranney.
Description: Durham, North Carolina : Carolina Academic Press, 2021. |
   Includes bibliographical references.
Identifiers: LCCN 2021041370 (print) | LCCN 2021041371 (ebook) |
   ISBN 9781531023331 (paperback) | ISBN 9781531023348 (ebook)
Subjects: LCSH: Torts--United States--History.
Classification: LCC KF1250 .R36 2021 (print) | LCC KF1250 (ebook) |
   DDC 346.7303--dc23/eng/20211004
LC record available at https://lccn.loc.gov/2021041370
LC ebook record available at https://lccn.loc.gov/2021041371

Carolina Academic Press
700 Kent Street
Durham, North Carolina 27701
(919) 489-7486
www.cap-press.com

Printed in the United States of America
2023 Printing

To Joe Kearney, Adrian Schoone, and Marquette Law School's faculty, staff, and students, past, present, and future

Contents

Acknowledgments	xi
Introduction	xiii
ONE *"Paltry Inconveniences:" Origins of American Tort Law*	3
Cross Currents of Legal Influence	5
Roots of American Tort Law: Property, Individualism, and Proximity	7
Tort Law and Property Rights	8
Individual Rights and Responsibilities: The Free-Labor Doctrine	10
Tempering Negligence by Degrees	11
Tort Business in the Courts	14
Three Small Rebellions	17
The Fellow-Servant Doctrine	17
Burden of Proof as to Contributory Negligence	20
Proximate Cause Revisited: Fire Cases	21
Early Legislative Intervention: Fencing Laws	23
Judges and Juries: Shifting Boundaries of Authority	24
Early Struggles and the Seven Bishops Principle	24
American Juries and Law-Finding	26
Judges, Juries and the Field Code	28
TWO *Leaps in the Dark: The Slow Softening of Fault-Based Law, 1870–1910*	33
The Changing Array of Accident Cases	35

The Push Against Contributory Negligence Begins	37
Distractions and Emergencies	39
Reinforcing Employers' Safe-Place Duties	41
The Continuing Struggle Over Proximate Cause	43
The Place of Children in the Tort System	45
Age-Specific Negligence	46
Parental Imputation	48
The Turntable Doctrine	49
The Rise of Employer Liability Laws and Safety Laws	51
Anti-Waiver Statutes	57
Safety Statutes	59
Judges Versus Juries in the Second Industrial Era	61
A Clash of Sympathies: Real or Imagined?	62
THREE *Saving Capitalism by Making it Good: Tort Law in the Progressive Era*	**67**
Workers Compensation: A Departure from Fault	71
Origins of Workers Compensation	71
The Movement Gains Strength	73
Workers Compensation Breaks Through	77
Workers Compensation Settles In	81
Comparative Negligence: The Socialization of Fault	86
Origins	87
Breakthroughs in Congress, Wisconsin and Mississippi	89
Product Liability Law: The Vertical Integration of Fault	92
The Inherent-Danger Rule	92
The Frontal Assault on Privity Begins	95
Judges and Juries in the Progressive Era	99
Judicialism and the Case Against Juries	99
Progressives and the Case Against Judges	99
Cabining the Jury: Directed Verdicts and JNOVs	102
Cabining the Jury: "Proper Evidence" and Scintillas	103
Streamlining the Jury	105

Contents   ix

FOUR   *The Golden Age of Tort Socialization, 1920–1970*   **107**

    The Rise of Safe Place Statutes   111
    From the Industrial Age to the Auto Age   112
        The Early Auto Age   113
        Socialization of Auto Accident Costs: The Columbia Plan   116
        The Family-Purpose Doctrine   117
        Liability to Auto Passengers   118
    Comparative Negligence: Slow-Growth Radicalism   120
        Early Growth   120
        The Triumph of Comparative Negligence   122
        Aggregation of Negligence   125
    Product Liability: Stopping Short of the Summit   127
        The Campaign Against Privity   127
        The Strict-Liability Campaign   130
    The Erosion of Civil Immunities   135
        Family Immunities   135
        Governmental and Charitable Immunities   137
        The Decline and Fall of Immunities, 1950–1970   140
    Continuing Confusion Over Causation   142
    Judges and Juries: An Old Struggle Takes New Forms   147

FIVE   *Through a Glass Darkly: Tort Law in the Age of Individualism, 1970–Present*   **153**

    The Big Four of Tort Reform   157
    New Battles Over Comparative Negligence: Joint and Several Liability   160
    Medical Malpractice: An Unlikely Flash Point   163
    Product Liability: Holding Back the Sea of Tort   168
        New Problems: Comparative Negligence and the Consumer-Expectations Standard   168
        The Rise of the Risk-Utility Standard   170
        Attack of the Contract Blob: The Economic Loss Doctrine   172
    Immunities Redux   176
        The Fluid Borders of Municipal Immunity   177

The Growth of Customized Immunities	179
The Resurrection and Reburial of No-Fault Auto Insurance	182
Judges and Juries in the Modern Era: Summary Judgment Triumphant	186

Appendix One *Survey of State Court Cross-Citations, 1800–1860* 193

Appendix Two *The Five-State Survey* 199

Appendix Three *Explanatory Notes* 213

Selected Bibliography 221
  Books 221
  Codes, Reports, Treatises and Dissertations 223
  Articles 225

Index 237

Acknowledgments

This is the second book that has been published as part of the Adrian Schoone Fellowship program at Marquette Law School (the first was *Wisconsin and the Shaping of American Law* in 2017). I am deeply grateful to Dean Joseph Kearney for his unfailing encouragement and support, and to Adrian Schoone for his generous gifts to the Law School that made this book possible. I hope they will find this book a useful contribution to the Schoone Fellowship's goal of making the mysteries of the law and its relationship to society more accessible to all.

This book has traveled a long path from conception to publication, and many other people have helped along the way. Sincere thanks to Professor Alex Lemann at Marquette for reading the book manuscript and providing valuable criticism and suggestions, and to others whose criticisms and comments likewise helped make this a better book. I am also grateful for the continuing support and encouragement of Professors David Ray Papke and Dan Blinka, as well as the late Gordon Hylton. Thanks also to Nancy Ranney, Esq. for her valuable comments on the manuscript and her advice from a practicing lawyer's perspective. Particular thanks to Professor (and Gratz College President) Paul Finkelman for his encouragement of this project and for his many writings that have helped me in my own work over the years.

I also owe a debt of sorts to a less benevolent presence. Some of the work on this book was done during the Covid pandemic of 2020–21. The limits that the pandemic placed on access to libraries and other traditional research sources impelled me to explore in detail the vast range of electronic resources now available to any scholar with Internet access. Those resources were essential to the making of this book, as were the collections of the Wisconsin Historical Society, the Marquette and University of Wisconsin libraries and the Wisconsin State Law Library. Last but certainly not least, I am grateful to Keith Sipe and Carol McGeehan at Carolina Academic Press for their encouragement and support, and to all the other staff members whose able work carried this book through the publication process.

Introduction

Why should not the sacrifices of all be taken at once as the burdens of all; not scattering by the way human wrecks to float as derelicts for a time, increasing the first cost till the accumulation disappears from view in the world of consumable things?... Only the lawmaking power can answer.

—Justice Roujet Marshall (Wisconsin) 1911[1]

Tort law, the law of how the costs of accidents and other harms should be allocated, is part of a larger American story. Individualism and self-reliance have always been core American values, but in the late nineteenth century a competing ethic emerged: that in an industrializing society increasingly dominated by large institutions and mass action, socialization of risk and accident costs was morally and practically imperative. The battle between these values has shaped American society from that time to the present. Tort law has been a faithful mirror of that battle.

American tort law was improvised from bits of the common law at the beginning of the industrial age. Since then, many of its parts have been regularly readjusted and lubricated, others have been redesigned, and new parts have been added to ease social friction in the joints and improve performance. As a result, the machine has been perennially complex and often confusing. The intricacies of tort law are difficult for laypersons to understand, and it has been a fertile field for academic and judicial disputation. Many scholars have described the intellectual and doctrinal history of tort law, but no one has attempted a comprehensive social history, an aspect at least as essential to an understanding of tort law's nature, its current controversies and its importance for Americans. This book tries to fill that gap.

---

1. *Houg v. Girard Lumber Co.*, 129 N.W. 633, 639 (Wis. 1911).

Tort law history can be loosely divided into five eras. The first began in the late eighteenth century, as the first signs of the industrial revolution appeared in the United States, and ended about 1870. During the pre-industrial era, the common law created injury liability rules primarily for traditional master-servant and kinship relationships. The industrial revolution brought people into regular contact with strangers, such as factory owners and railroads, for the first time and forced lawmakers to create new rules for injuries arising out of such contacts. Relying on free-labor ideals of individual responsibility and on an instrumentalist belief that the law should encourage business enterprise, early-nineteenth-century lawmakers created a contributory-negligence system that denied recovery to accident victims who were at fault in any way, no matter how minor. In the 1850s, several Midwestern and Southern states tried to soften the system's harsh effects by experimenting with comparative negligence, which allowed accident victims partly at fault to recover an amount reduced in proportion to their negligence; by repudiating the fellow-servant rule which exempted employers from liability when an employee was injured by another worker; and by expanding the scope of acts that were considered proximate causes for which the actor could be held liable.

The second era (1870–1900) reflected the maturation of the American industrial revolution. Railroad accidents dominated state court tort dockets at first, but by 1890 industrial accidents predominated. Americans increasingly realized that railroad and workplace injuries were a social problem, an inevitable byproduct of industrialization that could not be satisfactorily resolved by application of traditional fault principles. During the Granger revolt that swept the Midwest in the 1860s and 1870s, a handful of states eliminated the fellow-servant rule for railroads and their employees. In 1880, Great Britain enacted an employer liability statute eliminating the fellow-servant rule and several other employer defenses; several American states soon copied the statute. Industrial safety laws began to appear after 1880, but they were piecemeal reforms. Lawmakers hesitated to enact comprehensive safety codes, and state courts divided as to whether employers who violated safety laws were liable to injured workers. American reformers gradually began to look at socialization of workplace injury costs but opposition from employers and jurists who favored incremental reform, such as Thomas Cooley and Thomas Shearman, slowed progress.

Next, the book examines the Progressive Era's influence on tort law. Progressives played an important role in three major reforms: workers compensation, the rise of comparative negligence and expansion of manufacturers' liability for defective products. Beginning in the late 1880s, reformers made a close study of workplace injuries and gradually became convinced that such injuries were inevitable, not merely a product of individual fault, and should be handled through some form of social insurance. During the first decade of the twentieth century, they settled on a solution: workers compensation, which would impose absolute liability on employers but would cabin the benefits paid to workers and would virtually eliminate the risk and expense of workplace-accident litigation. They waged a masterly campaign to wean lawmakers, business leaders and the public from traditional concepts of fault. Male reformers such as Carroll Wright and John Commons made a rational, statistics-based case for reform, but Crystal Eastman's stories of the human cost of accidents to workers' families, set forth in her book *Work Accidents and the Law* (1910), the movement's most important publication, resonated with the public in a way that statistical studies could not. Workers compensation laws raised difficult constitutional issues and they appeared in an era when judges regularly struck down other Progressive laws. Reformers received a scare when New York's highest court struck down its state's workers compensation law in 1911, but courts in other states soon rejected the New York court's criticisms and upheld their states' laws, and in 1917 the U.S. Supreme Court gave its approval.

Progressives also struck new blows at contributory negligence. Between 1905 and 1908, Congress and several states enacted laws allowing negligent railroad workers a reduced recovery from their employers when their negligence was slight and the employers' negligence was gross. Several of the laws were soon modified to allow railroad workers to recover in all cases with only a proportional reduction of damages for their own fault, and by 1920 many other states had followed suit. In 1910 Mississippi enacted the first modern comparative negligence law applicable to all tort claims.

Socialization of the cost of product-related injuries also advanced during the Progressive era. The common-law privity doctrine, an instrumentalist doctrine developed by courts at the beginning of the industrial revolution, held that consumers could sue manufacturers of defective products that injured them only if they had purchased the product directly from the manufacturer. The doctrine worked well for a pre-industrial economy in which most products were locally made and sold, but not for the nationalized economy that arose after the Civil War. State courts made limited exceptions to privity as early as the 1850s for products deemed inherently dangerous, and beginning in the 1890s, an increasing number of courts cut through the framework of exceptions and gave all injured consumers the right to sue manufacturers directly.

The mid-twentieth century marked the peak of collectivist sensibilities in the United States. The rise of the automobile, the Great Depression and World War II imbued Americans with a sense of common experience and purpose that made them more receptive than ever before to socializing many of the costs of life, and those sentiments made themselves felt in tort law. Many states replaced piecemeal workplace safety statutes with omnibus statutes imposing a general duty on all businesses to make their premises reasonably safe, and in the process eliminated traditional employer defenses. Not all socialization efforts were successful: as the number of autos skyrocketed, reformers hoped that a no-fault system equivalent to workers compensation could be developed for auto accidents, but a plan developed by Columbia University researchers in the early 1930s failed to gain traction. Instead, auto accident costs were socialized to a limited extent through the spread of auto insurance and judicial expansion of auto owners' liability for negligence of other family drivers. During this golden age of accident cost socialization, American courts also chipped away at immunities created by nineteenth-century judges to insulate from liability relationships and institutions deemed socially essential, including spousal and parental relationships, charities and local governments, from liability for accidents.

Comparative negligence also spread, albeit slowly. In 1931, Wisconsin enacted a diluted comparative negligence system that allowed proportional recovery only to victims who were less than fifty percent at fault. Debate shifted away from the comparative merits of contributory and comparative negligence to the comparative merits of Wisconsin's diluted system and Mississippi's pure system, which allowed victims a proportional recovery regardless of their degree of fault. University of California law professor William Prosser emerged as a giant in the field of tort reform during the 1940s and 1950s; after he endorsed comparative negligence in 1953, the pace of adoption accelerated, and by 1970 all but a handful of states had abandoned contributory negligence. That was not all: between 1940 and 1970, Prosser executed one of the great tours de force of American legal history, using his writing skills and his influence within the American Law Institute to persuade nearly all states to move away from privity and impose "strict" (near-absolute) liability on manufacturers of defective products. But during the 1960s, several states warned that they were not altogether comfortable with elimination of fault concepts in such cases, signaling that the golden age of socialization might be coming to an end.

The 1960s, a time of great social unrest, ushered in the modern age of American culture and of tort law. The modern age has been dominated by a debate between those who support the right to express one's individuality no matter how unconventional it is, a belief referred to in this book as "expressive individualism," and those who believe that allegiance to traditional social mores and an emphasis on self-reliance and individual responsibility are paramount. That debate has also dominated modern tort law, most prominently in the "tort reform" movement, a collective label for a variety of traditionalist efforts to roll back accident-cost socialization. The movement has focused the general public's attention on tort law to an extent seldom matched in tort-law history. Just as labor unions and philanthropic organizations drew public attention to employers liability laws and workers compensation between 1880 and 1910 and consumer advocates drew attention to the flaws of privity during the early twentieth century, traditionalist groups including the Federalist Society, the U.S. Chamber of Commerce, the American Tort Reform Association and the American Legislative Exchange Council have waged a sophisticated campaign in support of tort reform since the 1970s.

The tort reform movement has had many facets. In the 1970s and again in the 1990s and 2000s, complaints about insurance crises supposedly caused by excessive tort damage awards were followed by demands for caps on awards, particularly in medical malpractice cases. Jurists and lawmakers sharply disagreed whether crises existed and if they did, whether they were caused by excessive awards or by economic cycles in the insurance business. States' responses varied widely: some states enacted liability-limiting laws, some did not. The laws have elicited many constitutional challenges, and American courts' responses have been mixed. Traditionalists have also had some success in limiting the reach of contributory negligence: they have persuaded some states to narrow the traditional doctrine of joint and several liability (holding that in cases involving multiple defendants, each defendant may be held liable for all defendants' collective portion of fault) and to choose diluted instead of pure comparative-negligence systems.

Traditionalists have also had success in other areas. They have persuaded many courts and lawmakers that consumer negligence should be preserved as a defense to product liability and that liability should be based on cost-effectiveness analysis rather than consumers' safety expectations. Traditionalists have also waged effective public campaigns painting product-liability plaintiffs as flouters of personal responsibility and painting their lawyers as predators. Many states have adopted an "economic loss doctrine" holding that plaintiffs who purchase products for commercial use must rely on contract rules, not more liberal strict-liability rules. Hopes for an equivalent to workers compensation in the auto-accident field briefly revived in the early 1970s but, as in the 1930s, eventually guttered out. The struggle between expressive individualism and traditionalist views has also surfaced in the field of legal immunities. Many courts and legislatures have revived municipal immunity, and a new generation of immunity statutes has arisen since 1970 to protect a new set of institutions deemed socially essential, ranging from participants in youth sports programs to churches accused of enabling sexually abusive practices by their clergy.

Tort law has evolved not only through the pronouncements of legislators and jurists but through its day-to-day use in the courtroom. The book examines tort law in the courtroom from two perspectives. First, it presents the results of a statistical survey of supreme court tort decisions of five sample states, New York, North Carolina, Wisconsin, Texas and California, at ten-year intervals from 1810 through 2010. This Five-State Survey is admittedly limited—analysis of all of the hundreds of thousands of tort cases that have made their way through American courts since independence would be a herculean task well beyond the book's scope—but the Survey is suggestive of how American accidents have changed in nature over time and how those changes have reflected larger social trends. In particular, it suggests that the movement in tort law away from nineteenth-century idealization of self-reliance to twentieth-century receptivity to socialization was accompanied by a judicial shift away from a mild tilt in favor of defendants to a mild tilt in favor of accident victims.

The book also examines the debate over the proper balance of power between judges and juries in the courtroom, a debate that has continued throughout American history and has had a deep influence on tort law. English common law gave judges the authority to determine what legal rules apply in a particular case but gave juries the authority to determine the facts (that is, what really happened) in cases where there was conflicting evidence. During the American colonial era, juries gained the right to determine the law in seditious libel cases. Nineteenth-century reformers tried to expand juries' law-finding powers, but they were blocked by Massachusetts chief justice Lemuel Shaw and other judicialists, who believed that judges should take a dominant role in deciding cases. American judges stoutly defended judges' power to take tort cases away from juries when they thought there could be only one proper legal outcome.

The struggle between judicialists and advocates of greater deference to juries intensified during the Progressive era. Many Progressives, most notably Theodore Roosevelt, were incensed by court decisions striking down Progressive reform laws as unconstitutional and they, along with prominent judges including North Carolina's Walter Clark and Arkansas' Henry Caldwell, urged limitation of judicial powers. Judicialists pushed back and even argued that juries should gradually be eliminated, as was happening in Great Britain. Judges gradually become more deferential to reform laws, but they have continued to defend their power to take cases away from juries and since the mid-twentieth century they have been aided by a powerful new tool: summary judgment.

Tort law's history demonstrates the resilience of American ideals of individual freedom and responsibility, ideals that survived the maturation of the industrial revolution, the Progressive era and the mid-twentieth-century heyday of collective sensibilities and that have revived and strengthened since 1970. But many of the socializing reforms of earlier eras have also survived notwithstanding the erosive effects of tort law's modern era: for example, contributory negligence, the demise of privity and the partial demise of fault in product liability cases have become thoroughly entrenched in the American legal landscape. Tort law is a product of constant improvisation, a machine that has proved sensitive, if not always immediately responsive, to social and economic trends. Those traits will continue to shape it and ensure its continuing importance in American life during the decades to come. It is hoped that the historical insights this book offers will enable readers to better understand both the course of tort law as it unfolds before them in the coming years and the social and economic forces that will shape that unfolding.

The Burdens of All

ONE

"Paltry Inconveniences"

Origins of American Tort Law

Upon no subject has the genius of our modern jurisprudence developed more complex and nice distinctions; ... no distinctions in the whole range of our jurisprudence are more disconnected and confused.

— American Law Register (1860)[1]

On January 22, 1863, death unexpectedly visited Mary Langhoff, a young Janesville, Wisconsin housewife and mother. Mary was raising three young daughters and an infant son on her own while her husband Herman served with the Army of the Potomac in Virginia. On her last day, Mary went to her neighbor, Elizabeth Hughes, to borrow some milk. In order to reach the Hughes home, she had to cross a double set of railroad tracks that came into Janesville from the north. At the end of her visit she turned toward the tracks and home, trying not to spill the milk.

Shortly before Mary began her errand, two Janesville-bound trains left Milton Junction, about eight miles to the north. The drivers decided to race each other along the double tracks to see who could reach Janesville first. Witnesses later testified that the trains were traveling about twenty-five miles per hour as they and Mary reached the crossing point, even though the state speed limit for trains was six miles per hour within the city. As the trains approached, Mary started running; she crossed the first track but then was hit and fell between the tracks. Mutilated and mortally wounded, she died a few minutes later.

Lawyers for Mary's estate, including future Wisconsin chief justice Edward Ryan, brought a wrongful-death lawsuit against the two railroads that had operated the

---

1. "The Doctrine of Negligence," 8 *American Law Register (O.S.)* 385, 385 (1860).

trains. At trial, the railroads asked judge William P. Lyon to grant a nonsuit—that is, dismiss the case because the evidence presented by Mary's estate showed conclusively that she had been negligent. The railroads based their request on the doctrine of contributory negligence, which held that a plaintiff who helped cause her accident in any way could not recover compensation for her injuries from another, even one whose negligence was greater than hers. Judge Lyon agreed that Mary had been negligent and he dismissed the estate's case without sending it to the jury.

Ryan then appealed, arguing that Mary's negligence was a question for the jury, not the judge. Wisconsin's supreme court agreed. Chief Justice Luther Dixon stated that the engineers undoubtedly were negligent in speeding and that a jury could conclude it was reasonable for Mary to believe, as she approached the crossing with the trains still some distance away, that they were obeying the speed limit and that she would have enough time to cross the tracks safely. In addition, she might not have been aware there were two trains. Dixon and his colleagues sent the case back to Judge Lyon for a new trial.[2]

At the end of the second trial, the jury concluded that Mary had not been negligent and awarded her estate the then-huge sum of $10,000. It was now the railroads' turn to appeal to the supreme court, and this time they prevailed. Dixon focused on evidence that Mary could have seen both trains and that she had paused briefly before crossing the track. "No prudent person," said Dixon, "would have attempted the passage under such circumstances; and the inference of negligence is so clear and unavoidable that no jury can be justified in returning a verdict for the plaintiff." He concluded with a curt admonition: "People who knowingly or deliberately take such risks must suffer the consequences of their own want of care."[3]

Mary Langhoff's case raises many questions for a twenty-first century reader. Why did the law bar her from any recovery when all admitted that the engineers' decision to speed contributed to her death? Why did the law give Judge Lyon power to take Mary's case away from the jury? Why did Chief Justice Dixon give Mary the benefit of the doubt on the first appeal, only to overturn the jury's decision in her favor and dismiss her case two years later? Dixon focused on Mary's decision to run after pausing and concluded that she could see both trains coming, but couldn't a jury have drawn a different conclusion from the evidence? Judge Lyon thought so: he rejected the railroads' request to overturn the verdict in Mary's favor at the end of the second trial before the railroads went to the supreme court.

Mary's case—that of a young mother who left behind children with a father far away and himself in peril—provides a particularly dramatic and tragic setting for these questions, which arose in many early American tort cases. Two overarching

---

2. *Langhoff v. Milw. & Prairie du Chien R. Co.*, 19 Wis. 489, 523–24 (1866); *see also Wis. Briefs & Cases*, Vol. 73, No. 16 (1865), Wis. State Law Library, Madison.

3. *Langhoff v. Milw. & Prairie du Chien R. Co.*, 23 Wis. 43, 44 (1868); *see also Wis. Briefs & Cases*, Vol. 102, No. 7 (1868).

debates dominated the early history of tort law: first, how the costs of injuries arising from contacts between strangers should be allocated among them, and second, what roles judges and juries respectively should have in allocating those costs. These debates were part of a larger discussion of American ideals. Did the benefits of freedom carry a corresponding obligation to bear life's misfortunes on one's own, or did others have an obligation to help alleviate those misfortunes? Were national ideals best achieved through direct democracy, including allocation of extensive power to juries, or a representative democracy in which judges and other political elites would speak for their fellow citizens?

Tort law underscored the difficulty of answering those questions. Contributory negligence quickly became the central principle of early tort law, but its triumph was not inevitable. Courts adopted it with little analysis of its underlying rationale and it soon became encrusted with exceptions. Judges' common-law powers over trial outcomes met an unprecedented challenge in England and America during the eighteenth and early nineteenth centuries, a challenge that went hand in hand with the democratizing impulses of the times, but here too there were countervailing forces. David D. Field's code of courtroom procedure for civil (non-criminal) cases, which most American states adopted during the second half of the nineteenth century, was promoted as a means of making law more friendly and accessible to laypersons, but in the end it helped ensure that judges would retain the upper hand in controlling tort case outcomes.

Cross Currents of Legal Influence

Most accounts of early American tort law focus on the origins of negligence in English cases and then turn to the adoption and occasional modification of English tort principles by American courts.[4] But another question, equally important, has seldom been addressed: to what extent did American federalism influence the early development of American tort law? Did each state follow a unique path in developing its tort law, or were there regional or nationwide patterns of reliance?

Writing in 1823, American lawyer and politician Charles J. Ingersoll observed that English influence remained stronger in American law than in other aspects of national life. He argued that English legal authorities "are received with a respect too much bordering on submission" and criticized "the colonial acquiescence in which they are adopted, too often without probation or fitness." Most modern scholars agree with Ingersoll's observation if not with his criticism.[5] Ingersoll's comments were accurate

---

4. *See, e.g.*, Robert J. Kaczorowski, "The Common-Law Background of Nineteenth-Century Tort Law," 51 *Ohio St. L.J.* 1127 (1990); Gary T. Schwartz, "The Character of Early American Tort Law," 36 *U.C.L.A. L. Rev.* 651 (1989); Fleming James, Jr., "Contributory Negligence," 62 *Yale L.J.* 691 (1953).

5. Charles J. Ingersoll, *A Discourse Concerning the Influence of America Upon the Mind* (1823), 35–36; Jerrilyn Marston, Note, "Creation of a Common Law Rule: The Fellow Servant Rule, 1837–

6 The Burdens of All

at the time he made them, but they became increasingly less so as the nineteenth century progressed. Reliance on English authority. As state courts matured and their own decisions increased in number, their reliance on those decisions and decisions of other state courts and federal courts increased correspondingly.[6]

FIGURE 1.1
Patterns of Judicial Influence in American State Courts, 1800–1860

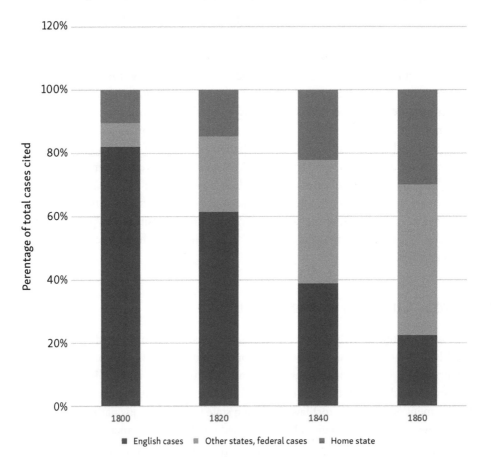

Two states, New York and Massachusetts, exercised outsize influence over American law during the early nineteenth century. They were among the first to authorize and fund publication of their appellate courts' decisions, and publishers in Boston, Albany and New York City disseminated those reports throughout the nation. New

---

1860," 132 *U. Pa. L. Rev.* 579, 589–90 (1984); Kaczorowski, "Common-Law Background," 1182; Schwartz, "Early American Tort Law," 676.

6. Figure 1.1 is derived from samples of supreme court decisions in each state taken from reports covering the years 1800, 1820, 1840 and 1860. The survey data and methodology are described in Appendix 1. The calculations are described in Appendix 3.

York Chancellor James Kent increased his state's influence through his *Commentaries on American Law*, first published in 1826, and between 1832 and 1845 Massachusetts's Joseph Story, when not attending to his duties as an associate justice of the U.S. Supreme Court, published a series of influential treatises on constitutional law, equity, and other subjects.[7] "The [New York] decisions ... have always come to us with a weight of authority," explained Vermont chief Justice Charles Williams, "and, in general, when a subject appears to have been thoroughly investigated by that court, I rest satisfied that they have come to a right conclusion."[8] The two states' influence moderated after 1850 but courts in new states, still in the early stages of legal development, continued to rely heavily on New York cases for guidance. As late as 1863, the justices in far-off Oregon explained that "the weight of authority, as well as of reason and sound policy, are in favor of [commercial] rule[s] as adopted in New York" because "[t]hat is the great commercial state."[9]

Roots of American Tort Law: Property, Individualism, and Proximity

Three themes stand out in early American tort law: the common law's emphasis on protection of property rights; the high importance that Anglo-American society and common law placed on individual rights and responsibilities; and the links that English and American jurists forged between tort liability and notions of proximity and causation. Many early tort cases involved injury to land. Courts were slow to fashion tort rules separate from traditional property-law principles governing such injuries, and elements of property law became permanently embedded in tort law. The contributory negligence doctrine reflected a core common-law value: individuals' rights would be protected, but they should not look to society or the law to relieve them of the consequences of their mistakes. Doing so would place inappropriate burdens on their fellow citizens, violate human dignity and undermine the free-labor ideal that was a cornerstone of nineteenth-century American thought. But many jurists balked at applying these principles in cases where a plaintiff's faults were minor or had not directly caused the injury at issue: they built conceptual structures involving degrees

---

7. *See* John T. Horton, *James Kent: A Study in Conservatism, 1763–1847* (1939); R. Kent Newmyer, *Supreme Court Justice Joseph Story: A Statesman of the Old Republic* (1985). Vermont justice Isaac Redfield also exerted national influence as a judge, as the author of the first American treatise on railroad law (1858) and as editor of the *American L. Rev.* (1861–76). David M. Gold, "Redfield, Railroads and the Roots of 'Laissez-Faire Constitutionalism,'" 27 *Am. J. Leg. Hist.* 254 (1983).

8. *Ives v. Hulet*, 12 Vt. 314, 335–36 (1840) (dissent). Supreme courts in other states made similar remarks. *See, e.g., Brinkerhoff v. Van Sciven*, 4 N.J. Eq. 251, 258 (N.J. 1842) (describing New York as "a people ... with whose laws we are, in many respects, identified"); *Myers v. Standart*, 11 Ohio St. 29 (1840).

9. *Kamm v. Holland*, 2 Or. 59, 60 (1863); *see also* Appendix 1.

of negligence and degrees of cause in an effort to temper contributory negligence without destroying it.

Tort Law and Property Rights

Tort law was first forged during the industrial revolution that began in England about 1750 and in the United States about 1800, but its origins were pre-industrial. For most people, life before the revolution involved little contact with strangers. Disputes arising out of interactions with family members, employers and local officials were resolved through common-law principles designed specifically for those relationships. Most people made their living either as owners or workers of land; property law and the law of master and servant governed that aspect of life. Disputes arising out of commercial relationships, the aspect of life perhaps most likely to involve contact with strangers, also had their own special rules, including contract and bailment law and rules for common carriers of goods and passengers.[10] Rules from each of those common-law fields would play a role in early tort law. The concepts of trespass *vi et armis* and trespass on the case were developed to cover injuries arising in other situations. Trespass *vi et armis* notionally applied to acts such as assault that were inherently wrongful, acts for which the common law held the actor absolutely liable. Trespass on the case applied to acts that were not inherently wrongful but were performed without proper care or regard for others' well-being: this was the first appearance of a concept akin to negligence in English law, but some early trespass *vi et armis* decisions also addressed lack of care. As a result, the issue of when acts causing injury should be evaluated in terms of negligence and in terms of strict liability became confused.[11]

That confusion continued into the early nineteenth century, and it was compounded by the fact that many early tort cases involved property-related injuries that made it difficult for courts to separate tort from property law. Two of the earliest American tort cases, both extensively relied on by courts in other states, illustrated the problem. In *Rust v. Low* (1809), Israel Rust's cattle escaped from his Massachusetts farm and wandered across two neighboring properties before ending up on Abigail Trask's land. Rust sued to get his cattle back from Trask; she then invoked common-law rules allowing landowners to keep possession of trespassing cattle. Rust argued that his cattle had not trespassed because they had come onto Trask's land from his neighbors'

---

10. For example the first book of William Blackstone's *Commentaries on the Law of England* (1765–69), perhaps the most widely-used treatise in both England and America during the century after its publication, was largely devoted to governmental powers; to taxation and local magistrates (Chapters 8–9); and to the law of master and servant (Chapter 14) and family relations (Chapters 15–17). Much of the rest of the treatise was devoted to real and personal property rights. *See also* Morton J. Horwitz, *The Transformation of American Law 1780–1860* (1977), 207–08; Lawrence M. Friedman, *A History of American Law* (2d ed. 1985), 299–302.

11. Kaczorowski, "Common Law Background," 1169–84; *Weaver v. Ward*, Hob. 134, 80 Eng. Rep. 284 (K.B. 1616); Blackstone, *Commentaries*, Book 3, Chapters 8 and 13; *see also* "The Doctrine of Negligence," 9 *Am. L. Reg. (O.S.)* 129 (1860).

property, not his own, and because Trask had not fenced her land as required by a 1785 state statute. After a lengthy discussion of common-law and statutory fencing rules, Massachusetts's supreme court concluded that Trask was entitled to keep the cattle because the cattle and Rust were trespassers in terms of both tort and property law. Fencing obligations applied only between adjoining landowners, and any tort claim Rust might have for loss of his cattle based on failure to fence could only be against Low, his immediate neighbor.[12]

Fifteen years later, in *Bush v. Brainard* (1823), New York's supreme court recast facts similar to those of *Rust* more explicitly in terms of tort. In *Bush*, the plaintiff's cow died after wandering onto Brainard's unfenced property and gorging on maple syrup that Brainard had tapped but had not yet stored. Chief Justice John Savage first analyzed the parties' rights in terms of property, stating that Brainard was obligated to maintain his property so as not to harm others, but he then pivoted to tort: "[I]t is necessary to inquire," he said, "not only whether the defendant has been guilty of culpable negligence on his part, but whether the plaintiff is free from a similar charge." Even though Brainard's leaving out the syrup was "gross negligence," Bush had "no right to permit his cattle to go at large there." *Bush* was the first American case to squarely address contributory negligence, but a lengthy comment appended by court reporter and future justice Esek Cowen made clear that the *Bush* court had been guided by *Rust*. Fencing statutes would continue to intertwine with tort law for many years, particularly during the early railroad era when collisions between locomotives and straying cattle were commonplace.[13]

Cases arising out of contacts between strangers, most commonly highway accidents involving pedestrians, wagons, sleighs and stagecoaches, began to appear in court reports regularly after 1820.[14] American courts rapidly abandoned concepts of trespass in favor of negligence as their preferred analytical tool. Negligence-based analysis had important practical advantages: negligence, a unitary term, eliminated the confusion related to categories of trespass and allowed room for future adjustment of underlying liability principles without any need to abandon the term itself. It took some time for American judges to formulate anything approaching a standardized definition of negligence. Many eventually gravitated to a description of negligence as a lack of ordinary care, following Massachusetts chief justice Lemuel Shaw's lead in *Brown v. Kendall* (1850). "Ordinary

---

12. 6 Mass. 90, 94–102 (1809). States used different names for their highest appellate courts, but all such courts are referred to in this book as "supreme courts" for clarity and simplicity.

13. 1 Cowen 78, 79–80 (N.Y. 1823); Horwitz, *Transformation of American Law 1780–1860*, 95.

14. Early cases in this category that were widely cited by other state courts include *Smith v. Smith*, 2 Pick. 621 (Mass. 1824), *Lane v. Crombie*, 12 Pick. 177 (Mass. 1831), and *Hartfield v. Roper*, 21 Wend. 615 (N.Y. 1839). Tort cases involving damage to neighboring property also continued to appear regularly. Influential cases included *Clark v. Foot*, 8 Johns. 421 (N.Y. 1811) (brush-burning); *Panton v. Holland*, 17 Johns. 92 (N.Y. 1819) (defendant's excavation of his own property undermined the foundations of a building on his neighbor's property); and *Livingston v. Adams*, 8 Cowen 175 (N.Y. 1826) (defendant's mill dam collapsed, resulting in flooding of neighbor's land).

care" represented a first step in defining negligence, but as Shaw himself noted, it left open the question: What constituted ordinary care? That definitional process would be never-ending, influenced as much by social as by legal forces.[15]

Individual Rights and Responsibilities: The Free-Labor Doctrine

The concept of negligence also fit well with the American free-labor doctrine, which celebrated individual self-reliance and hard work and held that success, defined in terms of both material prosperity and personal independence, would come to all who practiced those virtues. Free-labor adherents insisted that individual rights went hand in hand with individual responsibility, and they looked with suspicion on those who sought government assistance or any sort of wealth redistribution as a means of ameliorating social and economic inequality. The doctrine had its origins in sources as diverse as Adam Smith's *Wealth of Nations*, in which Smith described control over one's own labor as a fundamental property and liberty right, and antislavery orators including Abraham Lincoln, who praised the free-labor ethic in an 1859 speech:

> In these Free States, a large majority are neither hirers nor hired. Men...work for themselves..., taking their whole product for themselves, and asking no favor of capital on the one hand, nor of hirelings nor slaves on the other.... If any continue through life in the condition of the hired laborer, it is not the fault of the system, but because of either a dependent nature which prefers it, or of improvidence, folly or singular misfortune.[16]

The core principle of negligence was that defendants whose fault resulted in injury to another must take responsibility for their actions, but the contributory negligence doctrine held with equal firmness that those who were injured must do the same: if their actions contributed to their injuries in any way, they must bear the loss and the law would not help them, even against others who were more at fault than they were.[17] Some historians have pointed to two English cases, *Butterfield v. Forrester* (1809) and *Flower v. Adam* (1810) as the cases most responsible for implanting contributory negligence in American law, but American contributory negligence was largely homegrown.[18] One of the strongest judicial expressions of free-labor sentiment and support

---

15. *Brown*, 60 Mass. 292, 296 (1850) (stating that what is ordinary care "will vary with the circumstances of cases").

16. Adam Smith, *An Inquiry Into the Nature and Causes of the Wealth of Nations* (1776), Book 1, Chapter 10; Lincoln speech at Milwaukee, Wisconsin, September 30, 1859, in Roy P. Basler, ed., *Abraham Lincoln: His Speeches and Writings* (1946), 500–01.

17. William E. Forbath, "The Ambiguities of Free Labor: Labor and the Law in the Gilded Age," 1985 *Wis. L. Rev.* 767, 768–69, 779–86 (1985); *see* Eric Foner, *Free Soil, Free Labor, Free Men: The Ideology of the Republican Party Before the Civil War* (1970), Chapter 1.

18. *Butterfield*, 11 East 60, 103 Eng. Rep. 926 (K.B.1809); *Flower*, 2 Taunt. 214, 127 Eng. Rep. 1098 (C.P. (1810); *see* Kaczorowski, "Common-Law Background," 1189–92; James, "Contributory Negligence," 692–93; *see also* Figure 1.1 and accompanying text.

for the contributory negligence doctrine came from Cowen, now a member of New York's supreme court, in *Hartfield v. Roper* (1839), an influential early case. "[W]hen [a plaintiff] complains of wrong to himself," said Cowen, "the defendant has a right to insist that he should not have been the heedless instrument of his own injury. He cannot, more than any other, make a profit of his own wrong." American state courts occasionally cited *Butterfield* and *Flower* in their tort decisions but relied more frequently on *Hartfield* and other American authorities. And English courts moved away from contributory negligence more quickly than their American counterparts: as early as 1840 they began to limit the doctrine to cases in which a plaintiff's negligence had "substantially" contributed to his injury.[19]

The individualist mindset that dominated the common law and drove the free-labor doctrine during the nineteenth century made it difficult for most American jurists to conceive of, let alone adopt a comparative-negligence system that would allow injury victims to recover compensation from negligent defendants with some reduction for their own fault; but during the 1850s and 1860s a handful of states, most notably Illinois and Georgia, experimented with rudimentary comparative negligence systems. The experiments had only limited success: comparative negligence would not be seriously discussed in the United States for another half century and would not be widely adopted for another half century after that.[20] Until then, most states looked at tempering contributory negligence rather than rejecting it.

Tempering Negligence by Degrees

Some American courts tried to ameliorate the harsher aspects of contributory negligence by viewing it in terms of degrees. They formulated two degree-based scales, one based on remote and proximate cause and the other based on gross, ordinary and slight negligence. Vermont justice Isaac Redfield and his colleagues made the first important connection between causation and proximity in *Trow v. Vermont Central Railway Co.* (1852). *Trow* was a "livestock" case: the Vermont Central failed to erect

---

19. *Hartfield*, 21 Wend. at 620; W.R. Cornish and G. de N. Clark, *Law and Society In England* (1989), 495 and 495 n.72, citing *Sills v Brown*, 9 C. & P. 601 (1840) and stating that the "severer test" of pure contributory negligence "did not survive." In 1858, Isaac Redfield characterized *Hartfield* as an unusually harsh case and noted that other state courts had already tried to develop devices for tempering contributory negligence's inherent harshness. Redfield, *Treatise on the Law of Railroads* (1858), 330.

20. See *Aurora Branch R. Co. v. Grimes*, 13 Ill. 585 (1852) (applying contributory negligence); *Galena & Chi. Union R. Co. v. Jacobs*, 20 Ill. 478 (1858) (applying comparative negligence); *City of Lanark v. Dougherty*, 38 N.E. 892 (Ill. 1894) and *Lake Shore & Mich. S. R. Co. v. Hessions*, 37 N.E. 905 (Ill. 1894) (abandoning comparative negligence); Ga. Code (1860–62), §§ 2914, 2979 (adopting comparative negligence); *Macon & Western R. Co. v. Winn*, 26 Ga. 250 (1858); *Flanders v. Meath*, 27 Ga. 358 (1859). *See also* Chapter 3 and *Whirley v. Whiteman*, 38 Tenn. 609 (1858) (arguably endorsing comparative negligence); Leon Green, "Illinois Negligence Law," 39 *Ill. L. Rev.* 36, 46–54 (1944); E.A. Turk, "Comparative Negligence on the March—Part II," 28 *Chi.-Kent L. Rev.* 304, 305–13, 326–33 (1950).

fences along its right-of-way, and when Jones Trow's horse wandered onto the right-of-way it was struck and killed by a locomotive. Trow did not claim the engineer was at fault but based his negligence claim on the Vermont Central's failure to erect protective fencing. The railroad responded that Trow was contributorily negligent because he had failed to keep his horse under control and had frequently allowed it to wander onto the tracks before the day of the accident.[21]

Redfield and his colleagues held that Trow was as much at fault as the railroad because each party's negligence "was the remote cause of the injury, and equally contributed to the result." The justices explained that "remote negligence" meant negligence remote in time from the injury and that where both parties' negligence was remote the plaintiff could not recover. But they then carved an opening in the wall of contributory negligence: a plaintiff whose negligence was remote could recover if the defendant's negligence proximately caused his injury. The justices then sent the case back for a new trial, suggesting to Trow that he should consider making a claim against the engineer. If Trow could show that the accident "might have been avoided by the defendant, in the exercise of reasonable care and prudence"—in the words of later commentators, if the engineer had a "last clear chance" to avoid the collision—then the engineer's negligence would be considered a proximate cause and Trow could recover. Other courts soon endorsed the doctrine: if contributory negligence were applied without regard to proximity, Chief Justice Dixon argued, "[t]he bitterness and animosities which would be engendered on the part of those suffering wrongs would be productive of far greater evils than the paltry inconveniences to which companies may sometimes be subjected, could possibly counterbalance." Dixon did not say whether he would likewise consider a proximately negligent injury victim's loss to be a "paltry inconvenience," but the logic of his comment extended to both situations.[22]

Justice Isaac Redfield of Vermont. Engraved by A.H. Ritchie (1860). Courtesy Wikimedia Commons

---

21. 24 Vt. 487, 488–89 (1852).
22. 24 Vt. at 494–95; *Stucke v. Milw. & Miss. R. Co.*, 9 Wis. 202, 219–20 (1859).

Esek Cowen formulated a degrees-of-negligence scale in *Hartfield*.[23] A sleigh driver had run over a two-year-old child at the bottom of a hill even though he could have seen the child from some distance away; he argued that the parents had failed to supervise their child and that their negligence, imputable to the child, barred recovery. Some judges (Redfield comes to mind) might have refused imputation or concluded that the driver's conduct was proximate to the accident and the parents' conduct remote, which would have allowed the child to recover; but Cowen viewed the situation very differently. He rationalized that the driver must have been distracted by the need to manage his horses and sleigh. He then excoriated the parents and held that they were grossly (that is, willfully or recklessly) negligent, which would have barred recovery even if the driver had been ordinarily negligent (that is, had failed to exercise ordinary care), although in Cowen's view the driver was not negligent at all. Cowen couched his decision partly in terms of economic benefit: if drivers were held to a high standard of care, he reasoned, rural roads would "become of very little use" for the fast travel "for which they were principally intended." Cowen derived the distinction between gross and ordinary negligence from English bailment law, which provided that bailees (persons charged with the care of others' property) would be held to a standard of extraordinary, ordinary or no care depending on their relationship with the bailor (customer). English courts had previously indicated that the degrees of bailment care might be usefully translated into degrees of negligence, but *Hartfield* was the first American case in which that translation was made.[24]

Cowen's degrees-of-negligence framework was fashionable for a time, but unlike Cowen many courts used it to ease plaintiffs' legal burden, holding that ordinary negligence would not bar recovery from defendants guilty of gross negligence.[25] In the end, the framework proved too difficult to apply. Other courts began to criticize it in the 1850s, Cowen's successors repudiated it in 1862, and in 1869 Thomas Shearman and Amasa Redfield, the authors of the era's leading tort law treatise, effectively pronounced the framework dead.[26] Vermont's framework of remote and proximate cause

---

23. Fifteen years earlier, Redfield had hinted that in cases involving defendants whose business was public or partly public in nature, such as municipalities and railroads, plaintiffs should be able to recover even where the proximity of negligence was the same on both sides. *Hunt v. Town of Pownal*, 9 Vt. 411, 418 (1837).

24. *Hartfield*, 21 Wend. at 618–20, *see also Coggs v. Bernard*, 2 Ld. Raym. 909 (1703); Kaczorowski, "Common-Law Background," 1133–36. Typically, bailees acting for their own benefit (for example, for pay) were obligated to use extraordinary care, bailees acting both for their and the bailor's benefit (for example, where both sides had an interest in the property) were required to use ordinary care, and bailees acting for the bailor's benefit only were required to use only slight care.

25. *See, e.g., Kerwhacker v. Cleve., Columbus & Cinn. R. Co.*, 3 Ohio St. 172 (1854); *Evansville & Crawford R. Co. v. Lowdermilk*, 15 Ind. 120 (1860); *Whirley v. Whiteman*, 38 Tenn. (1 Head) 610 (1858).

26. *Neal v. Gillett*, 23 Conn. 437 (1855); *Wells v. N.Y. Cent. R. Co.*, 10 Smith (24 N.Y.) 181 (1862); *Wilds v. Hudson Riv. R. Co.*, 10 Smith (24 N.Y.) 430 (1862); *see also, e.g., Catawissa R. Co. v. Armstrong*, 49 Penn. St. 186 (1865); Thomas Shearman and Amasa Redfield, *A Treatise on the Law of Negligence* (1869), §§ 16, 37.

proved more durable, but American courts constantly struggled to define proximate cause. Early decisions adopting the Vermont framework produced definitions including acts "directly contributing" to an accident, acts after which the accident became unavoidable,[27] acts "which directly or by natural consequences conduced to the injury,"[28] and acts "simultaneous in operation with that of the defendants, of the same kind, immediate, growing out of the same transaction."[29] These efforts produced more confusion than clarity. Even luminaries such as Massachusetts chief justice Lemuel Shaw conceded that "[t]he whole doctrine of causation…is of profound difficulty, even if it may not be said of mystery,"[30] and tort law scholars such as Shearman and Redfield and Michigan chief justice Thomas Cooley were unable to cut the knot of confusion.[31] Proximate cause became a malleable concept, often tailored to fit individual cases based on judges' sensibilities, and by the middle of the twentieth century most American courts would openly acknowledge that fact.

Tort Business in the Courts

What types of tort cases came before state courts during the early years of American tort law? How did the mix of cases change over time? A survey of tort cases appearing at ten-year intervals in the highest courts of five states selected for geographical diversity, New York, North Carolina, Wisconsin, Texas and California, provides some useful clues.[32]

The Five-State Survey suggests that debt-related cases accounted for a substantial portion of early American tort litigation. During the early nineteenth century, many states allowed arrest and imprisonment of delinquent debtors at the request of their creditors in order to pressure them to pay their debts either directly or with the help of friends. Creditors could also obtain warrants from magistrates requiring sheriffs to seize debtors' assets without giving the debtor an opportunity to be heard prior to seizure. When mistakes were made, debtors often sued creditors and officials for

---

27. *Button v. N.Y. Cent. R. Co.*, 4 Smith (18 N.Y.) 248, 254, 258 (1858).
28. *Richmond v. Sacramento Vall. R. Co.*, 18 Cal. 351, 357 (1861).
29. *Isbell v. N.Y. & New Haven R. Co.*, 27 Conn. 393, 406 (1858).
30. *Marble v. City of Worcester*, 4 Gray (70 Mass.) 395, 398 (1855). For an example of the continuing confusion in one state, *see Pritchard v. La Crosse & Milw. R. Co.*, 7 Wis. 200 (1858) (attempting to equate proximate cause with gross negligence); *Stucke v. Milw. & Miss. R. Co.*, 9 Wis. 202 (1859; *Chi. & Nw. R. Co. v. Goss*, 17 Wis. 428 (1863); *Galpin v. Chi. & Nw. R. Co.*, 19 Wis. 637 (1865); *Fisher v. Farmers' Loan & Trust Co.*, 21 Wis. 74 (1866).
31. *See* Shearman and Redfield, *Treatise*, § 33 (stating that "proximate" means "near in the order of causation"); Thomas M. Cooley, *Treatise on the Law of Torts or the Wrongs Which Arise Independent of Contract* (1880), 68–69 (defining a proximate cause as one "from which…the injury followed as a direct and immediate consequence" and suggesting that the foreseeability of the harm might play a role in determining proximity).
32. Figure 1.2 is derived from the Five-State Survey. The Survey data and methodology are described in Appendix 2. The calculations for Figure 1.2 are described in Appendix 3.

wrongful imprisonment and wrongful seizure of assets. After 1840, as many states abolished imprisonment for debt and debt-collection assistance became a smaller part of local law enforcement, the number of debt-related tort cases dropped sharply.[33]

FIGURE 1.2

Five-State Survey: Types of Tort Cases, 1810–1870

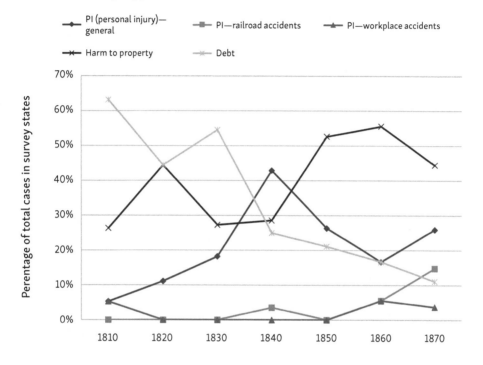

Property-related disputes also accounted for a large portion of early tort cases. Prior to 1860, most such disputes involved unauthorized encroachment on land by neighbors or their livestock. After that time, claims for new types of encroachment reflecting the industrial age appeared, such as landowner claims for damage caused by construction of railroads, streets and utility systems and by factories that produced noxious waste, and claims against railroads for loss of livestock that strayed onto their tracks. Personal-injury cases accounted for a smaller but significant portion of tort cases. Prior to 1850 most such cases involved claims for assault and battery arising out of fights, but after that time a steadily increasing number involved railroad and work-

---

33. *See generally* Peter J. Coleman, *Debtors and Creditors in America: Insolvency, Imprisonment, Debt, and Bankruptcy, 1607–1900* (1974). For examples of early cases *see Peters v. Henry*, 6 Johns. 121 (N.Y. 1810) and *Ballou v. Kip*, 7 Johns. 174 (N.Y. 1810).

place accidents. That increase would accelerate during the late nineteenth century as the United States continued to industrialize.[34]

Many legal historians, most notably J. Willard Hurst and Morton Horwitz, have used the concept of instrumentalism to explain early-nineteenth-century legal history. They argue that during that era "release of individual creative energy was the dominant value," one that embodied a "preference...for property put to creative new use rather than property content with what it is," and that legislators and courts shaped the law to accommodate that preference, rejecting the common law's traditional preference of landowners' rights where those rights and entrepreneurs' interests conflicted. Horwitz, relying mainly on court decisions in northeastern states, has argued that judges systematically favored railroads and other fledgling industrial-era enterprises over accident victims in tort cases, although studies of early-nineteenth-century tort decisions in other states have cast doubt on his conclusion.[35]

Railroads were regularly sued by employees, passengers, and bystanders who had been injured as a result of derailments and collisions at crossings and in freight yards. Railroads accounted for a large and growing portion of the American economy, thus, if state courts had wanted to shape the law instrumentally to promote economic growth, one would have expected them to reverse trial court decisions favoring plaintiffs more often than decisions favoring railroads. But the Five-State Survey, while not conclusive, suggests that any pro-railroad bias was weak at best. Plaintiffs prevailed in the trial court in nearly all of the Survey's railroad cases; state supreme courts upheld trial-court results in nearly sixty percent of those cases and sent thirty-seven percent back for a new trial, usually based on procedural errors at the first trial. They overturned trial-court decisions and awarded judgment to railroads on the merits in only five percent of cases, and they also occasionally reversed trial-court decisions in favor of railroads.[36]

---

34. The Five-State Survey cases on which these statements and Figure 1.3 are based are identified in Appendix 2.

35. Hurst, *Law and the Conditions of Freedom in the Nineteenth-Century United States* (1956), 7, 28; Horwitz, *Transformation of American Law 1780–1860* (1977), 16–30, 63–139; Gary T. Schwartz, "Tort Law and the Economy in Nineteenth-Century America: A Reinterpretation," 90 *Yale L.J.* 1717 (1981) (concluding that New Hampshire and California courts showed no instrumentalist bias); James L. Hart, Note, "Private Law and Public Policy: Negligence Law and Political Change in Nineteenth-Century North Carolina," 66 *N.C. L. Rev.* 421 (1988) (similar conclusion for North Carolina); Schwartz, "The Character of Early American Tort Law," 36 *UCLA L. Rev.* 641 (1989) (similar conclusions for Delaware, Maryland and South Carolina); Wex S. Malone, The Formative Era of Contributory Negligence," 41 *Ill. L. Rev.* 151 (1946) (similar conclusions for New York and Illinois); Nathan Honson, "Iowa Tort History, 1839–1869: Subsidization of Enterprise or Equitable Allocation of Liability?", 81 *Iowa L. Rev.* 811 (1996) (similar conclusion for Iowa).

36. *See* Appendix 3.

Three Small Rebellions

During the early years of American tort law, several issues sparked particular controversy: whether employers should be held liable for an employee's injuries caused by the negligence of fellow workers; whether the burden of proof as to contributory negligence should be placed on plaintiffs or defendants; and how far the concept of proximate cause should be extended in cases of damage caused by the spread of fire. Courts initially created rules in these areas favoring enterprise and requiring accident victims to bear the burden of economic growth, but dissent soon surfaced, and the ensuing controversies proved to be the opening of a larger debate over the allocation of accident costs that would transform tort law over the course of the next century.

The Fellow-Servant Doctrine

During the pre-industrial era, when most employers and employees had personal as well as workplace connections, the doctrine of *respondeat superior* governed employers' liability to injured workers for the negligence of fellow employees: employers were liable for all harm that their employees caused to others. During the eighteenth century, English judges gradually carved out an exception for workers' willful wrongdoing, and as corporations proliferated and employer-employee relationships became less intimate and more contractual, jurists increasingly suggested that existing doctrine was too paternalistic and should be further circumscribed. In *Priestley v. Fowler* (1837), Lord Abinger, the chief judge of England's Court of Exchequer, refused to hold an employer liable to a worker for an injury caused by the negligence of a fellow employee, and in *Farwell v. Boston & Worcester R. Corp.* (1842), Massachusetts chief justice Lemuel Shaw and his colleagues followed suit.[37]

In *Farwell*, a railroad engineer sued his employer after he was injured in a derailment caused by a switchman's negligence. Shaw recognized that in light of the rapid growth of railroads and worker injuries, his decision would have important economic and social consequences. Echoing free-labor principles, he concluded that engineer Farwell had agreed to assume the "natural and ordinary risks and perils incident to the performance of such services" in return for higher pay which reflected that risk. This was not mere rationalization: there is evidence that some railroad workers in high-risk positions received premium pay and that some railroads agreed to continue workers' employment or make severance payments and to cover part or all of their medical bills after injury. Injured workers could also seek compensation from negligent fellow workers as well as their employers, and this was not an entirely hollow remedy. Even

---

37. *Priestley*, 3 Mees. & W. 1, 150 Eng. Rep. 1030 (Exch. 1837); *Farwell*, 45 Mass. 49 (1842); Marston, "Fellow Servant Rule," 584–86; Joseph Story, *Commentaries on the Law of Agency* (2d ed. 1844), §§ 453d, 453e, 453f. Story reviewed *Priestley* and *Farwell* and suggested that employers should not be held liable for negligence of a worker's fellow employees unless the employer had directly participated in the negligence.

so, Shaw relied on general impressions of these alternative avenues of relief and made no effort to examine just how useful they would be.[38]

Shaw also reasoned that workers were in at least as good a position as employers to detect and prevent unsafe practices by their fellow workers: if their employer refused to remedy such practices, they could always quit and work elsewhere. Shaw recognized that workers could not always detect safety violations, for example those of workers in company departments different from their own. But because "it would be extremely difficult to establish a practical rule" determining when an injured worker did and did not have the power to prevent other workers' negligence, he would not allow any exceptions to the new fellow-servant doctrine. Shaw took pains to add that he and his colleagues were not abolishing *respondeat superior* altogether for worker injuries: if an employer violated a direct duty to the worker, such as its duty to hire reliable fellow workers and provide safe tools and equipment, it might still be liable.[39]

Many state courts endorsed Shaw's decision and adopted the fellow-servant doctrine in the 1840s and 1850s,[40] but the doctrine encountered resistance in the South and Midwest. Southern courts adopted the doctrine for white workers[41] but refused to extend it to enslaved workers. Slaveowners sometimes hired out slaves whose labor was not needed on the plantation to railroads, shipowners and small businesses, and the idea that slaves could refuse to work in unsafe conditions was antithetical to Southern notions of racial hierarchy. The real issue, as perceived by most Southern courts, was whether the loss from a hired slave's injury should fall on his owner or his employer. The issue first came up for decision in *Scudder v. Woodbridge* (1846), in which a planter who had hired out his slave Ned to work on a vessel plying Georgia's coastal waters sued the vessel's owner after Ned drowned due to another worker's carelessness. After explaining that the fellow-servant doctrine was not suited to

---

38. *Farwell*, 45 Mass. at 57–61; Robert J. Kaczorowski, "From Petitions for Gratuities to Claims for Damages: Personal Injuries and Railroads During the Industrialization of the United States," 57 *Am. J. Leg. Hist.* 261 (2017); Schwartz, "Early American Tort Law," 708–11; Peter Karsten, *Heart Versus Head: Judge-Made Law in Nineteenth-Century America* (1997), 116.

39. 45 Mass. at 57–60; Marston, "Fellow Servant Rule," 592–96; Alfred Konefsky, "'As Best to Subserve Their Own Interests': Lemuel Shaw, Labor Conspiracy and Fellow Servants," 7 *Law & Hist. Rev.* 219, 224–28 (1989).

40. See, e.g., *Murray v. S.C. R.R.*, 1 McMull. 385 (S.C.L. 1841); *Brown v. Maxwell*, 6 Hill 594 (N.Y. Ct. Corr. Errors 1844); *Ryan v. Cumberland Vall. R. Co.*, 23 Pa. St. 384 (1854); *Honner v. Ill. Cent. R. Co.*, 15 Ill. 550 (1854); *Mich. Cent. R. Co. v. Leahey*, 10 Mich. 193 (1862). Scotland's Court of Sessions rejected the fellow-servant doctrine for Scotland in 1862, but six years later the House of Lords held that the doctrine as set forth in *Priestley* applied throughout the United Kingdom. *Dixon v. Rankin*, 14 Cas. Sess. (N.S.) 480 (Scot. Ct. Sess. 1852); *Bertonshill Coal Co. v. Reid*, 3 Macq. H.L. 206 (H.L. 1858).

41. *See, e.g., Murray*, 1 McMul. 385 (S.C.L. 1841); *Scudder v. Woodbridge*, 1 Ga. 195 (1846); *Hubgh v. New Orleans & Carrollton R. Co.*, 6 La. Ann. 495 (1851); *Forsyth & Simpson v. Perry*, 5 Fla. 337 (1853); *Walker v. Bolling*, 22 Ala. 294 (1853); *Ponton v. Wilm. & Weldon R. Co.*, 51 N.C. 245 (1858); *Louisville & Nashville R. Co. v. Collins*, 63 Ky. 114 (1865).

slavery, Georgia chief justice Joseph Lumpkin held that the loss should fall on slave employers rather than owners.[42]

Curiously, Lumpkin justified the result as a matter of humanity to slaves rather than economic policy: many whites who worked alongside slaves, he said, were "destitute of principle and bankrupt in fortune" and employers were in the best position to protect hired slaves and compensate owners for loss. If employers were shielded from liability, "the life of no hired slave would be safe."[43] Most Southern courts sided with Lumpkin but viewed the issue less humanistically, as one of contract rather than tort: they reasoned either that slave hirers implicitly agreed to bear the loss when they entered into hiring agreements or that they were governed by bailment law which held bailees responsible for damage to property left in their care.[44] North Carolina adopted a different rule: Justice Thomas Ruffin, who like Lumpkin was one of the antebellum South's preeminent jurists, believed that slaveowners should protect themselves against loss when they contracted with hirers and that if they did not, they must bear the loss.[45]

Several Midwestern courts criticized Shaw's reasoning and cabined the fellow-servant doctrine for free workers. Ohio's supreme court was the first to do so. In *Little Miami Railroad Co. v. Stevens* (1851), Justice William Caldwell, speaking for the majority, rejected Shaw's contention that applying *respondeat superior* broadly would encourage workers to be careless and he criticized *Farwell* as "contrary to the general principles of law and justice." But the court was divided. Chief Justice Peter Hitchcock, taking Shaw's cue, drew a distinction between a company's failure to have its officials perform a direct duty to the worker such as giving notice of unsafe conditions, in which case *respondeat superior* would apply, and injury from acts of fellow servants. His colleague Rufus Spalding argued that the fellow-servant doctrine was "well settled law...founded in wisdom," and that deviation from the rule would produce "'alarming consequences' when carried into the practical details of business." The justices had very different images of workingmen: Caldwell wished to protect "innocent person[s] who had no control or management of the thing that produced it [the injury]," but

---

42. *Scudder*, 1 Ga. 195 (1846).

43. *Scudder*, 1 Ga. at 199; *see generally* Paul Finkelman, "Slaves as Fellow Servants: Ideology, Law, and Industrialization," 31 *Am. J. Leg. Hist.* 269 (1987).

44. *See, e.g., Forsyth & Simpson v. Perry*, 5 Fla. 337 (1853); *L. & N. R. Co. v. Yandell*, 56 Ky. 586 (1856); *Howes v. Steamer Red Chief*, 15 La. Ann. 321 (1860); *White v. Smith*, 12 Rich. 595 (S.C. 1860). Kentucky's supreme court continued to reject the fellow-servant doctrine for black and white workers alike long after most other state courts had accepted it. Karsten, *Heart Versus Head*, 121; Marston, "Fellow Servant Rule," 613; *see* Frederick Wertheim, Note, "Slavery and the Fellow-Servant Rule: An Antebellum Dilemma," 61 *NYU L. Rev.* 1112 (1986).

45. *Ponton v. Wilm. & Weldon R. Co.*, 6 Jones (51 N.C.) 245 (1858). Ruffin also believed that slaves' own negligence should be taken into account in determining where loss should fall. Alabama's supreme court avoided several opportunities to decide where the loss should fall, but it appeared to side with Ruffin on this point in at least one case. *Perry v. Marsh*, 25 Ala. 659 (1854); *see also Walker v. Bolling*, 22 Ala. 294 (1853) and *Cook & Scott v. Parham*, 24 Ala. 21 (1853).

Spalding warned against workers who, through "the negligence of others,...[would] grasp the treasures of the company, and procure a competency for life."[46]

Indiana's supreme court went in another direction: in *Gillenwater v. Madison & Indianapolis Railroad Co.* (1856), it limited the doctrine to cases where the victim and the fellow worker were in the same "department" and their concurrent negligence produced injury. The court left open the question of when workers would be considered to be in different departments.[47] The doctrine took a tortuous path in Wisconsin. In 1860, that state's supreme court rejected the doctrine altogether: Justice Byron Paine criticized as unrealistic Shaw's view that the doctrine would encourage workers to be more safety-conscious, and he argued that if a worker's only remedy against an employer's refusal to correct unsafe practices was to leave, eventually only careless workers would remain. But the following year Chief Justice Luther Dixon, who had supported Paine, changed his mind, "more from that deference and respect which is always due to the enlightened and well considered opinions of others, than from any actual change in my own views." Dixon, like other judges, had come to regard the fellow-servant doctrine as settled law notwithstanding Caldwell's and Paine's views; he did so based in part on U.S. Supreme Court justice Joseph Story's implicit endorsement of Shaw's decision in his treatise on agency law. The Wisconsin court reinstated the doctrine, although it would turn out that the battle was far from over.[48]

Burden of Proof as to Contributory Negligence

It was universally agreed that persons claiming they had been injured through another's negligence had the burden of proving that negligence in court. Burden of proof was not a mere theoretical construct: it had real consequences in the courtroom. It meant that defendants could win solely by successfully casting doubt on plaintiff's evidence without presenting evidence of their own, a tactic that was particularly useful in cases where the accident victim had been killed and could not give his version of events. The burden rule required juries to give the benefit of the doubt to defendants in close cases. The burden of proof as to contributory negligence was less settled: should defendants be required to prove the plaintiff's negligence, or should plaintiffs be required to prove their own lack of negligence as well as the defendant's negligence?

The first American decision of the issue came from Massachusetts's highest court, which in 1824 placed the burden on plaintiffs. Some states followed its lead, relying

---

46. *Stevens*, 20 Ohio 415 (1851), 431–35 (Caldwell), 436–37 (Hitchcock), 439–52 (Spalding).
47. *Gillenwater*, 5 Ind. 339 (1854).
48. *Chamberlain v. Milw. & Miss. Railroad Co.* 11 Wis. 238 (1860); *Moseley v. Chamberlain*, 18 Wis. 700, 704–05 (1861); Story, *Law of Agency*, §§ 453d, 453e, 453f; Marston, "Fellow Servant Rule," 597.

also on a similar holding in *Butterfield*,[49] but other states disagreed.[50] In 1859, New York's highest court issued an influential decision holding that there was no rule "of universal application" and that in many cases contributory negligence could be decided without focusing on which side had the burden of proof.[51] Legal writers, most notably Shearman and Redfield, criticized the Massachusetts rule as creating an improper presumption that plaintiffs were negligent: it was up to defendants to decide whether they wanted to make that argument, and if they did, they should prove it. During the late nineteenth century, many additional states, including some that had earlier followed the Massachusetts rule, changed course and placed the burden of proving contributory negligence on defendants.[52] By century's end, more than three-quarters of the states had followed suit and Shearman and Redfield deemed it "a waste of time to discuss the question further."[53]

Proximate Cause Revisited: Fire Cases

The first era of debate over proximate cause came to a close in a series of "sparks" cases in which cinders from fires or locomotive smokestacks spread and caused damage to adjoining property. It was generally agreed that those who started such fires were liable for damage to buildings, fields and other property with which the cinders had direct contact, but fires often spread due to wind from the first point of damage to adjoining buildings and fields, and the question of liability for such secondary damage was more difficult. The question assumed increasing urgency from the 1850s onward, as devastating urban fires became a regular occurrence. The great Chicago fire of 1871, which spread from a single stable and ultimately destroyed most of the city, was the best-known, but fires regularly destroyed large parts of other American cities and rural areas as well.[54]

---

49. *Smith v. Smith*, 2 Pick. 621 (1824); *see also, e.g., Merrill v. Hampden*, 26 Me. 234 (1847); *Aurora Branch R. Co. v. Grimes*, 13 Ill. 585 (1852); *Park v. O'Brien*, 23 Conn. 339 (1854).

50. *See, e.g., Lester v. Town of Pittsford*, 7 Vt. 158 (1835); *Beatty v. Gilmore*, 16 Pa. St. 463 (1851); Kaczorowski, "Common Law Background," 1196–97.

51. *Johnson v. Hudson Riv. Co.*, 20 N.Y. 64 (1859). An earlier New York decision had arguably leaned toward imposing the burden of proof on plaintiffs. *Harlow v. Humiston*, 6 Cow. 189 (N.Y. Err. & App. 1826).

52. For examples of states changing course compare *Chamberlain*, 7 Wis. at 431 with *Hunter*, 11 Wis. 167 (1860) and *Achtenhagen v. City of Watertown*, 18 Wis. 330, 332–33 (1863); compare also *Owings v. Jones*, 9 Md. 108 (1856) with *N. Cent. R. Co. v. State*, 31 Md. 357 (1869) and *Frech v. Phila., Wilm. & Balt. R. Co.*, 39 Md. 574 (1873). *See also* Shearman and Redfield, *Treatise* (2d ed. 1870), §§ 43–44 and *ibid.* (3d ed. 1888), §§ 107–108.

53. Shearman and Redfield, *Treatise* (5th ed. 1898), §§ 107–09.

54. Between 1850 and 1880 fires destroyed large parts of San Francisco (1851), Troy, New York (1862), Portland, Maine (1866), northeast Wisconsin and eastern Michigan (1871), Boston (1872) and Green Bay (1880). *See generally* Peter C. Hoffer, *Seven Fires: The Urban Infernos that Reshaped America* (2006).

In *Hart v. Western Rail Road Corp.* (1847), the first case of importance to address the secondary-damage issue, locomotive cinders set fire to the railroad's depot; the fire then spread and destroyed Hart's house which was located nearby. Massachusetts chief justice Shaw admitted that it was "difficult to lay down any general rule" of liability; he ultimately settled on the vague standard that fire originators should be liable for all damage resulting from a fire's spread "by ordinary and natural means," and held that the railroad was liable to Hart under that standard. In *Ryan v. New York Central Railroad Co.* (1866), locomotive sparks struck a building adjacent to the railroad's right-of-way and destroyed it; high wind then spread the fire to additional buildings, causing extensive destruction. New York justice (and future U.S. Supreme Court justice) Ward Hunt took a narrower view than Shaw. He and his colleagues agreed that the loss of the first building was the "ordinary and natural" result of the railroad's acts but argued that "in the second, third or twenty-fourth case...the destruction of the building was not a natural and expected result of the first firing."[55] Illinois chief justice Sidney Breese took a slightly different but equally narrow perspective, indicating that railroads' liability ended once owners of affected property, who must make reasonable efforts to stop fires from spreading to their property, were in a position to do so. Pennsylvania's supreme court followed suit in 1870.[56]

Other courts pushed back against the *Ryan* rule. In *Kellogg v. Chicago & Northwestern Railway Co.* (1870), Wisconsin chief justice Dixon rejected Hunt's approach and adopted foreseeability as a test of liability, an element that Shaw had alluded to in passing but that Dixon now made explicit for the first time. "It would be strange indeed," he said, "if the liability of a party...were to depend upon the fact whether he set fire at once to the property, or whether he set fire to some other combustible materials at some distance from it, but communicating with it, and which, it was apparent at the time, would inevitably, or almost inevitably, lead to its destruction."[57] By the end of the nineteenth century, Dixon's foreseeability formula was well established as the majority rule in sparks cases,[58] but it proved to be of limited use in non-sparks cases. Proximate cause would continue to be a controversial topic.

---

55. *Hart*, 13 Metc. 99, 104 (Mass. 1847); *Ryan*, 35 N.Y. 210, 212 (1866).

56. *Ill. Cent. R. Co. v. McClelland*, 42 Ill. 355 (1866); *Pa. R. Co. v. Kerr*, 62 Pa. St. 353 (1870).

57. *Kellogg*, 26 Wis. 223, 224–25, 236 (1870). Dixon's colleague Byron Paine argued unsuccessfully for Hunt's mechanistic rule, arguing that it was the only one that could provide certainty and predictability for litigants in such cases. 26 Wis. at 249 (dissent).

58. *See, e.g., Hoyt v. Jeffers*, 30 Mich. 181 (1874); Shearman and Redfield, *Treatise* (5th ed. 1898), § 666 and authorities there cited. The authors were early and vigorous critics of the *Ryan* rule: in 1874, before it had been widely rejected, they judged it "difficult to support upon any intelligible principle." Shearman and Redfield, *Treatise* (3d ed. 1874), § 327a.

Early Legislative Intervention: Fencing Laws

Jurists had long recognized that judge-made common law could be altered by legislatures through statutes. Early tort law was almost exclusively judge-made but beginning in the late eighteenth century legislatures began to intervene, for example, by enactment of agricultural fencing laws such as those cited in the *Rust* and *Bush* cases. They would do so with ever-increasing frequency thereafter.[59]

Another early legislative foray into tort law came in the form of railroad fencing laws. The common law did not require landowners to protect their property by fencing it: when livestock strayed, their owners had to bear the loss if they came to harm, and in addition were strictly liable for harm their livestock caused to others.[60] But English commoners and American colonists shared a strong sense of entitlement to free use of unenclosed lands, and on the American frontier, custom gave settlers a nearly unrestricted right to use such lands for grazing and other purposes. That sensibility was in tension with common-law rules; and railroad construction, which began in the eastern states in the early 1830s and by 1870 had produced a rail network that blanketed the Northeast and Midwest and was steadily expanding in the South and West, added a new dimension to the problem. Railroad rights-of-way ran alongside thousands of miles of farmland and pasture, and by the middle of the nineteenth century, train collisions with straying livestock had become a regular occurrence.[61] In 1848, New York's legislature required railroads to erect fences and cattle guards "suitable and sufficient" to prevent livestock from entering their rights-of-way. Until that was done, they would be liable to owners whose livestock they injured, but after construction was completed, common-law negligence rules would apply. Between 1848 and 1870, at least twelve other states, most in the Northeast and Midwest, adopted similar statutes; many Western states enacted similar laws soon after gaining statehood.[62]

---

59. Isaac F. Redfield, *The Law of Railways* (5th ed. 1878), §§ 127–128; Schwartz, "Early American Tort Law," 661 (referring to Delaware and South Carolina fencing laws); Honson, "Iowa Tort History," 816–17; Craig R. Heidemann, "Fencing Laws in Missouri: Confusion, Conflict, and a Need for Change," 63 *Mo. L. Rev.* 537, 538–42 (1998); *see also* Shawn E. Kantor and J. Morgan Kousser, "Common Sense or Commonwealth? The Fence Law and Institutional Change in the Postbellum South," 59 *J. S. Hist.* 201 (1993); R. Ben Brown, "The Southern Range: A Study in Nineteenth Century Law and Society," Ph.D. dissertation, University of Michigan, 1993.

60. Redfield, *Law of Railways* (5th ed.), §§ 127–128.

61. Jeffrey Omar Usman, "The Game Is Afoot: Constitutionalizing the Right to Hunt and Fish in the Tennessee Constitution," 77 *Tenn. L. Rev.* 57, 60–77 (1989); Paul M. Gates, *History of Public Land Law Development* (1968), 208–14; *see generally* James W. Ely, Jr., *Railroads and American Law* (2001).

62. 1848 N.Y. Laws, ch. 140; *see also, e.g.*, 1850 N.H. Laws, ch. 953; 1853 Ind. Laws, p. 113; 1855 Cal. Laws, p. 70; 1860 Wis. Laws, ch. 268; 1862 Iowa Laws, ch. 169;1865 Mo. Laws, ch. 63; 1867 Mich. Laws, ch. 67; 1867 Neb. Laws, pp. 88–89; 1874 Kan. Laws, ch. 94; Tex. Rev. Stats., § 4245 (1879). *See generally* Yasuhide Kawashima, "Farmers, Ranchers, and the Railroad: The Evolution of Fence Law in the Great Plains, 1865–1900," 30 *Gr. Plains Q.* 21 (Winter 2010); Shearman and Redfield, *Treatise* (3d ed. 1874), § 456; Redfield, *Treatise on the Law of Railroads*, §§ 127–128.

The new laws appeared to create a breach in the wall of contributory negligence by making railroads absolutely liable for livestock injuries on unfenced rights-of-way, but railroads' liability proved to be far from absolute. In *Corwin v. New York & Erie Railroad Co.* (1851), New York justice Richard Marvin and his colleagues noted that their state's statute reallocated the cost of livestock accidents to railroads and sounded a note of approval that was highly unusual in an instrumentalist era:

> [A] new state of things has arisen:... endangering the lives of all animals coming in contact with the moving mass, whether locomotive or cars, and at the same time putting in jeopardy the lives and limbs of all those who are connected with the train.... Was it safe to leave this important matter [fencing and guarding] to the thousand proprietors of lands along the sides of the road? Experience had shown that it was not...[63]

But Marvin left an opening for railroads: if a landowner undertook a "positive act increasing the danger to his cattle," he would not be allowed to recover. The question of what constituted "positive" landowner acts remained open, to be answered on a case-by-case basis. Many courts adopted Marvin's holding[64] and in 1861 Maryland's highest court gave another opening to railroads, holding that its state's fencing statute, similar to New York's, allowed contributory negligence as a defense. The statute, said the court, merely required the railroad to show that it had not been negligent in order to avoid liability. Other courts eventually applied Maryland's railroad-friendly gloss to their own fencing statutes, and in the end railroad fencing laws created only a modest chink in the contributory-negligence wall.[65] Still, they were a reminder that legislatures had the power to reallocate liability for accidents to meet changing social conditions and that judges such as Marvin might be sympathetic to the exercise of such power.[66]

Judges and Juries: Shifting Boundaries of Authority

Early Struggles and the Seven Bishops Principle

Tort law also provided a new front in a centuries-old struggle over the proper balance of power between judges and juries. Jury trials first appeared in England before the Norman conquest of 1066 as one of several modes of dispute resolution;

---

63. *Corwin*, 13 N.Y. 42, 47–48 (1855).

64. *Corwin*, 13 N.Y. at 48; *see also, e.g., Bartlett v. Dubuque & Sioux City R. Co.*, 20 Iowa 188 (1866); *Sika v. Chi. & Nw. R. Co.*, 21 Wis. 370 (1867); Shearman and Redfield, *Treatise* (3d ed. 1874), §§ 456, 471.

65. *Keech v. Balt. & Wash. R. Co.*, 17 Md. 32 (1861); *see also, e.g., Pgh., Ft. Wayne & Chi. R. Co. v. Methven*, 21 Ohio St. 586 (1871); *Cent. Br. R. Co. v. Lea*, 20 Kan. 353 (1878).

66. State railroad-fencing laws were not completely uniform, and the minor variations generated considerable litigation of their own. *See, e.g.*, 1860 Wis. Laws, ch. 268 (requiring railroad to fence along rights of way with exception for "depot grounds"); *Bennett v. Chi. & Nw. R. Co.*, 19 Wis. 158 (1865) (applying depot exception); *Fowler v. Farmers' Loan & Trust Co.*, 21 Wis. 77 (1866) (same).

they became the preferred mode after church authorities abolished the institution of trial by physical ordeal. Early jurors often had personal knowledge of the events at issue in a case and they provided evidence as well as participating in decisions; little distinction was made between determination of the true facts of a case and determination of whether those facts proved a violation of law. This gave jurors great power but also subjected them to risk: under the doctrine of attaint, they were subject to severe criminal penalties if the presiding judge believed they had erred in their verdict.[67] Starting in the fourteenth century, jurors' role as evidence providers withered. Courts limited their function to finding facts (for example, whether a trespass had occurred) and to issuing verdicts based on evidence presented by others and on judges' instructions as to the law they must apply (for example, the legal definition of a trespass). At the same time, opposition arose to attaint, which seemed unduly harsh in light of jurors' now-circumscribed powers. In *Bushell's Case* (1670), Chief Justice John Vaughan effectively abolished attaint when he rejected Crown officials' request to attaint a jury that had acquitted William Penn of sedition for preaching Quaker doctrines.[68]

Two decades later, the *Seven Bishops Case* (1688) opened a struggle over freedom of political speech that would last for nearly two centuries and would again change the balance of power between judges and juries. In the seventeenth century, the common law deemed any criticism of the Crown, no matter how truthful, to be seditious libel punishable by criminal penalties. The jury's role in libel prosecutions was limited to determining whether the words at issue had the meaning claimed by the Crown; judges would then decide whether the words were seditious and libelous. In early 1688, James II, the Catholic ruler of a nation where Anglican Protestantism had been the state religion for more than a century, abolished various anti-Catholic statutes by decree. When several Anglican bishops refused to read James's decree in their churches, Crown officials prosecuted them for libel. In accordance with prevailing practice, each of the presiding judges commented on the evidence and instructed the jury in the law; they allowed the jury to render a general verdict of guilt or innocence, but left no doubt that the law required a conviction. Nevertheless, the jury acquitted the bishops. The *Seven Bishops* verdict created a sensation, played a key role in James's downfall and exile later that year, and introduced the principle that juries had the right to determine both facts and law in seditious-libel cases.[69]

The *Seven Bishops* principle met strong resistance from James's successors and English judges. Libel prosecutions continued to be one of the Crown's preferred tools

---

67. Neil Vidmar and Valerie P. Hans, *American Juries: The Verdict* (2008), 21–25; Sir William Holdsworth, *A History of English Law* (7th ed. 1956), 1:312–50; Sir Frederick Pollock and Frederic W. Maitland, *The History of English Law Before the Time of Edward I* (2d ed. 1959), 1:138–49, 2:616–63.

68. Holdsworth, *History of English Law*, 338–50; Vidmar and Hans, *American Juries*, 27–30; *Bushell's Case*, 124 Eng. Rep. 1006 (1670).

69. 12 How. St. Tr. 183 (1688); Vidmar and Hans, *American Juries*, 30–32; James Oldham, *Trial by Jury: The Seventh Amendment and Anglo-American Special Juries* (2006), 28–35.

for quelling political dissent in England and the American colonies, but opponents put the *Seven Bishops* principle to good use, most famously in Philadelphia editor John Peter Zenger's 1735 libel trial. Andrew Hamilton, Zenger's lawyer, introduced the idea that only untrue statements could be libelous and that falsity was an issue of fact for the jury—an argument rejected by the judges who heard the case but implicitly accepted by the jury as law when it acquitted Zenger. The first phase of the struggle over the jury's law-finding role closed in 1792 when Parliament enacted a statute formally adopting the *Seven Bishops* principle.[70]

American Juries and Law-Finding

Efforts to extend the jury's law-finding role to other types of lawsuits began soon after American independence. The extension movement drew strength from larger political currents, including many Americans' post-independence distaste for all things English and their desire to shift power to legislatures, the branch of government most directly accountable to the people, and away from governors and judges who still carried a faint odor of monarchy and aristocracy; but it had only mixed success.[71] Pennsylvania inserted a *Seven Bishops* clause into its 1790 constitution giving juries law-determining powers in libel cases;[72] after that time nearly every new state did so as well, but only Georgia extended jury law-finding powers to cases other than libel prosecutions.[73] Many American judges opposed expansion of the jury's law-finding function, but some accepted a judge-deferential variant of the *Seven Bishops* principle under which jurors were allowed to apply the law to the facts and render a general verdict of liability or no liability, but were also required to follow instructions on the law that judges gave them. After 1790, as partisan divisions deepened, Jeffersonian antifederalists attacked the deferential model but it proved surprisingly durable, particularly after Chancellor Kent endorsed it in an influential 1804 decision. Many states formally adopted the deferential model for other cases, requiring jurors to apply law to the facts before them "under the direction of the court" or "as in other cases," thus

---

70. Norman Rosenberg, *Protecting the Best Men: An Interpretive History of the Law of Libel* (1986), 12–15; Vidmar and Hans, *American Juries*, 41–48; Oldham, *Trial By Jury*, 3; *see also* the discussion in *Sparf v. United States*, 156 U.S. 51 (1895), 129–42 (majority), 161–63 (dissent). An earlier Pennsylvania libel proceeding involving William Bradford (1690) had led to a result similar to that in the Zenger trial. Rosenberg, 34–36.

71. *See* Renee B. Lettow, "New Trial for Verdict Against Law: Judge-Jury Relations in Early Nineteenth-Century America," 71 *Notre Dame L. Rev.* 505, 506–07 (1996).

72. Pa. Const. (1790), art. IX, § 7. It did so largely in response to a controversial decision in which its supreme court went around the jury by using its contempt-of-court powers to punish sedition. *Respublica v. Oswald*, 1 Dallas 319 (Pa. 1788); Rosenberg, *Protecting the Best Men*, 60–67.

73. *See, e.g.,* Del. Const. (1792), art. I, § 5; Ky. Const. (1792), art. 12; Tenn. Const. (1796), art. XI, § 19; Ky Const. (1799), art. X, § 8; Ind. Const. (1816), art. I, § 1; Miss. Const. (1817), art. I, § 8; Conn. Const. (1818), art. I, § 7; Ill Const. (1818), art. VIII, § 23; Ala. Const. (1819), art. VI, § 14; Me. Const. (1820), art. I, § 4; Mo. Const. (1820), art. I, § 4; Ga. Const. (1777), art. XLI.

giving judges room to direct juries to follow their legal instructions and to overturn verdicts they believed to be erroneous.[74]

The distinction between the deferential model and the pure *Seven Bishops* principle was not academic: a judge whose statement of the law was binding on a jury had the right to overturn its general verdict if he believed the jurors had ignored his instructions, but a judge whose statement of the law was not binding had no such right.[75] The distinction was most fully debated in Indiana. In *Townsend v. State* (1828), Justice Jesse Holman held that jurors "must yield to the law as delivered by the Court" in all cases. Notwithstanding the Indiana constitution's *Seven Bishops* clause, Holman said, jury power to determine law was a "power[ ] of doing wrong" and "a violation of their oaths." Judicial instructions must be binding in order to achieve uniformity and predictability of the law, attributes essential to the success of an expanding and increasingly commercial nation.[76] Chief Justice Isaac Blackford disagreed, concluding that judicial instructions were "entitled to great deference and respect from the jury, but...not absolutely compulsory upon them"; but even Blackford agreed that judges retained the power to overturn verdicts contrary to their view of the law and to grant new trials. When Indiana held a constitutional convention in 1851, delegates responded to *Townsend* by inserting a clause giving juries power to determine the law in all cases. Indiana's supreme court promptly retorted that jurors still had a "duty to believe the law as laid down by the Court," but six years later, after a change of judges, the court reversed itself and affirmed that judicial instructions were advisory only. There things rested until the mid-twentieth century, when the court returned to the *Townsend* rule.[77]

A handful of other states experimented with extension of juries' law-finding powers through constitutional provisions and statutes, but the experiments eventually died at the hands of their courts, the most prominent example being Chief Justice Shaw's neutering of an 1855 Massachusetts statute extending the jury's law-finding power to all criminal cases. In *Commonwealth v. Anthes* (1856), Shaw stated the statute would be unconstitutional if interpreted to make the jury's law-finding power absolute: juries were bound to follow a judge's instructions as to the law in all cases. He argued this was necessary in order to preserve civil liberties as well as promote legal order and predictability: under the common law a court could not overturn a criminal acquittal

---

74. William E. Nelson, "The Province of the Judiciary," 37 *John Marshall L. Rev.* 325, 326–42 (2004); Lettow, "Judge-Jury Relations," 517–18; Julius Goebel, Jr., *History of the Supreme Court of the United States, Vol. I: Antecedents and Beginnings to 1801* (1971), 633–51; *People v. Croswell*, 3 Johns. 337 (N.Y. 1804); *see* "The Right of An Accused to Argument By Counsel Before the Jury, Both Upon the Law and the Fact," 6 *Am. Jurist* 237, 246 (1831).

75. Nelson, "Province of the Judiciary," 334–42; *Croswell*, 3 Johns. 337 (N.Y. 1804).

76. *Townsend*, 2 Blackford 151, 158–59 (1828).

77. 2 Blackford at 163 (Blackford dissent); *Carter v. State*, 2 Ind. 617 (1851); *Lynch v. State*, 9 Ind. 541 (1857); *Williams v. State*, 10 Ind. 503 (1858); Robert D. Rucker, "The Right to Ignore the Law: Constitutional Entitlement Versus Judicial Interpretation," 33 *Valparaiso L. Rev.* 449, 455–71 (1999).

under any circumstances, but retention of the law-finding power enabled judges to overturn erroneous convictions.[78]

Judges, Juries and the Field Code

Advocates of expanded jury powers also hoped their cause would draw strength from the movement to restate American law in the form of comprehensive written codes, a movement that originated in the 1780s and accelerated during the early nineteenth century. Two impulses drove the codification movement: a liberal-minded desire to simplify the written law and make it more accessible to ordinary citizens, thus reducing the power of legal elites and promoting a more direct form of democracy, and an essentially conservative desire to make the legal process more efficient, systematic and predictable. Liberals' hopes of democratizing American legal structures and reducing the role of judges and lawyers through codification were not fulfilled: as the nation and its economy grew and became more complex, it became clear that professional expertise was needed to administer the legal system under which they functioned.[79] The codification movement was more successful in achieving its goals of order and efficiency. After 1800, following Chancellor Kent's example, most states began compiling and publishing their supreme court decisions and statutes.[80] Many states' statutes included rules of court procedure for civil cases, including procedural devices that American judges had used to check juries since independence. Some of those powers were uniquely American; some had long histories in English law.

First was the power to order new trials. English judges had begun to use this power regularly after *Bushell's Case* eliminated their right to discipline erring juries through attaint. In theory, judges could order new trials for any reason, but most judges used

---

78. 1855 Mass. Laws, ch. 152; *Anthes*, 71 Mass. 185, 231 (1855). In 1827, Illinois enacted a statute giving juries the right to decide the law in all criminal cases; Illinois's supreme court gradually narrowed that right and ultimately held that the statute was unconstitutional. Rev. Code of Laws of Ill. (1827), pp. 162–63; *People v. Bruner*, 175 N.E. 400 (Ill. 1931). Maryland enacted a similar constitutional provision in 1851 which met a similar fate in the courts. Md. Const. (1851), art. XV, § 5; *Franklin v. State*, 12 Md. 236 (1858); *Stevenson v. State*, 423 A.2d 558 (Md. 1980); Gary J. Jacobsohn, "The Right to Disagree: Judges, Juries, and the Administration of Criminal Justice in Maryland," 1976 *Wash. U. L.Q.* 571 (1976). In 1895, a divided U.S. Supreme Court held that the law-finding function remained with the judge in all federal cases, including seditious-libel cases. *Sparf*, 156 U.S. 51 (1895).

79. Stephen N, Subrin, "David Dudley Field and the Field Code: A Historical Analysis of an Earlier Procedural Vision," 6 *L. & Hist. Review* 311, 316–17 (1988); *see* Charles M. Cook, *The American Codification Movement: A Study of Antebellum Legal Reform* (1981), 25–26, 100–50; Friedman, *History of American Law*, 401–07.

80. See G. Edward White, "The Chancellor's Ghost," 74 *Chi.-Kent L. Rev.* 229, 233–34 (1998); Horton, *Kent*, 139–161. Examples of early nineteenth-century statutory compilations include Robert and George Watkins, *Digest of the Laws of the State of Georgia* (1800); Harry Toulmin, *Collection of all the Public and Permanent Acts of the General Assembly of Kentucky* (1802); J.T. Buckingham, *Laws of the Commonwealth of Massachusetts* (1807); W. Johnston, *Compend of the Acts of Indiana* (1817); F. Baker, *Revised Code of the Laws of Mississippi* (1824); and Robert Blackwell, *Revised Code of the Laws of Illinois* (1827).

this power cautiously, typically when they concluded that evidence had been admitted erroneously or that flawed legal instructions had been given to the jury. New-trial orders became a preferred tool because they helped defuse charges that judges were taking too much power unto themselves: judges could point out that they were not deciding the case, merely sending it back to another jury. Only rarely did judges dismiss a case after overturning a verdict.[81]

A second important control device was the special verdict, that is, a verdict in which the jury was asked to answer a list (often quite lengthy) of questions about specific facts of the case. Prior to 1800, juries usually rendered general verdicts stating simply that they found in favor of a particular party. Judges had no way of examining the reasoning behind juries' general verdicts and accordingly had limited leeway to overturn them. Special verdicts gave judges more opportunity to find errors and overturn verdicts they believed were erroneous. Those who supported a strong judicial role pushed with much success for increased use of special verdicts after 1800.[82] They were helped by the near-universal impression among jurists and lawyers that juries were swayed too much by emotion and sympathy for accident victims. One state court commended the special verdict in terms that captured this view, terms that carried a faint but distinct suspicion of popular democracy:

> [Special verdicts] bring out the various facts separately, in order to enable the court to apply the law accurately, and to guard against any misapplication of the law by the jury. It is a matter of common knowledge, that a jury influenced by a general feeling that one side ought to recover, will bring in a verdict accordingly... And this does not imply intentional dishonesty in the jury... but rather a disposition to jump at results upon a general theory of right and wrong, instead of patiently grasping, arranging and considering details.[83]

A third important tool was the right to dispose of cases prior to verdict by granting motions of demurrer and nonsuit. If a defendant was willing to admit all of the facts that the plaintiff alleged in its written complaint and to rest its case on an argument

---

81. R.J. Farley, "Instructions to Juries—Their Role in the Judicial Process," 42 *Yale L.J.* 194, 200–04 (1932); Lettow, "Judge-Jury Relations," 509–19; James B. Thayer, *A Preliminary Treatise on Evidence at the Common Law* (1898), 169–74. New trials did not always result in legally satisfactory verdicts: "sometimes... persistent juries could just wear out judges." Lettow, "Judge-Jury Relations," 546; *see also* Malone, "Formative Era of Contributory Negligence," 162–64.

82. Thayer, *Preliminary Treatise on Evidence*, 217–20; Vidmar and Hans, American Juries, 31–33; Lettow, "Judge-Jury Relations," 544–47.

83. *Morrow v. Saline County Com'rs*, 21 Kan. 484, 503–04 (1879) (the author of the opinion was future U.S. Supreme Court justice David Brewer); W.W. Thornton, "Special Interrogatories to Juries," 20 *Am. L. Rev.* 366, 371 (1886). More recent commentators have agreed that jurors were plaintiff oriented. *See* James, "Contributory Negligence," 695; Malone, "Formative Era of Contributory Negligence," 156. A review of cases reported in the 1850s and several studies of trial-level verdicts in various communities support the conclusion that a majority of nineteenth-century verdicts were for plaintiffs but also suggest that verdicts for defendants were not uncommon. Schwartz, "Early American Tort Law," 667–68; Karsten, *Heart Versus Head*, 99.

that the law did not allow plaintiff to recover under those facts, it could file a demurrer motion. If the judge agreed with the defendant, the lawsuit was over: the plaintiff could not dig up more facts and try again unless the judge allowed it. Defendants used nonsuit motions to argue at trial, either after plaintiff had presented his evidence or after both sides had presented evidence, that the evidence was insufficient to prove plaintiff's case. Unlike demurrers, nonsuits allowed plaintiffs a real, if seldom used, chance to try again in a new lawsuit.[84] Another device was the directed verdict: if a judge believed at the close of plaintiff's trial evidence or of all trial evidence that one side or the other must prevail under the law, he could direct the jury to render a verdict in favor of that party. Directed verdicts were a blunt assertion of power over the jury, an assertion that might kindle public resentment, and judges used them sparingly.[85]

Another control device, softer than the others but often effective, was judges' right to give the jury their views on the evidence before sending the jury out to consider its verdict. Commenting on the evidence had become firmly entrenched in English practice long before American independence, but after independence some American states rebelled against it. In the 1790s, Tennessee and North Carolina allowed judges to summarize the evidence for juries but prohibited them from giving opinions about witnesses' credibility or suggesting to the jury what its verdict should be. The rebellion spread slowly at first,[86] but after 1860 it accelerated: by 1900 more than half of all states prohibited judges from giving any commentary about evidence or suggesting an appropriate verdict.[87]

Judges' powers increased in many states that adopted the civil procedure code introduced by David Dudley Field in New York in the mid-1840s. After New York's 1846 constitutional convention ordered a comprehensive recodification of the state's laws, Field, a member of an eminent, reform-minded family and a leading New York City lawyer, was appointed to a committee charged with developing a new civil procedure code. He led the way in preparing a partial code which was approved by New York's legislature in 1848.[88] The Code's clarity, the fact that it provided a ready-made set of procedural rules for states that did not have them, and New York's national legal influence all contributed to the Code's widespread success: between 1848 and 1870 twenty-six states adopted the Code.[89]

---

84. Thayer, *Preliminary Treatise on Evidence*, 234–38; Lettow, "Judge-Jury Relations," 521–22; Robert W. Millar, *Civil Procedure of the Trial Court in Historical Perspective* (1952), 298–304.

85. Lettow, "Judge-Jury Relations," 521–22; Millar, *Civil Procedure of the Trial Court*, 305–07.

86. Between 1800 and 1860, Mississippi (1822), Arkansas (1836), Illinois (1945), Georgia (1850) and Texas (1853) adopted similar provisions. Edson Sunderland, "The Problem of Trying Issues," 5 *Tex. L. Rev.* 18, 32–33 (1926).

87. Sunderland, "Trying Issues," 33–34, notes 25 and 27.

88. Subrin, "David Dudley Field," 313–19; 1848 N.Y. Laws, ch. 379. New York never adopted the completed Code in its entirety. See generally Henry M. Field, *Life of David Dudley Field* (1898), 68–96.

89. Subrin, "David Dudley Field," 316–17; Millar, *Civil Procedure of the Trial Court*, 54–55; Kellen Funk, "The Influence of the Field Code: An Introduction to the Critical Issues" and Funk, "Network Analysis: Finding the Regional Influences of Codification," both at Kellenfunk.org.

Field embodied both the liberal and conservative aspects of the codification movement. He believed that the new Code's rules simplified the law and would limit judicial discretion, make the law more accessible to non-lawyers and make litigation less expensive. But he also believed devoutly in precedent and legal order, and he viewed the Code as protective of existing legal boundaries between judges and juries. In fact, the Code shifted the boundary in favor of judges. It adopted the traditional rule that issues of law were to be determined by judges, made no mention of the *Seven Bishops* principle and provided that in any dispute, legal issues must be resolved before disputes of fact were addressed. The Code gave juries the right to decide fact issues only in disputes over real property and to a limited extent in divorce cases, but in a departure from existing boundaries, it stated that "every other issue is triable by the court." Judges were given discretion to order that other issues be decided by the jury, and in many states the force of custom was strong enough that judges continued to allow juries to decide nearly all fact issues. But their discretion to order otherwise was a potentially powerful new tool.[90]

The Field Code also codified other traditional judicial powers. It gave judges broad power in nearly all cases, including tort cases, to decide whether a jury would give a general or a special verdict and to dictate the wording of the questions to be answered by the jury. The Code also authorized use of demurrers and orders for new trials.[91] It is not clear whether the states that adopted Field's Code explicitly intended to expand judges' powers and cabin those of juries, or whether they viewed the Code simply as a means of ensuring legal order for the benefit of all. In his report to the New York legislature, Field emphasized efficiency but also emphasized a desire to prevent friction and misunderstandings between judges and juries and to make more accessible "the records of the Courts [which] have been sealed books to the mass of the people."[92] Field may have thought that New York's recent replacement of its appointive judicial system with popularly-elected judges would bring the judiciary closer to the people and reduce the need for jury trials, but the Code was adopted by elective and appointive states alike, and it seems unlikely that any such sanguine sentiment lay behind their decisions to adopt of the Code.[93]

---

90. 1848 N.Y. Laws, ch. 379, §§ 208–09, 212. County courts were authorized to try all issues of fact, although they were authorized to submit such issues to a jury upon request. *Ibid.*, § 35. *See generally, The Code of Civil Procedure of the State of New York, Reported Complete by the Commissioners on Practice and Pleadings* (1850).

91. 1848 N.Y. Laws, ch. 379, §§ 123–24, 204, 215–16.

92. A.P. Sprague, ed., *Speeches, Arguments and Miscellaneous Papers of David Dudley Field* (1884), 1:174 (committee first report, February 29, 1848), 1:291 (committee final report, December 31, 1849). Subrin, "David Dudley Field," 333–34; Wis. Const. (1848), art. VII, § 4.

93. A study of one state's tort decisions during the first years after it enacted the Field Code suggests that the statutory shift of power did not produce a revolution in the courtroom. Wisconsin adopted the Field Code in 1856. Between 1848 and 1870, most of the tort cases reaching its supreme court were appeals from judgments entered on jury verdicts. Only one-sixth of the tort cases reaching the supreme court were disposed of by trial-court judges without a jury verdict, and nearly half

By 1870, American states had put in place a basic legal framework for addressing injuries generated by the ever-increasing number of contacts between strangers in a steadily growing economy and society. But parts of the framework were in confusion, and it remained to be seen whether it would stand up as the nation continued to grow and change. Would the contributory negligence doctrine and the free-labor ideals it embodied survive in an economy increasingly dominated by large companies, one in which equality of bargaining power between corporations, workers and consumers was increasingly illusory? Would the balance of power in the courtroom, a hybrid shaped by pre-Field Code practice, the Code itself and trial judges' discretionary use of the numerous case-disposing tools available to them, achieve a workable balance between order and democracy? Events over the next thirty years, a little-studied but important period in the history of tort law, would provide answers.

---

of those were sent back for a jury trial. The cases and calculations on which this statement is based are described in Appendix 3.

TWO

Leaps in the Dark

The Slow Softening of Fault-Based Law, 1870–1910

If the judge... were to pass upon negligence as a question of law, he must, in doing so, be endeavoring to enforce a rule... which must take its final coloring from the experience, training, and temperament of the judge himself;... but because judges are men and men are different... it must be a very clear case, indeed, which would justify the court in taking upon itself this responsibility.

—Thomas M. Cooley (1880)[1]

Like most American judges, Luther Dixon wanted to build and maintain a body of tort law consisting of clear rules applied in a consistent fashion. Two cases brought home to him the fact that the task was considerably more difficult in practice than in theory.

On a sunny June day in 1862, thirteen-year-old Otto Achtenhagen's mother told him to take his little brother and go to a neighbor for butter and eggs. Otto walked onto a city bridge spanning the Rock River in Watertown, Wisconsin. A plank was missing from the middle of the bridge, but Otto did not see it: he fell through the hole into the river and was drowned, leaving a grieving family behind. Was Otto at fault in any way, which would mean that he could not recover damages from the city? The family's lawyer argued that the decision should be left to the jury, which might find that Otto had been understandably distracted by the need to keep an eye on his brother and had acted normally for a thirteen-year old. But at the close of the family's evidence, the trial judge granted a nonsuit and dismissed its case. On appeal, Dixon and his colleagues agreed: Otto had used the bridge before and must have known

---

1. Thomas M. Cooley, *A Treatise of the Law of Torts or Wrongs Which Arise Independent of Contract* (1880), 668–69.

about the hole, thus no jury could properly conclude that his failure to see it on the day of his death was excusable.[2]

Ten years later, a similar case came before Dixon and his colleagues. While walking down a Berlin sidewalk, James Barstow fell down an open cellar hatchway and was badly injured. Like the Achtenhagens, Barstow suffered a nonsuit at the close of his evidence, but this time the result was different on appeal. Barstow had been distracted by a greeting from an acquaintance driving a team and wagon on the other side of the street and this, said Dixon, might excuse his failure to mind the hatchway. Judges in the late nineteenth century were expected to present their decisions in formalistic, impersonal prose, stressing that they were mere interpreters of a fixed body of law, not law creators; expressions of doubt and appeals for legal reform were to be avoided.[3] But Dixon used the occasion to repent his decision in the Achtenhagens' case:

> [I]t has given me much trouble, and I have frequently had great doubts about its correctness when considering the same question since.... How could the court say, as a matter of law, that the fall of the boy through the hole was not without fault or negligence on his part, or that it was not purely accidental, or under circumstances in which no blame could attach to him?... [I]t was at best but a leap in the dark, and I think it was for the jury to take that leap.[4]

Dixon's expression of regret disturbed his more formalist colleague Orsamus Cole, who argued strenuously but not entirely convincingly that differences between Otto's and Barstow's conduct justified the different results. But Dixon was not alone: as will be seen, late-nineteenth-century American judges regularly departed from formalism in their opinions and recognized the policymaking element of their work.[5]

The decades following the Civil War are sometimes viewed as a period of stagnation, even reaction, in American tort law, a period in which judges preserved old rules based on notions of personal responsibility and fault that were proving increasingly ill-suited to a maturing industrial economy; but Dixon's confession of doubt revealed that deeper currents flowed beneath a formalistic surface. American courts had to address a constantly changing array of accidents that reflected the many technological advances of the late nineteenth century. The task of fitting this new array into the framework of tort law was a laborious one, and many courts recognized that accomplishing the fit required at least some adjustment of the framework. The

---

2. *Achtenhagen v. City of Watertown*, 18 Wis. 331, 331–32 (1864).

3. Lawrence M. Friedman, *A History of American Law* (1st ed. 1973), 333; Grant Gilmore, *The Ages of American Law* (1997), 60–64; Morton J. Horwitz, "The Rise of Legal Formalism," 19 *Am. J. Leg. Hist.* 251, 254–58 (1975); Donald W. Rogers, "From Common Law to Factory Laws: The Transformation of Workplace Safety Law in Wisconsin Before Progressivism," 39 *Am. J. Leg. Hist.* 177, 193 (1995).

4. *Barstow v. City of Berlin*, 34 Wis. 357, 362–63 (1874).

5. *Barstow*, 34 Wis. at 363 (Cole); *see* Brian Z. Tamanaha, "The Mounting Evidence Against the 'Formalist Age,'" 92 *Tex. L. Rev.* 1667 (2014).

courts left much of that task to their state legislatures, but when reform statutes were enacted, the courts were receptive and rejected most constitutional challenges. Tensions surrounding the proper balance of power between judges and juries in tort cases also rose as the volume and technological complexity of those cases increased. State supreme courts continued to use their power to overturn verdicts where they believed that the facts and existing tort rules compelled that result, but they used that power relatively sparingly.

The Changing Array of Accident Cases

The American industrial revolution, which had begun in the early nineteenth century with scattered water- and steam-powered factories and railroad construction in eastern states, entered a second phase around 1870. The Second Industrial Revolution was marked by the rise of large corporations and factories that relied on wage workers and increasingly sophisticated production and management techniques; it was also marked by proliferation of new technologies, by greatly increased use of coal and the introduction of electricity and oil as energy sources, and by completion of a national rail network.[6] In 1870, there were twice as many agricultural workers as manufacturing workers in the American workforce; American agricultural output and manufacturing output were roughly equal in value. The nation's population was just over thirty-eight million people; the industrial revolution was barely underway in the South, and much of the trans-Mississippi West was still unsettled. By 1910 manufacturing workers outnumbered agricultural workers by forty percent and industrial output, ranging from publishing and textiles in the Northeast to locomotives in Pennsylvania, food processing and machinery in the Midwest and mining and metal products in California, was worth more than twice as much as agricultural output. The nation's population had risen to ninety-two million people, nearly half of whom lived in the towns and cities where industry was concentrated, and all corners of America could now communicate with each other through a rail network of more than 200,000 miles, supplemented by a small but growing network of paved roads.[7]

These changes brought Americans ever more frequently into contact with each other and with potentially hazardous situations. The number of passenger and freight trains and the speeds at which they traveled rose steadily, creating an increased level of danger that crossing signs, whistles and other safety devices could never completely overcome. Electrified streetcars, which first appeared in New York in 1892 and spread to most major American cities by 1900, brought similar dangers, as did the new

---

6. See Alfred D. Chandler, Jr., *The Visible Hand: The Managerial Revolution in American Business* (1977), 79–376.

7. See *A Compendium of the Ninth Census of the United States* (1872), 594–95, 692, 796, 872; *Abstract of the Thirteenth Census of the United States Taken in the Year 1910* (1913), 137, 288–89, 437–38.

municipal electric systems that made them possible. Workplace machinery, ever more complex and dangerous, took an increasing toll: "the power was always turning—and it did not respond to shouts or to a hand, arm or body caught in a machine or belting or by the turning shafts."[8] During the Second Industrial Revolution, the number of tort cases coming before American courts increased sharply; they now included streetcar accidents, electrocutions, and workplace accidents involving ever more sophisticated factory and railroad equipment. These changes exerted a very real, if seldom-noted, influence on judicial behavior in the tort arena.

FIGURE 2.1
Five-State Survey: Types of Tort Cases, 1870–1920[9]

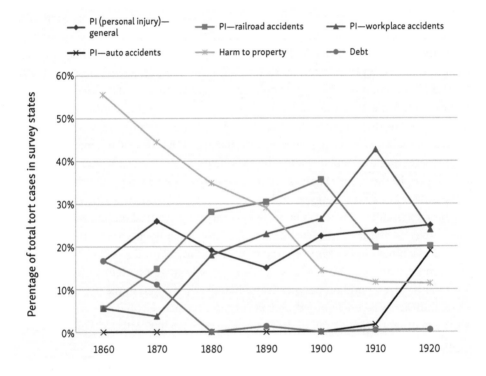

The Five-State Survey indicates that the changing mix of tort cases coming before American courts tracked social and technological change closely. In 1860, near the end of the American industrial revolution's first phase, disputes involving harm to property from such causes as excavation, construction of dams and pollution-generating activity on neighboring land dominated tort law. Disputes over executions against

---

8. Robert C. Nesbit, *The History of Wisconsin, Vol. III: Urbanization and Industrialization, 1873–1893* (1985), 224–25.

9. Figures 2.1 and 2.2 are derived from the Five-State Survey. The Survey data and methodology are described in Appendix 2. The calculations for Figures 2.1 and 2.2 are described in Appendix 3.

debtors were declining from earlier levels but still represented a significant share of tort cases. Railroad-accident and workplace-accident cases were beginning to appear in significant numbers, and during the ensuing decades they would come to dominate tort law. Railroad cases divided about equally between injuries to livestock wandering onto tracks, persons struck by trains and passengers injured in collisions or in boarding or alighting from trains. Trains and rail yards, factories, lumber operations and construction sites accounted for the largest number of workplace accidents. In 1900, workplace cases exceeded railroad cases for the first time, but in the 1910s they would diminish in number as workers compensation laws became popular. Railroad-employee accidents were at the intersection of the two categories, and they provided the catalyst for the most important legal reform of the era: employer liability laws.

FIGURE 2.2
Five-State Survey: The Rise of Railroad and Workplace Accidents

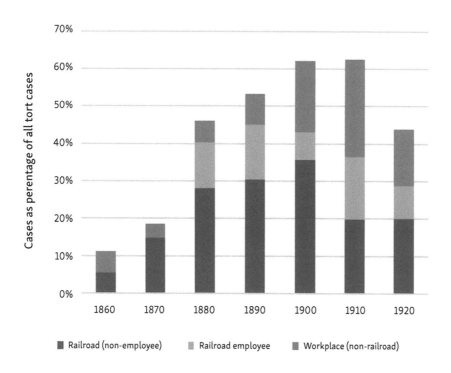

The Push Against Contributory Negligence Begins

By 1870, the free-labor principles that liability for injury cannot exist without fault, and that one whose own fault contributes to his injury should not be allowed to shift his loss to others, were firmly established in American tort law. Contributory negligence gave rise to an important corollary principle, assumption of risk. When Lord Abinger created the fellow-servant doctrine in *Priestley v. Fowler,* he stated that an employer was "bound to provide for the safety of his servant, to the best of [his] judgment, information, and belief";[10] but no workplace could ever be completely risk-free. In Abinger's view, workers knew this when they made their employment agreements, and being closer to the work than their employer, they were in a better position to assess its dangers. Abinger did not speak in terms of assumption of risk, but the principle followed inevitably from his reasoning, and other British and American judges soon made it explicit, sometimes in bluntly instrumentalist terms. In 1854, Pennsylvania justice Walter Lowrie explained:

> In what form shall we put [the safe-place duty], or how shall we define it? Is it that, when persons are employed to work for others, the employers are bound to see that the instruments of their work are and shall continue in a condition to be used with safety? ... [T]hen ... the engineer, the miller, the cotton-spinner, and the wool-carder have a guarantee for the accidents that may befall them in the use of the machinery which they profess to understand, and which they ought so to understand as to be able to inform their employers when it is out of order. If this be so, then the care and skill required of workmen is reduced very much below what is ordinarily expected of them.[11]

Nevertheless, by 1870 there were already signs that these principles were not a good fit for an industrializing America. Wage workers, mostly unskilled and dependent on corporations for their livelihood, now outnumbered craft workers whose special skills gave them greater job opportunities and greater ability to negotiate working conditions and other terms of employment, and the numerical disparity between the two groups was growing steadily. Wage workers often were a single part of a larger production process. They were dependent on other workers' proper performance of tasks over which they had no control, and on the proper functioning of machines whose inner workings and flaws were invisible or incomprehensible to them. Jurists and lawmakers began to question whether traditional notions of fault should be applied in such settings.[12]

As the number of work accidents rose, a faint but nagging sense also arose among jurists and the public that they might to some extent be an unavoidable byproduct of industrialization and economic growth. If accidents were inevitable, should fault continue to serve as a guiding principle for allocation of accident costs? Some jurists

---

10. 3 Mees. & W. 1, 6 (Exc. 1837).

11. *Ryan v. Cumberland Vall. R. Co.*, 23 Pa. 384, 385–86 (1854); *see also Ill. Cent. R. Co. v. Cox*, 21 Ill. 20 (1858).

12. John Fabian Witt, *The Accidental Republic: Crippled Workingmen, Destitute Widows, and the Remaking of American Law* (2004), 35–41; see also Kenneth S. Abraham, *The Liability Century: Insurance and Tort Law from the Progressive Era to 9/11* (2008), 28–52 (describing the rise of liability insurance and safety programs at the turn of the twentieth century); Robert J. Kaczorowski, "From Petitions for Gratuities to Claims for Damages: Personal Injuries and Railroads During the Industrialization of the United States," 57 *Am. J. Leg. Hist.* 261, 298–301 (2017).

defended the rule of no liability without negligence as a bulwark against governmental encroachment on private liberty and autonomy. Francis Hilliard, Thomas Cooley and Thomas Shearman and Amasa Redfield, all authors of leading nineteenth-century treatises on tort law, took a softer approach. They suggested that adherence to the no-liability-without-negligence rule provided the best answer *if* negligence were defined as a lack of ordinary care. The ordinary-care standard would still impose the loss on victims in truly faultless accidents, but the irreducible looseness of the term "ordinary" would give juries some leeway to take accidents that others might see as faultless out of that category, for example by finding negligence in acts of an employer or exonerating an injured worker from contributory negligence where others might not.[13]

The rationale suggested by Hilliard, Cooley and Shearman and Redfield was quickly recognized as imperfect, not least by the authors themselves: their idea of jury leeway grated against the formalist ideal that law should be neutral, consistent and predictable. The liberty-oriented argument proved more durable, but it clashed with the rising perception that workplace accidents were inevitable.[14] During the Second Industrial Era, American judges responded to these tensions by making regular efforts to soften the free-labor principles articulated in *Priestley* and its progeny without breaking with them altogether.

Distractions and Emergencies

Two softening devices, the distraction rule and the emergency rule, emerged at the beginning of the Second Industrial Era. They were applied mainly in railroad, highway and sidewalk accident cases, but later proved useful in workplace accident cases as well. As early as 1860, the argument was made to Massachusetts's supreme court that people are often distracted by their own thoughts or unexpected events happening nearby and that in such situations, their failure to be mindful of hazards is not inconsistent with ordinary care and should not be treated as negligence. The court, which was often skeptical of tort reform, rejected the argument, stating that it was "equivalent to a positive declaration that [the plaintiff] was utterly incautious"; but a few years later, the justices relented: juries could consider distraction as an excuse for what would otherwise be contributory negligence.[15] Beginning in the early 1870s,

---

13. Francis Hilliard, *The Law of Torts or Private Wrongs* (4th ed. 1874), 1:122–23, 137–38; Cooley, *Law of Torts*, 659–87; Thomas G. Shearman and Amasa Redfield, *Treatise on the Law of Negligence* (5th ed. 1898), §§ 42–43; Witt, *Accidental Republic*, 46–49.

14. Witt, *Accidental Republic*, 46–52.

15. *Gilman v. Inhabitants of Deerfield*, 15 Gray 577, 581 (Mass. 1860); compare *Smith v. City of Lowell*, 88 Mass. 39 (1863) (indicating that plaintiffs were not required to be constantly attentive to their surroundings); *Weare v. Inhabitants of Fitchburg*, 110 Mass. 334, 339 (1872) (stating: "Previous knowledge of the existence of the defect, and a residence in its immediate neighborhood, are not conclusive" of contributory negligence).

other state courts also endorsed the idea of distraction as a defense against claims of contributory negligence, and by the turn of the century the idea was widely accepted in American courts, although some suggested that its use should be sparing and that the duty to observe one's surroundings was nearly absolute.[16]

Late-nineteenth-century courts also recognized that plaintiffs might be confronted with an emergency (for example, an unexpected but imminent train collision) that required them to make an instant choice between several risky alternatives (such as jumping off or staying with the train). In such cases, a choice that proved mistaken would not be treated as failure of ordinary care. The emergency rule first appeared in an early-nineteenth-century English case and an 1839 U.S. Supreme Court decision. The concept of contributory negligence was not fully matured at that time, and both courts viewed the emergency rule as the basis for a cause of action against the creator of the emergency,[17] but during the 1850s and 1860s, courts reframed the rule as a defense against claims of contributory negligence. Alabama's supreme court was one of the first to do so: in 1853 it explained that mistaken choices of action under "circumstances of excitement, confusion and danger brought about by the negligent acts of the defendants" would not constitute contributory negligence.[18] New York's highest court endorsed the rule in 1857, and even the Massachusetts court indicated that the rule was appropriate.[19] Other courts soon followed suit, and the emergency rule encountered little judicial resistance.[20]

---

16. *See Wheeler v. Town of Westport*, 30 Wis. 392 (1872) (doctor stumbled over boulders in a highway while hastening to respond to a nighttime emergency call); *Barstow*, 34 Wis. 357 (1874) (pedestrian fell down open sidewalk hatchway while talking with a friend); *Cohen v. Eureka & Palisade R. Co.*, 14 Nev. 376 (1879) (plaintiff was distracted by his surroundings and did not see train coming). Other examples of cases in which the rule was applied liberally include *Van Praag v. Gale*, 40 P. 555 (Cal. 1895) (plaintiff walked into an elevator shaft while reading a newspaper; court emphasized that the shaft had been closed earlier but was not closed at the time of the accident); *Le Beau v. Telephone & Telegraph Construction Co.*, 67 N.W. 339 (Mich. 1896) (pedestrian was distracted by nearby construction at time of injury); *City of Meridian v. McBeath*, 32 So. 53 (Miss. 1902) (plaintiff was distracted by approaching streetcar); *West Kentucky Telephone Co. v. Pharis*, 78 S.W. 917 (Ky. 1904) (plaintiff was worried about her sister's illness and visibility was poor). For an example of a case taking a narrow view of the rule, see *Dale v. Webster County*, 41 N.W. 1 (Iowa 1888) (plaintiff walked onto bridge and fell off it while reading a newspaper). *See generally* Shearman & Redfield, *Treatise* (5th ed. 1898), § 376.

17. *Jones v. Boyce*, 1 Stark. 493, 171 Eng. Rep. 640 (N.P. 1816); *Stokes v. Saltonstall*, 38 U.S. 181 (1839).

18. *Cook v. Parham*, 24 Ala. 21. (1853). *Cook* involved a slaveowner's claim against defendant for loss of his slave; as in other such cases, the court considered the slaveowner's economic interest more than humanity toward slaves in determining who should bear the loss. *See* Chapter 1, notes 41–45 and accompanying text.

19. *Ingalls v. Bills*, 9 Metc. 1 (Mass. 1846); *Hegan v. Eighth Ave. R. Co.*, 15 N.Y. 380 (1857).

20. Other early cases adopting the rule include *Frink v. Potter*, 17 Ill. 406 (1856); *Sw. R. Co. v. Paulk*, 24 Ga. 356 (1858); *Jeffersonville R. Co. v. Swift*, 26 Ind. 459 (1866); and *Schultz v. Chi. & Nw. R. Co.*, 44 Wis. 638 (1878). *See also* Shearman & Redfield, *Treatise*, § 89 (4th ed. 1888) and authorities there cited.

Reinforcing Employers' Safe-Place Duties

As workplace accidents grew in number, both British and American courts refined the safe-place duty of employers that Lord Abinger had articulated in *Priestley*. During the 1850s and 1860s, they forged a consensus: in addition to ensuring that workplaces and equipment were safe when originally provided to workers, employers must also eliminate defects and hazards brought to their attention.[21] Whether that duty included a continuing obligation to inspect workplaces and equipment for hazards proved to be a more difficult question. In *Warner v. Erie Railroad Co.* (1868), New York's highest court answered it by applying the ordinary-care standard: if an employer monitored equipment "with frequency, and with such tests and custom and experience have sanctioned and prescribed," that would excuse the employer from liability if the equipment later failed. For instrumentalist reasons, the court refused to impose a continuous duty of monitoring on employers: that would come too close to an absolute standard of care, which would "carry their corporate liability beyond reason" and impose an "intolerable burden." Thus, the extent of an employer's obligation to monitor equipment depended on industry custom—a custom set by employers themselves.[22] Other states soon adopted the *Warner* standard,[23] although a few courts indicated that a duty of continuous inspection should be adopted and others described the duty of inspection in terms so strong as to suggest that more than ordinary care was required.[24]

Priestley did not address whether employers' safe-place duty included an obligation to hire competent workers, but it left an opening for such a holding, which British and American courts promptly supplied.[25] Again, the difficult question was whether the duty to monitor workers' competence continued after they were hired. In 1855, Ohio's supreme court held that employers would be liable for continuing to employ workers after they had been "shown to be incompetent or unsuitable," but in 1868 the House of Lords held, and New York's highest court suggested in *Warner*, that the employer's

---

21. *See, e.g., Keegan v. W. R. Corp.*, 4 Selden 175 (N.Y. 1853); *Carle v. Bangor & Piscataquis Canal & R. Co.*, 43 Me. 269 (1857); *Hallower v. Henley*, 6 Cal. 209 (1856); *Indpls. & Cinn. R. Co.*, 10 Ind. 554 (1858); *Hard v. Vt. & Can. R. Co.*, 32 Vt. 473 (1860); *Snow v. Housatonic R. Co.*, 8 Allen 441 (Mass. 1864); *Chi. & Nw. R. Co. v. Swett*, (45 Ill. 197 (1867).

22. *Warner*, 39 N.Y. 468, 475–76 (1868).

23. *See, e.g., Columbus & Indpls. Cent. R. Co. v. Arnold*, 31 Ind. 174 (1869); *Houston & Tex. Cent. R. Co. v. Dunham*, 49 Tex. 181 (1878); *Norfolk & W. R. Co. v. Jackson's Adm'r*, 8 S.E. 370 (Va. 1888); Shearman & Redfield, *Treatise* (5th ed. 1898), § 194a.

24. *See, e.g., Chi. & Nw. R. Co. v. Swett*, 45 Ill. 197 (1867); *Davis v. Cent. Vt. R. Co.*, 55 Vt. 84 (1882); *Peschel v. Chi., Mpls. & St. Paul R. Co.*, 21 N.W. 269, 274–78 (Wis. 1885) (dissent of Justice David Taylor suggesting that unconditional duty should be imposed).

25. *See, e.g., Mad Riv. & Lake Erie R. Co. v. Barber*, 5 Ohio St. 541 (1856); *Frazier v. Pa. R. Co.*, 38 Pa. 104 (1861); *Hutchinson v. York, Newcastle & Berwick R. Co.*, 5 Ex. 343 (Exc. 1850); *Wigmore v. Jay*, 5 Ex. 354 (Exc. 1850); *see also* Thomas Bevan, *Negligence In Law* (3rd ed. 1908), 663–65 (discussing British cases).

duty ended after the hiring process was completed.[26] A few states agreed with New York, but others did not. In 1867, Illinois chief justice Sidney Breese pointed out that safety was a public, not merely a private matter: in an age where railroads and other large corporations had "countless lives and unnumbered property committed daily to their care," it was essential to ensure that companies employ train crews and other workers who would continually fulfill that trust and avoid "destruction of life and property in their path, as they sweep in their terrific power over our State."[27]

Most courts that refused to impose a continuing duty of care to monitor employees' reliability adopted a corollary that mitigated the harsh effects of that refusal. In 1862, England's Court of Exchequer held that if a worker warned his employer of a dangerous workplace condition and the employer promised to fix it, that would trigger a grace period during which the worker could continue to work in the presence of the condition without being held to have assumed the risk of injury. American jurists supported the grace-period rule as a matter of justice, noting that "the dependent position of servants generally makes it reasonable to hold any notice on their part sufficient, however timid and hesitating, so long as it plainly conveys to the master the idea that a defect exists, and that they desire its removal." The rule quickly gained acceptance in nearly every British and American court and was soon extended to cover warnings about problematic fellow workers.[28]

The grace-period rule generated collateral questions: how long should the grace period be, and how specific did the employer's promise to remedy the problem have to be in order to justify reliance on the worker's part? Most American courts applied a general rule of reasonableness to both questions, with an important qualifying condition: even if a promise had been made to remedy the condition at issue, a worker could not invoke the grace-period rule if the condition was obviously and imminently hazardous.[29] In cases of injury resulting from latent defects in machinery and equipment that were unknown to both employer and worker, courts generally applied free-labor

---

26. *Mad River*, 5 Ohio St. at 561; *Wilson v. Merry*, L.R. 1 Sc. App. 326 (H.L. 1868); *Warner*, 39 N.Y. at 479 (citing *Wilson* with approval and stating: "the duty of the master was to select proper and competent persons to do the work…, and when he had done that, he had performed his whole duty").

27. *See, e.g., Heine v. Chi. & Nw. R. Co.*, 17 N.W. 420, 422–23 (Wis. 1883) (agreeing with *Warner*); *Ill. Cent. R. Co. v. Jewell*, 46 Ill. 99, 101–02 (1867).

28. *Clark v. Holmes*, 7 H. & N. 937 (Exc. 1862); Shearman & Redfield, *Treatise* (2d ed. 1870), § 96; Francis Wharton, *A Treatise on the Law of Negligence* (1874), §§ 220–21; *see also, e.g., Kroy v. Chi., R.I. & Pac. R. Co.*, 32 Iowa 357 (1871); *Snow v. Housatonic R. Co.*, 8 Allen 441 (Mass. 1864); Francis H. Bohlen, "Voluntary Assumption of Risk: II," 20 *Harv. L. Rev.* 91 (1906) (citing cases).

29. *See, e.g., Greenleaf v. Ill. Cent. R. Co.*, 29 Iowa 14 (1870); *East Tenn., Va. & Ga. R. Co. v. Gurley*, 12 Lea 46 (Tenn. 1883); *see also* Shearman & Redfield, *Treatise* (5th ed. 1898) §§ 185, 185b; Wharton, *Treatise on Negligence* (2d ed. 1878), §§ 206, 208–09.

principles, holding that the worker would be deemed to have assumed the risk and must bear his own loss.[30]

The Continuing Struggle Over Proximate Cause

Causation continued to be a fundamental part of tort law as the nineteenth century drew to a close: there would be no liability for injury unless the defendant was at fault *and* that fault had caused the injury. But causation was not always straightforward, and it became less so as Americans moved from pre-industrial life to life in an integrated national economy, a life daily impacted by actions of large institutions located far away from their communities, operating through intermediaries who often were equally remote. Early- and mid-nineteenth-century judges had struggled mightily to devise a standard delineating those parts of causal chains that would trigger legal liability and those that would not, but they had only limited success. The rule laid down by Chief Justice Dixon in the *Kellogg* case, a rule centered on foreseeability, came closest: whether a given act caused an injury would be judged primarily in terms of whether the actor could reasonably have foreseen that the act would lead to the injuries for which compensation was claimed.[31]

Kellogg proved highly influential—forty years later, Shearman and Redfield stated that "[f]ew cases have been so often cited, quoted from and approved"—but it proved difficult to apply. Dixon's rule did not make foreseeability the exclusive test of causation and liability: physical and temporal proximity of act to injury could also be considered, and the subjective nature of foreseeability and the vast variety of circumstances that led to accidents all but guaranteed that uncertainty would continue. Courts that emphasized foreseeability in the wake of *Kellogg* used a variety of phrases to address the physical and temporal component of the analysis: the words "natural," "direct," "probable" and "proximate" cause appeared often, either singly or in combination.[32] The terminology varied from decision to decision even within individual states.[33]

---

30. Wharton, *Treatise* (2d ed. 1878), §§ 209–211; see, e.g., *Paulmier v. Erie R. Co.*, 34 N.J.L. 151 (1870); *Gibson v. Pac. R. Co.*, 46 Mo. 163 (1870); *Chi. & Alton R. Co. v. Platt*, 89 Ill, 141 (1878); *Ballou v. Chi. & Nw. R. Co.*, 11 N.W. 559 (Wis. 1882); *Atchison, Topeka & S. Fe R. Co. v. Ledbetter*, 34 Kan. 326 (1885).

31. *Kellogg v. Chi. & Nw. R. Co.*, 26 Wis. 223, 224–25, 236–38 (1870).

32. Shearman & Redfield, *Treatise* (6th ed. 1913), § 26 n.7; see, e.g., *Lake v. Milliken*, 62 Me. 240, 242 (1873) ("natural and proximate consequence"); *Ehrgott v. City of N.Y.*, 96 N.Y. 264, 281 (1884) (same); *Henry v. S. Pac. R. Co.*, 50 Cal. 176, 183, 1875 WL 1559 (1875) ("natural and probable consequence"); *Doggett v. Rich. & Danville R. Co.*, 78 N.C. 305, 307–08, 1878 WL 2336, at *2 (1878) ("natural and probable consequence"); *Pgh. S. R. Co. v. Taylor*, 104 Pa. 306, 315–16 (same).

33. Compare, e.g., *Ehrgott*, 96 N.Y. at 281, ("natural and proximate consequence"); *Lowery v. Manhattan Ry.*, 99 N.Y. 158 (1885) (an "ordinary and natural," "expected" or "necessary and usual result"); and *Frace v. N.Y., York, L.E. & W.R. Co.*, 143 N.Y. 182, 189 (1894) ("natural and direct result").

Dixon's own state was not immune from confusion. During the 1890s and the first decade of the twentieth century, his successors veered between tests that mentioned only foreseeability; that combined foreseeability with "natural consequence" and, later, "natural and probable" consequence; and that focused on "efficient," "responsible and efficient" and "real producing" causes.[34] "It is somewhat strange," a frustrated Justice John Winslow exclaimed in 1899, "that false notions of what constitutes proximate cause...became so grounded in many professional minds that the real philosophy of the subject cannot apparently be grasped and understood, notwithstanding the many clear elucidations of it given by this court."[35] Winslow's subsequent efforts to clear up confusion also failed,[36] and eventually Wisconsin trial judges settled on a jury instruction the supreme court had recommended in 1897 that referred to foreseeability and "natural cause."[37] They did so more out of a desire for consistency than out of admiration of the supreme court's work, and their decision to parrot the instruction to juries without elaboration or explanation may have served as a tacit invitation to jurors to use their own judgment in evaluating causation issues.

Early in the Second Industrial Era, a few courts recognized that causation standards were as much a matter of policy as logic. In 1865, Pennsylvania justice David Agnew argued that such standards must allow for the fact that occasional error and lack of foresight are an ineradicable part of life:

> ...otherwise [humans] would often be run into a chain of consequences wholly foreign to their intentions....To visit upon them *all* the consequences of failure would set society upon edge, and fill the courts with useless and injurious litigation. It is impossible to compensate for all losses, and the law therefore aims at a just discrimination, which will impose upon the party causing them, the proportion of them that a proper view of his acts and the attending circumstances would dictate.[38]

But who would determine the "proper view" of causation? American judges consistently made clear that they would retain ultimate control. New York's highest court sent that signal by consistently defending the rule of limited liability for fire damages based on "ordinary and natural" cause which it had established in *Ryan v. New York Central Railroad Co.* (1866). More than thirty years after *Ryan* was decided, Justice Albert Haight conceded that juries had a role in determining causation but emphasized the court's continuing belief that physical proximity was crucial to causation, at

---

34. *See, e.g., Jackson v. Wis. Tel. Co.*, 60 N.W. 430, 431, 433 (Wis. 1894); *Block v. Milw. St. R. Co.*, 61 N.W. 1101 (Wis. 1895); *Sheridan v. Bigelow*, 67 N.W. 732 (Wis. 1896).

35. *Baxter v. Chi. & Nw. R. Co.*, 80 N.W. 644, 648–49 (Wis. 1899)

36. *See, e.g., Wills v. Ashland L., P. & St. R. Co.*, 84 N.W. 998 (Wis. 1900); *Decker v. McSorley*, 86 N.W. 554 (Wis. 1901); *Eichmann v. Buchheit*, 107 N.W. 325 (Wis. 1906).

37. *Deisenreiter v. Kraus-Merkel Malting Co.*, 72 N.W. 735, 737 (Wis. 1897).

38. *Fleming v. Beck*, 48 Pa. 309, 313 (1865); *see also Doggett*, 78 N.C. at 307–08 and *Ehrgott*, 96 N.Y. at 281 (expressing similar sentiments).

least in fire cases. "[W]here is the line to be drawn?" he asked. "Shall it be one mile, two miles or ten miles distant from the place of the original starting of the fire? Who is to specify the distance?" Haight made clear that he and his colleagues would decide. In his view, the *Ryan* rule, which effectively limited juries' leeway in evaluating causation, "is wiser and more just and...we ought not to depart from it. The limitation may be somewhat arbitrary, but it recognizes the principle that we should live and let live. Fires often occur from the trivial acts of most prudent persons."[39]

Thus, at the end of the Second Industrial Era, causation doctrine was a soup composed of judicial logic, judicial policy and jury sentiment, all loosely united under the label of proximate cause. Jurists recognized the label's imprecision and flaws but clung to it because they could not find anything better. "This old form of words may not have originally meant what is now intended," Shearman and Redfield explained, but "it is now immovable...and is the form so long in use that its rejection would make unintelligible nearly all reported cases on the question involved."[40] Judges and jurists would continue to wrestle with causation during the twentieth century, edging ever closer to frank acknowledgment that causation, like other elements of tort law, turned heavily on policy and on changing social conditions.

The Place of Children in the Tort System

Accidents in which children were killed or severely injured appeared with depressing frequency in late-nineteenth-century court reports. Judges and jurists grappled with the questions of whether children should be held to the same standard of negligence as adults and whether lax parental supervision that allowed a child to enter an area of danger should be treated as contributory negligence that barred the child from recovering. Their evolving answers reflected larger shifts in Americans' attitudes toward children.

During America's colonial and early republican eras, most adults took a distinctly unsentimental view of children. Congregationalists and other dissenting Protestant denominations, important cultural forces in the Northeast and Midwest, regarded children, like adults, as beings imbued with original sin who could expect salvation only if they were among God's elect. Many adults coped with high early-childhood death rates by distancing themselves emotionally from their and others' children. Attitudes began to change after the great religious revivals of the early nineteenth century: revivalists rejected the doctrines of original sin and election and promoted a warmer, more personal Christianity toward children and adults alike. But the view that children should make their own way in the world from an early age remained strong. Child labor was an accepted and essential part of the agricultural economy that

---

39. *Ryan*, 35 N.Y. 210 (1866); *Hoffman v. King*, 160 N.Y. 618, 627–29 (1899).
40. Shearman & Redfield, *Treatise* (6th ed. 1913), § 26; *see ibid.* (4th ed. 1888), § 26 (same).

dominated the pre-industrial age, and textile mills and other early industries often hired whole families including young children. Thus, it seemed only natural, as well as economically necessary for many working families, to include children in the work-force, and that reinforced traditional views of children as adults in miniature. Children accounted for a large percentage of the American industrial work force throughout the last half of the nineteenth century and well into the twentieth century.[41]

By the 1840s, the industrial revolution was producing a sizable upper middle class whose children did not need to work in order to ensure economic survival. Members of that class began to take a sentimental, protective view of children, one that would eventually generate a movement to shift children from the industrial work force into schools. That movement would not gain real momentum until the turn of the century—child labor remained too important to the American economy to allow its elimination—but in the meantime it triggered widespread judicial reexamination of parents' and children's place in tort law.[42]

Age-Specific Negligence

In *Hartfield v. Roper* (1839), Esek Cowen not only helped lay the foundation for American contributory negligence doctrine but also threw his court's influence behind the traditional view that children should be held to the same standard of negligence as adults.[43] But soon afterward, in *Lynch v. Nurdin* (1841), England's Lord Chief Justice Thomas Denman suggested for the first time that children should be held to an age-specific standard of negligence; and in *Birge v. Gardiner* (1849), in which a child pulled at a fence and was injured when it fell on him, Connecticut's supreme court became the first American court to side with Denman and reject Cowen's view. "The plaintiff was a child, without judgment or discretion," said Chief Justice Samuel Church, "and it was [for] to the jury to say, whether such a child ought to be chargeable with fault so as to defeat his recovery; or whether or not the acts done by him, were not rather the result of childish instinct, which the defendant might easily have foreseen."[44] In *Robinson v. Cone* (1850), a nationally influential

---

41. Viviana Zelizer, *Pricing the Priceless Child* (1985), 25–28, 66–70; Hugh D. Hindman, *Child Labor: An American History* (2002), 22–26, 28–36; Paula S. Fass and Mary Ann Mason, eds., *Childhood in America* (2000), 237–48; Mary Lynn Stevens Henninger et al., *A Century of Childhood 1820–1920* (1984), 2–8, 122–27. In 1870, more than 700,000 children ages 10 to 14 worked in factories, comprising nearly 6 percent of the total workforce. In 1910 the figures were 1.6 million and 4.3 percent respectively. Hindman, *Child Labor*, 34.

42. Hindman, *Child Labor*, 40–45; John R. Commons, ed., *History of Labour in the United States, 1896–1932* (1935), 3:457–60.

43. 21 Wend. 615, 618–19 (N.Y. 1839).

44. *Lynch*, 1 Q.B. 29 (Q.B. 1841); *Birge*, 19 Conn. 507, 512 (1849). British courts never formally adopted Denman's suggestion as a rule: several courts rejected it, and the tide did not turn in favor of *Lynch* in Great Britain until the early twentieth century. See *Mangan v. Atterton*, L.R. 1 Ex. 239 (Exc. 1866); *Hughes v. Macfie*, 2 H. & C. 744 (Exc. 1863); Bevan, *Negligence*, 161–63.

decision authored by Isaac Redfield, Vermont's supreme court concurred, and during the 1870s, New York's highest court edged away from *Hartfield* and agreed that the extent of a defendant's duty of care toward a child should depend on the child's age.[45] Most states followed suit, although a few, most notably Massachusetts, continued to reject an age-specific standard.[46]

Other questions remained. One-year-old toddlers and twenty-year-old factory workers were both minors, but their cognitive and judgmental capacities were very different; how would tort law address these differences? A few courts set a minimum-threshold age, usually seven, below which a child could not be found negligent under any circumstances, or an adult-threshold age, usually eighteen, at which minors would be held to the same standard of care as adults. Pennsylvania justice Edward Paxson believed judges had a duty to set threshold ages: the issue could not be left to jurors because that "would give us a mere shifting standard, affected by the sympathies or prejudices of the jury in each particular case." Paxson held that his state's adult-threshold age should be the same for tort and criminal responsibility: namely, fourteen for boys and age twelve for girls.[47] Pennsylvania and some other states combined minimum and adult-threshold ages with legal presumptions: children between the minimum age and the adult threshold age would be presumed incapable of negligence, but defendants could overcome the presumption by showing that a child was unusually bright or was on notice of the danger at issue.[48] Most state courts avoided thresholds and presumptions altogether: they left it to juries to determine the cognitive and judgmental ability of an injured child and whether he had exercised due care, while reserving the right to take the issue from the jury and decide it as a matter of law in exceptional cases.[49]

---

45. *Robinson*, 22 Vt. 213 (1850); *O'Mara v. Hudson Riv. R. Co.*, 38 N.Y. 445 (1868); *Thurber v. Harlem Br., Morrisania & Fordham R. Co.*, 60 N.Y. 326 (1875); *see also* Shearman & Redfield, *Treatise*, §§ 70, 73; Charles F. Beach, Jr., *A Treatise on the Law of Contributory Negligence, or Negligence as a Defense* (2d ed. 1892), § 136.

46. *See, e.g., Holly v. Boston Gas Light Co.*, 74 Mass. 123, 132 (1857) (stating that a nine-year-old girl injured in a gas explosion "had no right to expose herself carelessly or willfully to its [the gas light system's] injurious effects"); *Wright v. Malden & Melrose R. Co.*, 4 Allen 283 (Mass. 1862); *Gallagher v. Johnson*, 130 N.E. 1 (Mass. 1921). Several treatise writers criticized Massachusetts severely on this point. Shearman & Redfield, *Treatise* (2d ed. 1870), § 48a n. 2; Beach, *Contributory Negligence*, § 141.

47. *Nagle v. Allegheny Vall. R. Co.*, 88 Pa. St. 35, 39–40 (1879). *See also, e.g., Dicken v. Liverpool Salt & Coal Co.*, 23 S.E. 582 (W.Va. 1895) (holding that a two-year-old child cannot be negligent as a matter of law).

48. *Nagle*, 88 Pa. St. at 39–40.

49. *See, e.g., Schmidt v. Milw. & St. Paul R. Co.*, 23 Wis. 186 (1868); *Ky. Cent. R. Co. v. Gastineau's Adm'r*, 83 Ky. 119 (1885); *Westbrook v. Mobile & Ohio R. Co.*, 6 So. 321 (Miss. 1889); Beach, *Contributory Negligence*, § 136 and cases there cited.

Parental Imputation

When young children were killed or injured, defendants routinely claimed that the injury was due to inadequate parental supervision. Would parents' negligence be imputed to children so as to bar them from recovery? The debate was initially framed by Justice Cowen in *Hartfield*, who said it should be imputed, and by Justice Redfield in *Robinson*, who said it should not be. Some courts agreed with Cowen: in Massachusetts, Justice Pliny Merrick held that a nine-year old girl poisoned by a leaky gas pipe could not recover because her father had not taken action to fix the problem. To hold otherwise, he reasoned, would contravene established patterns of family authority: the daughter "was entitled to the benefit of [her father's] superintendence and protection, and was consequently subject to any disadvantages resulting from the exercise of that parental authority which it was both his right and duty to exert."[50] But Redfield's view ultimately prevailed. In 1858, Tennessee's supreme court denounced Cowen's view in distinctly humanistic terms as "opposed to...every principle of reason and justice," a view which "is, literally, to visit the transgression of the parent upon the child." Other states soon followed suit, and in 1875 Cowen's successors edged away from his view, holding that at the least, parental negligence would not be imputed to very young children.[51]

Some courts professed support for Cowen's view but softened it by encouraging juries to consider the practical difficulties of parenting when weighing parents' conduct—a practice endorsed by most late-nineteenth-century commentators and courts.[52] For example, when a sixteen-month-old boy crawled onto railroad tracks and was killed, Wisconsin's supreme court refused to condemn his mother, who had left him in the care of a ten-year-old sibling. "Some consideration," said Justice William Lyon, was "due to the fact that the family were poor, and it was doubtless necessary, in carrying on their domestic affairs, that the services of each member of the family should be fully utilized." New York justice Robert Earl went further, stating that no negligence could be imputed to a parent who allowed her four-year-old son to play in the street after warning him to watch out for traffic. "Hundreds of young children," said Earl, "are permitted, with general safety, and must be permitted in cities to amuse themselves upon the sidewalks, and they cannot always be attended by persons of discretion."[53]

---

50. *Holly*, 74 Mass. at 132.

51. *Whirley v. Whiteman*, 38 Tenn. 610, 620 (1858); *see also, e.g., City of St. Paul v. Kuby*, 8 Minn. 154 (1863); *Boland v. Mo. R. Co.*, 36 Mo. 484 (1865); *Thurber*, 60 N.Y. at 333–34; *see also* Note, "Contributory Negligence on the Part of an Infant," 4 *Am. L. Rev.* 405, 412–13 (1870).

52. *See, e.g., Pgh., Allegheny & Manchester R. Co. v. Pearson*, 72 Pa. St. 169 (1872); *Isobel v. Hannibal & St. Joseph R. Co.*, 60 Mo. 475 (1875); *Walters v. Chi., R.I. & Pac. R. Co.*, 41 Iowa 71 (1875); Beach, *Contributory Negligence*, § 136.

53. *Hoppe v. Chi., Milw. & St. Paul R. Co.*, 21 N.W. 227, 231 (Wis. 1884) (Lyon); *Birkett v. Knickerbocker Ice Co.*, 110 N.Y. 504, 507 (1888) (Earl); *see also, e.g., Chi. & Alton R. Co. v. Gregory*, 58 Ill. 226 (1871).

The Turntable Doctrine

American courts paid increased attention to children as the nineteenth century drew to a close, perhaps prompted in part by the ever-growing number of workplace cases involving children that appeared on their dockets. Beginning in the 1870s, many courts held that employers' safe-place duties included a duty of particular care to inform child workers of workplace hazards and to allow for the "tendency to thoughtlessness" among young boys.[54] But children who were injured when they played with equipment or structures on public or private property faced another obstacle: legally, they were trespassers, and the common law shielded owners from liability to trespassers unless the owners had deliberately or recklessly created the hazard.[55] In 1841, Lord Chief Justice Denman suggested in *Lynch v. Nurdin* that relaxed standards of negligence for children should be linked to toughened standards of care for property owners, and in 1872 U.S. Supreme Court Justice Ward Hunt took the first steps to convert that suggestion into law. During his previous service as a New York justice, Hunt had written the decision in which his state moved away from *Hartfield* and adopted an age-specific standard of negligence for children. After his promotion to the federal high Court, he affirmed that standard and held that a railroad was liable to a child who had been injured while playing on a turntable (a rotating circular platform used in rail yards to turn locomotives and cars around) that was not guarded.[56]

Three years later, Minnesota's supreme court became the first state court to adopt Hunt's holding. Justice George Young disclaimed any intent to interfere with property owners' rights or to make them insurers of children, but he viewed turntables as a natural temptation to children's instincts of play, instincts of which property owners were surely aware. When an owner "sets before young children a temptation which it has reason to believe will lead them into danger," said Young, "it must use ordinary care to protect them from harm."[57] The rule became known as the "turntable" doctrine and, as it was expanded to other hazards on private property, as the "attractive nuisance" doctrine.

The doctrine was highly controversial. Several states soon followed Hunt's and Minnesota's lead,[58] but other courts and commentators sharply criticized the doctrine as an unwarranted invasion of landowners' traditional common-law rights to use their property as they saw fit. "The youthful innocence of the child does

---

54. *See, e.g., Coombs v. New Bedford Cordage Co.*, 102 Mass. 572 (1869); *Hickey v. Taaffe*, 105 N.Y. 26 (1887); *Neilon v. Marinette & Menominee Paper Co.*, 44 N.W. 772 (Wis. 1890).

55. *See, e.g., Morgan v. City of Hallowell*, 57 Me. 375 (1869); *Gramlich v. Wurst*, 86 Pa. St. 74 (1878); *E. Ky. R. Co. v. Powell*, 33 S.W. 629 (Ky. 1895).

56. *Lynch*, 1 Q.B. at 35–36; *O'Mara*, 38 N.Y. at 448–49; *Sioux City & Pac. R. Co. v. Stout*, 84 U.S. (17 Wall.) 657, 660–61 (1872).

57. *Keffe v. Milw. & St. Paul R. Co.*, 21 Minn. 207, 212 (1875).

58. *See, e.g., Kan. Cent. R. Co. v. Fitzsimmons*, 22 Kan. 686 (1879); *Fink v. Mo. Furnace Co.*, 10 Mo. App. 61 (1881); *Evansich v. Gulf, Colo. & S. Fe R. Co.*, 57 Tex. 126 (1882); *Union Stock Yards & Transit Co. v. Rourke*, 10 Ill. App. 474 (1881).

not make restrictions on the right of user less damaging to the owner," said one commentator, and Michigan justice Frank Hooker raised the specter that homeowners would not be able to leave even the smallest object on their lawns and would have to worry constantly about encroaching children. Hooker's colleague Robert Montgomery disagreed: he indicated that protection of children took priority over protection of property rights but also argued that owners would be liable only if there was "something calculated to allure a child of tender years." "You may call the doctrine... the result of evolution of the law, or what you please," said Montgomery, but "[i]t is a humane doctrine."[59]

Courts that adopted the turntable doctrine reflected the continuing shift in nineteenth- and early-twentieth-century views of children. In 1904, Wisconsin's supreme court justified its adoption of the doctrine for injuries on public property with a sentimental statement reflective of the new upper-middle-class perspective on children: one who wished to "wholly stop the flow of childish spirits while on the highway, and turn the little ones into men and women before their time," said Justice Winslow, "must either have had no childhood of his own or must have forgotten the fact."[60] But early-nineteenth-century views of children were slow to die out altogether, particularly in lawsuits against corporations perceived as performing essential social and economic functions. Many Americans reacted emotionally, and sometimes violently, to children's deaths in train and streetcar accidents; but others, like the author of a 1904 *New York Times* article, took a purely instrumentalist view: the transportation advantages of modern life "cannot be retarded to enable heedless children to get out of the way."[61] By 1900, most states had made some allowance for children's immaturity in their tort laws, but courts still took cases away from juries and ruled that children had been contributorily negligent as a matter of law in situations that make the rulings shocking to modern sensibilities.[62] That is not altogether surprising. The movement to eliminate child labor and with it,

---

59. Jeremiah Smith, "Liability of Landowners to Children Entering Without Permission," 11 *Harv. L. Rev.* 349, 352 (1898); William L. Prosser, "Trespassing Children," 47 *Cal. L. Rev.* 427, 430–33 (1959); *Ryan v. Towar*, 87 N.W. 644 (Mich. 1901), 646–47 (Hooker), 652 (Montgomery). At least one court took a middle path: it agreed to a broad rule of liability for attractions on public property, which it viewed as public nuisances for which tort law had long held owners liable, but it rejected liability for attractions on private property. This served as a gateway to later adoption of the doctrine for attractions on private property as well. See *Klix v. Nieman*, 32 N.W. 223 (Wis. 1887) (rejecting turntable doctrine); *Busse v. Rogers*, 98 N.W. 219, 222 (Wis. 1904) (adopting doctrine for attractions on public property, and suggesting that the court might eventually extend the doctrine to private property); *Angelier v. Red Star Yeast & Products Co.*, 254 N.W. 351 (Wis. 1933).

60. *Busse*, 98 N.W. at 222.

61. "Children in the Streets," *N.Y. Times*, December 9, 1904, p. 8, quoted in Zelizer, *Priceless Child*, 37.

62. *See, e.g., Tishacek v. Milw. Elec. R. & Light Co.*, 85 N.W. 971, 972–73 (Wis. 1901) (holding that a five-year-old girl who had run up to a streetcar line and stopped in the driver's sight but had then suddenly run across the line and had been struck and killed could not recover, and stating that "children of an age to be permitted to care for themselves upon city streets [must] exercise some measure of precaution when danger is actually observed by them").

utilitarian views of children had only just begun; it would not fully take hold for another decade, and even then it would face stiff constitutional resistance from the U.S. Supreme Court.[63] Railroads and streetcar companies would eventually launch a national safety campaign that greatly reduced crossing injuries for adults and children alike, but that campaign would not begin in earnest until the early 1910s. By then, workers compensation and child protection laws were appearing, laws that would transform negligence law and would moot many of the nineteenth-century legal battles over children's place in tort law.[64]

Walter McDougall and Paul West, *New York World*, March 18, 1900. The cartoon addresses streetcar and scaffolding accidents, both prolific sources of late-nineteenth-century tort litigation, as well as an enduring stereotype in American history: predatory lawyers. Courtesy Wikimedia Commons.

The Rise of Employer Liability Laws and Safety Laws

It was not only courts that wrestled with allocation of liability for railroad and workplace injuries. Legislatures did so as well, and in a much more public way. Between 1870 and 1910, many states enacted employer liability laws that ranged from codification of judicially created tort rules to elimination of the fellow-servant doctrine and other employer defenses. The laws were a barometer of changing American attitudes toward concepts of fault and allocation of accident liability.

The employer-liability-law movement arose out of a broader legal reaction to railroads that had begun in the 1850s. Before the Civil War, American states and municipalities had subsidized railroad construction heavily through purchases of railroad stock, bond issues and outright grants. Railroad subsidies were regularly challenged by disgruntled taxpayers and unlucky local governments that had invested in failed railroad ventures. The challenges did not succeed—state supreme courts almost uniformly held that railroads were so important to the economy that governmental subsidies served a public purpose—but their failure left a residue of popular ill will

---

63. Commons, *History of Labour*, 3:457–60; *Hammer v. Dagenhart*, 247 U.S. 251 (1918); *Bailey v. Drexel Furniture Co.*, 259 U.S. 20 (1923).

64. Zelizer, *Priceless Child*, 40–44.

toward railroads.[65] During and after the Civil War, railroads, buoyed by improved economic conditions, consolidated their lines and enacted complex and often discriminatory freight and passenger rates, acts that were economically defensible but deeply unpopular. They also gained a reputation for poor treatment of customers, a problem evidenced by the steady stream of tort suits filed by passengers who had been ejected from trains over fare disputes or had been denied help and shelter while waiting for trains.[66] Mark Twain deemed the problem worthy of satire in *The Gilded Age* (1873), and Charles Francis Adams Jr., a descendant of two presidents and a national authority on railroad management, complained publicly that railroad employees' manners "are probably the worst and most offensive to be found in the civilized world."[67]

The end of the 1860s brought both legislative and judicial reaction. In 1869, Massachusetts created the first state railroad commission, with Adams at its head, and other states soon followed. Most legislatures declined to give their commissions power to limit rates or correct abusive practices and confined them to investigating such matters and recommending reforms to lawmakers. But other states, particularly in the Midwest, went further. In 1869 and 1870, the Michigan, Wisconsin and Iowa supreme courts, speaking through Cooley, Dixon and Iowa justice John F. Dillon—all jurists of national reputation—reversed their legal course, holding that railroads should be viewed as private rather than public enterprises and that public subsidies were unconstitutional except in very limited circumstances.[68] Between 1870 and 1875, Midwestern states enacted a series of "Granger laws" creating more powerful railroad regulatory agencies and limiting rates and rate discrimination. Their supreme courts and ultimately the U.S. Supreme Court upheld the laws, thus laying a foundation for modern regulatory government in America.[69]

---

65. Carter Goodrich, *Government Promotion of Canals and Railroads* (1960), 51–120; Charles Fairman, *History of the Supreme Court of the United States, Vol. 6: Reconstruction and Reunion, 1864–1888* (1971), 918–1116; *see, e.g., Nichol v. Town of Nashville*, 28 Tenn. 252 (1848); *Sharpless v. Mayor of Phila.*, 21 Pa. St. 147 (1853).

66. During the 1860s and 1870s, such incidents accounted for roughly two percent of all tort cases in the five Survey states. See Appendix 2.

67. Mark Twain (Samuel L. Clemens) and Charles Dudley Warner, Jr., *The Gilded Age: A Tale of Today* (1873), ch. 29; Adams, "The Granger Movement," 120 N. Am. Rev. 394, 402 (1873)

68. *Hanson v. Vernon*, 27 Iowa 28 (1869); *People v. Twp. Board of Salem*, 20 Mic. 465 (1870); *Whiting v. Sheboygan & Fond du Lac R. Co.*, 25 Wis. 167 (1870); *see also* Alan R. Jones, *The Constitutional Conservatism of Thomas McIntyre Cooley: A Study in the History of Ideas* (1987), 16–26, 48–53; Clyde Jacobs, *Law Writers and the Courts: The Influence of Thomas M. Cooley, Christopher G. Tiedeman, and John F. Dillon Upon American Constitutional Law* (1973).

69. 1871 Ill. Laws, pp. 618, 636, 640; *People v. Munn*, 69 Ill. 80 (1873), *aff'd*, 94 U.S. 113 (1877); *see also* 1871 Minn. Laws, chs. 32, 34; *Blake v. Winona & St. Peter R. Co.*, 19 Minn. 418 (1872) *aff'd*, 94 U.S. 113 (1877); 1874 Wis. Laws, c. 273; *Potter Law Case (State ex rel. Atty. Gen. v. Chi. & Nw. R. Co.)*, 35 Wis. 425 (1874); Solon J. Buck, *The Granger Movement* (1913), 102–08; George W. Miller, *Railroads and the Granger Laws* (1971), 107–16, 126–31, 161–65; Joseph A. Ranney, *Wisconsin and the Shaping of American Law* (2017), 73–78.

Midwestern Grangerites included tort law in their reform efforts. Iowa's legislature enacted the nation's first employer liability law in 1862. The law effectively eliminated the fellow-servant doctrine for railroads by making them "liable for all damages sustained by any person, including employees of the company in consequence of any neglect of the [company's] agents"; it also prohibited railroads from forcing workers to waive injury claims as a condition of employment.[70] Wisconsin and Kansas enacted similar employer liability laws in 1874. The laws did not abolish fault altogether: railroads could still invoke employee contributory negligence and assumption of risk as defenses.[71] The laws were an important step toward shifting the cost of accidents to employers, but only a partial one: legislators focused exclusively on railroads and gave little thought to eliminating the fellow-servant doctrine for other employers.

Railroads challenged all three states' employer liability laws, arguing that the laws violated constitutional guarantees of equal protection by singling out railroads for regulation and that they interfered with railroads' constitutional liberty and property rights to operate their businesses as they pleased and to contract with employees on terms of their own choosing. All three states' supreme courts summarily rejected the challenges. Liability laws limited to railroads did not violate guarantees of equal protection of the laws, they said: railroads and the safety hazards they posed were unique in many respects, therefore they could be the subject of laws limited to their field. Nor did the laws violate employers' liberty, property or contract rights: those arguments had been dealt with in their earlier Granger law decisions, which affirmed in strong terms state power to regulate corporations. Wisconsin chief justice Edward Ryan had emphasized in his Granger law decision that state power was an essential check on the threat that concentrated corporate power posed to democratic values. He had warned railroads that public discontent must be heeded: regulatory laws were akin to "the surgeon's wholesome use of the knife, to save life, not to take it"; and he now underscored that warning. The U.S. Supreme Court also agreed, upholding Kansas's employer liability law in *Missouri Pacific Railroad Co. v. Mackey* (1888) and Iowa's law in *Minneapolis & St. Louis Railroad Co. v. Herrick* (1888).[72]

---

70. 1862 Iowa Laws, c. 169. In 1856 Georgia had enacted a law abolishing the fellow-servant doctrine for railroad workers, "who cannot possibly control those who should exercise care and diligence in the running of trains." 1855–56 Ga. Laws, p. 155. The law was similar to the Iowa law, except that the quoted language apparently limited its scope to train operators. See Marland C. Hobbs, "Statutory Changes in Employers' Liability," 2 *Harv. L. Rev.* 212 (1888). The territories of Wyoming and Montana also enacted early employer liability laws. Montana went the furthest, extending to employees the enhanced duty of care that railroads owed passengers. Mont. Rev. Stats (1879), p. 471, § 318; Wyo. Comp. Laws (1876), p. 512, ch. 97; Hobbs, "Statutory Changes," 220.

71. 1874 Wis. Laws, ch. 173; 1874 Kan. Laws, ch. 93; Donald J. Berthrong, "Employer's Liability Legislation in Wisconsin, 1874–1893," 34 *Sw. Soc. Sci. Q.* 57, 59–60 (1953).

72. *Potter Law Case*, 35 Wis. at 580 (1874) (upholding Wisconsin's Granger law); *Ditberner v. Chi., Milw. & St. Paul R. Co.*, 2 N.W. 69 (1879); *McAunich v. Miss. & Mo. R. Co.*, 20 Iowa 338 (1866); *Mo. Pac. R. Co. v. Haley*, 25 Kan. 35 (1881); *Mo. Pac. R. Co. v. Mackey*, 6 P. 291 (Kan. 1885), aff'd, 127 U.S. 205 (1888); *Herrick*, 127 U.S. 210 (1888).

New employer liability laws appeared in various forms after 1880. As with many other aspects of tort law, American lawmakers looked to Great Britain for guidance. During the 1860s, British trade unions and social reformers began criticizing common-law tort defenses, particularly the fellow-servant and assumption-of-risk doctrines, and recommended their abolition. Support for reform gradually grew, and after extensive debate, Parliament enacted the Employers' Liability Act of 1880. The 1880 Act was not limited to railroads but applied to a broad variety of industries. It eliminated common-law defenses available against workers where a worker's injury resulted from workplace and equipment defects; from negligence of vice-principals, that is, officials and supervisors with authority to direct workers; from a worker's compliance with a boss's order; from acts of fellow employees undertaken in compliance with company rules or a boss's order; or from acts of railroad workers in charge of locomotives, trains and signal points. Alabama adopted the 1880 Act nearly verbatim in 1885 and Massachusetts (1887), Colorado (1893) and Indiana (1893) soon followed suit.[73]

Between 1880 and 1910, approximately nineteen other states and territories fashioned their own employer liability laws. Some followed the early Midwest model, eliminating the fellow-servant doctrine for specified railroad personnel, usually engineers, train crews and switch operators.[74] Some states adapted one or two of the 1880 Act's categories of exemption from the fellow-servant doctrine or combined categories with codification of other softening features introduced by American courts.[75] Other states took unique paths, most notably Maryland: in 1902, it abolished the fellow-servant doctrine for miners and quarry and streetcar workers and provided that they could recover half the value of their injuries from their employer even if they were contributorily negligent. Employers would be exempted from the law if they agreed to pay premiums to a benefit fund administered by the state insurance commissioner for

---

73. 43 & 44 Vict. c. 42 (1880); 1885 Ala. Laws, p. 115; 1887 Mass. Laws, c. 270; 1893 Colo. Laws, c. 77; 1893 Ind. Laws, c. 130; see Conrad Reno, *A Treatise on the Law of Employers' Liability Acts* (1896), 363–77.

74. *See* 1891 Fla. Laws, c. 4071; La. Rev. Stats. (1897), § 2320; 1887 Minn. Laws, c. 13; Mo. Laws, p. 96; 1897 N.C. Laws, c. 56; 1903 N.D. Laws, c. 151; 1903 Or. Laws, p. 29; 1897 Tex. Laws, c. 6. The 1856 Georgia statute also fell in this category; *see* footnote 70 above.

75. *See* Ark. Rev. Stats. (1893), § 6659; Ariz. Terr. Rev. Stats. (1901) § 2767 (fellow-servant doctrine inapplicable if the employer had prior notice of the fellow worker's incompetency); Cal. Civ. Code (1909) § 1970 (doctrine inapplicable if fellow-servant hiring was negligent); Conn. Rev. Stats. (1901) § 4702 (doctrine inapplicable to vice-principals' negligence); 1893 N.M. Terr. Laws, c. 28 (similar to Arizona law); 1897 N.Y. Laws, c. 56 (doctrine inapplicable to vice-principals' negligence; employers liable for workplace defects); 1902 Ohio Laws, p. 114 (similar to New York law); 1903 Or. Laws, p. 20 (fellow-servant doctrine inapplicable to negligence of vice-principals and railroad crew members); S.C. Const. (1895), art. IX, § 15 (similar to Oregon law; doctrine also inapplicable to workers in different departments); Va. Const. (1902), § 162 (similar to South Carolina law).

workers killed in accidents, or if they created a company death-benefit fund approved by the commissioner.[76]

During the late nineteenth and early twentieth centuries, mining companies consistently and vigorously opposed expansion of workers' rights. Strikingly, and perhaps not coincidentally, many of the states that failed to enact liability laws were states in which mining interests were powerful.[77] None of the Midwestern states that had pioneered employer liability statutes for railroads expanded their statutes to apply to all industries in line with the British model. That seems curious, but it is consistent with a broader American pattern: most states that enacted employer liability laws created basic statutes reflecting their choice among these options and then left them in place, making only marginal adjustments in subsequent legislative sessions. Wisconsin was a rare exception. In 1880 its legislature repealed the state's 1874 law, but labor unions protested and campaigned for the law's restoration. They gained support from conservatives such as Frank Flower, the head of the state's Bureau of Labor and Industrial Statistics, who "f[ou]nd a sentiment in favor" of reinstating the old law and argued that "[o]ur laws as well as justice should keep pace with the advance of civilization." In 1889 and 1893, the legislature enacted limited laws barring application of the fellow-servant doctrine to acts of certain railroad supervisors and equipment operators. During the Progressive era, Governor Robert La Follette criticized these laws as "makeshift provision[s]...drawn...in the interest of the [railroad] companies with the purpose of modifying as little as possible the common law on the subject," and in 1903 Progressives expanded the laws to cover all accidents that involved "risk or hazard peculiar to the operation of railroads."[78]

---

76. 1902 Md. Laws, ch.139. In 1904 a lower state court struck down the law on the ground that it impermissibly delegated legislative power to the commissioner and deprived employers of the right to a jury trial. The decision was not appealed, and no further reform took place in Maryland until the advent of workers compensation. George E. Barnett, "The Maryland Workmen's Compensation Act," 16 Q. J. Econ. 591 (1902); Barnett, "The End of the Maryland Workmen's Compensation Act," 19 Q. J. Econ. 320, 320–22 (1905). In 1890, Mississippi codified the vice-principal and departmental exceptions to the fellow-servant doctrine and abolished the assumption-of-risk defense except for conductors and engineers. Miss. Const. (1890), § 193. In 1903, Montana codified the vice-principal and departmental exceptions and applied them to miners as well as railroad workers. 1903 Mont. Laws, c. 83.

77. See Figure 2.3; see generally Priscilla Long, *Where the Sun Never Shines: A History of America's Bloody Coal Industry* (1989).

78. 1880 Wis. Laws, c. 232; 1889 Wis. Laws, c. 438; 1893 Wis. Laws, c. 220; 1903 Wis. Laws, c. 448; Berthrong, "Employers' Liability Law," 60–68; Wis. Bur. of Lab. and Ind. Stats., *Second Biennial Report* (1886), xlv–xlvi; Wis. Sen. J., 97–98 (La Follette address to legislature, January 15, 1903).

FIGURE 2.3
The Evolution of Employer Liability Laws, 1860–1904[79]

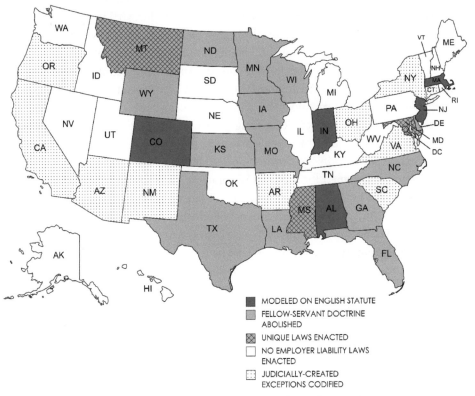

(Map generated from a template provided by courtesy of mapchart.net)

Post-1880 employer liability laws continued to elicit constitutional challenges, usually on the ground that the lines they drew between covered and non-covered workers were arbitrary and violated federal and state constitutions' equal-protection clauses. American courts rejected most of these challenges. The U.S. Supreme Court effectively put an end to challenges to laws limited to railroad employees in 1888 in *Mackey* and *Herrick*; later statutes that varied from the Iowa and Kansas employer liability laws in minor respects were challenged but were upheld by state supreme courts based on *Mackey* and *Herrick*.[80] In *Tullis v. Lake Erie & Western Railway Co.* (1899), the federal

---

79. *See* Carroll D. Wright, *Tenth Special Report of the Commissioner of Labor: Labor Laws of the United States, With Decisions of Courts Relating Thereto* (1904), and Reno, *Law of Employers' Liability*. Figure 2.3 is based on information in these sources.

80. *Mackey*, 127 U.S. 205 (1888); *Herrick*, 127 U.S. 210 (1888); *see Coley v. N.C. R. Co.*, 40 S.E. 195 (N.C. 1901); *Bodie v. Chas. & W. Carolina R. Co.*, 39 S.E. 715 (S.C. 1901); *Lewis v. N. Pac. R. Co.*, 92 P. 469 (Mont. 1907); Reno, *Law of Employers' Liability*, § 28; John Fabian Witt, "The Long History of State Constitutions and American Tort Law," 36 *Rutgers L.J.* 1159, 1181–82 (2005).

high Court upheld Indiana's law adopting the 1880 British Act's classifications, and courts in several other states with laws based on the 1880 Act rejected challenges to those laws based on *Tullis*.[81] A few employer liability laws did not survive challenge. In 1903 Mississippi's supreme court struck down a law that abolished the fellow-servant doctrine for all corporations, concluding that the law's omission of individual employers was unconstitutionally arbitrary, but it agreed that employer liability laws could validly target railroads and other businesses that involved a special degree of hazard.[82]

Employer liability laws that survived constitutional challenges were sometimes cabined by narrow judicial construction. Courts uniformly held that the laws did not eliminate contributory negligence as a defense.[83] Some liability laws codified the grace-period rule, providing that workers would not be subject to an assumption-of-risk defense even if they knew of a hazardous condition if they gave notice to the employer or the employer promised to fix the problem; but courts enforced these laws grudgingly, indicating that worker protections would not apply if the hazard posed an imminent threat of injury or the employer delayed repairs unduly.[84] Many cases involved injuries to workers who had followed instructions from persons not regularly authorized to give them orders or to control safety conditions, and courts frequently held that such persons were protected by state liability laws that incorporated the British Act's categories excluding employees of similar description from the fellow-servant doctrine.[85]

Anti-Waiver Statutes

During the late nineteenth and early twentieth centuries many American railroads established worker benefit plans, participation in which was often compulsory, or informally provided temporary support for injured workers and their families. Some also provided jobs for permanently disabled workers. They did so out of paternalism and out of a desire to avoid the costs and risks of litigation, but they and other

---

81. *Tullis*, 175 U.S. 348 (1899); *see Ryalls v. Mechanics' Mills*, 22 N.E. 766 (Mass. 1889); *Colo. Milling & Elev. Co. v. Mitchell*, 58 P. 28 (Colo. 1899); *Quigley v. Lehigh Vall. R. Co.*, 79 A. 458 (N.J. 1911).

82. *Ballard v. Miss. Cotton Oil Co.*, 34 So. 533 (Miss. 1903), *Bradford Const. Co. v. Heflin*, 42 So 174 (Miss. 1906). Indiana's supreme court agreed. *Bedford Quarries Co. v. Bough*, 80 N.E. 529 (Ind. 1907).

83. *See* Reno, *Law of Employers' Liability*, § 151; *see also, e.g., Mobile & B. R. Co. v. Holborn*, 84 Ala. 133 (1888); *Daugherty v. Midland Steel Co.*, 53 N.E. 844 (Ind. App. 1899).

84. Reno, *Law of Employers' Liability*, §§ 218, 239; *see, e.g., Kroy v. Chi., R.I. & P. R. Co.*, 32 Iowa 357 (1871), *Indpls. & St. L. R. Co. v. Watson*, 14 N.E. 721 (Ind. 1887).

85. Reno, *Law of Employers' Liability* (2d ed. 1903), §§ 249–50; *see, e.g., Hartford v. N. Pac. R. Co.*, 64 N.W. 1033, 1033–34 (Wis. 1895); *St. L. & S.F. R. Co. v. Guin*, 68 So. 78 (Miss. 1915). Some courts also held that the laws did not apply to railroads in receivership, although more courts held that they did. *See, e.g., Henderson v. Walker*, 55 Ga. 481 (Ga. 1875) and *Turner v. Cross*, 18 S.W. 578 (Tex. 1892) (holding that their states' laws did not cover receivers); *Sloan v. Cent. Iowa R. Co.*, 16 N.W. 331 (Iowa 1883), *Rouse v. Harry*, 40 P. 1007 (Kan. 1895) and *Malott v. Shimer*, 54 N.E. 101 (Ind. 1899); *Powell v. Sherwood*, 63 S.W. 485 (Mo. 1901) (all holding that laws applied to receivers).

employers also tried to protect themselves by inserting waiver clauses in their workers' contracts. These included absolute-waiver clauses requiring workers as a condition of employment to waive all right to file lawsuits in case of injury, and benefit-receipt clauses requiring workers to waive such rights if they accepted the guaranteed but limited benefits that company plans provided.[86]

Britain's 1880 Act did not prohibit such clauses, and nineteenth-century British courts generally upheld both types of clauses as consistent with free-labor principles of liberty of contract,[87] but American legislatures and courts gave the clauses a cooler reception. Between 1860 and 1910, at least nineteen states enacted anti-waiver statutes prohibiting absolute-waiver clauses and, in some cases, benefit-receipt clauses.[88] American courts generally upheld benefit-receipt clauses in the absence of prohibitory statutes[89] but many struck down absolute-waiver clauses even in the absence of statutes, reasoning that because they required workers to give up legal rights that had not yet sprung into existence, they were contrary to public policy and void.[90] Judicial hostility to absolute-waiver clauses insulated prohibitory statutes limited to such clauses from any serious constitutional challenge, but American courts divided over statutes prohibiting benefit-election clauses. Some courts upheld their states' prohibitory statutes, stating that such clauses were against public policy because they required workers to elect a remedy prior to injury without providing any immediate benefit in return.[91] Other courts upheld benefit-election clauses, reasoning that benefit election operated as a voluntary settlement between employers and workers.[92] In

---

86. One scholar has concluded that after 1880, railroads and their employees inclined more toward litigation. Railroads did so because of increasing pressure to reduce costs and increase efficiency; workers did so because they feared that acceptance of paternalistic benefits would threaten their independence and bargaining power as to other issues. See Kaczorowski, "From Petitions for Gratuities to Claims for Damages," 266–78, 282–98.

87. *See e.g., Griffiths v. Dudley*, 9 Q.B. Div. 357 (Q.B. 1882); *Clements v. London & Nw. R. Co.*, 2 Q.B. (Eng.) 482 (Q.B. 1894).

88. *See, e.g.,* 1893 Wis. Laws, c. 220; 1903 Wis. Laws, c. 448. *See also, e.g.,* Ark. Rev. Stat. (1894), § 6660; Colo. Const. (1876), art. XV, § 15; 1891 Fla. Laws, c. 4071; Ga. Code (1895), § 2613; Mass. Stats., § 106:16; Miss. Const. (1890), § 193; Mont. Const. (1889), art. XV, § 16; 1903 N.D. Laws, c. 131; 1897 N.Y. Laws, c. 56; 1903 Or. Laws, p. 20; 1897 Tex. Laws, c. 6; Va. Const. (1902), § 162; Wyo. Const. (1890), art. XIX, § 1.

89. *See, e.g., Graft v. Balt. & Ohio R. Co.*, 8 A. 206 (Pa. 1887); *Spitze v. Balt. & Ohio R. Co.*, 23 A. 307 (Md. 1892); *Eckman v. Chi., B. & Q. R. Co.*, 48 N.E. 496 (Ill. 1897); *Chi., B. & Q. R. Co. v. Bell*, 62 N.W. 314 (Neb. 1895); *Beck v. Pa. R. Co.*, 43 A. 908 (N.J. 1899). None of these states had statutes limiting the validity of such clauses.

90. *See, e.g., Kan. Pac. R. Co. v. Peavey*, 29 Kan. 169 (1883); *Lake Shore & Mich. S. R. Co. v. Spangler*, 8 N.E. 467 (Ohio 1886); *Little Rock & Ft. Smith R. Co. v. Eubanks*, 3 S.W. 808 (Ark. 1887); *Johnson's Adm'x v. Richmond & Danville R. Co.*, 11 S.E. 829 (Va. 1890); *Hissong v. Richmond & Danville R. Co.*, 8 So. 776 (Ala. 1891); *see also* Reno, *Employers' Liability Laws*, §§ 7–9.

91. *See, e.g., Pa. Co. v. Chapman*, 77 N.E. 248 (Ill. 1905); *Atl. Coast Line R. Co. v. Beazley*, 45 So. 761 (Fla. 1907); *Barden v. Atl. Coast Line R. Co.*, 67 S.E. 975 (N.C. 1910).

92. *See, e.g., Pgh., Cinn., Chi. & St. L. R. Co. v. Cox*, 45 N.E. 641 (Ohio 1896); *Colaizzi v. Pa. R. Co.*, 101 N.E. 859 (N.Y. 1913).

1908, Congress explicitly banned use of benefit-election clauses by railroads engaged in interstate commerce, which led to a sharp reduction in their use. The U.S. Supreme Court upheld the 1908 law, and nearly all state courts followed its lead thereafter.[93]

Safety Statutes

Workplace safety statutes grew in tandem with employer liability laws. Between 1870 and 1910 most states, particularly those at an advanced stage of industrialization, enacted safety statutes, but they did so in haphazard fashion. Early safety laws were directed at individual problems and were often enacted in reaction to a particularly bad factory fire or explosion. New York provides a good example. Labor groups, most notably the New York City-based Workingmen's Assembly, and philanthropic groups began advocating for workplace reform in the late 1870s, but they focused primarily on reduced hours and improved working conditions for women and children, not on workplace safety. During the early 1880s they turned their attention to safety issues, and in 1886 they persuaded New York's legislature to enact a workplace law that established a factory-inspection system but said nothing about workplace physical conditions and safety devices. The following year the legislature enacted limited equipment-safety rules and in 1889, after a fire engulfed Rochester's Steam Gauge and Lantern Factory Works and killed thirty-eight people, the legislature enacted the state's first fire-escape laws. Wisconsin provides another example: two years after an 1883 fire destroyed Milwaukee's Newhall House hotel and killed seventy-one people, its legislature expanded an existing safety-ladder law and required fire escapes and fireproof construction in hotels and factories. Additional safety statutes appeared sporadically throughout the 1890s and early 1900s.[94] Less industrialized states did not enact workplace safety laws until the twentieth century, and no state would attempt to create a comprehensive industrial safety code until 1911, when Wisconsin established an Industrial Commission charged with preparing and enforcing such a code.[95]

Like the core tort concepts of fault-based liability and contributory negligence, the late-nineteenth-century piecemeal legislative approach to safety was a product of the era's focus on individual responsibility. That focus also shaped the early work of state labor bureaus. During the two decades after Massachusetts created the first such bureau in 1869, twenty more states, prodded by organized labor, created similar

---

93. 35 U.S. Stats. 65 (1908); *Chi., B. & Q. R. Co. v. McGuire*, 219 U.S. 549 (1911); see Note, "Validity of Contract Providing that Acceptance of Benefits from Relief Association Shall Bar Action Against Employer," 12 A.L.R. 477 (1921), § V and cases there cited.

94. 1886 N.Y. Laws, ch. 409; 1887 N.Y. Laws, ch. 462; 1889 N.Y. Laws, ch. 560; Fred R. Fairchild, "The Factory Legislation of the State of New York," *Pubs. of Am. Econ. Assn.*, 3d ser., Vol. 6 (November 1905), 29–35, 44–56, 78–80; 1878 Wis. Laws, c. 212; 1885 Wis. Laws, chs. 50, 247, 375; Nesbit, *History of Wisconsin: Urbanization and Industrialization*, 453.

95. *See, e.g.*, N.C. Gen. Stats. (1908), Tex. Rev. Civ. Stats. (1911) and Cal. Civ. Code (1905) (all containing little or no safety legislation); 1911 Wis. Laws, c. 485; *see* Rogers, "Common Law to Factory Laws," 197.

bureaus.[96] Many states gave their bureaus power only to monitor workplace conditions and suggest improvements; very few lawmakers were prepared to give the bureaus power to create and enforce safety regulations. One state commissioner rationalized that safety issues could be handled through the criminal-law system: "[I]f any artisan in an unsafe building... shall complain to the district attorney, that officer will at once, if a good case is presented, proceed against the offender." Workers, he said, "having an adequate remedy in their own hands... cannot justly complain that the state makes no effort to protect them."[97]

Though early safety statutes were sketchy, still, they were available for enforcement. Beginning in the 1880s, the question arose whether violation of such statutes would impose absolute liability on employers in case of worker injury, or whether employers could still assert contributory negligence as a defense. American courts had useful precedents to look to: during the 1860s and 1870s, many had considered that question in the context of statutes requiring railroads to fence their rights of way. Several states, most notably New York, had interpreted their fencing statutes to impose absolute liability on railroads whose failure to fence led to livestock and crossing accidents. To do otherwise, reasoned Justice Rufus Peckham, would effectively nullify fencing statutes, because owners whose livestock strayed onto tracks could almost always be considered contributorily negligent.[98] Other courts refused to go that far, holding that violation of fencing statutes was sufficient to establish negligence on the railroad's part but that contributory negligence was still a defense,[99] and in some cases holding that imposition of liability regardless of fault was unconstitutional.[100]

American courts divided over the effect of workplace safety laws in much the same manner. A majority of courts that considered the issue held that workplace safety laws did not bar use of contributory negligence and assumption-of-risk defenses against injured adult workers unless the laws contained explicit wording to that effect; they were reluctant to undermine traditional concepts of fault through liberal statutory interpretation.[101] Courts in some states were not so reluctant: they liberally construed

---

96. Commons, *History of Labour*, 3:628; *see* Fairchild, "Factory Legislation of New York," 24–27.

97. Arthur J. Altmeyer, *The Industrial Commission of Wisconsin: A Case Study in Labor Law Administration* (1932), 13; Rogers, "Common Law to Factory Laws," 196–97; Wis. Bureau of Labor Statistics, *First Biennial Report, 1883–84* (1884), at 167–68, 170.

98. *Shepard v. Buff., N.Y. & Erie R. Co.*, 35 N.Y. 641 (1866). Other early cases upholding absolute liability included *Jeffersonville, Madison & Indpls. R. Co. v. Ross*, 37 Ind. 545 (1871) and *Wilder v. Me. Cent. R. Co.*, 65 Me. 332 (1876); *see also, e.g., Ill. Cent. R. Co. v. Crider*, 19 S.W. 618 (Tenn. 1892).

99. *See, e.g., Curry v. Chi. & Nw. R. Co.*, 43 Wis. 665 (1878); *Jolliffe v. Brown*, 44 P. 149 (Wash. 1896). After *Curry* was decided, Wisconsin's legislature amended the state's fencing law to preclude contributory negligence as a defense. 1881 Wis. Laws, c. 193; *see Quackenbush v. Wis. & Mich. R. Co.*, 22 N.W. 519 (Wis. 1885) (upholding 1881 law).

100. *See, e.g., Zeigler v. S. & N. Ala. R. Co.*, 58 Ala. 594 (1877); *Bielenberg v. Mont. Union R. Co.*, 20 P. 314 (Mont. 1889); *see also* Witt, "State Constitutions and Tort Law," 1177–78.

101. *See, e.g., Thompson v. Edward P. Allis Co.*, 62 N.W. 527, 529 (Wis. 1895); *Knisley v. Pratt*, 148 N.Y. 372 (1896); *Langlois v. Dunn Worsted Mills*, 57 A. 910 (R.I. 1904); *Mika v. Passaic Print Works*,

safety statutes to preclude employers from asserting contributory negligence and assumption of risk based on building and equipment defects. Those defenses, said Kansas justice Henry Mason, were at bottom based on a worker's express or implied agreement to be responsible for the risks that attended unsafe machinery, and such an agreement could hardly be said to exist if the legislature had placed that responsibility on the employer through a safety statute.[102]

Many courts that allowed contributory negligence and assumption of risk as defenses to claims by adult workers made an exception as to employers who hired children in violation of minimum-age statutes. New York took the lead. Minimum-age statutes, Justice Haight explained in 1903, were intended to reduce child labor and protect vulnerable children from harm; they represented a legislative determination that children did not possess the judgment required for industrial work and, thus, could not be charged with contributory negligence.[103] Most other states eventually followed suit,[104] but a minority, led by Massachusetts, did not, holding that use of liability defenses against children would not be barred unless that was explicitly done by statute.[105]

Judges Versus Juries in the Second Industrial Era

The widespread adoption of David D. Field's civil procedure code in the 1850s and 1860s underscored the delicacy of the balance of power between judges and juries that existed at the dawn of America's Second Industrial Era. Where witnesses' accounts of an accident differed, juries had broad power to decide what actually happened. Their fact-finding power extended to issues central to the outcome of many tort cases, for example, whether employers' actions were consistent with the ordinary level of care observed in their industries. But judges had broad countervailing powers: if they concluded there was no real dispute as to the facts or as to the proper legal outcome that

---

70 A. 327 (N.J. 1908); *Jones v. Am. Caramel Co.* 74 A. 613 (Pa. 1909).

102. *W. Furniture & Mfg. Co. v. Bloom*, 90 P. 821 (Kan. 1907); *see also, e.g., Kilpatrick v. Gr. Trunk R Co.*, 52 A. 531 (Vt. 1902) and *Narramore v. Clev., Cinn., Chi. & St. Louis R. Co.*, 96 F. 298 (6th Cir. 1899) (William Howard Taft, J.).

103. *Marino v. Lehmaier*, 66 N.E. 572 (N.Y. 1903); *see generally* Lindley D. Clark, *The Law of the Employment of Labor* (1911), 129–32.

104. See, e.g., *Perry v. Tozer*, 97 N. W. 137 (Minn. 1903); *Ornamental Iron & Wire Co. v. Green*, 65 S. W. 399 (Tenn. 1901); *Sipes v. Mich. Starch Co.*, 100 N. W. 447 (Mich. 1904); *Am. Car & Foundry Co. v. Armentraut*, 73 N. E. 766 (Ill. 1905); *Lenahan v. Pittston Coal Mining Co.*, 218 Pa. St. 311 (1907); *Leathers v. Blackwell's Durham Tobacco Co.*, 57 S. E. 11 (N.C. 1907); *Sanitary Laundry Co. v. Adams*, 183 Ky. 39, 208 S.W. 6, 7 (1919) (collecting cases).

105. *Berdos v. Tremont & Suffolk Mills*, 95 N.E. 876 (Mass. 1911); *see also, e.g., Sterling v. Union Carbide Co.*, 105 N.W. 755 (Mich. 1905); *Robin v R.J. Reynolds Tobacco Co.*, 53 S.E. 891 (N.C. 1906). Michigan and North Carolina later modified their positions. *See also* Note, "Construction of Child Labor Statutes," 23 *Yale L.J.* 175 (1913) (criticizing the *Marino* decision and arguing that no exception should be made unless explicitly stated in a child-labor statute).

the facts required, they could take the case from the jury using tools such as nonsuits, directed verdicts and orders for new trials. In cases that went to the jury, judges could shape the verdict questions that ultimately would determine a case's outcome. In some states they could also give the jury their analysis of the evidence, which could effectively dictate the jury's decision.

A Clash of Sympathies: Real or Imagined?

How actively did judges assert their powers, and how did the balance of power between judges and juries affect the outcome of tort cases during the Second Industrial Era? Jurists accepted as a truism that juries were unduly sympathetic to accident victims and, in the words of one state judge, were "apt to find...corporations liable for losses and injuries under circumstances where an individual would not be held responsible." Another writer was less restrained, denouncing "[t]he flagrant disregard by jurors in [workplace accident] actions of their oaths" which "has given ground for the impression...that the jury cannot now be relied upon to secure a just determination of the facts between employer and employee."[106] That picture was exaggerated—studies of Second Industrial Era trial courts in various states suggest that any jury predisposition toward plaintiffs was mild at best[107]—but it rang true to many American judges, and it may have prompted them and their colleagues to assert their powers more vigorously as a counterbalance.

Many members of the public noticed and disapproved of this judicial attitude. Andrew Bruce, a law professor and future North Dakota supreme court justice, agreed that "the tendency is steadily growing toward a stricter control of the jury by the courts," and he worried that this would soon produce a crisis:

> If judges are now limiting the employer's liability, it is largely because rightly or wrongly they have come to believe that there is abroad a conspiracy against capital and employers...Justifiable, however, as these tendencies may be, there can be no doubt of their unpopularity. An injured man can rarely be brought

---

106. *Pike v. Chi., Milw. & St. Paul R. Co.*, 40 Wis. 583, 586–87 (1876) (Justice Orsamus Cole); James R. Burnet, "Critical Opinions Upon Recent Employers' Liability Legislation in the United States," 50 *J. Soc. Sci.* (1902), 53–54.

107. *See* Randolph E. Bergstrom, *Courting Danger: Injury and Law in New York City, 1870–1910* (1992), 138 (about two-thirds of New York City trial-court jury verdicts favored plaintiffs, but more than half of all cases were decided on procedural grounds or by settlement); Lawrence M. Friedman, "Civil Wrongs: Personal Injury Law in the Late 19th Century," 1987 *Am. Bar Found. Rsch. J.* 351 (1987) (study of Alameda County, California state trial court and federal trial court for Northern District of California; roughly half of cases resulted in verdicts for plaintiffs); Lawrence M. Friedman and Thomas D. Russell, "More Civil Wrongs: Personal Injury Litigation, 1901–1910," 34 *Am. J. Leg. Hist.* 295, 308 (1990) (same courts, similar result); Frank W. Munger, "Social Change and Tort Litigation: Industrialization, Accidents, and Trial Courts in Southern West Virginia, 1872–1910," 36 *Buff. L. Rev.* 75, 99–100 (50–60 percent of verdicts in trial courts for three West Virginia counties were for plaintiffs).

to see the justice of a verdict which is returned against him by a jury. Much less can he be induced to acquiesce when a Supreme Court judge, whom he has not seen and who knows only of the case as it is presented to him on the printed record, is responsible for his overthrow. As things now are, it is perhaps not an exaggeration to say that every personal injury case is a factor in the increase of social discontent.[108]

But judges were also aware they were not infallible. Luther Dixon's open confession of a change of heart was rare but not unique, and no less an eminence than Thomas Cooley warned that judges must think carefully before taking cases away from a jury:

> [W]hen the judge decides that a want of due care is not shown, he necessarily fixes in his own mind the standard of ordinary prudence, and...turns [the plaintiff] out of court upon his opinion of what a reasonably prudent man ought to have done under the circumstances. He thus makes his own opinion of what would be generally regarded as prudence a definite rule of law. It is quite possible that, if the same question of prudence were submitted to a jury collected from the different occupations of society, and perhaps better competent to judge of the common opinion, he might find them differing with him as to the ordinary standard of proper care.[109]

As has been seen, Second Industrial Era judges were faced with constant challenges to traditional concepts of fault and individual responsibility. They were loyal to those concepts but occasionally softened them by creating rules such as relaxed standards of care for children and their parents and common-law safe-place duties tailored to industrial realities. Did these softening impulses also make them less eager to use their powers and more deferential to juries? Examination of the Second Industrial Era tort decisions in the Five-State Survey yields suggestive if inconclusive information.

First, state supreme court judges were not always required to make a final decision whether an injury victim should prevail and receive compensation. About one-third of the Survey cases involved procedural issues, for example, whether a jury's verdict had been tainted by improper admission of evidence, by erroneous instructions from the trial judge or by a poorly-crafted set of verdict questions that did not reach all of the issues in the case. Supreme courts sent nearly all such cases back for a new trial rather than deciding them on the merits. Occasionally they made clear what they thought the final outcome should be, but in most cases they reinforced the jury's role as the ultimate decider of who was at fault.[110]

---

108. Bruce, "Employers' Liability in the United States," 32 *Forum* 48–49 (1902).

109. *Det. & Milw. R. Co. v. Van Steinburg,* 17 Mich. 99, 120 (1868); *see also* Beach, *Contributory Negligence* (2d ed. 1892), § 126.

110. The proportions of cases involving procedural issues were: 34% (1870), 28% (1880), 31% (1890), 39% (1900), 37% (1910) and 31% (1920). Trial courts, too, issued procedural decisions regularly: during the survey years, roughly 15% to 20% of all tort cases reaching supreme courts involved trial-court procedural decisions. See Appendix 3 for the data on which these calculations are based.

However, a numerical "shift" scale can be used to evaluate plaintiffs' success in Five-State Survey courts during the Second Industrial Era, and to test whether the concerns of Bruce, Cooley and others about judicial reaction against juries perceived to be overly friendly to plaintiffs were justified. The strongest shifts occurred when a supreme court overturned a trial-court decision for one party and decided for the other party on the merits without sending the case back for a new trial. In Figure 2.4, which is based on the Five-State Survey cases for the years indicated, a value of +2 is assigned to supreme court reversals in favor of plaintiffs on the merits and, at the other end of the spectrum, a value of –2 to reversals in favor of defendants on the merits. Lesser shifts, when a supreme court reversed a trial-court merits decision and sent the case back for a new trial or reversed a trial-court decision allowing the tort case to go to trial and issued its own decision on the merits, represented a real but less extreme setback for the party that had prevailed in the trial court; these shifts are assigned values of +1 if they benefited plaintiffs and –1 if they benefited defendants. Cases in which supreme courts affirmed trial courts' procedural and merits decisions resulted in no change in either party's position, and they are assigned a value of zero.[111]

It is not unreasonable to conclude that Second Industrial Era appellate courts issuing a relatively high proportion of decisions reflecting strong or intermediate shifts in defendants' favor were instinctively inclined to scrutinize jury and trial-court decisions favoring plaintiffs more closely than decisions favoring defendants. Likewise, courts issuing a relatively high proportion of decisions reflecting strong or intermediate shifts toward plaintiffs might well have empathized with accident victims. Such empathies may have colored judges' views of the facts in the cases that came before them and of where those facts fit into the legal framework that governed liability in each case. Figure 2.4 suggests that collectively, the Five-State Survey supreme courts tilted modestly but consistently toward defendants throughout the Second Industrial Era. The collective tilt changed surprisingly little from decade to decade.[112]

---

111. The overall shifts for the five Survey states in the aggregate were: -0.273 (1870), -0.307 (1880), -0.327 (1890), -0.283 (1900), -0.359 (1910), and -0.402 (1920). The shift index is explained in more detail in Appendix 3. The cases on which Figure 2.4 is based are listed in Appendix 2 and the shift calculations are described in Appendix 3.

112. There was significant variation between the states during the Second Industrial Era. The average shift for each state, based on all Survey cases for that state during the era (1870–1920), was, in order of defendant friendliness, New York, –.411; Texas, –.348; Wisconsin, –.281; California, –.218; and North Carolina, –.176. The calculations are described in Appendix 3. The reasons for these variations and their significance must remain a matter of speculation until more detailed research is done.

FIGURE 2.4
Five-State Survey: Shift Distributions, 1870–1920

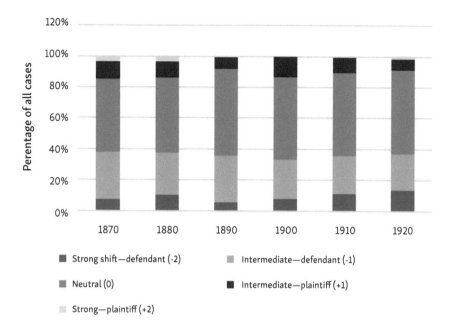

What accounts for this mild judicial tilt toward defendants? Figure 2.4 suggests that Bruce's and Cooley's concerns were justified, that some judges did believe juries were overly friendly to plaintiffs and that they needed to check that tendency. But it is likely that the institutional conservatism of law also affected the tilt. Plaintiffs ask the law to change things by remedying an alleged wrong; but law is structured to foster predictability and stability, values often at odds with change. Law places the burden on plaintiffs to show that courts should make their requested change. Late-nineteenth-century judges placed high importance on these institutional values; they consistently asserted and defended their power to rein in juries who might override such values with their own notions of justice in order to help sympathetic plaintiffs.

One courtroom practice that changed during the Second Industrial Era was trial judges' custom of giving juries their views on the evidence and the merits of a case. As discussed in the previous chapter, the British common-law practice of allowing judges to comment freely on the evidence, which was based on a concomitant assumption that juries should defer to judges as Crown officials, did not take deep root in a less hierarchical America. Between the end of the American Revolution and 1860, a handful of states allowed judges to sum up evidence for juries but prohibited them from giving their views as to its effect or as to what the verdict should be.[113] The

---

113. During this period, North Carolina (1795), Tennessee (1796), Mississippi (1822), Arkansas (1836), Illinois (1845), Georgia (1850) and Texas (1853) adopted such provisions. Edson R. Sunderland, "The Problem of Trying Issues," 5 *Tex. L. Rev.* 18, 32–33 (1926).

anti-instruction movement accelerated after 1860, and by 1900 more than half of all states prohibited or discouraged judges from engaging in either activity, some by statute or constitutional amendment[114] and some through directives from their supreme courts.[115] Most such courts made it clear that their decisions were based on the need to show respect for jury independence, but some also emphasized the practical side: the more a trial judge opined on a case to the jury, the more risk he ran that his judgment would be reversed on appeal.[116] Trial judges took note, and judicial editorializing gradually disappeared.

At the dawn of the twentieth century, the superstructure of American tort law was much the same as it had been forty years earlier. The core principles of individual responsibility and of liability as a function of fault remained firmly in place. Legislative and judicial efforts to soften the sometimes-harsh effects of those principles had produced some changes at the margin, but Progressives now were gaining power in many states in tandem with a steadily growing popular feeling that the old concepts of responsibility and fault were not suited to the new age of wage workers, mass production and ever-changing industrial technology. Progressives increasingly came to believe that mere softening of traditional tort principles was not enough. Change would have to come through legislation, and it would have to be fundamental.

---

114. *See, e.g.,* Nev. Const. (1864), art. VI, § 12 (stating that "[j]udges shall not charge juries in respect to matters of fact, but may state the testimony and declare the law"); S.C. Const. (1868), art. IV, § 26 (same); Wash. Const. (1889), art. IV, § 16 (similar).

115. *See, e.g., Whitelaw's Ex'r v. Whitelaw*, 1 S.E. 407, 409–10 (Va. 1887) (stating: "It lies at the foundation of jury trials that by their verdict the jury shall determine the issue joined upon their consciences without outside influence or coercion from the court or elsewhere. The province of the court is to instruct the jury upon questions of law, and express no opinion, make no comments concerning the facts, whether conflicting or not; there can be no particular circumstances which will justify the court in doing either"). *See also McDuff v. Det. Eve. J. Co.*, 47 N.W. 671 (Mich. 1890); *United Rys. & Elec. Co. of Balt. v. Carneal*, 72 A. 771 (Md. 1909).

116. Sunderland, "Trying Issues," 33–34, notes 25 and 27; *Horr v. C.W. Howard Paper Co.*, 105 N.W. 668, 671 (Wis. 1905) (stating that "When a trial judge has both the industry and the courage to undertake to so promote the cause of justice, we are far from suggesting criticism or disapproval [but t]he attempt is nevertheless accompanied with danger").

THREE

Saving Capitalism by Making it Good
Tort Law in the Progressive Era

Accidents to workmen... are all but inevitable.... Heretofore these losses have been borne by the injured workmen themselves, by their dependents, or by the state at large. It was the belief of the Legislature that they should be borne by the industries causing them, or, perhaps more accurately, by the consumers of the products of such industries. That the principle thus sought to be put into effect is economically, sociologically, and morally sound, we think must be conceded.... Indeed, so universal is the sentiment that to assert to the contrary is to turn the face against the enlightened opinion of mankind.

—Justice Mark Fullerton (Washington), 1911[1]

The Progressive movement was a tree of many branches. Between 1890 and 1920, it produced fundamental legal change in elections, taxation, utility regulation and the workplace—and, what is less well-known, in American tort law. The work of Carroll Wright and Crystal Eastman, both of whom played important roles in the era's restructuring of tort law, illustrates Progressivism's diffuse nature.

Wright was born into an upper-middle-class New England family in 1840. Like other members of his class, he viewed the labor movement with more detachment than sympathy, but as a devout Universalist he believed in a "practical religion" which counseled faith in humanity's ability to progress toward perfection, and he viewed statistical study and social science as keys to that perfection. In 1873, after serving in the Civil War and in the Massachusetts legislature, he was appointed to head the state's recently created Bureau of Labor Statistics. Wright quickly made the bureau a leader

---

1. *State ex rel. Davis-Smith Co. v. Clausen*, 117 P. 1101, 1113–14 (Wash. 1911).

in the study and quantification of industrial conditions, a source of information useful to reformers who wanted to change the state's employer liability laws, and in 1885 he was chosen to head the newly-created United States Bureau of Labor.[2]

Under Wright's leadership, the Bureau issued a steady stream of studies and reports on labor conditions. In 1893, it published one of the earliest American reports on the new no-fault workers compensation systems then arising in Europe, and in 1898 it sponsored William Willoughby's *Workingmen's Insurance,* the first treatise to advocate adoption of such systems in America and to explain how that might be done. In 1903, as public interest started to grow, the Massachusetts legislature asked Wright to head a committee to propose legislation, and the following year he and his fellow members proposed a no-fault compensation plan that would give workers "a more certain, even if more moderate, compensation" than would litigation under existing employer liability laws. Wright made the point that many industrial accidents were the result of bad luck, not employer or worker fault, and that traditional tort-law fault concepts were not adequate to meet the social problem of industrial accidents. But Wright did not use his statistical expertise to analyze accidents and their costs in any detail, and the committee's thorough but dispassionate argument for its plan failed to persuade the legislature to take immediate action. Something more was needed.[3]

Crystal Eastman did more than anyone else to fill that need. Eastman came from a world similar to Wright's, but she brought an element of intimacy and feeling to her reform work that Wright lacked. Raised in Massachusetts and New York in a family of reform-minded activists, she was a member of the first generation of American women given a genuine opportunity to make their mark in the professions. In 1907, after earning graduate degrees in sociology and law, she attracted the attention of the Russell Sage Foundation and was hired to work on a survey of industrial conditions in Pittsburgh's steel mills. The Pittsburgh Survey became a model for other social research projects, and after recounting some of her conclusions in magazine articles, Eastman published *Work Accidents and the Law* (1910), generally regarded as the Survey's most influential report. *Work Accidents* was unlike anything previously seen in reform literature. Eastman combined statistical and policy analysis with stories of the post-accident lives of individual workers and their families, stories told in an intimate style that spoke of the poverty and desperation that followed in the wake of injuries. The book's impact was enhanced by its tasteful typeface and layout; by drawings and photographs of affected workers and families created by Joseph Stella and Lewis Hine, both major American artists; and by its dramatic statistical illustrations, including a "death calendar" showing the number of work-related deaths in Pittsburgh each

---

2. James Leiby, *Carroll Wright and Labor Reform: The Origin of Labor Statistics* (1960), 10–15, 18–30, 62–65.

3. John Graham Brooks, *Fourth Special Report of the Commissioner of Labor: Compulsory Insurance in Germany* (1893); Willoughby, *Workingmen's Insurance* (1898); 1903 Mass. Laws, ch. 87; [Massachusetts] Committee on Relations Between Employer and Employee, *Report* (1904), 44–45; Leiby, *Wright and Labor Reform,* 69–80; John Fabian Witt, *The Accidental Republic: Crippled Workingmen, Destitute Widows, and the Remaking of American Law* (2004), 10–11, 63.

day from July 1906 through June 1907 and a statue of a worker diagrammed to show the average compensation paid for each limb lost in an industrial accident.[4] *Work Accidents* brought the problem of industrial injuries home to upper-middle-class Americans without whose support change could not occur, and it added weight to arguments for workers compensation in ways that Wright and others who wrote in a more masculine style could not match.[5]

VALUATIONS PUT ON MEN IN PITTSBURGH IN 1907
Actual amounts paid as compensation by employers to twenty-seven workmen permanently injured in Allegheny County, April, May, June, of that year
For loss of an eye,........ $200, $150, $150, $100, $75, $50, $50, $48, 0, 0, 0.
For loss of an arm,........ $300, 0, 0.
For loss of two fingers,.... $100, $100, 0, 0, 0, 0, 0.
For loss of leg,........... $225, $175, $150, $100, $55, 0.
[For relative significance of these figures see Chapter VIII.]

Illustration from Crystal Eastman, *Work-Accidents and the Law* (1910), showing amounts voluntarily paid by Pittsburgh employers for workers' loss of limbs. Courtesy of Cornell University and Hathitrust.

---

4. Crystal Eastman, "The Temper of the Workers Under Trial," 21 *Charities and the Commons* 561 (January 2, 1909); Eastman, "A Year's Work Accidents and Their Costs," ibid., 1147 March 6, 1909); Eastman, *Work Accidents and the Law* (1910), frontispiece, 126; Witt, *Accidental Republic*, 126–30; Jason R. Puskar, *Accident Society: Fiction, Collectivity and the Production of Chance* (1999), 154–62, 176–83; Lawrence J. Friedman and Mark D. McGarvie, eds., *Charity, Philanthropy and Civility in American History* (2003), 211–12, 236–37.

5. Wright's work on workers compensation was secondary to his other work in statistics, labor relations and education and came near the end of his life. He died in 1909 and did not see the reform he had advocated six years earlier come to fruition. Eastman's life turned in a different direction after 1910. She moved to Wisconsin in 1912 to work on an unsuccessful campaign for women's suffrage; she then returned to New York, where she became an important figure in national women's rights, pacifist and civil liberties circles before her untimely death in 1928. Leiby, *Wright and Labor Reform*, 123–206; Robert E. Humphrey, *Children of Fantasy: The First Rebels of Greenwich Village* (1978), 158, 166; Amy Aronson, *Crystal Eastman: A Revolutionary Life* (2019), 97–278.

Employer liability laws, which softened and partially eliminated traditional tort defenses in workplace accident cases, were viewed as the answer to perceived injustices in the tort system for much of the late nineteenth century, but by 1900 an increasing number of reformers and jurists were calling for more fundamental change: a move away from traditional notions of fault in workplace accident cases and perhaps other areas of tort law as well. The free-labor ideal of individual autonomy and responsibility tenaciously maintained its presence in tort law, but gradually the idea gained ground that accidents should be viewed as an unavoidable concomitant of urbanization and industrialization, the price to be paid for the benefits of a modern society. That led irresistibly to the question: should payment of that price be socialized?

Progressives did not have a unitary political creed, but they did have some core principles, several of which meshed nicely with socialization of accident costs. One was that democracy and economic security were interdependent: in the words of Wisconsin's Charles McCarthy, "the state must protect and invest in the life and happiness of the individual in order that the greatest prosperity [for all] might come from it." Another was an abiding faith that this could best be achieved through management by experts. "Industrial democracy will never accomplish its purpose" of increasing production and consumption, warned Herbert Croly, a leading Progressive intellectual, "unless science can be brought increasingly to its assistance...in a most liberal measure."[6] That sentiment provided an opportunity for older Progressives such as Wright and younger ones such as Eastman to help reconfigure tort law through social science.

The Progressive-era struggle over socialization of tort law took place largely through three movements: to replace traditional tort law in the workplace with workers compensation systems; to replace contributory negligence with comparative negligence systems in which a negligent victim's recovery would be reduced in proportion to his negligence but not eliminated altogether; and to eliminate rules of privity that had barred consumers from making claims against negligent product manufacturers. Like other Progressive-era reform movements, these movements originated in the late nineteenth century but gained momentum around 1900 and achieved significant success during the twenty years that followed. During the years following Wright's Massachusetts report, an ever-increasing stream of popular and legal articles on industrial accidents, together with studies such as Eastman's, impelled many states to take action. The first workers compensation laws were enacted in 1910–11; after a brief scare when New York's highest court struck down its state's law, supreme courts in Massachusetts, Washington, Wisconsin and elsewhere upheld their states' workers compensation laws. By 1920, the U.S. Supreme Court had given its blessing to several types of compensation laws, more than half of the states had enacted such laws, and traditional negligence principles were largely a thing of the past in the American workplace.

The same pattern applied to comparative negligence. Two states, Georgia and Illinois, had experimented as early as the 1850s with exceptions to contributory negligence that allowed limited forms of comparison and recovery by victims who were

---

6. McCarthy, *The Wisconsin Idea* (1912), 162; Croly, *Progressive Democracy* (1914), 397.

partly at fault. The turn of the twentieth century brought a burst of comparative negligence laws for railroad workers: Wisconsin enacted the first such law in 1907, and the following year Congress inserted a comparative negligence provision in the Federal Employers Liability Act (FELA), which a number of states copied. Comparative negligence progressed more slowly than did workers compensation: some lawmakers rejected it outright, and others were reluctant to extend it beyond occupations that were viewed as especially hazardous.

The bar of privity between manufacturers and consumers had begun to erode as early as the 1850s, but many scholars have identified a Progressive-era New York court decision, *MacPherson v. Buick Motor Co.* (1916), as a transformative case that definitively abolished the privity bar and turned products liability law in a new direction. That is an exaggeration: *MacPherson*'s contribution was to articulate directly a broad no-privity rule that courts in several other states had worked on since the early 1890s. After *MacPherson* was decided, many other states eventually repudiated the privity rule, but they did not rush to do so.

The Progressive era also marked another chapter in the debate over the proper balance of power between judges and juries. There were regular Progressive rumblings of discontent against judges perceived to be hostile to reform, but several prominent jurists, most notably Wisconsin chief justice John Winslow, waged an effective public relations campaign in which they explained that court decisions striking down or cabining reform laws were based on genuine constitutional scruples, not political agendas. Judges across the ideological spectrum continued to defend their right to take cases away from juries where the facts of the case and applicable law made the result clear, and they resisted all efforts to shift the balance of power in the jury's direction. At the end of the Progressive era (1920), the judge-jury balance of power differed little from what it had been in 1890.

Workers Compensation: A Departure from Fault

Origins of Workers Compensation

In 1884, German Chancellor Otto von Bismarck created the world's first compensation system that abandoned the concept of fault in the workplace. Unions and employer associations were powerful forces in German politics, and Bismarck hoped the new system would defuse worker discontent and promote cooperation between the two groups, which was essential to his goal of making Germany a world power. Bismarck initially proposed a state-run compensation system financed entirely by taxes, but he eventually decided that a compulsory system funded by employers' mutual insurance associations and administered by workers' sickness associations would be more economically and politically successful.[7]

---

7. P. Tecumseh Sherman, "Can the German Workmen's Insurance Law Be Adapted to American Conditions?," 61 *U. Pa. L. Rev.* 67, 68–70 (1912).

England continued to rely on its 1880 employer liability Act, but criticism of the Act's patchwork nature grew steadily, and in 1897 Parliament abandoned the Act for a workers compensation system. Parliamentary supporters of the new system, including Joseph Chamberlain and future prime minister Herbert Asquith, stressed that accidents should be viewed as an inevitability rather than as a product of carelessness, and they used a military analogy that was to become popular among American reformers. "If…a soldier in the army of industry is wounded or dies he is entitled in the one case to a pension, and in the other case that his dependents are to be provided for," said Asquith, and "you cannot leave the application of that principle to chance, as to whether the captain of the company is solvent or insolvent."[8] The 1897 English law was limited to railroad and mine workers and other selected occupations, but it was extended to nearly all workers in 1906. Participation in the new system was compulsory: employers were made liable for worker injuries regardless of fault, and workers were foreclosed from bringing suit under the common law. But the law allowed more choice than its German counterpart: employers could choose whether to self-insure or obtain outside insurance, and they and their employees could opt out of the law by creating mutual benefit societies.[9]

The American workers compensation movement had its origins in the creation of state labor bureaus. In the years after the Civil War, state lawmakers became increasingly aware of the social and economic problems that industrialization was creating, but their instinct was to study and quantify those problems before responding substantively. Massachusetts created the first state labor bureau in 1869, and during the following two decades nineteen other states followed suit. In 1882, the Massachusetts legislature instructed Wright and his bureau to study and report on employer liability measures.[10] Wright's 1882 study merely compiled existing liability laws, but it sparked his interest in the subject and in 1892, after becoming the U.S. Commissioner of Labor, he commissioned a federal study of the German workers compensation system. The study recommended that Americans wait to see if the German system would succeed before proceeding with similar reform, but Wright emphasized that the subject was important, and the study attracted national attention.[11]

Shortly after the English system went into effect, the influential Social Reform Club of New York City made its own study of workers compensation and prepared a bill for a rudimentary form of no-fault compensation that was introduced in New York's 1898 legislature. The bill did not pass, but public interest continued to grow, and reformers

---

8. Wis. Bur. of Lab. and Ind. Stats. (WBLIS), *1907–08 Report*, 122–34 (reprint of Chamberlain speech), 134–43, 138 (reprint of Asquith speech); Witt, *Accidental Republic*, 63–65.

9. Sherman, "German Workmen's Insurance Law," 68–72 (1912); "Employers' Liability," 66 *Contemp. Rev.* [London] 137 (1894); 60 & 61 Vict. ch. 87 (1897); 6 Edw.7 ch. 58 (1906); WBLIS, *1907–08 Report*, 121–37; R. Newton Crane, "Injury Actions and Workmen's Compensation in England," 18 *Green Bag* 216 (1906).

10. John R. Commons, ed. *History of Labour in the United States 1896–1932* (1935), 3:628; J.E. Rhodes, "Inception of Workmen's Compensation in the United States," 11 *Me. L. Rev.* 35, 35–37 (1917); Leiby, *Wright and Labor Reform*, 10–13, 36–38, 65–68.

11. Brooks, *Fourth Special Report*; Rhodes, "Inception of Workmen's Compensation," 38–39.

began to argue that the United States was falling behind Europe. Willoughby's treatise appeared the same year; it surveyed existing European systems, private employer and union insurance plans for American workers, and existing employer liability laws. Willoughby concluded that existing American laws and private plans were an insufficient response to the problem of accidents. He noted that Europe had adopted workers compensation "only after experience had demonstrated that [existing systems] gave rise to intolerable litigation, and that practically the employees were but slightly benefited." Although workers compensation had "barely enter[ed] upon the stage of discussion" in the United States, he urged the nation to note Europe's experience and follow its example.[12]

An early but short-lived legislative breakthrough occurred in 1902 when Maryland enacted a law providing for a crude, highly limited form of workers compensation and comparative negligence. The law provided that miners and quarry and streetcar workers could recover half the value of their injuries from their employer even if they were contributorily negligent. The law was struck down as unconstitutional because it did not provide for trial by jury of compensation disputes, but its enactment signaled that American lawmakers were ready to take up workers compensation in earnest.[13] The Wright committee's report to the 1903 Massachusetts legislature marked an inflection point. Even though the committee failed to persuade lawmakers to adopt workers compensation, its report marked the first time a comprehensive system had been directly recommended to a legislature, and Wright's reputation caused lawmakers in Massachusetts and elsewhere to take notice.[14]

The Movement Gains Strength

The workers compensation movement accelerated after 1904, both in state capitals and in the forum of public opinion. The American Association for Labor Legislation (AALL) and the National Civic Federation, influential organizations that counted both reformers and industrialists as members, concluded that workers compensation provided a better answer to the workplace-accident crisis than existing tort law, and they began promoting workers compensation throughout the nation; they were soon joined by the National Association of Manufacturers (NAM).[15] Articles describing the hazards workers faced in industries such as coal, steel and railroads, the prevalence

---

12. Rhodes, "Inception of Workmen's Compensation," 39–40; Willoughby, *Workingmen's Insurance*, iii, 328–59.

13. 1902 Md. Laws, ch. 139; George E. Barnett, "The Maryland Workmen's Compensation Act," 16 Q. J. Econ. 591 (1902); Barnett, "The End of the Maryland Workmen's Compensation Act," 19 Q. J. Econ. 320, 320–22 (1905).

14. Rhodes, "Inception of Workmen's Compensation," 39–46; Robert Asher, "Workmen's Compensation in the United States, 1880–1935" (Ph.D. thesis, University of Minnesota, 1971), 88–97; *see also* Willoughby, *Workingmen's Insurance*; 1898 Mass. Laws, ch. 78; Massachusetts Bur. of Stats. of Lab., *Thirty-First Annual Report, Part II* (1901); 1902 Md. Laws, ch. 139; 1903 Mass. Laws, ch. 87.

15. James Weinstein, "Big Business and the Origins of Workers Compensation," 8 *Lab. Hist.* 156, 162–65 (1967); Asher, "Workmen's Compensation," 190–220; Commons, *History of Labour*, 570–72.

and human cost of accidents, and the failings of employer liability law began to appear regularly in popular magazines such as *Outlook*, *McClure's* and *Overland* that were sympathetic to Progressive causes.[16] Scholarly journals and highbrow general-circulation magazines such as *Atlantic Monthly* and *North American Review* also educated their readers about the nature and advantages of workers compensation, and the New York Charity Organization Society published supportive articles written by Eastman and other reformers in its *Charities and the Commons* magazine (later renamed *Survey*).[17] Theodore Roosevelt also supported the cause in speeches and articles, most notably in a 1907 speech given at the tricentennial celebration of the founding of Jamestown and in a 1908 special message to Congress.[18]

Crystal Eastman, ca. 1914. From the records of the National Woman's Party, via Wikimedia Commons.

---

16. *See, e.g.*, Clarence M. Mark, "Waste Heap of Industry," 50 *Overland Monthly* 122 (February 1907); Arthur B. Reeve, "Is Workmen's Compensation Practicable?", 85 *Outlook* 508 (March 2, 1907); John Graham Brooks, "Moralized Insurance," 39 *Collier's Mag.* 25 (June 15, 1907); Lancelot Packer, "The Hazards of Industry: Should the Workman Bear the Whole Burden?", 92 *Outlook* 319 (June 5, 1909); John M. Gitterman, "The Cruelties of Our Courts," 35 *McClure's Mag.* 151 (June 1910).

17. *See, e.g.*, Frank A. Vanderlip, "Insurance for Working-Men," 181 *N. Am. Rev.* 921 (December 1905); Josiah Strang, "Our Industrial Juggernaut," 183 *N. Am. Rev.* 1030 (November 1906); Frank W. Lewis, "Employers Liability," 103 *Atl. Monthly* 57 (January 1909); Frank W. Taussig, "Workmen's Insurance in Germany: Some Illustrative Figures," 24 *Q. J. Econ.* 191 (1909); *see also* Epaphroditus Peck, "The Massachusetts Proposition for an Employers' Compensation Act," 14 *Yale L.J.* 18, 18–19 (1904); Ernest Freund, "Constitutional Aspects of Employers Liability Legislation," 19 *Green Bag* 80, 80–83 (1907).

18. Rhodes, "Inception of Workmen's Compensation," 48; Witt, *Accidental Republic*, 3.

Reformers who shared Carroll Wright's love of data also contributed to the campaign. New York's labor statistics bureau presented a brief statistical study of accident rates in hazardous occupations in its 1899 annual report, and Wisconsin's bureau devoted more than one hundred pages of its 1904 report to an article by Milwaukee attorney William D. Kerr, who elaborated on Wright's arguments and used statistics to lay out the case for a new system. Kerr noted the scarcity of industrial-accident data but collected and presented federal railroad-accident statistics and studies from New York, Illinois and Germany, which collectively showed shockingly high rates of injury and deaths in various industries.[19] He recognized that some American critics viewed workers compensation, particularly compulsory workers compensation, as socialistic, but he argued that view was unfounded. The public must bear the cost of accidents whether through increased product prices or taxation, and, he said, a workers compensation system would greatly reduce the transactional costs exacted by predatory plaintiffs' lawyers and profit-hungry insurers.[20]

Kerr concluded his article by appealing to labor. In 1904, American unions were concentrating on protective workplace legislation for women and children and on a campaign against use of court injunctions against strikers, and some unions were wary of workers compensation. Kerr recognized that many workers still considered themselves autonomous craftsmen rather than wage earners and viewed workers compensation as carrying a taint of government paternalism and charity. He implored them to move beyond that view: compensation for industrial accidents was "an item distinctly apart from wages," a social obligation to labor at a time when labor, "through no fault of its own, [could be] overtaken by adverse circumstances which are beyond its means to regulate."[21]

Momentum continued to build. In 1905, an Illinois legislative committee addressed an issue that would give reformers continuing concern: whether employers and workers should be compelled to participate in workers compensation systems or whether participation should be voluntary. The Illinois committee raised concerns about the constitutionality of a compulsory system: imposing liability for accidents on employers regardless of their fault and depriving both sides of the right to litigate might be viewed by judges as an infringement of liberty and property rights and of the right to try disputes to a jury. The committee recommended that any Illinois law be voluntary, but it also prepared and attached to its report a model law for a compulsory system. The Illinois legislature did not enact either proposal, but the committee's model law was widely circulated and proved useful to other legislatures.[22]

---

19. WBLIS, *1903–04 Report*, 425–27; *Seventeenth Annual Report of the Bureau of Labor Statistics of the State of New York for the Year 1899* (1899), 564–78.

20. WBLIS, *1903–04 Report*, 452. Kerr noted that in the United States, 70% of employers' insurance premiums went to pay administrative costs but in Germany, only 23% did. *Ibid.*, 526.

21. *Ibid.*, 538.

22. Charles R. Henderson, "Workingmen's Insurance in Illinois," *Proceedings of the First Annual Meeting, Am. Assn. for Labor Legis.* (1907), 79–81; WBLIS, *1907–08 Report*, 117–20; Witt, *Accidental Republic*, 46–47, 137.

In 1907, Wisconsin's bureau published a detailed statistical analysis of industrial accidents in its state. The bureau's work during this period was heavily influenced by University of Wisconsin professor John Commons, a nationally recognized authority on industrial economics and labor reform who was gaining recognition as one of the leading intellectual lights of Progressivism. The Russell Sage Foundation hired Commons to assist with the Pittsburgh Survey, and in that role, he absorbed Crystal Eastman's view that many accidents were best attributed to hazards of the industry, not employer or employee fault. Commons soon came to view workers compensation as a part of his decades-long crusade to "save Capitalism by making it good," and his views influenced lawmakers in Wisconsin and elsewhere.[23] Commons' stamp appeared with particular clarity on a detailed economic calculation in the Wisconsin bureau's 1907 report showing that workers compensation would deliver more benefit to workers at lower cost to employers than the traditional tort system.[24]

The momentum for reform reached critical mass in 1909: in that year Wisconsin's bureau published a supplemental study reinforcing its views, Crystal Eastman published the first results of her Pittsburgh research, and Minnesota's bureau published an article similar to Kerr's 1904 article, with statistics for its state.[25] Studies and articles favoring workers compensation were appearing in ever-increasing numbers, and hardly any writers now defended existing employer liability systems. Labor leaders such as the United Mine Workers' John Mitchell were overcoming their initial skepticism as to workers compensation: they concluded that trading accident litigation rights for guaranteed, if limited, compensation would likely benefit workers, and for the first time they openly favored workers compensation. Many American business associations had reached the same conclusions as the AALL and NAM, and they too turned their energies toward shaping new systems rather than opposing them.[26]

---

23. Commons, *Myself: The Autobiography of John R. Commons* (1934, reprint 1963), 101–06, 140–43; Robert S. Maxwell, *La Follette and the Rise of the Progressives in Wisconsin* (1956), 80–82; James Leiby, *A History of Social Welfare and Social Work in the United States* (1978), 118–22; Witt, *Accidental Republic*, 126–30.

24. WBLIS, *1907–08 Report*, 2–70; Bureau, *1909–10 Report*, 71–72. The Bureau found that 52 percent of all accidents surveyed were due to hazards of the industry; 23 percent and 11 percent were the fault of workers and employers respectively; in 7 percent, both employer and worker were at fault; and 6 percent were due to the negligence of fellow servants. WBLIS, *1907–08 Report*, 2.

25. Eastman, "Temper of Workers"; Eastman, "A Year's Work: Accidents and Their Costs"; Eastman, "Employers Liability: A Criticism Based on Facts" (Pamphlet, Am. Assn. for Lab. Legis., 1909); Eastman, "The Temper of the Legislature of the State of Wisconsin"; *Report of the Special Committee on Industrial Insurance, 1909–1910* (IIC Report), 91–129; Don D. Lescohier, "Industrial Accidents and Employers Liability in Minnesota," in Minn. Bur. of Lab., Inds. & Comm., *Twelfth Biennial Report 1909–10* (1909), 125–34.

26. John Mitchell, "Automatic Compensation—The Injured Workman's Right," 17 *Am. Federationist* 971 (1910).

Most strikingly, a handful of judges temporarily abandoned the neutrality that judicial formalism required; they openly expressed their unhappiness with the existing system and their desire for change. Wisconsin justice Roujet Marshall provided the most notable example. Marshall was devoted to free-labor principles; he consistently applied a critical eye to Progressive reform measures and defended his court against charges that it favored employers over injured workers, but he became increasingly frustrated with the harsh results that existing tort law often produced in workplace-accident cases. In *Houg v. Girard Lumber Co.* (1910), Marshall and his colleagues overturned a jury verdict in favor of a lumber-mill worker whose foot had been caught and mangled in a sprocket, holding that the evidence compelled a finding of contributory negligence, but Marshall added an appendix in which he bluntly made the case for workers compensation:

> Why [should] not inevitable incidents of activities upon which all depend to satisfy demands of legitimate human desire, be laid at once upon the subject of consumption where they must in the end inevitably go for final liquidation? ... Why should not the sacrifices of all be taken at once as the burdens of all; not scattering by the way human wrecks to float as derelicts for a time, increasing the first cost till the accumulation disappears from view in the world of consumable things? ... Only the lawmaking power can answer. At its door lies the duty to do so, and will lie any sin there may be in not laboring to that end.[27]

It was well established in common law that legislatures had nearly unlimited power to modify tort rules of recovery; thus, Marshall did not see workers compensation as a threat to his core judicial values. In 1908, he quietly contacted acquaintances in the Wisconsin legislature to offer help in drafting a workers compensation law, and he subsequently played a behind-the-scenes role in the drafting process.[28] More judges would echo Marshall's unhappiness with the existing system, if not his activism, when they were asked to strike down their states' newly-enacted workers compensation laws.

Workers Compensation Breaks Through

In 1909, the New York, Wisconsin and Minnesota legislatures created committees to study the workers compensation models reformers had advanced and to propose laws for enactment. Fifteen other states followed suit in 1910 and 1911.[29] New York was the

---

27. *Houg*, 129 N.W. 633, 639 (Wis. 1911) (Marshall); *see also Driscoll v. Allis-Chalmers Co.*, 129 N.W. 401, 408 (Wis. 1911) (similar comments by Chief Justice John Winslow).

28. Robert Asher, "The 1911 Wisconsin Workmen's Compensation Law: A Study in Conservative Labor Reform," 57 *Wis. Mag. of Hist.* 123, 126–29 (Winter 1973–74); Roujet D. Marshall, *Autobiography of Roujet D. Marshall* (1923), 2:53–59, 239–46; Joseph A. Ranney, "Shaping Debate, Shaping Society: Three Wisconsin Chief Justices and Their Counterparts," 81 *Marq. L. Rev.* 923, 937 (1998).

29. 1909 N.Y. Laws, ch. 518; 1909 Wis. Laws, ch. 518; Robert Asher, "The Origins of Workmen's Compensation in Minnesota," 44 *Minn. Hist.* 142, 146 (Winter 1974); Shawn E. Kantor and Price V. Fishback, "How Minnesota Adopted Workers' Compensation," 2 *Indep. Rev.* 557 (1998). In 1910 and

first to complete the study-and-enactment process. Its commission, headed by state senator Jonathan Wainwright with Eastman serving as secretary, conducted hearings throughout the state in 1909. It also examined European compensation systems and the history of employer liability in America and compiled detailed industrial-accident statistics for New York. The tone of the commission's report echoed Wright more than Eastman: the report focused on the existing tort system's economic inefficiency and its tendency to promote labor unrest, with little direct discussion of the need to alleviate injured workers' suffering.[30]

The committee concluded that reform should be introduced gradually, and it made two proposals. The first was a workers compensation system limited to hazardous occupations such as railroad, construction and electrical work; workers would be allowed to opt out of the system and rely on existing remedies, but employers would not. Injured workers would be paid according to a statutory schedule based on the severity of their injuries. The committee also proposed a separate system that employers and workers could mutually agree to join. The voluntary system would make employers liable for all machinery- and premises-related hazards, but it was not a no-fault system: it preserved the fellow-servant doctrine in reduced form. After brief debate, the legislature enacted both proposals with little change in June 1910.[31]

A legislative rush followed: between March and July 1911, nine other states across the country enacted workers compensation laws.[32] Like New York, other early-adopting states wrestled with many questions of detail, most importantly whether the new systems should apply to all businesses or only to limited industrial categories and whether they should be compulsory or voluntary. Nearly all early-adopting states viewed their new laws as an experiment and chose to limit them to hazardous occupations. Some laws' lists of hazardous occupations were short, but some were so extensive as to encompass nearly all industrial work.[33] Most states exempted farm workers and domestic servants from the laws, categories which accounted in 1910 for

---

1911 New Jersey, Pennsylvania, Maryland, West Virginia, Ohio, Michigan, Iowa, Missouri, Texas, Nebraska, Oregon and Washington created similar commissions. U.S. Department of Labor, Bulletin No. 203, *Workmen's Compensation Laws of the United States and Foreign Countries* (1917), 14–31.

30. [New York] Commission to Enquire Into the Question of Employers' Liability ("Wainwright Commission"), *First Report* (1910), 1–55.

31. Wainwright Commission, *First Report*, 50–58; 1910 N.Y. Laws, chs. 352, 674.

32. 1911 Kan. Laws, ch. 218 (March 14, 1911); 1911 Wash. Laws, ch. 74 (March 14); 1911 Nev. Laws, ch. 183 (March 24); 1911 Cal. Laws, ch. 399 (April 8); 1911 N.H. Laws, ch. 163 (April 15); 1911 Wis. Laws, ch. 50 (May 3); 1911 Ill. Laws, p. 314 (June 10); 1911 Ohio Laws, p. 524 (June 15); 1911 Mass. Laws, c. 751 (July 28). These laws are referred to in subsequent footnotes as "1911 [state] WC Law."

33. *See, e.g.,* 1911 Cal. WC Law, § 4; 1911 Nev. WC Law, § 3; 1911 Kan. WC Law, § 6; 1911 Ill. WC Law, § 2; 1911 Ohio WC Law, § 20-1; 1911 Wash. WC Law, § 2.

more than forty percent of the American workforce; a few states also exempted small businesses.[34]

Whether the new systems should be compulsory or voluntary was a more difficult issue. Many legislators shared the concern of Illinois' 1905 committee that in an age where American courts were suspicious of reforms that imposed limits on employers' freedom and were protective of traditional concepts of fault, compulsory systems imposing liability on employers without fault would be held unconstitutional. They addressed that concern by creating voluntary systems from which both employers and employees could opt out and rely on common-law remedies. Among the early-adopting states, only New York, Nevada and Washington, whose legislature stressed the economic and equitable need to "withdraw [industrial disputes] from private controversy," enacted compulsory systems.[35]

The voluntary states gave employers powerful carrot-and-stick incentives to join their new systems. Nearly all workers compensation laws established fixed rates of payment for temporary and permanent work-related injuries and for deaths and set absolute limits on total recovery.[36] In an age of ever-improving risk statistics and risk-assessment techniques, the fixed rates and caps enabled employers to calculate and predict their accident-related costs with some certainty, and that was worth a great deal. The stick was that employers who refused to join would be deprived of their common-law defenses of assumption of risk and fellow-servant liability, which would give juries freer rein to render verdicts in injured workers' favor and would reduce judges' power to overturn those verdicts. Conversely, workers whose companies elected to join the system had an incentive to do likewise: if they did not, the company could invoke contributory negligence and other existing defenses against them.[37] Several voluntary states also encouraged participation by providing that employers and workers would be deemed to have chosen to participate in the new system unless they specifically notified the state otherwise.[38]

The workers compensation movement received a temporary setback in late March 1911, when New York's highest court struck down its state's workers compensation law in *Ives v. South Buffalo Railway Co.*[39] *Ives* brought the constitutional worries of workers compensation supporters to a boil, even though a careful reading of the decision revealed that it did not pose as grave a threat as feared. Speaking for the court, Justice

---

34. *See, e.g.,* 1911 Kan. WC Law, §§ 6, 8 (agricultural workers and companies with five or fewer employees); 1911 Ohio WC Law, § 20-1; *Thirteenth Census of the United States: Abstract of the Census* (1913), 285, 437.

35. *See* 1911 Wash. WC Law, § 1; 1911 Nev. WC Law, § 1.

36. *See, e.g.,* 1911 Kan. WC Law, § 11; 1911 Ill. WC Law, §§ 4–5; 1911 Wash. WC Law, § 5.

37. Asher, "Wisconsin Workmen's Compensation Law," 136–37; *see, e.g.,* 1911 Ohio WC Law, § 21-1; 1911 Wis. WC Law, §§ 2394-1, 2394-4.

38. *See, e.g.,* 1911 Ill. WC Law, § 1; 1911 Wis. WC Law, §§ 2394-6, 2394-8 (imposing notice requirement on workers but not employers).

39. 94 N.E. 431 (N.Y. 1911).

William Werner rejected an attack on the New York law's abolition of traditional tort defenses, adhering to the principle that the legislature had nearly unlimited power to modify tort rules. Werner also rejected an argument that applying a uniform rule to all covered employers regardless of the degree of worker hazard in their businesses violated constitutional equal-protection guarantees, and he also declined to consider a challenge based on the law's failure to provide for trial by jury. But Werner drew the line at the law's compulsory elimination of fault. Imposing liability on an employer "who has omitted no legal duty and has committed no wrong...based solely on a legislative fiat that his business is inherently dangerous," said Werner, "...is taking the property of A and giving it to B, and that cannot be done under our constitutions." Werner conceded that the law was supported by "cogent economic and sociological arguments" and appealed to "a recognized and widely prevalent sentiment." The court considered the law's constitutionality only under New York's state constitution, not the U.S. Constitution, and Werner hinted that amendment of New York's constitution and revision of the statute might resolve the flaws the court had found.[40]

The *Ives* decision created an uproar which grew louder when, the day after the decision was issued, a fire broke out at the Triangle Shirtwaist Factory in Manhattan. The factory's fire escape doors were illegally locked, and as a result 146 trapped garment workers died, either of asphyxiation or of injuries from leaping out of windows.[41] Legislatures on the verge of enacting their own workers compensation laws pressed on with the enactment process. Massachusetts lawmakers asked their supreme court to give an advisory opinion whether their proposed elective law would pass constitutional muster, and lawsuits were soon filed in Washington and Wisconsin to test the validity of those states' new laws.

In May 1911, the Massachusetts court advised its legislature that the state's proposed elective law would be constitutional, and in September Washington's supreme court upheld its state's compulsory law.[42] In a terse opinion, Massachusetts's justices pointed to the legislature's broad power to modify tort rules and found that the proposed law's exemption of farm workers and servants from its scope was reasonable. They also stressed that the law's voluntary feature eliminated any concern about deprivation of liberty or property rights or lack of a jury trial. That saving feature was not available to Washington's justices, but they did not need it. In *State ex rel. Davis-Smith Co. v. Clausen* (1911), the court, speaking through Justice Mark Fullerton, rejected Werner's argument that legislatures could not impose liability without fault. Fullerton pointed out that in the past many railroad fencing statutes upheld by American courts had done just that. Washington's new law, even though compulsory, was well within

---

40. 94 N.E. at 437–40.

41. *See* Witt, *Accidental Republic*, 175–77; Arthur F. McEvoy, "The Triangle Shirtwaist Factory Fire of 1911: Social Change, Industrial Accidents, and the Evolution of Common-Sense Causality," Am. Bar Found. (1993).

42. *In re Opinion of Justices*, 96 N.E. 308 (Mass. 1911); *State ex rel. Davis-Smith Co. v. Clausen*, 117 P. 1101, 1113–14 (Wash. 1911).

the scope of the state's police power to promote public safety and welfare. That fact, he said, justified any collateral limitation the law imposed on employers' and workers' freedom to contract as they saw fit, and it justified the legislature's decision not to provide for trial of compensation disputes by jury. Fullerton carefully refrained from denouncing *Ives* but said openly that "we have not been able to yield our consent to the view there taken."[43]

In November, Wisconsin's supreme court followed suit in *Borgnis v. Falk Co.* (1911). Like their Massachusetts and Washington counterparts, Wisconsin's justices adhered to a broad view of legislative power to modify common-law tort defenses and rejected an equal-protection challenge to the state's new law. They agreed with the Massachusetts court that because the new law was elective, it did not violate employers' or workers' property and liberty rights or deprive them of any right to a jury trial.[44] *Borgnis* served as a showcase for Roujet Marshall's and Chief Justice John Winslow's competing constitutional philosophies. Winslow viewed himself as a "constructive conservative": he believed that constitutions must be interpreted flexibly in light of modern conditions, a philosophy which he distilled in a famous passage in *Borgnis*. To say that a constitution's "general provisions [must] be construed and interpreted by an eighteenth century mind in the light of eighteenth century conditions and ideals," said Winslow, was "to command the race to halt in its progress, to stretch the state upon a veritable bed of Procrustes."[45] Marshall agreed that the new law was well within the scope of the legislature's established authority to modify tort law and that because it was elective it did not violate due process, but as a committed constitutional originalist, he viewed Winslow's discourse on constitutional flexibility as misguided and dangerous. "If the constitution is to efficiently endure," he argued, "the idea that it is capable of being re-squared, from time to time, to fit new legislative or judicial notions of necessities... must be combated whenever and wherever advanced."[46]

Workers Compensation Settles In

Emboldened by these decisions, eleven additional states adopted workers compensation laws in 1912 and 1913, and by 1920 such laws were in place throughout all regions of the United States except the deep South.[47] The Washington supreme court's

---

43. *Opinion of Justices*, 96 N.E. at 309; *Clausen*, 117 P. at 1113–14.
44. *Borgnis*, 133 N.W. 209, 216–17 (Wis. 1911).
45. *Borgnis*, 133 N.W. at 215–16; *see also, e.g.,* Winslow, "The Patriot and the Courts," (Address to Loyal Legion of Milwaukee, February 3, 1909), 9; Winslow, "An Understanding Heart: Does the American Judge Possess It?," 31 *Survey* 17 (October 4, 1913), both in Winslow Papers, Wisconsin Historical Society (WHS). Winslow took the Procrustes metaphor from the Greek myth of a giant who racked too-short victims and mutilated too-tall victims in order to fit all to his iron bed.
46. *Borgnis*, 133 N.W at 223–24 (1911); Asher, "Wisconsin Workmen's Compensation Law," 139–40.
47. Lindley D. Clark and Martin C. Frincke, Jr., *Workmen's Compensation Legislation of the United States and Canada* (1921), 9.

decision also encouraged several states to switch from elective to compulsory systems.[48] Events in New York following *Ives* underscored the strength of the tide. Legal commentators criticized Werner's statement that there could be no liability without fault, pointing out, as had Justice Fullerton, that absolute liability had long played a role in both the common law and statutory law. Theodore Roosevelt made *Ives* a centerpiece of his argument for recall of unpopular court decisions during his unsuccessful 1912 campaign to regain the presidency, and in order to put all doubt to rest, the AALL launched a campaign to amend state constitutions to authorize workers compensation. The AALL's campaign bore fruit in five states including New York, whose voters ratified a workers-compensation amendment in 1913 and subsequently rejected Werner's bid to become chief justice. In 1915 New York's legislature enacted a new elective system, which the state's highest court subsequently upheld.[49]

FIGURE 3.1
The Spread of Workers Compensation[50]

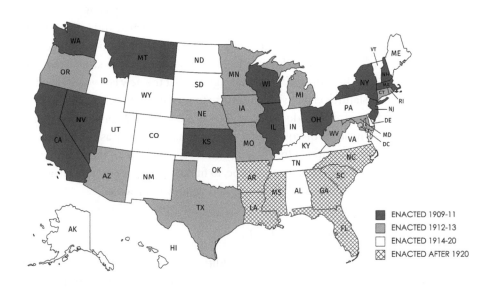

(Map generated from a template provided by courtesy of mapchart.net)

---

48. *See, e.g.*, 1911 Cal WC Law, § 1; 1913 Cal. Laws, ch. 176.

49. Witt, *Accidental Republic*, 175–82; Andrew Bruce, "The New York Employers' Liability Act," 9 *Mich. L. Rev.* 684, 694–95 (1910); James Parker Hall, "The New York Workmen's Compensation Act Decision," 19 *J. Polit. Econ.* 694, 697 (1911); Editors, "The Recall of the Ives Decision," 4 *Bench & Bar (N.S.)* 1 (1913); N.Y. Const. (1894, amended 1913), art. XIX, § 1; 1915 N.Y. Laws, chs. 167, 674; *Jensen v. S. Pacific R. Co.*, 109 N.E. 600 (N.Y. 1917).

50. Figure 3.1 is compiled from Clark and Frincke, *Workmen's Compensation Legislation*, 9.

The workers compensation tide did not completely exorcise the specter of constitutional challenge, particularly for compulsory laws. In 1909, Montana had enacted a limited compensation system that required mining companies and their workers to contribute to a state insurance fund that paid fixed sums for injury and death, but at the end of 1911 its supreme court struck down the law on the ground that unlike other compensation laws it did not grant employers exemption from common-law liability or any other benefit in return for their forced contributions.[51] In 1914, Kentucky's supreme court struck down its state's elective law by a 4–3 vote based on a state constitutional provision that prohibited enactment of any limits on damages for personal injury or property damage. The court also criticized the legislature's decision to require employers and workers to give notice if they wished to opt out of the statute, concluding that this effectively made the law compulsory and deprived all parties of their freedom of contract.[52]

In 1915, California's supreme court upheld both its state's 1911 elective law and a superseding 1913 compulsory law, but Justice Lucien Shaw, a well-respected jurist whose reputation extended beyond his state, raised two disturbing and potentially important points of doubt in his concurring opinion. Shaw argued that California's compulsory law was saved only by the fact that, like Washington's law, it required employers to pay premiums into a common, state-administered fund as a sort of tax. He reasoned that if the law had required employers to procure insurance or assume liability individually (as was the case in many other states), that would impermissibly have allowed imposition of liability without fault and, thus, would have created an unconstitutional taking of property. Shaw also believed that the legislature could not constitutionally provide benefits to workers who were entirely responsible for their injury without any fault of others. Such workers could perhaps be compensated through general public welfare programs, but not by forcing employers to pay.[53]

---

51. *Cunningham v Nw. Improv. Co.*, 119 P. 554 (Mont. 1911); 1909 Mont. Laws, ch. 67.

52. *Ky. St. J. Co. v Workmen's Comp. Bd.*, 170 S.W. 1166 (Ky. 1914); 1914 Ky. Laws, ch. 73; Ky. Const. (1851), § 54. Two years later, Pennsylvania's supreme court peremptorily rejected a challenge to that state's elective law based on a state constitutional provision similar to Kentucky's. *Anderson v. Carnegie Steel Co.*, 99 A. 215 (Pa. 1916); Pa. Const. (1838), art. III, § 21.

53. *W. Indemnity Co. v. Pillsbury*, 151 P. 398 (Cal. 1915), 406–07 (Shaw concurrence).

Despite these setbacks and doubts, after *Ives* every new workers compensation law, whether elective[54] or compulsory,[55] survived constitutional challenge except for Montana's 1909 law and Kentucky's 1914 law; and both of those states promptly enacted new laws that their supreme courts upheld.[56] Arguments used by opponents in the early Massachusetts, Washington and Wisconsin cases—legislative lack of power to alter tort law and abolish traditional employer defenses, violation of due process by departing from a fault-based system, and deprivation of the right to trial by jury—were regularly raised but uniformly rejected.[57] Equal-protection challenges also continued to arise in a variety of forms. Some states excluded small companies from their workers compensation laws, partly because they believed workers in small companies were in closer contact with their employer's operations and, thus, had more opportunity to guard against hazards, and partly because small employers complained loudly that they had limited resources and could not easily pass on insurance costs to consumers. State supreme courts uniformly rejected equal-protection challenges to such classifications;[58] they also rejected challenges to laws that limited workers compensation to listed occupations deemed to be hazardous, deferring to legislators' choices of classification.[59] In some states, opponents argued that laws requiring employers and workers

---

54. Decisions upholding elective laws include *State ex rel. Yaple v. Creamer*, 97 N.E. 602 (Ohio 1912); *Sexton v. Newark Dist. Tel. Co.*, 86 A. 451 (N.J. 1913); *Debeikis v, Link-Belt Co.*, 104 N.E. 211 (Ill. 1914); *Shade v. Ash Grove Lime & Portland Cement Co.*, 139 P. 1193 (Kan. 1914); *Matheson v. Mpls. St. R. Co.*, 148 N.W. 71 (Minn. 1914); *Hunter v. Colfax Consol. Coal Co.*, 154 N.W. 1037 (Iowa 1915); *Mackin v. Detroit-Timkin Axle Co*, 153 N.W. 49 (Mich. 1915); *Wheeler v. Contoocook Mills Corp.*, 94 A. 265 (N.H. 1915); *Evanhoff v. State Indus. Acc. Comm.*, 154 P. 106 (Or. 1915); *Jensen*, 109 N.E. 600 (N.Y. 1915); *Anderson*, 99 A. 215 (Pa. 1916); *Sayles v. Foley*, 96 A. 340 (R.I. 1916); *De Francesco v. Piney Mining Co.*, 86 S.E. 777 (W.Va. 1916); and *Middleton v. Tex. P. & L. Co.*, 185 S.W. 556 (Tex. 1916). *See generally* Clark and Frincke, *Workmen's Compensation Legislation*, 69–90.

55. Decisions upholding compulsory laws include *Pillsbury*, 151 P. 198 (Calif. 1915); *Solvuca v. Ryan & Reilly Co.*, 101 A. 710 (Md. 1917); *Anderson v Hawaiian Dredging Co.*, 24 Hawaii 97 (1917); and. *Inspiration Consol. Copper Co. v. Mendez*, 166 P. 278 (Ariz. 1917).

56. *Greene v. Caldwell*, 186 S.W. 648 (Ky. 1916); *Shea v. North-Butte Mining Co.*, 179 P. 499 (Mont. 1919).

57. Examples include the following. **Rejecting argument of no power to change tort law:** *Debeikis*, 104 N.E. 211 (Ill. 1914); *Matheson*, 148 N.W. 71 (Minn. 1914); *Contoocook Mills*, 94 A. 265 (N.H. 1915); *Middleton*, 185 S.W. 556 (Tex. 1916). **Rejecting argument of deprivation of right to jury trial:** *Opinion of Justices*, 106 N.E. 1 (Mass. 1911); *Creamer*, 97 N.E. 602 (Ohio 1912); *Sexton*, 86 A. 451 (N.J. 1913); *Hunter*, 154 N.W. 1037 (Iowa 1915), *Debeikis*; *Shea*, 179 P. 499 (Mont. 1919); *Sayles*, 96 A. 340 (R.I. 1916). **Rejecting argument that absence of fault component violated due process and freedom of contract:** *see* the cases previously cited in this note. *See generally* Clark and Frincke, *Workmen's Compensation Legislation*, 72–79, 95–99.

58. *Borgnis*, 133 N.W. at 217–18; *see also, e.g., Sexton*, 86 A. 451 (N.J. 1913); *Matheson*, 148 N.W. 71 (Minn. 1914); and *Mackin*, 153 N.W. 49 (Mich. 1915).

59. *See, e.g., Johnston v. Kennecott Copper Corp.*, 248 F. 407 (9th Cir. 1918) (Alaska law limited to miners); *Middleton*, 185 S.W. 556 (Tex. 1916), *aff'd*, 249 U.S. 152 (1919) (law excluded cotton-gin workers); *Mailman v. Record Foundry & Mach. Co.*, 106 A. 606 (Me. 1919) (law excluded loggers).

who wished to opt out to give written notice amounted to coercion and violated their rights to due process of law, but most courts other than Kentucky's disagreed.[60]

Several of the unsuccessful state-court challenges made their way to the U.S. Supreme Court, and in 1917 the Court issued three decisions involving New York's new workers compensation law and Washington's and Iowa's laws. The decisions ended virtually all doubt as to the constitutionality of both elective and compulsory workers compensation.[61] In an era when the high Court scrutinized reform laws closely and often skeptically, the absence of skepticism in its workers compensation decisions was striking. Justice Mahlon Pitney firmly endorsed the view that employers' traditional tort defenses—which, in his view, were "of comparatively recent origin" and not worthy even of designation as traditional—could be freely altered by the legislature.[62] The image of workers as soldiers in the battle for industrial production, deserving of care if they fell, resonated with Pitney and his colleagues; they also accepted the view that accidents should be viewed in terms of inevitability and risk rather than individual fault.[63]

The high Court had no difficulty rejecting other common arguments against workers compensation laws. Such laws did not violate employers' and workers' property rights, said Pitney: they were designed to address a genuine social problem, and although each side was compelled to forego former advantages, each received new benefits in return. Echoing Lucien Shaw's critique, Pitney indicated that a constitutional boundary line still existed: no system could set aside old rules "without providing a reasonably just substitute," but he also indicated that the Court would take an indulgent view of what that included.[64] The Court held that there was little difference for constitutional purposes between elective and compulsory systems: given workers compensation's compelling public purpose, even compulsory systems would pass muster if charges to employers were "reasonable in amount" and "fairly distributed."[65] Pitney also rejected equal-protection challenges to the laws, again indicating that the Court would be highly deferential to state legislatures' classification decisions, and he firmly rejected challenges based on the lack of trial by jury: initial determination of

---

60. *See, e.g., Mackin*, 153 N.W. 49, 52 (Mich. 1915); but see *Kentucky State Journal*, 170 S.W. 1166 (Ky. 1914) (criticizing notice requirements).

61. *N.Y. Cent. R. Co. v. White*, 243 U.S. 188 (1917) (upholding New York's elective second law); *Mt. Timber Co. v. Washington*, 243 U.S. 219 (1917) (upholding Washington's compulsory law); *Hawkins v. Bleakly*, 243 U.S. 210 (1917) (upholding Iowa's elective law). In 1915 the Court had sent an early signal of encouragement to supporters, holding that Ohio's exclusion of small employers from its workers compensation system was a reasonable classification. *Jeffrey Mfg. Co. v. Blagg*, 235 U.S. 571 (1915).

62. *White*, 243 U.S. at 198–202; *Hawkins*, 243 U.S. at 213; *Mt. Timber*, 243 U.S. at 239–40.

63. *White*, 243 U.S. at 203; *Mt. Timber*, 243 U.S. at 239–40.

64. *White*, 243 U.S. at 201–03; *Mt. Timber*, 243 U.S. at 238, 240–41.

65. *Mt. Timber*, 243 U.S. at 238.

compensation awards by administrative tribunals was appropriate, and nearly all laws allowed court review of tribunal decisions.[66]

In 1919, the high Court finished mapping the basic constitutional parameters of workers compensation when it addressed unusual features of the Texas and Arizona systems. Texas's law allowed employers to elect before their workers whether they would join the system, but it made the system compulsory for all workers whose employers so elected. Pitney upheld this apparent discrimination, reasoning that employers and workers made different types of investments in the industrial system, that both sides benefited from the security the system provided, and that uniformity among workers, even compelled uniformity, would promote harmony.[67] Arizona tested the limits of the Court's tolerance: the state's constitution mandated a system that was compulsory for employers but allowed workers to elect their remedy at any time before or after an injury, thus depriving employers of a large part of the predictability that had made workers compensation attractive to them. Some states had recognized the problem and had required workers to elect before they were injured;[68] but in *Arizona Copper Co. v. Hammer* (1919), the Court narrowly upheld Arizona's law. Four dissenters argued that the law violated employers' due process and equal protection rights: "[W]hile the employer is declared subject to new, uncertain and greatly enlarged liability" notwithstanding use of the utmost care, Justice James McReynolds complained, "nothing has been granted him in return."[69] *Arizona Copper* was a reminder that the Court would not grant legislatures unlimited leeway in replacing fault-based tort systems, but it also confirmed the Court's strong blessing on the workers compensation movement.

Comparative Negligence: The Socialization of Fault

The movement from contributory negligence to comparative negligence received less publicity than the workers compensation movement, but in the end, it created a more profound change. At first blush, workers compensation was the more radical of the two—it eliminated the relationship between fault and recovery, whereas comparative negligence merely altered that relationship—but unlike comparative negligence, it was limited to a single area of social and economic endeavor. Ironically, workers compensation's limited scope contributed to its success. Workplace injuries were distinctive, easy to publicize, and conducive to a specialized solution that could be standardized for all employers and workers. By contrast, there were no special types of accidents that called out for application of comparative negligence. Nevertheless, American jurists were uneasy about the inequities of contributory negligence from its inception.

---

66. *Hawkins*, 243 U.S. at 215–18; *Mt. Timber*, 243 U.S. at 235, 239–40; *White*, 243 U.S. at 208.
67. *Middleton v. Tex. P. & L. Co.*, 249 U.S. 152 (1919).
68. *See, e.g.*, 1911 Wis. WC Law, § 2394-8; Asher, "Wisconsin Workmen's Compensation Law," 136–37.
69. *Ariz. Copper Co.*, 250 U.S. 400 (1919), 450 (McReynolds dissent).

Origins

Comparative negligence first attracted national attention and achieved prominence during the Progressive era, but its origins go back to the mid-nineteenth century. In the wake of Esek Cowen's 1839 *Hartfield* decision, many American state courts developed a tripartite scale of "slight," "ordinary" and "gross" negligence. The classification, which was adapted from English bailment law, was a prime example of pre-industrial property law's influence on early tort law. Some judges, including Cowen and Luther Dixon, suggested that grossly negligent defendants would not be allowed to invoke contributory negligence as a defense in cases where the plaintiff's negligence was slight; but the terms' meanings, and whether they really added anything to existing law, were unclear. Critics labeled the scale "a troublesome and unnecessary refinement"; they argued that there was only one type of negligence, and that what constituted negligence varied with the circumstances of each case.[70] Cowen's and Dixon's judicial successors agreed with the critics and retreated from the tripartite scale, but the confusion already created cleared up only slowly,[71] and the slight-gross distinction would resurface as comparative negligence evolved.[72]

In the 1850s, Georgia's supreme court, which had already shown its skepticism of contributory negligence by limiting the fellow-servant doctrine, took the first step toward modern comparative negligence. Chief Justice Joseph Lumpkin, a jurist of national reputation who viewed the use of degrees of negligence as "impracticable,"[73] was the chief inventor. In *Macon & Western Railroad Co. v. Winn* (1856), he endorsed the "last clear chance" rule, holding that if an accident victim was negligent but the defendant then had a last clear chance to prevent injury and did not, the victim could recover notwithstanding his own earlier negligence. Lumpkin then added that "[h]e who is most negligent, can never ask a court for compensation [but] he who is least so, may or may not, according to the facts and circumstances of the case." These statements did not necessarily conflict with contributory negligence but soon afterward, in *Flanders v. Meath* (1859), Lumpkin explained that his decision in *Winn* really meant that "when both parties are in fault, but the defendant most so, the fault of the plaintiff

---

70. *Hartfield v. Roper*, 21 Wend. 615 (N.Y. 1824); *Galpin v. Chi. & Nw. R. Co.*, 19 Wis. 637, 643 (1865) (stating: "[I]f the negligence of the [livestock] owner be slight and remote, and that of the company gross and the immediate cause of the injury, I think that the owner may recover"); Shearman and Redfield, *Treatise on the Law of Negligence* (3d ed. 1874), §§ 16–17; Cooley, *Law of Torts*, 630–31; Charles F. Beach, *Contributory Negligence* (2d ed. 1892), §§ 17–18.

71. *See Fero v. Buff. & State Line R. Co.*, 22 N.Y. 209 (1860); *Wells v. N.Y. Cent. R. Co.*, 24 N.Y. 181 (1862); *Randall v. Nw. Tel. Co.*, 11 N.W. 419, 423 (Wis. 1882). Chapter 1, notes 25–26 and accompanying text.

72. Dixon's fusion of degrees of negligence and cause in *Galpin* confused Wisconsin trial judges, forcing the state's supreme court to instruct them repeatedly that "a rule of weighing the comparative negligence of the parties has never been adopted in this state." *Randall*, 11 N.W. at 423; *see also* 1911 Cal. WC Law, § 1; 1911 Nev. WC Law, § 1.

73. *Scudder v. Woodbridge*, 1 Ga. 195 (1846); *Macon & W. R. Co. v. Davis*, 18 Ga. 679, 684 (1855); *see* Chapter 1.

may go in mitigation of damages." That was the breakthrough, and two years later a committee charged with re-codifying Georgia's statutes added a comparative negligence law that incorporated the *Flanders* holding.[74]

Illinois supreme court justice Sidney Breese and his colleagues also experimented with comparative negligence in the 1850s, but their experiment was less successful. In 1852, they too adopted the last-clear-chance rule, but unlike their Georgia counterparts they equated initial negligence with remote cause and subsequent failure to prevent an accident with proximate cause, thus complicating a concept of causation that was already confusing to many litigants.[75] In *Galena & Chicago Union Railroad Co. v. Jacobs* (1858), Breese tried to clarify the situation. "The true doctrine," he said, "... is, that in proportion to the negligence of the defendant, should be measured the degree of care required of the plaintiff...where there are faults on both sides, the plaintiff shall recover, his fault being to be [sic] measured by the defendant's negligence." Breese injected the slight-gross distinction for good measure: a plaintiff, he said "need not be wholly without fault" provided that his "negligence is comparatively slight, and that of the defendant gross."[76] Most Illinois trial courts interpreted these statements as a departure from Cowen's slight-gross negligence scale and as a directive to implement comparative negligence, but subsequent supreme court decisions, including some written by Breese, put that interpretation in question: the court suggested that in the *Jacobs* case Breese had merely tried to reaffirm the last-clear-chance rule, albeit awkwardly. In 1894, the court finally put the matter to rest by formally rejecting comparative negligence.[77]

Early gestures toward comparative negligence were muddled because the concept elicited conflicting feelings. Georgia's and Illinois's efforts reflected a general unease over contributory negligence, a feeling that it was unjust to deny an injury victim whose lapse had been minor any right to recover, even from a defendant whose lapse had been the primary cause of accident and injury. In 1886, Florida chief justice George McWhorter flatly denounced contributory negligence as "unjust and inequitable." As McWhorter saw it, "[t]he law says you were both at fault and draws from that premise the conclusion that one alone must bear all the damage, provided that one is the plaintiff." A year later Florida's legislature, perhaps influenced by his statement, copied and adopted Georgia's comparative negligence statute.[78]

---

74. *Winn*, 19 Ga. 440, 446 (1856); *Flanders*, 27 Ga. 358, 362 (1859); R.H. Clark, T.R.R. Cobb and D. Irwin, *Code of the State of Georgia* (1861), § 2979; *see also* 1855–56 Ga. Laws, p. 155; Francis S. Philbrick, "Loss Apportionment in Negligence Cases: Part II," 99 *U. Pa. L. Rev.* 766, 778–80 (1951); Charles Hilkey, "Comparative Negligence in Georgia," 8 *Ga. B. J.* 51, 56–59 (1945).

75. *Moore v. Moss*, 14 Ill. 106 (1852); *Joliet & N. Ind. R. Co. v. Jones*, 20 Ill. 221 (1858); *see* Leon Green, "Illinois Negligence Law," 39 *Ill. L. Rev.* 36, 44–47 (1944); Philbrick, "Loss Apportionment," 780–81.

76. *Jacobs*, 20 Ill. 478, 496–97 (1858).

77. *City of Lanark v. Dougherty*, 38 N.E. 892 (Ill. 1894); Green, "Illinois Negligence Law," 52–53.

78. *L. & N. R. Co. v. Yniestra*, 21 Fla. 700, 737 (1886); 1887 Fla. Laws, ch. 3744.

McWhorter's sentiment was close kin to the sentiments that produced employer liability laws and to the growing view of workplace accidents as products of inevitability and risk. But free-labor views of fault and individual responsibility proved durable, and other jurists worried that comparative negligence would tilt the balance of power in the courtroom too much toward juries. Georgia's supreme court considered the extent to which judges could cabin juries' apportionment of negligence and ultimately concluded that the comparative-negligence system gave them no means of doing so: "For the apportionment of damages according to the relative fault of the parties," said Justice Logan Bleckley, "there seems to be no standard more definite than the enlightened opinion of the jury." The specter of expanded jury power prompted legal traditionalists to resist comparative negligence and prompted moderates to explore more indirect means of helping accident victims. Kansas supreme court justice (and future U.S. Supreme Court justice) David Brewer exemplified traditionalists' attitude, explaining that "many considerations, especially the difficulty of apportioning the damages and determining to what extent the wrong of the respective parties was instrumental in causing the injury, uphold the rule so universally recognized, that where the wrong, the negligence of both parties, contributes to the injury, the law will not afford relief."[79]

Breakthroughs in Congress, Wisconsin and Mississippi

A breakthrough came shortly after 1900; once again, the path to reform ran along rails. Between 1905 and 1907, three states enacted degree-based negligence statutes allowing railroad workers a recovery, albeit a reduced one, in cases where a worker's negligence was slight and the employer's was gross.[80] In 1906, after four years of deliberation, Congress enacted a Federal Employer Liability Act (FELA) that also applied the degrees-of-negligence approach. Section 2 of the law provided that a railroad worker's negligence would not bar recovery "where his contributory negligence was slight and that of the employer was gross in comparison," and that the worker's damages award would be reduced "in proportion to the amount of negligence attributable" to him.[81] Section 2's origin, like that of the 1905–07 state statutes, was unclear. Georgia senator Augustus Bacon claimed that it was derived from his state's comparative negligence law, but Indiana representative Edgar Crumpacker, a leading critic, viewed the bill as "revolutionary"; others believed the bill was merely a modest tweaking of existing state laws.[82]

---

79. *Ga. R. & Banking Co. v. Neely*, 56 Ga. 540, 544 (1876); *Kan. Pac. R. Co. v. Potter*, 14 Kan. 37, 50–51 (1874).

80. 1905 Ohio Laws, ch. 195; 1907 Neb. Laws, ch. 192; 1907 N. Dak. Laws, ch. 203.

81. 34-1 U.S. Stats. 232, § 2 (1906); *Cong. Rec.*, 59th Cong. 1st Sess., 1742–43 (January 30, 1906).

82. *Cong. Rec.*, 59th Cong. 1st Sess., 1747 (Bacon); 4605–06 (Crumpacker); *see also ibid.*, 4607 (statement by Rep. Robert Lee Henry of Texas that the bill only "modifies and mitigates" contributory negligence).

The FELA passed by a comfortable margin with bipartisan support, but in early 1908 the U.S. Supreme Court struck it down on the narrow ground that it was not limited to interstate commerce, as the federal Constitution required. The high Court did not rule on whether Section 2's change in tort liability rules violated due process, but it referred to earlier cases upholding state employer liability laws, thus giving supporters hope that an amended law would withstand court scrutiny.[83] In the meantime, Wisconsin's 1907 legislature enacted a law for railroad workers that contained the first truly modern formulation of comparative negligence. The Wisconsin law stated that:

> [I]n all cases where the jury shall find that the negligence of the company... was greater than the negligence of the employee so injured, and contributing in a greater degree to such injury, then the plaintiff shall be entitled to recover, and the negligence, if any, of the employee so injured shall be no bar to such recovery.[84]

This formulation jettisoned contributory negligence and degree systems in favor of a simple balancing test, one that gave juries much more latitude than did the old rules. That fact did not go unnoticed. Edward Hyzer, a railroad lobbyist, argued during pre-enactment hearings that comparative negligence would allow juries to render verdicts "according to caprice" and would risk a "return to barbarism." But the formulation preserved an important free-labor element: accident victims could socialize the cost of their injuries only if they were not primarily at fault. If their fault equaled or exceeded the defendant's, they must take full responsibility and they could not recover any damages.[85]

When FELA supporters introduced a new bill in Congress in 1908, they modified the comparative negligence section (now section 3 of the bill) substantially. Like Wisconsin's 1907 law, the new bill dropped all reference to degrees and provided that contributory negligence would no longer be a bar to recovery; but unlike Wisconsin's law, it adopted "pure" comparative negligence, allowing partial recovery even where a plaintiff's negligence equaled or exceeded the defendant's negligence. There was lively debate in the House Judiciary Committee, which was assigned the task of evaluating the bill. The committee rejected criticisms similar to Hyzer's; it concluded that comparative negligence was "nearer ideal justice" than contributory negligence, a fact that outweighed any practical difficulties of comparison. Opponents also argued that the law should be confined to extrahazardous railroad jobs, but supporters replied impatiently that it was too late to raise the issue: the law would apply to all railroad

---

83. *Employers' Liability Cases*, 207 U.S. 463, 491–92, 496–501 (1908). Article I, § 8 of the U.S. Constitution grants Congress the power "to regulate Commerce with foreign Nations, and among the several States, and with Indian Tribes."

84. 1907 Wis. Laws, ch. 254.

85. *Ibid.*; Hyzer, "Argument on Negligence Bills Pending Before the Legislature of 1907," pamphlet, WHS. In 1913 the legislature amended the 1907 law to confirm that plaintiffs' damages would be reduced in proportion to their negligence. 1913 Wis. Laws, ch. 644.

employees, from engineers to shipping clerks. In the end, the new FELA passed with large majorities in both houses.[86]

Both the Wisconsin law and the 1908 FELA elicited constitutional challenges. The Chicago, Milwaukee & St. Paul Railroad (Milwaukee Road) challenged the Wisconsin law after its employees Michael Kiley, a fence builder whose eye had been put out by a flying staple, and John Zeratsky, a brakeman injured in a train collision, secured judgments against it. The railroad made an equal-protection challenge in Kiley's case, arguing that the legislature had improperly extended the law to railway employees engaged in nonhazardous jobs and had improperly ignored other hazardous businesses. The supreme court disagreed, holding that unique nature of railroads and their hazards justified singling them out for special legislation. In Zeratsky's case, the Milwaukee Road tried another line of attack. The 1907 law required juries to determine whether each party's negligence "directly contributed to the injury," and the railroad argued this violated the long-standing rule that defendants could be held liable only if their negligence proximately caused injury. The court again disagreed: it interpreted "direct contribution" as meaning proximate cause. The Milwaukee Road also argued that juries must be given standards for making comparisons and that there would be no standard unless the old three-degree system was read into the law, an invitation that the court summarily declined.[87]

Justice Marshall was the lone dissenter in the *Kiley* and *Zeratsky* cases, and his dissents illustrated the limits of many conservative judges' tolerance for tort reform. Marshall was willing to decouple fault from liability if, as with workers compensation, that was done by creating a system formally separated from tort law and directed to a distinct social problem; but comparative negligence was different. The 1907 law did not identify railroads as an institution uniquely in need of comparative negligence, and in his view, the law violated equal-protection guarantees because it was not limited to hazardous railroad jobs. The specter of uncontrolled jury discretion in negligence apportionment was also very much on Marshall's mind: the law's "direct contribution" standard, he argued, allowed juries to hold railroads liable no matter how remote their negligence or how proximate the plaintiff's to the accident. But Marshall could not persuade his colleagues, and in *Mondou v. New York, New Haven & Hartford Railroad Co.* (1912), the U.S. Supreme Court unanimously rejected a challenge to the 1908 FELA that was based on an equal-protection argument similar to that made in the *Kiley* case.[88] The FELA proved to be an important early catalyst for comparative negligence. Between 1908 and 1920, sixteen states enacted "little FELA"

---

86. *Cong. Record*, 60th Congress, 1st Sess., 4426–39 (House of Representatives, April 6, 1908), 4526–38 (Senate, April 9, 1908); 53 U.S. Stat. 1404 (1908).

87. *Kiley v. Chi., Milw. & St. Paul R. Co.* 119 N.W. 309 (Wis. 1909); *Zeratsky v. Chi., Milw. & St. Paul R. Co.*, 123 N.W. 904 (Wis. 1909).

88. *Kiley*, 119 N.W. at 312–313 (Marshall dissent); *Zeratsky*, 123 N.W. at 910–13 (Marshall dissent); 35 U.S. Stat. 65 (1908); *Mondou*, 223 U.S. 1, 52–53 (1912).

laws covering railroad workers in intrastate service, all containing comparative-negligence provisions modeled on Section 3.[89]

In 1910, Mississippi became the first state to enact a comparative negligence law for all personal injury cases. It adopted the "pure" formula of the 1908 FELA rather than Wisconsin's diluted formula, which denied recovery to plaintiffs whose negligence equaled or exceeded the defendant's negligence. Opponents challenged the law's constitutionality, arguing that determination of degrees of negligence was a judicial function that could not be delegated to juries. Mississippi's supreme court rejected the argument: in its view, negligence apportionment was really a determination of fact, a function traditionally given to juries, and judges retained their power to overturn apportionments that were unsupported by evidence.[90] But elsewhere, reluctance to eliminate contributory negligence in non-railroad cases remained strong. No other state would adopt comparative negligence for all personal injury cases until 1931, and no other state would adopt pure comparative negligence until 1971.[91] This lingering reluctance, together with questions about how negligence should be compared in situations involving multiple defendants, would shape the evolution of comparative negligence after 1920, a process that would be slow and halting.

Product Liability Law: The Vertical Integration of Fault

The Inherent-Danger Rule

Another area of tort law transformed during the Second Industrial Revolution and the Progressive era was product liability law. The common-law rule of privity held that consumers harmed by an unsafe or defective product could seek compensation from those who were "in privity" with them, that is, had sold the product to them directly, but not from a manufacturer who had sold the product to an intermediate merchant.[92] Consumers were also expected to examine goods before buying them and to assume

---

89. 1909 Tex. Laws, p. 279; 1910 Ohio Laws, p. 197; 1911 Kan. Laws, ch. 239; 1911 Mont. Laws, ch. 29; 1911 Nev. Laws, § 183; 1911 S. Dak. Laws, ch. 206; 1913 Fla. Laws, ch. 651; 1913 Neb. Laws, ch. 124; 1913 N.C. Laws, ch. 6; 1913 Wyo. Laws, ch. 132; 1915 Iowa Laws, § 2071; 1915 Minn. Laws, ch. 187; 1915 N. Dak. Laws, ch. 207; 1916 Va. Laws, p. 762; 1916 S.C. Laws, c. 29; 1918 Ky. Laws, ch. 52. In addition, three states extended the FELA model to certain hazardous occupations other than railroading. See 1911 Or. Laws, ch. 3 (building and construction trades); 1912 Ariz. Laws, ch. 89 (mining, manufacturing and transportation); 1919 Ark. Laws, p. 734 (mining). See also A. Chalmers Mole and Lyman P. Wilson, "A Study of Comparative Negligence: Part II," 17 *Corn. L.Q.* 604, 608–13 (1932). Congress extended the FELA model to maritime workers in 1920. 41 U.S. Stat. 988 (1920). Two states enacted laws that, like Wisconsin's, limited recovery to workers whose negligence was less than that of the employer. 1915 Mich. Laws, § 5497; 1919 Ark. Laws, p. 143.

90. 1910 Miss. Laws, ch. 135; *Natchez & S. R. Co. v. Crawford*, 55 So. 596 (Miss. 1911).

91. 1931 Wis. Laws, ch. 242; 1971 R.I. Laws, ch. 206.

92. David G. Owen and Mary J. Davis, *Owen and Davis on Products Liability* (2014), §§ 1:9–1:10; *Holcombe v. Hewson*, 170 Eng. Rep. 1194 (N.P. 1810); *Gardiner v. Gray*, 171 Eng. Rep. 46 (K.B. 1815).

all risk of injury after the goods passed out of the seller's hands, although there were exceptions for some foods and drugs and sellers and buyers could negotiate for contractual warranties of quality and fitness for a particular use.[93]

These rules worked satisfactorily during America's pre-industrial and early industrial eras, when most Americans made their own tools, clothing, furniture, food and other essential products or bought them directly from local artisans, but the Second Industrial Revolution brought the privity rule into question. Mass manufacture of goods for regional, national and international markets was a central feature, indeed a central purpose of that revolution. Manufacturers enlisted an army of intermediate sellers as mass markets became the norm, and a rising consumer culture required manufacturers to appeal directly to customers through product branding and advertising in order to succeed. Beginning in the 1850s, products of regional and national manufacturers, labeled as such, occupied an ever-increasing amount of shelf space in the department stores that were becoming common in large cities and in country and village general stores throughout the United States. Advertising agencies dedicated to national and regional product promotion began to appear in the 1870s, as did mail-order giants such as Sears, Roebuck & Co. (founded in 1872) and Montgomery Ward & Co. (founded in 1888), who created the first truly national product distribution systems.[94]

The increasingly direct nature of communication between manufacturers and consumers, and increasing popular recognition that intermediary sellers were no more than a link between them, raised two important questions: first, should product liability be governed by contract rather than tort law, and second, should the law eliminate privity rules and make manufacturers directly liable to consumers for defective products? Because pre-industrial England and America had never viewed product quality as exclusively a matter of contract, early-industrial-era British and American courts did not fence off product liability from tort law. But they saw no reason to modify privity either. In *Winterbottom v. Wright* (1842), the first important case to address the issue, Lord Abinger defended privity in instrumentalist terms similar to those he had used to establish the fellow-servant doctrine in *Priestley v. Fowler*. Without privity, he said, "the most absurd and outrageous consequences, to which I can see no limit, would ensue."[95]

---

93. *See, e.g., Seixas v. Woods*, 2 Caines 48 (N.Y. 1804); Owen and Davis, *Products Liability*, §§ 1:7–1:9; *see also, e.g.,* William Blackstone, *Commentaries on the Law of England* (1765–69), 4:157–61 (discussing laws prohibiting false weights and measures, prohibiting reconstitution of "dead victuals" in new forms and regulating the quality of baked goods, wine and meat); *The Acts of Assembly Now In Force, in the Colony of Virginia* (1752), 371–73 (1748 law for inspection of pork, beef, flour, tar, pitch and turpentine); 1784 Mass. Laws, ch. 50 (prohibiting sale of adulterated, "diseased, corrupted or unwholesome provisions"); 1785 N.Y. Laws, ch. 35 (labeling of flour).

94. Lawrence B. Glickman, ed., *Consumer Society in American History: A Reader* (1999), 1–4; *see also, e.g.,* E.S. Turner, *The Shocking History of Advertising!* (2012).

95. *Winterbottom*, 10 Mees. & W. 109, 152 Eng. Reports 402 (Exch. 1842); *Priestley v. Fowler*, 3 Mees. & W. 1 (1837); *see* Chapter 1.

After *Winterbottom*, the steady shift to mass production, to regional and national product distribution and a to consumer-oriented economy created subtle but powerful currents against privity and it soon began to erode, albeit slowly. In *Thomas v. Winchester* (1852), New York's highest court, relying heavily on pre-industrial food-and-drug statutes and court decisions that had imposed heavy responsibilities on drug manufacturers, held that a manufacturer who had mistakenly filled a bottle labeled as dandelion extract with belladonna was directly liable to a consumer poisoned by the drug even though the consumer had purchased the bottle from a pharmacist.[96] American courts interpreted *Winchester* not as challenging the concept of privity but as creating an exception for products deemed inherently dangerous. Between 1860 and 1900, the courts carved out additional exceptions for other poisonous drugs, for food, and for fuel and illuminating oils such as kerosene and naphtha, which could explode when mixed improperly or stored at high temperatures.[97] Many of the products so classified were not, strictly speaking, inherently dangerous but only became so if stored or used improperly. This was a tacit expansion of the scope of liability envisioned by *Winchester*, and courts that participated in that expansion sometimes obscured its nature by referring interchangeably to "inherently" and "imminently" dangerous products.

Accidents involving construction equipment became increasingly frequent as the industrial age advanced,[98] and beginning in 1882 with the New York case of *Devlin v. Smith*, courts created another privity exception for construction equipment defects, based on the premise that manufacturers knew exactly how their equipment would ultimately be used. Some early cases also suggested it would be appropriate to make manufacturers directly liable to consumers where they actually knew of the product defect or overlooked a visible defect. But the emerging consumer economy raised a broader question: should courts also eliminate privity where the manufacturer didn't actually know of the defect but could have discovered it through ordinary care — in other words, where the manufacturer was negligent? Judges in some early construc-

---

96. *Winchester*, 6 N.Y. 452 (1852). The court had first affirmed the privity rule in *Mayor of Albany v. Cunliff*, 2 N.Y. 165 (1849), reasoning that when manufacturers relinquished possession of their products, they relinquished control, and that all subsequent injury would necessarily arise from use of the product. 2 N.Y. at 180–81.

97. *See, e.g., Davidson v. Nichols*, 93 Mass. 514 (1866) (chemicals with explosive properties); *Wellington v. Downer Kerosene Oil Co.*, 104 Mass. 64 (1870) (naphtha); *Hourigan v. Nowell*, 110 Mass. 470 (1872) (illuminating oil); *Elkins, Bly & Co. v. McKean*, 79 Pa. 493 (1875) (same); *Bishop v. Weber*, 1 N.E. 154 (Mass. 1885) (food). Other early product-liability cases created exceptions for agricultural and industrial machinery, although these exceptions were not universally adopted. *See, e.g., Loop v. Litchfield*, 42 N.Y. 351 (1870) (sawmill balance wheel); *Heizer v. Kingsland & Douglass Mfg. Co.*, 19 S.W. 630 (Mo. 1892) (crop thresher); *compare Losee v. Clute*, 51 N.Y. 494 (1873) (refusing to eliminate privity as to industrial boiler).

98. In 1900 and 1910, construction cases accounted for roughly fifteen percent of all workplace-accident cases in the Five-State Survey. *See* Appendix 3.

tion-equipment cases arguably did so, but they shied away from saying as much: instead, they chose to slot their cases into the imminent-danger category.[99]

The Frontal Assault on Privity Begins

The first direct attack on privity occurred in *Heaven v. Pender*, an English construction-equipment case decided the year after *Devlin*. Master of the Rolls William Brett, relying on the industrial-era concept that duties of care were not confined to pre-industrial, status-based relationships but potentially extended to everyone directly harmed by a wrongdoer's conduct, suggested that where "everyone of ordinary sense would...recognize at once" that absent use of "ordinary care and skill with regard to the condition of the thing supplied...there will be danger of injury to the person...for whose use the thing is supplied," then failure to use ordinary care would render the supplier liable to anyone injured by the product.[100] Brett's colleagues declined to adopt his suggestion as law, but other courts took notice and in *Schubert v. J.R. Clark Co.* (1892), another construction-equipment case, Minnesota's supreme court became the first American court to squarely eliminate privity for manufacturer negligence. The *Schubert* court declined to rely on the imminent-danger doctrine and adopted Brett's rule: companies that offered a defective product, said Justice Daniel Dickinson, would be "deemed to have anticipated that...it would come to the hands of a purchaser, either directly from the defendant [manufacturer] or from some intermediate dealer, for actual use, and with the consequences which actually were suffered." Standing alone, that statement might have fit within the imminent-danger or actual-knowledge exceptions, but Dickinson put the court's intent to forge new ground beyond doubt:

> [I]t would be difficult to distinguish such a case [where the manufacturer did not sell directly to the consumer] in principle from one where the transaction is directly between the wrongdoer, then knowing the danger, and the party who is injured. If any distinction is to be made it must rest upon grounds of expediency, the arbitrary fixing of a limit to the liability of the wrongdoer, but we consider that in principle the defendant should be held to responsibility for an injury resulting proximately...from its confessedly negligent act, which was such as to expose another to great bodily harm. [101]

---

99. *Devlin*, 89 N.Y. 470 (1882); *see also, e.g., Bright v. Barnett*, 60 N.W. 418 (Wis. 1894) (defective construction plank; court stressed that the planks in question had visible knots and that the manufacturer had failed to follow customary testing procedures before supplying the planks); *Casey v. Hoover*, 89 S.W. 330 (Mo. App. 1905) (manufacturer of defective bridge held liable to traveler); *Steele v. Grahl-Peterson Co.*, 109 N.W. 882 (Iowa 1906) (construction company held liable to passerby injured by collapse of defective work).

100. 11 Q.B.D. 503 (Ct. App. 1883).

101. *Schubert*, 51 N.W. 1103, 1105–06 (Minn. 1892). Jurists took notice of *Schubert*, but a handful of earlier decisions had eliminated privity in cases where a manufacturer deceptively advertised its product as safe, and some jurists incorrectly placed *Schubert* in this category. *See McCaffrey v. Mossberg & Granville Mfg. Co.*, 50 A. 651 (R.I. 1901); *see also* Charles Loring, "Liability of a Man-

The steady advance of the consumer economy and Progressives' focus on food and drug safety played important roles in privity's continuing erosion after *Schubert*. Beginning in the 1880s, product-safety statutes appeared with increasing frequency,[102] and between 1900 and 1915 most states enacted laws regulating the manufacture and sale of oleomargarine, narcotics, commercial feeds and fungicides.[103] Support for a federal food-and-drug act (FDA) grew rapidly after 1900: popular magazines such as the *Ladies Home Journal* and *Collier's Weekly* devoted extensive space to the topic, and Upton Sinclair's book *The Jungle* (1906), describing horrific dangers and health hazards in the meat-packing industry, became a best seller. A series of experiments conducted under U.S. Department of Agriculture chief chemist Harvey Wiley starting in 1902, known as the "poison squad" tests, also dramatized the hazards of mislabeled and adulterated drugs and attracted national attention. In Washington, President Roosevelt and North Dakota Senator Porter McCumber pressed for Congressional enactment of an FDA applying to nearly all food- and drug-related products in interstate commerce, and in 1906, Congress complied. Between 1906 and 1911, no fewer than forty states enacted "little FDA" laws for intrastate commerce that borrowed heavily from the federal model. Food and drug laws were one of the few categories of reform laws that escaped judicial criticism during the era: judges of all political faiths agreed that such regulation fell squarely within the states' police power over public health.[104]

The pure-food-and-drug movement's advance during the Progressive era did not immediately convince American judges to abandon privity in product-liability cases but it made them more open to doing so, and after 1900, jurists and a few courts began to edge toward *Schubert*. In 1906, an unsigned article in the *Harvard Law Review*, relying in part on *Schubert*, called openly for abolition of privity in cases involving manufacturer negligence as well as those involving defects known to the manufacturer, and in 1913 Thomas Shearman and Amasa Redfield suggested in their influential tort-law treatise that privity should be eliminated in all cases where "it is contemplated

---

ufacturer or a Vendor to Persons With Whom He Has No Contractual Relations for Negligence in the Construction or Sale of Chattels," 58 *Cent. L.J.* 365, 367 (1904) (characterizing *Schubert* as an "expansive" application of the imminent-danger rule). Examples of early deceptive-advertising cases include *Loop*, 42 N.Y. 351 (1870); *Elkins*, 79 Pa. 493 (1875); *Heizer*, 19 S.W. 630 (Mo. 1892); and *Lewis v. Terry*, 43 P. 398 (Cal. 1896) (folding bed).

102. *See, e.g.*, 1880 Wis. Laws, chs. 252, 269 (oil and food analysis and inspection); 1881 Wis. Laws, ch. 40 (labeling of dairy products); 1882 Wis. Laws, ch. 167 (pharmacist licensing and drug labeling); 1883 Ind. Laws, §§ 6800–01 (oleomargarine); 1893 Colo. Laws, ch. 125 (oleomargarine); 1895 Tenn. Laws, ch. 101 (oleomargarine); 1897 Wis. Laws, ch. 375 (bakery sanitation). *See* James Westervelt, *American Pure Food and Drug Laws* (1912), 260–1450 for a detailed listing and description of such laws.

103. *See* Westervelt, *Pure Food and Drug Laws*, passim.

104. 34 U.S. Stats. 768 (1906); C.C. Regier, "The Struggle for Federal Food and Drugs Legislation," 1 *L. & Contemp. Probs.* 3, 3–14 (1933); Arthur D. Herrick, *Food Regulation and Compliance* (1944), 4–9. State "little FDA" laws are compiled and exhaustively described in Westervelt, *Pure Food and Drug Laws*, 260–1450.

that the thing shall be resold."[105] In *Watson v. Augusta Brewing Co.* (1905), Georgia's supreme court held a soda bottler directly liable to a consumer who swallowed broken glass inside the bottle, stating that privity "does not matter" because the public, for whom the product was intended, had "the right to rest secure in the assumption that [it] will not be fed on broken glass."[106] New York's highest court, where the erosion of privity had begun more than fifty years earlier, inched toward abolition in *Torgesen v. Schultz* (1908) and *Statler v. George A. Ray Manufacturing Co.* (1909), cases which involved, respectively, an exploding seltzer siphon and an exploding coffee urn. In *Torgesen,* the court spoke favorably of Brett's opinion in *Pender* and stated broadly that manufacturers must "take reasonable care to prevent the article sold from proving dangerous when subjected only to customary usage." In *Statler,* it went a step further: manufacturers of products "liable to become a source of great danger to many people if not carefully and properly constructed," said Justice Charles Hiscock, were "chargeable with knowledge of defective and unsafe construction" whether or not they had actual knowledge.[107]

In 1916, the New York court made another important contribution to the erosion process in *MacPherson v. Buick Motor Co.,* holding Buick directly liable to a driver who was injured when one of his auto's wooden-spoked wheels broke. Justice Benjamin Cardozo, who would finish his career by joining the U.S. Supreme Court and would become one of the most celebrated American jurists of the twentieth century, reviewed his court's previous decisions and held in forceful, direct prose that their logic compelled complete abolition of privity in all cases of manufacturer negligence. Cardozo explained that:

> If the nature of a thing is such that it is reasonably certain to place life and limb in peril when negligently made, it is then a thing of danger. Its nature gives warning of the consequences to be expected. If to the element of danger there is added knowledge that the thing will be used by persons other than the purchaser, and used without new tests then, irrespective of contract, the manufacturer of this thing of danger is under a duty to make it carefully.[108]

This was too much for Chief Justice Willard Bartlett, who had authored the *Torgeson* decision. He noted that a Buick vendor, not Buick, had made the defective wheel, and he argued that seltzer siphons and coffee urns were inherently dangerous (being

---

105. Note, "Tort Liability of Contractor or Vendor to Parties Not Privy to the Contract," 19 *Harv. L. Rev.* 372 (1906); Shearman and Redfield, *Treatise* (6th ed. 1913), § 117a.

106. *Watson,* 52 S.E. 152, 153 (Ga. 1905). *See also Clement v. Crosby & Co.,* 111 N.W. 745, 746 (Mich. 1907), in which Michigan's supreme court allowed a plaintiff to proceed on a traditional claim of knowing concealment of the compound's dangerous properties but suggested that a claim of negligence might have been sufficient.

107. *Torgesen,* 84 N.E. 956, 957 (N.Y. 1908); *Statler,* 88 N.E. 1063, 1064 (N.Y. 1909).

108. *MacPherson,* 111 N.E. 1050, 1052 (N.Y. 1916). As to Cardozo's place in American law, *see, e.g.,* Richard A. Posner, *Cardozo: A Study in Reputation* (1990); Andrew L. Kaufman, *Cardozo* (2000).

intended for use under pressure) in a way that autos were not. But those of Bartlett's colleagues who had joined in the *Torgeson* and *Statler* decisions did not see it that way, and they agreed with Cardozo.[109]

Most modern scholars regard *MacPherson* as a watershed case, the case that definitively pulled down the barrier between manufacturers and consumers in personal injury cases,[110] but the *Schubert* and *Watson* cases put that in question; and, consistent with the gradual nature of privity's erosion, *MacPherson*'s rise to fame was slow. *MacPherson* received immediate attention from writers in Harvard's and Yale's law journals: one writer viewed it as a potentially transformative case, but others viewed it as merely creating a new category of imminently-dangerous products.[111] No other state supreme court would abolish privity in reliance on *MacPherson* until 1927,[112] and the first law review article anointing it a watershed case did not appear until 1929.[113] Privity eroded substantially during the Progressive era due to Progressives' receptivity to socialization of accident costs and industrialization's role in breaking down economic walls between manufacturers and consumers, but at the end of the era it was still alive, if enfeebled, in most states. Privity's death would be a major focus of attention in the American legal community during the decades to come.

---

109. *MacPherson*, 111 N.E. at 1958 (dissent). In *Olds Motor Works v. Shaffer*, 140 S.W. 1047 (1911), Kentucky's highest court held that an auto manufacturer was liable to a consumer under circumstances very similar to those of *MacPherson*, but it did not formally abolish privity.

110. *See, e.g.*, Warren A. Seavey, "Mr. Justice Cardozo and the Law of Torts," 52 *Harv. L. Rev.* 372, 376-79 (1939); James A. Henderson, Jr., "MacPherson v. Buick Motor Company: Simplifying the Facts While Reshaping the Law," in Robert L. Rabin & Stephen D. Sugarman, eds., *Torts Stories* (2003), 52-68; Kenneth Abraham, "Prosser's *The Fall of the Citadel*," 100 *Minn. L. Rev.* 1823, 1826-28 (2016); Posner, *Cardozo*, 108-09.

111. Note, "Negligence—Liability of Manufacturers to Third Parties—Nature of the Goods as Test—MacPherson v. Buick Motor Co.," 25 *Yale L.J.* 679 (1916) (viewing *MacPherson* as supporting a new category of imminently dangerous products); Note, "Torts—Negligence—Liability of a Manufacturer," 32 *Harv. L. Rev.* 89 (1918) (same); Note, "Torts—Negligence—Liability of Contractor to Third Party," 27 *Yale L.J.* 961 (1917) (viewing *MacPherson* as potentially transformative).

112. *McLeod v. Linde Air Prods. Co.*, 1 S.W.2d 122 (Mo. 1927) (faulty oxygen tank valve). The first judicial endorsement of *MacPherson* came in a 1917 federal case, *Cadillac Motor Car Co. v. Johnson*, 221 F. 805 (6th Cir. 1917). Prior to 1927, several state courts spoke favorably of *MacPherson* but did not squarely endorse its blanket abolition of privity. *See Travis v. Rochester Bridge Co.*, 118 N.E. 694 (Ind. App. 1918); *Jones v. Gulf States Steel Co.*, 88 So. 21 (Ala. 1921); *Collette v. Page*, 114 A. 136 (R.I. 1921); *Martin v. Studebaker Corp.*, 133 A. 384 (N.J. 1926); *White Sewing Mach. Co. v. Feisel*, 162 N.E. 633 (Ohio App. 1927). Some courts rejected *MacPherson*. *See, e.g., Windram Mfg. Co. v. Boston Blacking Co.*, 131 N.E. 454, 455 (Mass. 1921) (citing *MacPherson* as an example of a "tendency...in some recent cases" but refusing to abandon privity).

113. Francis H. Bohlen, "Liability of Manufacturers to Persons Other Than Their Immediate Vendees," 45 *L.Q. Rev.* 343, 359-66 (1929). A 1932 article referred to *MacPherson* as one of a cluster of recent cases abolishing privity. Note, "Liability of Manufacturers," 10 *Tex. L. Rev.* 520 (1932).

Judges and Juries in the Progressive Era

Judicialism and the Case Against Juries

The struggle over the proper balance of power between judges and juries in tort and other cases continued during the Progressive era on a number of fronts. The era began with talk of eliminating all use of juries in civil cases. Many judicialists—that is, persons instinctively and intellectually inclined to favor a strong role for judges and a limited role for juries in the legal system, including future president and federal chief justice William Howard Taft, Harvard law professor and former Nebraska supreme court commissioner Roscoe Pound, and University of Michigan law professor Edson Sunderland—argued that the average juror did not have the education or ability needed to correctly decide the many complex and technical issues that were appearing in industrial-era lawsuits. Others argued that although juries had served at the United States' founding as a bulwark against government encroachment on civil liberties, American democracy was now well established and no longer had need of them in that role.[114] But jury defenders were equally numerous and equally vocal. Federal circuit judge Henry Clay Caldwell argued that juries were an essential counterbalance to the ever-present risk of judicial overreaching and that complaints of courtroom inefficiency and delay were largely due to judicial, not jury errors. Other judges supported the jury system for more pragmatic reasons: "[I]t brings the people to the courts to assist in trials," said one trial judge, "and prevents the class feeling that would probably arise if all cases were tried by the judges." Most judicialists conceded that formal elimination of juries in civil trials was not possible because "[t]he American of the present day feels that it is an almost inherent right of society."[115]

Progressives and the Case Against Judges

Beginning in the 1890s, federal and state judges, many of whom believed devoutly in free-labor principles and conceived property and liberty rights and freedom of contract in broad terms, closely scrutinized reform laws addressing political corruption, taxation, workplace safety, utility regulation and other pressing social issues. They upheld most reform laws, as the workers compensation experience illustrated,

---

114. *See* Renee Lettow Lerner, "The Rise of the Directed Verdict: Jury Power in Civil Cases Before the Federal Rules of 1938," 81 *Geo. Wash. L. Rev.* 448, 453–55, 520–22 (2013); Andrew Kent, "The Jury and Empire: The Insular Cases and the Anti-Jury Movement in the Gilded Age and Progressive Era," 91 *S. Cal. L. Rev.* 375, 396–406 (2018); *see also* Lawrence Irwell, "The Case Against Jury Trials in Civil Actions," 54 *Cent. L.J.* 243 (1902).

115. Henry C. Caldwell, "Trial by Judge and Jury," 33 *Am. L. Rev.* 321, 322, 341 (1899); William H. Blymyer, "The Jury System in Civil Cases the Greatest Drag in Delaying Justice," 26 *Green Bag* 203, 203 (1914); George Clementson, "A Plea for Non-Unanimous Verdict In Civil Actions," *Reports of Wis. St. Bar Assn. 1902–03* (1903), 107–08. Clementson was a Wisconsin circuit judge.

but they struck down enough laws to elicit Progressive ire.[116] *Lochner v. New York*, a 1904 U.S. Supreme Court decision that struck down a law limiting bakers' hours of work despite evidence that their overlong hours affected public health, became the Progressives' leading specimen of judicial overreach, but there were many others.[117]

Progressives who felt that judges went too far in scrutinizing reform laws eventually launched a movement to curb judicial power through popular recall of judges and of court decisions. In 1908, Oregon became the first state to provide for recall of judges; several other states followed suit, and the movement reached a climax in 1912.[118] During that year, Ohio voters ratified a new constitution explicitly authorizing judicial recall as well as several other Progressive reform measures that had previously been struck down by the state's supreme court, and Theodore Roosevelt made recall of unpopular decisions a key theme of his campaign to regain the presidency as the Progressive Party's candidate. "When [the people] have definitely decided on a given policy they must have public servants who will carry out the policy," Roosevelt argued, not judges whose "prime concern was with the empty ceremonial of perfunctory legalism, and not with the living spirit of justice." Roosevelt privately hoped that judges would make recall measures unnecessary by engaging in self-correction, but he warned that judicial overreaching was "turning large classes of people against the life, liberty and property clauses" and toward socialism.[119]

Several prominent judges responded publicly to these criticisms, including North Carolina chief justice Walter Clark and Wisconsin's John Winslow. Clark joined the critics and went further than many of them: he attacked judicial overreach at its root, arguing that judges had no authority to review and overturn legislative decisions. Clark's position had a respectable pedigree, having been supported by a line of distinguished nineteenth century judges. The issue had been settled against him by the

---

116. *See, e.g.,* Edward Keynes, *Liberty, Property, and Privacy: Toward a Jurisprudence of Substantive Due Process* (1996), 97–115; Michael Les Benedict, "Laissez-Faire and Liberty: A Re-evaluation of the Meaning and Origins of Laissez-Faire Constitutionalism," 3 *L. & Hist. Rev.* 293, 328–30 (1985); Owen M. Fiss, *History of the Supreme Court of the United States, Vol. 8: Troubled Beginnings of the Modern State, 1888-1910* (1993).

117. *Lochner*, 198 U.S. 45 (1904). For examples of other decisions cited by Progressives as examples of judicial overreach, *see* Gilbert E. Roe, *Our Judicial Oligarchy* (1912), 40–43, 117–20, 129–31, 142–45; William L. Ransom, *Majority Rule and the Judiciary* (1912), 16–17; Edith M. Phelps, *Selected Articles on the Recall: Including the Recall of Judges and Judicial Decisions* (1915), 82–94, 154–61.

118. Or. Const. (1908), art. II, § 18. Other states that enacted judicial recall measures included California, Arizona, Colorado, North Dakota and Wisconsin. Cal. Const. (1911), art. II, § 15; Ariz. Const. (1912), art. VIII, § 1; Colo. Const. (1912), art. XXI, § 1; N.D. Const. (1920), art. III, §§ 1, 10; Wis. Const. (1926), art. XIII, § 12. *See also* Thomas Goebel, *Government by the People* (2002), 65–68.

119. Clarence E. Walker, *Proceedings and Debates of the Constitutional Convention of the State of Ohio* (1912), 384–86 (Roosevelt), 669 (comments by William Jennings Bryan to convention regarding judges); Ohio Const. (1912), II:38 (recall provision); Sidney M. Milkis, *Theodore Roosevelt, The Progressive Party, and the Transformation of American Democracy* (2009), 56–96, 91 (quoting Roosevelt campaign address at Omaha, Nebraska, April 27, 1912); *see also* Gilbert E. Roe, *Our Judicial Oligarchy* (1912), v–vi, 117–21, 207–19.

mid-nineteenth century,[120] but as the number of decisions striking down reform laws increased, he felt compelled to speak out. Between 1906 and 1915, Clark argued in a series of speeches and articles that use of the judicial power to strike down reform laws was directly responsible for Progressives' ire and for the recall movement. He singled out *Lochner* for particular criticism, charging that it "was in truth based upon unwillingness to curb the power of the employer over the employee," and he intimated that recall was an appropriate solution: all branches of government, he said, "are subject to only one reviewing body and that is the Sovereign—the people themselves."[121]

Progressives as a whole were far from united on judicial recall. The conservative image of judges as detached appliers of rules divorced from politics meshed with the broad Progressive vision of a government administered by experts based on scientific principles, and Winslow, who became Wisconsin's chief justice in 1907, took great care to promote that image. Winslow was sensitive to complaints of judicial overreach but he was a firm judicialist at heart, wary of efforts to limit judicial power. In 1909, he embarked on a campaign of speeches and articles designed to explain conservatives and Progressives to each other and to promote his vision of constructive conservatism. Winslow urged conservatives to bear in mind that "as individual life has more and more given place to crowded community life, the rights and privileges once deemed essential to the perfect liberty of the individual are often found... to breed wrong and injustice to the community at large," language that he would echo in the *Borgnis* case. But he also reminded Progressive critics that "[j]udges are sworn to protect and support... constitutions as they are, and not as they would like to see them"—language that echoed in the supreme court's workplace-injury decisions as the transition to workers compensation drew near.[122]

---

120. Judges who opposed judicial review included Pennsylvania chief justice John Gibson and Maryland chancellor Theodorick Bland. *See Eakin v. Raub*, 12 Serg. & Rawle 330, 355 (Pa. 1825) (Gibson); *Evans v. Randall* (Baltimore County Court, 1816) (Bland), quoted in Charles G. Haines, *The American Doctrine of Judicial Supremacy* (1932), 265; *see generally* Haines, *passim* and Renee B. Lettow, "New Trial for Verdict Against Law: Judge-Jury Relations in Early Nineteenth-Century America," 71 *Notre Dame L. Rev.* 505, 506–07 (1996).

121. Walter Clark, "Some Defects in the Constitution of the United States," 13 *Mich. L. Rev.* 263, 277–82 (1906); Clark, "Government by Judges," address delivered at Cooper Union, New York City (January 27, 1914); Clark, Letter , 19 *Law Notes* 178, 179 (December 1915); Clark, "Back to the Constitution," 3 *Va. L. Rev.* 214, 220 (1915).

122. Winslow, "The Patriot and the Courts," 9, 12; *see Borgnis*, 133 N.W. at 215–16; *Houg*, 129 N.W. at 639; *Driscoll*, 129 N.W. at 408. For other examples of Winslow's campaign, see Winslow, "Understanding Heart"; and Winslow, "The Judicial Recall: Is it a Remedy or a Nostrum?," speech to Kansas Conference on Charities and Correction (no date, probably 1914) and Winslow, "Some Tendencies of Modern Legislation and Judicial Decisions" (lecture notes, May 3, 1916), both in Winslow Papers, WHS.

Cabining the Jury: Directed Verdicts and JNOVs

Winslow believed that popular dissatisfaction with judges was due in part to poorly organized court systems and outdated civil procedure rules that created inefficiency, delay and unnecessary litigation costs. He did not want to return to the old English system in which judges dominated civil trials—"American courts have indeed avoided the Scylla of absolutism," he commented—but in his view, the real question was "whether in doing so they have not fallen into the Charybdis of weakness" by creating a system in which trial judges were "hardly more than a moderator."[123]

The close balance of power between judicialists and their Progressive critics and the depth of feeling on each side meant that judicialists would have to approach any further cabining of jury power by indirect paths. Several such paths were already in use, most importantly nonsuits and directed verdicts. At the close of evidence at trial, any party could ask for a nonsuit if it believed the plaintiff had not proved his case, or the judge could order a nonsuit on his own initiative if he held that belief. The case would then be dismissed, but the plaintiff would have a chance to collect more evidence and pursue a new lawsuit and trial if he wished. Demurrers also appeared in the mid-nineteenth century, in the form of motions made by defendants shortly after commencement of the lawsuit to dismiss the plaintiff's complaint because it did not state facts or legal theories that supported recovery. Directed verdicts, which a judge could order a jury to render either at a defendant's request or on his own initiative, provided no second chance. The jury would be told that the plaintiff's case had failed and that it must give a verdict against him, which the judge would then certify as a judgment.[124] Nonsuits and new trials contributed heavily to the rapid growth of court caseloads and resultant complaints at the end of the nineteenth century. American courts responded by gradually abandoning nonsuits in favor of directed verdicts, and during the Progressive era they developed a refinement: judgments notwithstanding the verdict (JNOVs), which allowed a jury to issue a verdict based on its own views but then permitted the judge to reject it and issue a contrary judgment if he disagreed. The advantage of JNOVs was that if the judge was proved wrong on appeal, the jury's verdict could be reinstated without need for a new trial.[125]

Jury defenders were not slow to recognize that the rise of directed verdicts and JNOVs meant a reduction of jury power, and they pushed back: between 1912 and 1923, several state legislatures prohibited directed verdicts entirely or in part. But the

---

123. Winslow, "The Twentieth-Century Lawyer" (address given to Northwestern University Law School Alumni Association, April 25, 1912), 3–4, in Winslow Papers, WHS.

124. James B. Thayer, *A Preliminary Treatise on Evidence At the Common Law* (1898), 169–74, 234–38; Robert W. Millar, *Civil Procedure of the Trial Court in Historical Perspective* (1952), 298–301; Note, "The Changing Role of the Jury in the Nineteenth Century," 74 *Yale L.J.* 184, note 77 (1964); Douglas G. Smith, "The Historical and Constitutional Contexts of Jury Reform," 25 *Hofstra L. Rev.* 377, 453–54 (1996); Lerner, "Rise of Directed Verdict," 458–67.

125. Millar, *Civil Procedure in Historical Perspective*, 305–06; Lerner, "Rise of Directed Verdict," 502–05.

prohibitive laws met stiff judicial opposition. Virginia's supreme court got around its state's law by indirection, allowing judges to give juries instructions that effectively dictated the verdict or to strike all evidence presented by a party that had not established its case. Minnesota's supreme court upheld a law that authorized directed verdicts only where both sides agreed; it did so in part because the legislature had also authorized JNOVs, but Wisconsin's supreme court viewed a similar law as an attack on "the very essence of judicial power; that is, the power to determine under the law the rights of parties properly before it." Collectively, these cases signaled that American judges would aggressively protect their right to take cases away from juries where they believed the proper result was obvious.[126]

Cabining the Jury: "Proper Evidence" and Scintillas

The tools that judges could use to take a case from the jury were well-known but the standard that courts should use to determine when it was appropriate to take a case from the jury was less certain, and it too was a focus of attention during the Progressive era. Some early American courts had rejected the English rule, which allowed judges to take cases away from juries unless there was evidence "upon which the jury can *properly* find a verdict," in favor of the "scintilla" rule, holding that a case must go the jury where there was "*any* evidence...tending to prove each material fact put in issue."[127] At the advent of the American industrial age, New York courts began moving back toward the English rule in a series of railroad accident cases, based largely on instrumentalist concerns that juries were predisposed in favor of accident victims and against defendant corporations.[128] New York judges were uncertain how to define the circumstances under which a jury could "properly" find for a plaintiff so as to make judicial intervention inappropriate, but they gradually moved toward a definition encompassing cases in which "honest, intelligent and impartial men may rationally differ."[129]

During the 1850s and 1860s, American elites became increasingly distrustful of juries and receptive to a more active role for judges, due partly to the steadily increasing presence of recent immigrants in American politics on juries and partly to a desire

---

126. Lerner, "Rise of Directed Verdict," 503–05; 1912 Va. Laws, ch. 52; *see Small v. Va. R. & P. Co.*, 99 S.E. 525 (Va. 1919); *Barksdale v. S. R. Co.*, 148 S.E. 683 (Va. 1929); 1913 Minn. Laws, ch. 245; *Zimmerman v. Chi. & Nw. R. Co.*, 151 N.W. 412 (Minn. 1915); 1923 Wis. Laws, ch. 31; *Thoe v. Chi., Milw. & St. Paul R. Co.*, 195 N.W. 407, 409 (Wis. 1923).

127. Lerner, "Rise of Directed Verdict," 475–78. English and American courts expressed the two rules with many minor variations of form. The phrases quoted here, which are found at M.A. Foran, "The Scintilla Rule and Its Relations to Trial by Jury," 4 *W. Res. L.J.* 143, 144 (Nov. 1898), give the gist of the difference.

128. Lerner, "Rise of Directed Verdict," 478–79, citing, inter al., *Stuart v. Simpson*, 1 Wend. 376 (N.Y. Sup. Ct. 1828) and *Haring v. N.Y. & Erie R. Co.*, 13 Barb. 9 (N.Y. Gen. Term 1852); *see also* Chapter 2.

129. Lerner, "Rise of Directed Verdict," 483; *Ernst v. Hudson Riv. R. Co.*, 39 N.Y. 61, 68 (1868) (concurrence).

to eliminate court congestion. In *Pleasants v. Fant* (1874), the U.S. Supreme Court gave voice to their distrust and encouraged a return to the English standard: it held that federal courts must take cases from juries if, after "conceding to all the evidence offered the greatest probative force, which...it is *fairly entitled* to, it is [not] sufficient to justify a verdict."[130] Some state courts adopted the *Fant* standard,[131] but others adhered to the scintilla rule.[132]

Renewed debate broke out in several legal journals during the Progressive era. Supporters of the English rule relied heavily on Justice Samuel Miller's statement in *Fant* that allowing cases with clear outcomes to go to juries would be an "idle exercise," a waste of court time and resources. They criticized the scintilla rule as a tool for delay and coercion of defendants, and argued that English rule was necessary to safeguard the rule of law against the vagaries of popular passion.[133] Supporters of the scintilla rule replied that Miller had later reconsidered his views in *Fant*, and they praised the rule as "the personified sentinel of the right of trial by jury," one essential to true justice. "[T]he judicial mind," said one supporter, "cannot...deduce truth from facts as well as the ordinary intelligent man, who sees things, from perhaps a lower intellectual plane, as they really are, and who understands human nature, because he is more in contact with it."[134] A number of jurists questioned whether the dispute had any real meaning. Harvard law professor James Bradley Thayer sided with jury defenders, but he could "hardly believe that the difference is, at bottom, anything more than a difference over words."[135]

Both the English standard and the scintilla rule were inherently elastic and left openings for judges to exercise their own discretion in sending cases to or withholding them from the jury. Given that elasticity, courts' actions showed the true rule in each state more clearly than their words. The Five-State Survey indicates that late-nineteenth-century trial judges and supreme court justices made extensive use of their powers to take tort cases from juries, and that such use did not diminish during the Progressive era. Throughout the period from 1860 to 1920, trial judges in cases included in the Survey disposed of more than one-tenth of all tort cases that came before them through demurrers, nonsuits and directed verdicts. Most of the

---

130. Lerner, "Rise of Directed Verdict," 475–78, 488–90; *Fant*, 89 U.S. 116, 122 (1874).

131. *See, e.g., Paine v. Gr. Trunk R. Co. of Canada*, 58 N.H. 611 (1879); *Conley v. McDonald*, 40 Mich. 150 (1879).

132. *See, e.g., Penticost v. Massey*, 81 So. 637 (Ala. 1919); Jerome A. Holtzman, "Alabama's Scintilla Rule," 28 *Ala. L. Rev.* 592, 602–07 (1977).

133. James Troup, "Should the Scintilla Rule Be Abolished?", 4 *W. Res. L.J.* 117, 119–21 (October 1898); Samuel C. Graham, "Directing Verdicts," 16 *Va. Law Reg.* 401, 402–03, 406 (October 1910).

134. Foran, "Scintilla Rule," 151; M.J. Fulton, "Directing Verdicts," 16 *Va. L. Reg.* 241, 241–45 (August 1910).

135. Letter from Thayer to editors, reprinted in "The Scintilla Rule—A Symposium," 4 *W. Res. L.J.* 169, 177 (December 1898). *See also* John H. Wigmore, *A Treatise on the System of Evidence in Trials at Common Law* (1905), 4:§ 2494 (stating that "There is no virtue in any form of words" for stating the rule).

remaining cases resulted in jury verdicts that trial judges accepted, but in roughly forty percent of those cases their supreme courts disagreed and ordered either judgment for the party that had lost at trial or a remand to the trial court, thus giving the losing party either an outright victory or another chance at it. In sum, judges directed the outcomes of more than half of all tort cases covered in the Survey; juries were allowed to make their decisions without interference in less than half.[136]

FIGURE 3.2
Five-State Survey: Judicial Deference to Juries, 1860–1920[137]

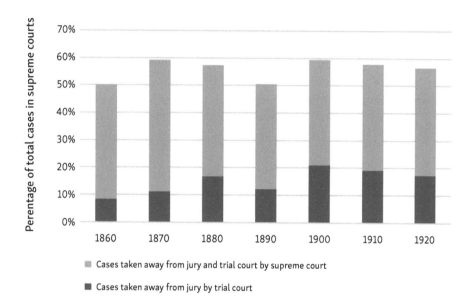

- Cases taken away from jury and trial court by supreme court
- Cases taken away from jury by trial court

Streamlining the Jury

Two additional jury-related movements, to eliminate the traditional requirement for unanimous verdicts in civil cases and to allow juries of reduced size, promoted Progressive ideals of efficiency. Those issues were less controversial than directed verdicts, JNOVs and the scintilla debate because they bid fair to make trials faster and

---

136. See Figure 3.2 and Appendices 2 and 3; *see also* Henry Billings Brown, "The Administration of the Jury System," 17 *Green Bag* 623, 625 (1905) (stating that "As a matter of practice, I have found that about fifty per cent of the cases should be taken from the jury"). Brown had served as a federal trial judge before joining the U.S. Supreme Court.

137. The cases on which Figure 3.2 is based are described in Appendix 2; the calculations are described in Appendix 3. "Cases taken away from jury by trial court" includes cases disposed of by trial courts through demurrer, nonsuits and directed verdicts. "Cases taken away from jury and trial court by supreme court" includes cases in which trial courts entered judgment on jury verdicts but the supreme court then overturned the judgment and either entered judgment of its own or sent the case back for a new trial.

more efficient and they did not pose any evident threat to jury power. Idaho was the first state to eliminate the unanimity requirement (1891) and by 1914, fourteen states had followed suit. Most required a three-fourths vote for a verdict.[138] Reduced-size provisions differed widely in detail: Georgia set a minimum of five jurors in 1877, and during the next forty years approximately sixteen states set minimums ranging from three jurors upward. Some states allowed reduced juries only if all parties to a lawsuit consented; others provided for reduced numbers in all cases.[139]

The vigorous debates of the Progressive era over judicial power, judicial hostility to reform and the usefulness of juries in the industrial age did not change the judge-jury balance of power in most states, but they did make one thing clear: judges would stoutly defend their role as masters in matters of law, including the right to take cases from the jury where the law made the proper outcome clear. No reform impulse would be allowed to interfere with that right. But the line between judges' and juries' roles, between matters of law and fact, remained blurry, with the potential to shift as the twentieth century unfolded and presented new social and legal challenges.

---

138. Idaho Const. (1891), art. I, § 7; John B. Phillips, "Modifications of the Jury System," 16 *Green Bag* 514, 514 (1904). The circumstances under which non-unanimous verdicts were allowed in civil cases varied among states. *Ibid*.

139. Phillips, "Modifications," 519–20; *see, e.g.*, Ga. Const. (1877), art. VI, § 18 (reduced jury only with consent); 1913 Wis. Laws, ch. 441 (consent required); 1977 Wis. Laws, ch. 187, § 95 (at least six jurors required).

FOUR

The Golden Age of Tort Socialization, 1920–1970

Any rule which operates to limit liability for a wrongful act must be derived from judicial policy, and its limits cannot be defined by any formula capable of automatic application, but must rest in the sound discretion of the court.

—Chief Justice Marvin Rosenberry (Wisconsin), 1931[1]

When John Crawford reported for work as a brakeman at the Natchez & Southern Railroad's yards in Natchez, Mississippi, on a hot July morning in 1910, he had no idea that he was about to become the standard-bearer for a quiet revolution in American tort law. Crawford was ordered to help a switch engine crew assemble cars for a train, using the link-and-pin couplings built into the Natchez & Southern's cars. Each car had a pivoting socket at one end and a U-shaped link at the other end; workers had to guide a car's link into the socket of the next car and then insert a heavy vertical pin through both link and socket in order to hold them together. When Crawford encountered a flatcar with a socket stuck to one side that couldn't be moved into position, he jumped on the switch engine's running board and tried to move the socket into position with his foot. As he did so the socket pivoted, trapping Crawford's foot against the switch engine's platform which rammed into the flatcar. Crawford's foot was mangled and eventually was amputated.[2]

Crawford sued the Natchez & Southern for negligently providing the defective coupling that caused his injuries, and the case followed a common pattern: the railroad denied liability and argued that the accident had resulted from Crawford's own negligence. At trial, the railroad asked the judge to give the jury a traditional instruc-

---

1. *Osborne v. Montgomery*, 234 N.W. 372, 378 (Wis. 1931).
2. *Natchez & S. R. Co. v. Crawford*, 55 So. 596 (Miss. 1911).

tion that "if they believe that the plaintiff's own negligence caused or contributed to his injury, then they must find for the defendant." At an earlier time, the instruction likely would have been given and would have doomed Crawford's case. But the judge refused to give the instruction: Mississippi's legislature had just enacted the nation's first pure comparative negligence law, providing that contributory negligence would not bar a plaintiff from recovering but would only reduce the amount of damages he was entitled to recover. The jury concluded that the railroad was negligent; it did not exonerate Crawford from contributory negligence but accounted for that negligence by awarding him a reduced amount of $2,000 in damages. The Natchez & Southern appealed and challenged the new statute's constitutionality, but Mississippi's supreme court gave the challenge short shrift. The statute, said Justice William Anderson, fell within the legislature's power to modify the rules of tort law and did not confer judicial power on juries. John Crawford's case was the first comparative-negligence case to reach Mississippi's supreme court. It received no fanfare, but it marked the beginning of the end for a contributory negligence regime that had dominated American tort law for nearly a century.[3]

The shift to comparative negligence was one of several ways in which tort law responded, often haltingly, to the impulses toward collective action and collective security that played a central role in American society from roughly 1920 to 1970. The idea that risk was an unavoidable part of modern life and that sometimes socialization of accident costs was the best way to address it had appeared in American political discourse as early as the 1880s, and legal gestures toward such socialization—workers compensation laws, limited comparative-negligence systems for railroad workers, and a handful of court decisions extending manufacturers' liability for negligence to ultimate consumers as well as direct purchasers of their products—appeared soon afterwards. But Americans' approach to socialization and collective action changed shape repeatedly as the twentieth century progressed.

The 1920s marked the first time that a majority of Americans lived in cities and suburbs, a world which created closer interpersonal contact than their rural fellow citizens enjoyed. Automobile ownership skyrocketed, and states and the federal government created a nationwide system of highways that brought auto owners new opportunities for contact with others. During the same decade, radio evolved from a novelty into a national communications network: by 1930, hundreds of stations broadcast news and entertainment programs, many of them distributed nationwide, to more than thirteen million households. Radio owners in places like rural Mississippi might not have felt great kinship with voices broadcasting from New York City, but they acquired a degree of familiarity and even comfort with that previously alien world. In 1933, during the depths of the Depression, President Franklin Roosevelt took advantage of

---

3. *Crawford*, 55 So. at 598–600. The court relied heavily on an earlier Wisconsin decision upholding that state's 1907 law creating a limited comparative-negligence system for railroad workers. Ibid. at 598, citing *Kiley v. Chi., Milw. & St. Paul R. Co.*, 119 N.W. 309 (Wis. 1909); *see* Chapter 3.

that familiarity in his "fireside chat" broadcasts to quell a widespread sense of panic that was threatening to change the Depression from an economic crisis into something much worse. Movies, many of which were distributed and exhibited by regional and national theater chains, created another common experience for Americans.[4] The 1920s also saw a national consumer economy come into full flower. The prosperity of that decade enabled millions of middle-class Americans to buy nationally distributed and branded products ranging from automobiles and household appliances to a wide variety of food, beverages, clothing and personal-use products. Consumer demand shrank during the Depression, but the national consumer model remained in place and would flourish again after World War II.[5]

The Depression created a sense of shared struggle among many Americans and made them more receptive to socialization of risk than ever before. Franklin Roosevelt's New Deal made modest redistributions of wealth in order to provide work and hope to hard-pressed Americans; most viewed this as an effort not to destroy capitalism but to save it from past excesses.[6] Early Depression-era socializing measures included state mortgage moratoria, which temporarily deferred the flow of funds from straitened homeowners to creditors; agricultural programs that imposed production quotas on farmers, treating them as a collective, in return for subsidies that came from another collective group, namely taxpayers; and industrial relief programs that promoted collective action by major industries to regulate their own production levels and business practices. Three programs enacted at the height of the New Deal involved more direct forms of asset redistribution for collective security. State unemployment compensation programs, which spread rapidly after Wisconsin enacted the nation's first program in 1932, taxed employers in order to enable millions of laid-off workers to avoid destitution; the federal Social Security program (1935) used similar redistributive methods to provide security for old and infirm Americans as well as the unemployed; and the Norris-La Guardia Act (1932) and Wagner Act (1935) gave formal legitimacy to collective organizing and bargaining by workers for higher wages and better workplace conditions.[7]

---

4. John A. Heitmann, *The Automobile and American Life* (2009), 24–34, 44–50, 76–80, 135–39; David Blanke, *Hell on Wheels: The Promise and Peril of America's Car Culture, 1900–1940* (2007), 27–31; U.S. Census Bureau, *Historical Statistics of the United States: Colonial Times to 1970* (1975), 796 (radio stations and radio use); Jim Cox, *American Radio Networks: A History* (2009); Amos Kiewe, *FDR's First Fireside Chat: Public Confidence and the Banking Crisis* (2007).

5. Robert N. Mayer, *The Consumer Movement: Guardians of the Marketplace* (1989), 19–26; *see also* E.S. Turner, *The Shocking History of Advertising!* (1953).

6. William E. Leuchtenburg, *Franklin D. Roosevelt and the New Deal* (1963), 84–92, 163–66; David M. Kennedy, *Freedom from Fear: The American People in Depression and War. 1929–1945* (2001), 363–80; Stephen W. Baskerville and Ralph Willett, eds., *Nothing Else to Fear: New Perspectives on America in the Thirties* (1985), 18–27; Alonzo Hamby, *Liberalism and Its Challengers: From FDR to Bush* (2d ed. 1992), 4–5; Alan Brinkley, *Liberalism and its Discontents* (1998), 86–88.

7. Leuchtenburg, *New Deal*, 130–33, 150–52; Kennedy, *Freedom from Fear*, 26–27, 290–92, 257–72; Joseph A. Ranney, *Wisconsin and the Shaping of American Law* (2017), 141–56.

World War II marked the height of American collectivist spirit. The federal government controlled and collectivized the nation's economy to an unprecedented extent in order to win the war. Military service and work in war plants brought millions of Americans from different regions and walks of life together for the first time and gave them a sense of national unity and purpose, a sense that remained in place after the war's end. Postwar events bolstered the collectivist spirit: the Cold War, with its specter of world domination by Russian and Chinese Communism, gave Americans a new common enemy and created a culture that celebrated the nation's moral and economic superiority. That culture also encouraged a life built around group activities including work, school, and civic, religious and recreational groups. The collectivist spirit was also reinforced by continued expansion of the nation's automobile culture, capped by the construction of an interstate highway system beginning in the mid-1950s, and by the rise of national television networks that by 1960 reached ninety-five percent of American households. Millions relied on CBS's Walter Cronkite and other news anchors to explain national and world events to them, and they trusted those anchors to an extent that is almost inconceivable to internet-age Americans.[8]

American tort law responded to these socializing forces in a variety of ways. There was little intellectual opposition to comparative negligence, the most direct and probably the most important step toward socialization of accident costs, but American states were slow to adopt it. By 1970, only six states had joined Mississippi and Wisconsin in doing so, and several of those states preserved an element of traditional free-labor sensibility by allowing accident victims to recover only from those more negligent than themselves. When auto accidents displaced workplace injuries as the primary source of tort litigation, some jurists drew an analogy between the two and proposed that a no-fault system akin to workers compensation be developed for auto cases, but they had little success.

More modest socialization measures met with greater success. Omnibus safe-place statutes imposed upon business owners a general duty to make their premises safe for others and to comply with state safety regulations. The statutes did not impose absolute liability on owners but they did make it easier for accident victims to establish owner liability. The privity rule, holding that negligent manufacturers of defective products were liable only to direct purchasers, eroded only slowly during the first years after Benjamin Cardozo's decision in *MacPherson v. Buick Motor Co.* (1916), but during the 1950s, courts began to abandon privity at an increasingly rapid rate and in the 1960s, University of California law professor William Prosser persuaded many states to go one step further: manufacturers would now be strictly liable to consumers for product

---

8. James T. Patterson, *Grand Expectations: The United States, 1945–1974* (1997), 16–17, 327–30; George Marsden, *The Twilight of the American Enlightenment: The 1950s and the Crisis of Liberal Belief* (2014), 22–24, 108–12; Census Bureau, *Historical Statistics*, 42, 795–996 (radio and television stations and use); *See also* Robert D. Putnam, *Bowling Alone: The Collapse and Revival of American Community* (2000); James Baughman, *The Republic of Mass Culture: Journalism, Film, and Broadcasting in America Since 1941* (1997); Douglas Brinkley, *Cronkite* (2012).

defects, no matter how carefully they made their product, if it reached the consumer "without substantial change in the condition in which it [was] sold."[9] Other traditional immunities, including rules barring family members from suing each other for injuries and limiting the liability of charitable institutions and local governments, eroded in tandem with the privity rule. By 1970, the American tort-law system was spreading the costs of accidents much more widely than it had in 1920, and it was flirting with further socialization. But reform had largely been kept within the confines of a fault-based system, and it would remain there during the years to come.

The Rise of Safe Place Statutes

In 1911 Wisconsin Progressives enacted landmark laws that coupled a safe-place statute, requiring nearly all employers to furnish "employment...[and] a place of employment" which shall be as "free[ ] from danger...as the nature of the employment will reasonably permit," with creation of a commission charged with developing a comprehensive system of industrial safety regulations. Prior to 1911, American states had addressed workplace safety in piecemeal fashion, sporadically enacting laws that addressed isolated safety issues in reaction to recent fires and other disasters.[10] Wisconsin was the first state to shift to an omnibus workplace-safety system.

John Commons, who played a key role in formulating the 1911 laws as well as other Progressive reforms, was particularly proud of his work on the safe-place statute. He had feared that the courts would interpret any such statute as imposing absolute liability on employers for accidents and accordingly would strike it down as violative of constitutional liberty and property rights, but "[a]fter many conferences," he and his colleagues devised the "reasonably permit" clause which they believed would "raise the standards above the ordinary" but would also allow the law to survive constitutional challenge.[11] In 1913, Wisconsin's supreme court held not only that the statute was constitutional but that it overrode the prevailing late-nineteenth-century rule that use of devices conforming to prevailing industry practice was sufficient to insulate employers from liability. Something more than conformity to custom was needed to show that a workplace was as safe as conditions "reasonably permitted." Commons had achieved his goal.[12]

During the next two decades, at least seventeen other states enacted omnibus safe-place statutes. Some followed Wisconsin's model, requiring places of employment to

---

9. Am. L. Inst., *Restatement (Second) of Torts* (1964) (hereinafter "*Restatement 2d*"), § 402A.
10. 1911 Wis. Laws, ch. 485, §§ 1021b-1, 1021b-2, 1021b-8; *see* Chapter 2, notes 94–97 and accompanying text.
11. John R. Commons, *Myself: The Autobiography of John R. Commons* (1934, reprint 1963), 154–55.
12. *Rosholt v. Worden-Allen Co.*, 144 N.W. 650 (Wis. 1913); *Sparrow v. Menasha Paper Co.*, 143 N.W. 317 (Wis. 1913).

be "safe" and defining safety as the highest degree of safety that the circumstances would reasonably permit.[13] Other states adopted variants of a more limited safe-place statute, adopted by Massachusetts in 1913, that empowered its industrial commission to "determine what suitable... requirements for the prevention of accidents shall be adopted or followed" in places of employment.[14] Some states combined the two models.[15] But American courts also placed safe-place statutes firmly within the framework of common-law negligence. Most held that violation of a safety statute was sufficient to establish that an employer was negligent, but that employers could still assert contributory negligence and assumption of risk as defenses unless the statute in question explicitly barred the use of such defenses or imposed criminal penalties for safety violations. The courts more readily cut off employer defenses in cases involving injury or death of children employed in violation of child labor laws, a situation in which the victims commanded special sympathy.[16] By the early 1930s, it was clear that safe-place laws represented an important though not a conclusive step toward shifting the burden of accidents from victims toward businesses, and, thus, toward socialization of accident costs. The heightened liability standards that flowed from safe-place statutes, the stream of new safety regulations issued by state industrial commissions and legislative constriction of traditional common-law defenses gave accident victims powerful and permanent new advantages in the courtroom.

From the Industrial Age to the Auto Age

During the first decade of the twentieth century, advocates of workers compensation had argued their case based mainly on the inevitability of accidents and economic efficiency, but workers compensation promised an additional, less publicized benefit: the hope that removal of industrial-accident cases from tort law would reduce court caseloads. That hope proved evanescent; it soon dissipated with the entry of automobiles into American life. Lawsuits by workers against their employers continued to appear for a time after the 1910s, in part because many of the

---

13. 1913 Cal. Laws, ch. 176, § 52; 1913 New York Laws, ch. 145; 1913 Ohio Laws, ch. 871; 1915 Colo. Laws, ch. 180, § 4(i); 1917 N.H. Laws, ch. 183; 1917 Utah Laws, ch. 100; 1919 Nev. Laws, ch. 225; 1920 Or. Laws, ch. 48; *see generally* John R. Commons, *History of Labour in the United States 1896–1932* (1935), 3:653.

14. 1913 Mass. Laws, ch. 813; *see also* 1917 Idaho Laws, ch. 81; 1923 Tenn. Laws, ch. 7; 1925 Ariz. Laws, ch. 83 (allowing commission to promulgate regulations only upon petition); 1929 Md. Laws, ch. 426; 1929 Neb. Laws, ch. 138.

15. *See* 1913 Pa. Laws, ch. 267; 1915 Mont. Laws, ch. 96; 1919 Wash. Laws, ch. 130.

16. *See* Note, "Contributory Negligence as Defense to Actions Based on Statutes," 25 *Harv. L. Rev.* 463 (1912); Thomas Shearman and Amasa Redfield, *Treatise on the Law of Negligence* (6th ed. 1913), §§ 241a–241c; William L. Prosser, "Comparative Negligence," 51 *Mich. L. Rev.* 465, 470–71, notes 27–29 (1953); *see also, e.g., Am. Car & Foundry Co. v. Armentraut*, 73 N.E. 766 (Ill. 1905); *Lenahan v. Pittston Coal Mining Co.*, 67 A. 642 (Pa. 1907); *Pinoza v. N. Chair Co.*, 140 N.W. 84 (Wis. 1913) (all involving violation of child labor laws).

early workers compensation laws covered only limited categories of workers, but by 1940, such lawsuits had virtually disappeared. Auto accident cases came to dominate American courts' tort dockets: from the 1930s to the 1960s, they accounted for roughly half of all tort cases included in the Five-State Survey. Safe-place cases, usually brought against employers by customers or contractors injured on their premises, consistently accounted for another ten to thirty percent of tort cases. Railroad and streetcar accident cases, which had dominated mid-nineteenth century tort law but had declined during the late nineteenth century, continued their decline, although they never completely disappeared.

FIGURE 4.1
Five-State Survey: Types of Tort Cases, 1920–1970[17]

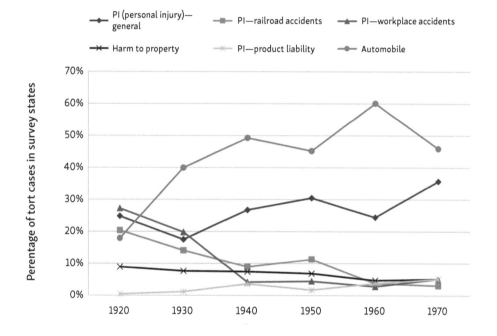

The Early Auto Age

The automobile's rise as a presence in tort law corresponded to its rise as a presence in twentieth-century American life. Experimental motor vehicles first appeared in Europe and the United States in the 1890s. Their potential superiority to horses for

---

17. The cases on which Figure 4.1 is based are described in Appendix 2; the calculations are described in Appendix 3. Automobile accident cases also dominated tort dockets in courts not covered in the Survey. *See, e.g.,* Patterson H. French, *The Automobile Compensation Plan: A Solution for Some Problems of Court Congestion and Accident Litigation in New York State* (1933), 17–18, 25 (survey showing that automobile cases accounted for 62 to 71% of all trial-court litigation in various New York counties).

purposes of farm-to-market, city and interurban travel quickly became apparent, but producing affordable, reasonably reliable autos proved difficult at first. Prior to 1910, autos were generally regarded as a luxury suitable only for wealthy Americans; subsequent improvements such as Charles Kettering's invention of the self-starter to replace hand cranks and, most important, Henry Ford's adoption of assembly-line techniques for mass auto manufacturing eventually brought autos within the economic reach of middle-class Americans. The rise of the auto is best summarized by one historian's conclusion that "most Americans first read about the car by 1900, first saw one in action by 1910, first rode in one by 1920, and first owned a car by 1930." Autos gripped the American imagination: they embodied speed, physical power and the freedom to go where one wanted. They enabled city dwellers to commute to work and contributed to the rapid suburban growth that marked the 1910s and 1920s. Farmers and other rural Americans also came to rely on autos and trucks as an economic and social lifeline to the rest of the world.[18]

Lawmakers quickly recognized the need to accommodate this flood of new machines and the accidents that followed in its wake. They had little difficulty fitting automobile law into the traditional framework of tort rules governing highway accidents. Thomas Cooley and other nineteenth-century jurists who had shaped tort law as it pertained to roads had recognized that roads would be used in ever-changing ways, and nineteenth-century laws requiring railroads to observe speed limits and use whistles, bells and other devices to alert others to their presence provided guidance for auto laws.[19] In 1901, Connecticut became the first state to enact speed limits for autos, and during the next fifteen years nearly all states enacted rudimentary "rules of the road." Early laws focused on speed limits and basic safety equipment such as headlights, brakes, and horns and other warning devices. Many states also codified the common-law principle that all highway users would have "equal rights," and required motorists to register their vehicles.[20] Between 1910 and 1925, Congress and the states appropriated millions of dollars to construct new roads and upgrade existing highways. This good-roads movement responded to existing demand but also fueled additional demand for autos and auto travel.[21]

---

18. James J. Flink, *The Automobile Age* (1990), 131–38; Heitmann, *Automobile and American Life*, 19–47; Blanke, *Hell on Wheels*, 1–4, 17–24, 27–30, 42.

19. *Macomber v. Nichols*, 34 Mich. 212, 217 (1876) (stating: "[L]ocomotion upon the public roads has hitherto been chiefly by means of horses and similar animals, but persons using them have no prescriptive rights, and are entitled only to the same reasonable use of the ways which they must accord to all others. Improved methods of locomotion are perfectly admissible, if any shall be discovered, and they cannot be excluded from the existing public roads, provided their use is consistent with the present methods").

20. *See* C.P. Berry, *The Law of Automobiles* (7th ed. 1935), §§ 2.64–2.67, 2.71, 2.141–2.155.

21. Heitmann, *Automobile and American Life*, 74–85; Flink, *Automobile Age*, 170–79; Blanke, *Hell on Wheels*, 30–31. The most important early federal highway acts were the Good Roads Act, 39 U.S. Stats. 355 (1916), and the Federal Highway Act, 42 U.S. Stat. 212 (1921).

FIGURE 4.2
United States: Autos and Auto Accidents, 1920–1970[22]

	Registered Automobiles	Auto Accidents	Fatalities
1920	8,131,522	N/A	12,500
1930	23,034,753	N/A	32.900
1940	27,465,826	6,100,000	34,501
1950	40,339,077	8,300,000	34,763
1960	61,671,390	10,400,000	38,137
1970	89,243,557	16,000,000	54,633

The proliferation of autos and highways produced collisions, injuries and deaths in startling numbers. Injury and death rates were particularly high during the first years of the auto age, due partly to the fact that early autos posed extensive safety risks: closed-cab autos did not become common until the late 1920s, and early tires were flimsy and prone to frequent blow-outs. Auto design improvements reduced death rates in proportion to the number of autos and miles driven, but the total number of deaths increased as auto use grew. How could the toll be reduced? Americans were not sure. At first, free-labor views of individual responsibility prevailed: careless drivers were seen both as the source of the problem and as holding its solution. Auto experts and the press denounced drivers who caused accidents as "motorized morons" and "road hogs"; and state legislatures prohibited driving under the influence of alcohol and enacted ever more elaborate rules of the road.[23]

But auto accidents proved to be a surprisingly intractable problem, one which public shaming and increased driver regulation failed to solve. The public rejected efforts to portray careless drivers as outlaws: in its view, most accidents involved ordinary citizens and resulted from bad judgment or bad luck, not outrageous behavior. Furthermore, many Americans instinctively viewed traffic police as an affront to the values of freedom and independence that autos represented, and they viewed traffic courts, sometimes with justification, as nests of corruption, incompetence and class bias. By the early 1930s, reformers realized that their efforts to reduce accidents by shaming had failed, and they redirected their energies to what became known as "the three E's": engineering, education and improved traffic-code enforcement. Transportation planners tried to minimize opportunities for collision by constructing one-way streets and divided highways. They also made extensive use of sidewalks and pedes-

---

22. Census Bureau, *Historical Statistics*, 719–20; Federal Highway Administration, Table, "State Motor Vehicle Registrations By Years, 1900–1995," at https://www.fhwa.dot.gov/ohim/summary95/mv200.pdf. Figure 4.2 does not include accidents involving only buses and trucks. Federal and state agencies did not begin compiling comprehensive accident statistics until the late 1930s.

23. Flink, *Automobile Age*, 383–84; Blanke, *Hell on Wheels*, 38–42, 52–55, 91–94, 112–13, 116–18; Edward C. Fisher, *Vehicle Traffic Law* (1973 rev. ed.), 2–4.

trian crossings, because collisions between autos and pedestrians were a large part of the accident problem: pedestrians took the legal doctrine of equal road-use rights seriously, but many motorists felt at some level that pedestrians should yield to their greater power and their desire for speedy, uninterrupted travel. Reformers also promoted formal driver education and laws that made such education a requirement for driver licensing; uniform national traffic rules, a movement that gained little success prior to the 1960s; and more user-friendly traffic courts.[24]

Socialization of Auto Accident Costs: The Columbia Plan

For tort law's purposes, the most important aspect of the "three E's" movement was that it reflected a shift from a free-labor-oriented view to a more socialized view of auto accidents. During the 1920s and early 1930s, reformers gradually accepted the fact that accidents were an inherent risk of auto use and, thus, could be viewed as a price that must be paid for the benefits of the automobile age. From this, reformers drew parallels between auto and industrial accidents and considered whether an equivalent of workers compensation could be devised for automobiles.[25] Calls for a no-fault system for auto accidents arose as early as 1916, and in 1932 Columbia University's Council for Research in the Social Sciences studied the issue closely and formulated a model no-fault plan. The Columbia Plan would impose absolute liability for accidents on auto owners regardless of the extent of their involvement but, like workers compensation, it would also insulate them from tort litigation and would limit victims' compensation. Victims could recover their medical expenses, lost income and other economic losses but would be allowed no compensation for their pain and suffering, an item that the Council believed was too difficult to measure and control.[26]

The Columbia Plan had little success. A bill embodying most of its features was introduced in New York's legislature in 1938 but failed, and the Plan was not introduced in any other state legislature.[27] The primary obstacle to a no-fault auto accident system was that auto owners, unlike employers, had no customers to whom they could pass on their costs. State-sponsored compensation funds and compulsory auto insurance were suggested as funding mechanisms, but the former seemed to many lawmakers to be too close to overt socialism. Laws requiring drivers to purchase auto

---

24. Blanke, *Hell on Wheels*, 53–55, 91–98, 113–14, 118–30, 168–73; Fisher, *Vehicle Traffic Law*, 14–17.

25. Blanke, *Hell on Wheels*, 4–6, 91–98; French, *Automobile Compensation Plan*, 45–49, 104–86.

26. French, *Automobile Compensation Plan*, 44–45, 111–205; George H. Priest, "The Invention of Enterprise Liability: A Critical History of the Intellectual Foundations of Modern Tort Law," 14 *J. Leg. Stud.* 461, 470–74 (1985).

27. Samuel H. Hofstadter, "A Proposed Automobile Accident Compensation Plan," 328 *Ann. Am. Acad. Pol. & Soc. Sci.* 53, 59 (1960); Ernest C. Carman, "Is A Motor Vehicle Accident Compensation Act Advisable," 4 *Minn. L. Rev.* 1 (1919); French, *Automobile Compensation Plan*, 33–37, 44–48; Kenneth Abraham, *The Liability Century: Insurance and Tort Law from the Progressive Era to 9/11* (2008), 72–74.

insurance at prescribed minimum levels of coverage or to verify that they were able to pay accident costs out of their own resources as a condition of licensure appeared in many states during subsequent decades, but legislators could not bring themselves to require substantial levels of coverage or to couple such requirements with a no-fault system.[28] Socialization of accident costs through insurance would remain largely a matter of individual choice.

The Family-Purpose Doctrine

The ultimate lesson of the Columbia Plan was that any socializing of auto accident costs would have to be done incrementally and indirectly. In addition to enacting insurance laws, some states partially socialized accident costs within families by requiring parents to sponsor their children's driver's license applications and making them vicariously liable for any damage the young drivers caused. But the "family purpose" doctrine was the most important of the incremental socializing measures. Beginning about 1912, some courts expanded auto owners' liability by creating a legal presumption that autos were intended to be used by the entire family. They reasoned that the pleasure and convenience family members gained from auto use was also the owner's (usually the husband and father's) "affair and business." Accordingly, when family members used the auto with his explicit or tacit permission, they became his agents and he would be legally liable for any injuries they caused.[29]

The new doctrine represented a major expansion of agency law, and it was controversial. Courts that adopted the doctrine generally refrained from characterizing it as a policy response to the automobile age but they had difficulty reconciling it with traditional rules of agency, and they were criticized by many traditionalist judges. Even though "every good father makes it his 'business,' ... to furnish so far as he can, for use by the members of his family, all those things that will contribute to their convenience and pleasure," said California justice Frank Angelotti, still, that did not mean that a family member who used the car "exclusively on a mission of his

---

28. Massachusetts enacted the first compulsory-insurance law applicable to all drivers in 1925. The law was challenged as a violation of drivers' liberty and property rights but was upheld as a legitimate exercise of the state's power to promote safety. 1925 Mass. Laws, ch. 346; *In re Opinion of the Justices*, 147 N.E. 681 (Mass. 1925). During the 1920s and early 1930s, several other states enacted compulsory-insurance laws limited to auto owners with poor driving records. *See, e.g.,* 1924 N.Y. Laws, ch. 534; 1925 Conn. Laws, ch. 183; 1927 N.H. Laws, ch. 54; 1929 N.J. Laws, ch. 116; 1929 Iowa Laws, ch. 118; 1931 Wis. Laws, ch. 478. *See also* Abraham, *Liability Century*, 74–77; J.P. Chamberlain, "Compulsory Insurance of Automobiles," 12 *A.B.A.J.* 49 (1926); Note, "Financial Responsibility of Owners and Operators of Motor Vehicles," 30 *Colum. L. Rev.* 109 (1930).

29. Early cases in which courts adopted the family-purpose doctrine include *Daily v. Maxwell*, 133 S.W. 351 (Mo. App. 1911); *Stowe v. Morris*, 144 S.W. 52 (Ky. 1912); *McNeal v. McKain*, 126 P. 742 (Okla. 1912); *Kayser v. Van Nest*, 146 N.W. 1091 (Minn. 1914); and *Griffin v. Russell*, 87 S.E. 10 (Ga. 1915). *See also* Abraham, *Liability Century*, 72–74; Norman D. Lattin, "Vicarious Liability and the Family Automobile," 26 *Mich. L. Rev.* 846 (1928).

own," such as a personal errand or a date, was acting as the father's agent; and based on that logic, nearly half the states rejected the family-purpose doctrine.[30] Courts that adopted the family purpose doctrine often justified their decisions by stating, erroneously, that they were simply following the majority rule; this prompted one commentator to gibe that the doctrine was created "[b]y a wave of the wand, and by means of a fictional shellac for permanence."[31] Some adopting courts relied on state statutes imposing vicarious liability on owners who loaned their autos to others,[32] and a few frankly admitted that they were motivated by practical considerations. As early as 1918, one justice argued that:

> [T]he practical administration of justice between the parties is more the duty of the court than the preservation of some esoteric theory concerning the law of principal and agent. If owners of automobiles are made to understand that they will be held liable for injury to person and property occasioned by their negligent operation by infants or others who are financially irresponsible, they will doubtless exercise a greater degree of care in selecting those who are permitted to go upon the public streets with such dangerous instrumentalities.[33]

Even traditionalist courts allowed a degree of flexibility: in close cases, they often deferred to jury determinations that a particular use of the family car benefited the owner as well as the driver, thus allowing accident victims to recover from solvent owners under traditional agency rules.[34] As family auto insurance became more widely available, the debate over the family-purpose doctrine gradually became moot.

Liability to Auto Passengers

Another important battle over socialization involved drivers' liability to their passengers. Passengers entered autos as guests, and under the common law, hosts were liable to invited guests if they caused an accident through lack of "ordinary

---

30. *Spence v. Fisher*, 193 P. 255, 257 (Cal. 1920). At least eighteen states adopted the family-purpose doctrine and at least twenty-two states rejected it. See Lattin, "Vicarious Liability," 847–50, notes 6–8.

31. Lattin, "Vicarious Liability," 847; *see also* Note, "The Family Purpose Doctrine in Virginia," 24 *Va. L. Rev.* 931 (1938) (supporting the family-purpose doctrine but arguing that courts should squarely defend it on policy grounds).

32. *See* Note, "Automobiles—Statutory Liability of Owners for the Negligence of Persons Operating Automobiles With The Owner's Consent," 21 *Minn. L. Rev.* 823 (1937) (an article apparently authored or edited by William Prosser); Note, "The Responsibility of Vehicle Owners: An Exception to the Law of Agency," 38 *Harv. L. Rev.* 513, 517 (1925) (arguing that the family-purpose doctrine should be enacted by legislatures rather than by judges' "confusing and tortured misapplication of insufficient older theories").

33. *King v. Smythe*, 204 S.W. 296, 298 (Tenn. 1918).

34. *See, e.g.*, *Tyree v. Tudor*, 106 S.E. 675 (N.C. 1921) (holding that son's taking girlfriend to a dance was a family purpose); *Zeidler v. Goelzer*, 211 N.W. 140 (Wis. 1926) (holding that children's trip to a park was a family purpose).

care."³⁵ During the early years of the automobile era many courts applied the ordinary-care rule in auto cases, but a feeling grew among jurists and lawmakers alike that if applied literally, the rule could lead to unfairness. Drivers performed a gratuitous service for passengers, and surely they should receive some recompense in the form of reduced exposure to liability. Accordingly, some courts held that ordinary care was limited to "active negligence," that is, driver conduct that created dangers over and above the usual risks that motorists faced on public streets and highways.³⁶ Other courts were uncomfortable with any reference to an ordinary-care standard, and held that drivers would be liable only for intentionally or recklessly putting passengers at risk. Passengers would be deemed to assume the risk of ordinary carelessness on a driver's part, such as failure to maintain an auto in good condition or a tendency to drive fast.³⁷ During the 1910s and 1920s, many legislatures enacted statutes immunizing drivers from liability to passengers, with limited exceptions for drunk driving and intentional harm.³⁸ Oregon went the furthest, creating immunity without exceptions, but it returned to the immunity mainstream after its supreme court struck down the law as violative of a clause in the state constitution creating the right to a remedy for harms.³⁹

But advocates of a true ordinary-care rule, one more friendly to passengers and more likely to socialize the cost of accidents, persisted. C.P. Berry, the author of a leading early automobile-law treatise, argued in 1924 that "[i]t is a matter of every day occurrence in every part of the country for persons of ordinary prudence to rely greatly upon the person in control of the vehicle" and that "[i]t would be strange, indeed, to require every person in a vehicle to keep the same lookout that the driver naturally keeps." Some courts explicitly or tacitly agreed, holding that almost any deviation from strict compliance with rules of the road would violate the ordinary-care standard and affirming jury verdicts that reflected that view.⁴⁰ The spread of comparative negligence laws during the mid-twentieth century allowed a finer calibration of fault than did contributory negligence and reduced the need to protect drivers with

---

35. Prosser, *Handbook of the Law of Torts* (1st ed. 1941), §§ 76, 78.

36. *See, e.g., Pigeon v. Lane,* 67 A. 888 (Conn. 1907), the first decision to use the "active negligence" label; *Rappaport v. Stockdale,* 199 N.W. 513 (Minn. 1924); Berry, *Law of Automobiles* (7th ed. 1935), § 5.104.

37. *Massaletti v. Fitzroy,* 118 N.E. 168 (Mass. 1917); *Epps v. Parrish,* 106 S.E. 297 (Ga. App. 1921); *Heiman v. Kloizner,* 247 P. 1034 (Wash. 1926).

38. *See, e.g.,* 1913 Cal. Laws, Motor Vehicle Act, § 141-3/4; 1919 Iowa Laws, ch. 275; 1927 Conn. Laws, ch. 308; 1929 Del. Laws, ch. 225; 1929 Mich. Laws, No. 19; 1930 Ky. Laws, ch. 85; 1930 S.C. Laws, No. 659.

39. 1927 Or. Laws, ch. 342; *Stewart v. Houk,* 271 P. 998, 272 P. 893 (Or. 1928); 1929 Or. Laws, ch. 401.

40. Berry, *Law of Automobiles* (4th ed. 1924), p. 494; Arthur W. Blakemore, "Is the Law Fair to the Motor Vehicle?," 65 *U.S. L. Rev.* 20, 25 (1931) (arguing that "[t]he practical situation is that driving a car is a one-man job"); *see also, e.g., O'Shea v. Lavoy,* 185 N.W. 525 (Wis. 1921).

high walls of immunity, and beginning in the late 1950s many courts returned to a true ordinary-care standard for drivers.[41]

Traditional negligence principles and reluctance to fully socialize auto accident costs proved surprisingly durable as the automobile age progressed. Nearly all states flatly rejected the idea of characterizing autos as dangerous instrumentalities, a tack that would have fit comfortably into existing tort law and would have allowed imposition of near-absolute liability on drivers.[42] Some courts incrementally socialized auto accident costs by holding that violation of vehicle safety statutes automatically constituted negligence, thus easing accident victims' burden of proof; but other states held that such violations were nothing more than evidence of negligence which a jury could consider, and every state allowed drivers to invoke contributory or comparative negligence as a defense.[43] Between 1920 and 1970 many state supreme courts struggled with heavy workloads, but renewed calls for a no-fault system that would have eliminated auto cases from those workloads were met with a curious judicial silence. It is unclear whether that silence reflected a belief that auto accidents, unlike workplace injuries, did not lend themselves to socialization and extrajudicial resolution, or a belief that free-labor notions of individual responsibility must be preserved and that socialization of auto accident costs should be accomplished through insurance and other private means rather than legal change.

Comparative Negligence: Slow-Growth Radicalism

Early Growth

By 1920, comparative negligence had a foothold in tort law, but the foothold was tenuous. American states had two comparative-negligence models they could look to: Wisconsin's 1907 diluted model, which allowed contributorily negligent railroad workers to recover damages only if their employer's negligence was greater than their own, and the "pure" model reflected in the 1908 Federal Employers Liability Act and Mississippi's 1910 comparative negligence statute, which allowed plaintiffs to recover regardless of their degree of negligence but reduced their damages in proportion to that negligence. Among these pioneering efforts, the FELA had the greatest short-term impact. Between 1908 and 1920, sixteen states adopted "little

---

41. *See, e.g., Meistrich v. Casino Area Attractions, Inc.*, 155 A.2d 90 (N.J. 1959); *McConville v. State Farm Mut. Auto. Insurance Co.*, 113 N.W.2d 14 (Wis. 1962); *Buletao v. Kauai Motors, Ltd.*, 406 P.2d 867 (Hawai'i 1965); *Parker v. Redden*, 421 S.W.2d 586 (Ky. 1967); Kyle Graham, "The Diffusion of Doctrinal Innovations in Tort Law," 99 *Marq. L. Rev.* 75, 104–05 (2015).

42. *See, e.g., Lewis v. Amorous*, 159 S.E. 338 (Ga. App. 1907); *Colborne v. Detroit United Ry.*, 143 N.W. 32 (Mich. 1913); *State v. Goldstone*, 175 N.W. 892 (Minn. 1920); Fisher, *Vehicle Traffic Law*, 8–10.

43. *See* authorities collected in. Prosser, "Comparative Negligence," 470–71, and Berry, *Law of Automobiles* (5th ed. 1926), § 215, notes 9–16.

FELA" laws applying the FELA model to intrastate railroads.[44] Three states extended the FELA model to selected hazardous occupations other than railroading, and in 1920 Congress extended it to maritime workers.[45] Two states also adopted Wisconsin's diluted model.[46]

Sentiment for expansion of comparative negligence grew slowly after 1920. A few more states adopted little-FELA laws,[47] but the American Bar Association (ABA) illuminated the depth of resistance to change when, in 1925, it considered whether to recommend extension of comparative negligence to property-damage claims arising out of maritime accidents. Opponents argued that apportionment was unjust because negligence could not be measured with perfect precision, and that the task of apportionment would impose substantial new burdens on judges and juries. They reasoned that any injustice that contributory negligence systems inflicted on victims who were only slightly at fault was illusory because judges and juries overlooked slight negligence as a practical matter. Supporters replied that courts that had administered FELA cases and early state comparative negligence laws had had no difficulty with apportionment issues and had not had to take on extra work, but in its final report (1929), the ABA recommended that comparative negligence not be expanded.[48] Two states felt that pure comparative negligence went too far but were uneasy about denying slightly negligent plaintiffs all chance of recovery; they enacted laws applying comparative negligence in cases where the plaintiff's negligence was found to be "slight."[49]

In 1931, Wisconsin joined Mississippi in extending comparative negligence to all torts. The 1931 law's most prominent supporter was Joseph Padway, a veteran labor lawyer who would soon become chief counsel for the American Federation of Labor. Padway's work had given him close acquaintance with worker injury cases under the FELA and Wisconsin's 1907 law; he likely concluded that comparative negligence was serving workers well and should be made universal. A bill to create a state-administered no-fault auto insurance system had been introduced in the previous legislature,

---

44. *See* the cases cited at Chapter 3, note 89. Mississippi's 1910 law may have been inspired in part by the FELA. William H. McMullen, Note, "Torts—Effect of Mississippi's Comparative Negligence Statute on Other Rules of Law," 39 *Miss. L.J.* 493 (1968).

45. 1911 Or. Laws, ch. 3 (building and contracting trades); 1912 Ariz. Laws, ch. 89 (hazardous work in mining, manufacturing and transportation); 1919 Ark. Laws, p. 734 (mining companies); 41 U.S. Stat. 988 (1920); *see also* A. Chalmers Mole and Lyman P. Wilson, "A Study of Comparative Negligence: Part II," 17 *Cornell L.Q.* 604, 608–13 (1932).

46. 1915 Mich. Laws, § 5497; 1919 Ark. Laws, p. 143; *see* Prosser, "Comparative Negligence," 479.

47. Ill. Rev. Code (1927), ch. 114, § 323; 1907 Neb. Laws, p. 192; 1910 Ohio Laws, ch. 197; 1937 Colo. Laws, p. 513.

48. Mole and Wilson, "A Study of Comparative Negligence: Part I," 17 *Cornell L.Q.* 333, 348–49 (1931); "Report of Committee on Admiralty," 54 *A.B.A. Rep.* 278 (1929).

49. 1913 Neb. Laws, ch. 124; 1941 S.D. Laws, ch. 160; *see also* Prosser, "Comparative Negligence," 470.

and conservatives dropped their opposition to comparative negligence in order to head off its passage, but they persuaded lawmakers to retain a diluted system.[50]

Jurists took note of Wisconsin's new law, but during the next three decades the comparative negligence movement stagnated for reasons that are not entirely clear. Comparative-negligence bills were introduced in the 1930 New York legislature and in Minnesota, Pennsylvania, Michigan and Illinois in the 1940s, but none passed.[51] Nearly all legal commentators who addressed comparative negligence viewed it favorably, including William Prosser, the leading tort reformer of the age; but Prosser devoted his energies mainly to products liability law, and none of his colleagues saw fit to launch a comparable crusade for comparative negligence.[52] The conservative impulses that had persuaded the ABA in the 1920s not to recommend expanded use of comparative negligence continued to hold sway.[53]

The Triumph of Comparative Negligence

Interest in comparative negligence revived in the 1950s and early 1960s. An increasing number of commentators argued that no evidence had surfaced in comparative-negligence states to support concerns about juries' abuse of apportionment power or increased court workloads, and that it was inappropriate to encourage the overlooking of slight negligence as a substitute for comparative negligence.[54] They also redoubled their criticism of contributory negligence as unjust. In 1953, Prosser memorably described it as:

> [A] rule which visits the entire loss caused by the fault of the two parties on one of them alone, and that one the injured plaintiff, least able to bear it, and quite

---

50. See Joseph A. Padway, "Comparative Negligence," 16 *Marq. L. Rev.* 3, 4 (1931); Gerald P. Hayes, "Rule of Comparative Negligence and Its Operation in Wisconsin," 23 *Ohio St. Bar Assn. Rep.* 233, 234 (1950); Prosser, "Comparative Negligence," 466 n. 6; 1931 Wis. Laws, ch. 244.

51. Prosser, "Comparative Negligence," 466.

52. *See, e.g.,* Charles O. Gregory, *Legislative Loss Distribution in Negligence Actions* (1936), 59–65; Prosser, *Handbook* (1st ed. 1941), § 53; Note, "Comparative Negligence in Pennsylvania," 17 *Temple L.Q.* 276 (1943); Robert A. Leflar, "The Declining Defense of Contributory Negligence," 1 *Ark. L. Rev.* 1, 16–20 (1947).

53. *See* John J. Haugh, "Comparative Negligence: A Reform Long Overdue," 49 *Or. L. Rev.* 38, 41–43 (1969).

54. Francis S. Philbrick, "Loss Apportionment in Negligence Cases: Part II," 99 *U. Pa. L. Rev.* 766 (1951); Prosser, "Comparative Negligence" (1953); Fleming James, Jr., "Contributory Negligence," 62 *Yale L.J.* 691 (1953); Note, "Tort—Comparative Negligence Statute," 18 *Vand. L. Rev.* 327 (1964); Fowler Harper and Fleming James, Jr., *The Law of Torts* (1956), §§ 27.2-4, 27.10; James, "Contributory Negligence"; Frank E. Maloney, "From Contributory to Comparative Negligence: A Needed Law Reform," 11 *U. Fla. L. Rev.* 135, 160–63, 174 (1958); *see also* Haugh, "Comparative Negligence." Prosser took a fairly detached view of comparative negligence in the first edition of his *Handbook*; he became progressively more supportive in his 1953 article and in the second (1955) and third (1964) editions of his treatise. Prosser, *Handbook* (1st ed. 1941), § 53; *Handbook* (2d ed. 1955), § 54; *Handbook* (3d ed. 1964), § 66.

possibly much less at fault than the defendant who goes scot free. No one has ever succeeded in justifying that as a policy, and no one ever will.[55]

Perhaps equally important, socialization was now proceeding rapidly on other fronts. Prosser was making rapid headway in persuading state courts to expand manufacturers' liability for defective products; state courts were beginning to warn that they would abolish traditional liability immunities enjoyed by family members, charitable institutions and local governments if their legislatures did not do so; and for the first time since the 1930s, there were new calls to consider a no-fault compensation system for auto injuries. Many legislators and jurists now came to view comparative negligence not as a curiosity, but as a line of defense against more thoroughgoing socialization of tort law and as a means of preserving at least a core element of fault in the law.[56]

Isolated voices, including future U.S. Supreme Court justice Lewis Powell, continued to defend contributory negligence, based largely on their continuing suspicion of juries. Juries' perceived penchant for overlooking slight plaintiff negligence was tolerable, but in cases of more evenly balanced negligence they could not be relied on to reduce damages in proportion to the plaintiff's negligence. Contributory negligence gave judges an essential tool to check unreasonable jury verdicts; replacing it with comparative negligence, said one insurance executive, would remove "the last bar...to complete chaos in our courts" and would pave the way for complete socialization of accident costs. Supporters of comparative negligence continued to insist that such fears were largely fantasy, and opponents eventually turned their energies toward persuading legislatures to adopt diluted rather than pure systems.[57]

The 1960s and 1970s witnessed change of unprecedented rapidity in many areas of law; comparative negligence was one of them. Between 1969 and 1984, thirty-seven states adopted comparative negligence, some by statute and some by court decision. Some states adopted Mississippi's pure model allowing all plaintiffs to recover something regardless of the extent of their negligence.[58] Other states adopted Wisconsin's

---

55. Prosser, "Comparative Negligence," 469.

56. *See* Abraham, *Liability Century*, 69–70, 92–100; G. Edward White, *Tort Law in America: An Intellectual History* (1980), 167–68; Hofstadter, "Proposed Automobile Accident Compensation Plan," 59; *Hilen v. Hays*, 673 S.W.2d 713, 718 (Ky. 1984) (stating that courts "must accommodate justice by evolution or anticipate revolution").

57. Frederick S. Benson, "Comparative Negligence—Boon or Bane," 23 *Ins. Counsel J.* 204, 214 (April 1956); Lewis F. Powell, Jr., "Contributory Negligence: A Necessary Check on the American Jury," 43 *A.B.A.J.* 1005 (1957); Prosser, "Comparative Negligence," 469, 508–09; Arthur Best, "Impediments to Reasonable Tort Reform: Lessons from the Adoption of Comparative Negligence," 40 *Ind. L. Rev.* 1, 11–15 (2007).

58. *See* 1971 R.I. Laws, ch. 206; 1973 Wash. Laws (Ex. Sess.), ch. 138; 1975 N.Y. Laws, ch. 69; 1979 La. Laws, No. 431; 1984 Ariz. Laws, ch. 237; *see also, e.g., Hoffman v. Jones*, 280 So.2d 431 (Fla. 1973); *Li v. Yellow Cab Co.*, 532 P.2d 1226 (Cal. 1975); *Kaatz v. State*, 540 P.2d 1037 (Alaska 1975); *Kirby v. Larson*, 256 N.W.2d 400 (Mich. 1979); *Scott v. Rizzo*, 634 P.2d 1234 (N.M. 1979); *Alvis v. Ribar*, 421 N.E.2d 886 (Ill. 1981); *Gustafson v. Benda*, 661 S.W.2d 11 (Mo. 1983); *Hilen*, 673 S.W.2d 713 (Ky.

49-percent diluted model, limiting recovery to victims who were less negligent than the persons they sued (put another way, in a two-party case the victim had to show that she was no more than 49 percent responsible and the defendant was at least 51 percent responsible for the accident).[59] Still others adopted a 50-percent diluted model, allowing plaintiffs to recover damages in cases where the parties' negligence was equal.[60]

FIGURE 4.3
States Adopting Comparative Negligence, 1910–1984[61]

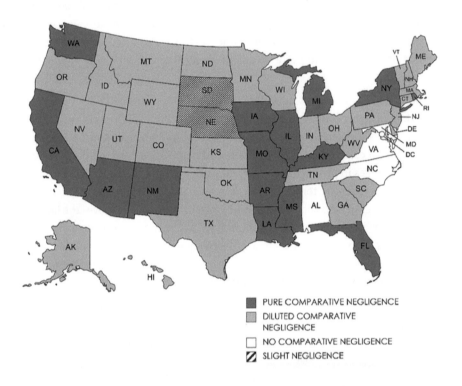

(Map generated from a template provided by courtesy of mapchart.net)

1984). For a comprehensive survey of comparative negligence laws enacted between 1969 and 1984, see Best, "Impediments to Reform."

59. See 1971 Colo. Laws, ch. 125; 1971 Idaho Laws, ch. 186; 1973 N.D. Laws, ch. 78; 1973 Utah Laws, chs. 710–12; 1973 Wyo. Laws, ch. 28; 1974 Kan, Laws, ch. 239; *Bradley v. Appalachian P. Co.*, 256 S.E.2d 879 (W.Va. 1979).

60. See 1969 Hawaii Laws, ch. 227; 1969 Mass. Laws, ch. 761; 1969 N.H. Laws, ch. 227; 1969 Minn. Laws, ch. 624; 1970 Vt. Laws, Act 234; 1971 Or. Laws, ch. 668; 1973 Conn. Laws, Act 73-622; 1973 Nev. Laws, ch. 787; 1973 N.J. Laws, ch. 146; 1973 Okla. Laws, ch. 30; 1973 Tex. Laws, ch. 28; 1975 Mont. Laws, ch. 60; 1976 Pa. Laws, ch. 152; 1979–80 Ohio Laws, p. 594; 1983 Ind. Laws, p. 1930; 1984 Del. Laws, ch. 384; 1984 Iowa Laws, ch. 193 see generally Victor E. Schwartz, *Comparative Negligence* (1986), §§ 1.1, 2.1. Wisconsin moved from a 49-percent model to a 50-percent model in 1971. 1971 Wis. Laws, ch. 47.

61. The map is derived from information in Schwartz, *Comparative Negligence*, §§ 1.1 and 2.1 and Best, "Impediments to Reform," 17.

In some states, reform involved a tug-of-war between courts and legislatures. Typically, the supreme court would suggest that the time had come for reform but would invite the legislature to act first. If the legislature did not do so, the court would adopt comparative negligence after concluding (as did nearly all state courts) that the contributory-negligence system had been created by judges, not legislators, and therefore judges could change it.[62] Most legislatures that enacted comparative-negligence statutes favored diluted systems, which preserved an element of fault. This represented a victory of sorts for insurance companies and traditionalists who, as in Wisconsin, had decided to seek diluted comparative negligence rather than oppose it altogether.[63]

By contrast, nearly all courts that adopted comparative negligence favored the pure model. Some judges supported that model on instrumentalist grounds: contributory negligence had been developed in the early industrial age to support the imperative of economic development at the expense of accident victims, they said, and it had no place in a mature industrial economy. Other judges favored the pure model because they believed it would avoid elements of arbitrariness and inefficiency inherent in diluted systems. They were particularly critical of 49-percent dilution: it seemed unjust that victims who were 49 percent responsible for an accident could recover more than half of their damages, but those who were 50 percent responsible could recover nothing. Cases in 49-percent states in which defendants and victims were held equally negligent often resulted in appeals. Many judges who voted for a pure model reasoned that appeals would be less likely under a pure system, which would give nearly all victims at least some recovery.[64]

Aggregation of Negligence

Comparative negligence raised collateral issues, the most important of which was aggregation of negligence. When a plaintiff and multiple defendants were each found negligent under a diluted comparative-negligence system, should the plaintiff's negli-

---

62. Examples of states falling in this category include: Illinois, *see Maki v. Frelk*, 239 N.E.2d 445 (Ill. 1968) (deferring to legislature); *Alvis*, 421 N.E.2d 886 (Ill. 1981) (adopting pure comparative negligence); 1986 Ill. Act 84-1431 (adopting the 50% rule); Missouri, *see Steinman v. Strobel*, 589 S.W.2d 293 (Mo. 1979) (deferring to legislature); *Gustafson*, 661 S.W.2d 11 (Mo. 1983) (adopting comparative negligence in face of legislative inaction); New Mexico: *City of Albuquerque v. Redding*, 605 P.2d 1156 (N.M. 1980) and *Scott*, 634 P.2d 1234 (N.M. 1981); *see also Hilen*, 673 S.W.2d 713 (Ky. 1984) (implicitly criticizing legislature for failure to act).

63. Best, "Impediments to Reform," 11–12, 17–19; Prosser, "Comparative Negligence," 466 n. 8, 484.

64. Prosser, "Comparative Negligence," 469–75; *Li*, 532 P.2d at 1243. The criticism was not unfounded. For example, between 1931 and 1970, Wisconsin's supreme court considered at least 20 cases in which the jury had found the parties equally negligent and 11 cases in which the trial court had found the plaintiff at least 50 percent negligent as a matter of law. The court upheld most of the jury verdicts but reversed about half of the trial judges' decisions for a variety of reasons. The cases and calculations are described in Appendix 3. Only one state supreme court, West Virginia's, endorsed a diluted system, and it did not do so until the late 1970s. *Bradley*, 256 S.E.2d 879, 885 (W. Va. 1979).

gence be compared to each defendant individually, or should the defendants' negligence be lumped together? Many diluted-comparative-negligence statutes allowed plaintiffs to recover if their negligence was less than (or equal to) "the person against whom recovery is sought," thus leaving it up to courts to decide whether the term "person" referred to defendants individually or collectively.[65] Lumping defendants' negligence together would give victims a better chance of recovery because if individual comparisons were made, there was always a possibility that some defendants would be found less negligent than the victim, in which case the victim could not recover from them. The issue was also important because many cases involved both solvent and insolvent defendants. For example, an auto passenger might sue both the solvent driver of the car in which he was riding and the uninsured, insolvent driver who had hit his host's car. If the insolvent driver was primarily at fault and the host driver was partly at fault but less so than the passenger, individual comparison would limit the victim to an uncollectible judgment while the host driver escaped liability altogether.

Wisconsin was the first state to adopt a diluted comparative-negligence model and unsurprisingly, its supreme court was the first to address the aggregation issue. In *Walker v. Kroger Grocery & Baking Co.* (1934), the court opted for individual comparison, interpreting the 1931 law's reference to "the person against whom recovery is sought" as limited to a single individual.[66] The *Walker* rule soon came under attack from Prosser and other jurists, and in *Walton v. Tull* (1962), Arkansas's supreme court rejected it as inconsistent with comparative negligence's true goal, namely improved socialization of accident costs. "We cannot adopt a narrow construction of our comparative negligence statute in the vain hope of avoiding inequitable situations due to insolvency," stated Justice George Rose Smith. "Obviously either the plaintiff or the solvent defendant must suffer, and the loss has traditionally fallen upon the wrongdoer."[67] Courts that addressed the aggregation issue in the years immediately following the *Walton* decision adopted Wisconsin's individual-comparison rule,[68] but after 1975, as pro-socialization sentiment took firm hold in other areas of tort law, more courts sided with Arkansas and aggregate comparison.[69]

---

65. *See, e.g.,* 1931 Wis. Laws, ch. 242; 1955 Ark. Stats., ch. 191.

66. *Walker*, 252 N.W. 721, 727–28 (Wis. 1934). The court also noted that victims could find solace in the common-law rule of joint and several liability, which provided that a plaintiff could recover all of his damages (less his own negligence) from any defendant who was more negligent than he was. 252 N.W. at 727-28.

67. *Walton*, 356 S.W.2d 20, 27 (Ark. 1962).

68. *Marier v. Mem. Rescue Service, Inc.*, 207 N.W.2d 706 (Minn. 1973); *Van Horn v. Wm. Blanchard Co.*, 438 A.2d 552 (1981).

69. *See* J. Evans and A.M Swarthout, "Comparative Negligence Rule Where Misconduct of Three or More Persons Is Involved," 8 A.L.R.3d 722 (1966, rev. 2021) and authorities there cited; *Mt. Mobile Mix, Inc. v. Gifford*, 660 P.2d 882, 886–87 (Colo. 1983) (adopting aggregation rule and collecting cases and statutes on both sides).

Product Liability: Stopping Short of the Summit

In 1960 William Prosser, appropriating a metaphor first used by Benjamin Cardozo in the early 1930s, painted product liability law as a "citadel" whose walls of privity protected manufacturers from liability to consumers injured by their products—in Prosser's view, a citadel now under siege by the forces of socialization. Prosser's metaphor captured the imagination of scholars and lawmakers alike and played an important role in his largely successful campaign to bring down the citadel walls altogether. It still provides a useful framework for analyzing the course of product liability law during the mid-twentieth century.[70]

The Campaign Against Privity

The first attackers had appeared at the citadel walls in the 1850s. They were few in number and had a limited objective: to excavate an entrance, namely an exception to privity for inherently dangerous products such as drugs, food and illuminating oils, while disclaiming any intent to raze the walls on a broad scale. Prosser and other scholars portrayed Cardozo's 1916 *MacPherson* decision, abolishing privity in his state for all cases of manufacturer negligence that resulted in personal injuries, as the first major breach of the walls, but Minnesota's supreme court had made the first such breach in 1892, and during the decade preceding *MacPherson* several other courts had widened it.[71] *MacPherson* reinforced the breach and sounded a bugle call for additional troops, but they arrived slowly.

The campaign against privity after 1920 was driven mainly by debates between jurists and judges, conducted through law review articles and court decisions, but economic prosperity and the flowering of a national consumer culture during the 1920s helped build popular support for the cause. Electric appliances such as vacuum cleaners, washing machines, ovens and toasters were first invented between 1890 and 1910. By 1925, more than half of American homes were wired for electricity; the market for such appliances boomed, and accidents and litigation followed in their wake. Accidents involving other consumer products also continued to increase. Soda bottles, which were prone to contamination and cracking, and automobiles were particularly frequent subjects of litigation. As the novelty of the stream of new products wore off, many consumers moved past their initial reaction of unalloyed

---

70. William L. Prosser, "The Assault Upon the Citadel (Strict Liability to the Consumer)," 69 *Yale L.J.* 1099, 1099 (1960), citing Cardozo in *Ultramares Corp. v. Touche*, 174 N.E. 441, 445 (N.Y. 1931); see also Prosser, "The Fall of the Citadel (Strict Liability to the Consumer)," 50 *Minn. L. Rev.* 791 (1966); Kenneth S. Abraham, "Prosser's Fall of the Citadel," 100 *Minn. L. Rev.* 1823 (2016).

71. *MacPherson*, 111 N.E. 1050 (N.Y. 1916); Prosser, "Assault Upon the Citadel," 1100–01; Note; "Torts—Negligence—Liability of Contractor to Third Parties," 27 *Yale L.J.* 961 (1917); Francis H. Bohlen, "Liability of Manufacturers to Persons Other Than Their Immediate Vendees," 45 *L.Q. Rev.* 343, 359–66 (1929); *Schubert v. J.R. Clark Co.*, 51 N.W. 1103 (Minn. 1892); *see* Chapter 3.

gratitude and took a more clear-eyed approach that put a premium on good value and product safety. After Frederick Schlink's *Your Money's Worth* (1927) and *One Hundred Million Guinea Pigs* (1933) became best-selling books, Schlink founded Consumers' Research, the first organization dedicated to evaluating product quality and safety and disseminating its findings to a broad readership. *Consumer Reports* magazine, founded by Schlink's rival Arthur Kallet, first appeared in 1936 and soon became popular.[72]

American consumers thus came to feel that they had a direct stake in product safety, and they became impatient with distinctions between manufacturer and seller liability. That impatience helped lay the groundwork for further assaults on the citadel of privity. State courts outside New York began mentioning *MacPherson* with approval in the early 1920s but many hesitated to formally abolish privity, perhaps because they were reluctant to court controversy unnecessarily, and they continued to fit as many cases as they could into the framework of privity exceptions for inherently dangerous products.[73] Some courts signaled that they might be willing to eliminate privity in cases where the manufacturer actually knew a particular product was defective, but they balked at extending the exception to cases where manufacturers did not know of but could have discovered a defect.[74] A few courts eliminated privity in cases involving manufacturers' design defects[75] and products that caused property damage rather than human injury.[76]

In 1934 the American Law Institute (ALI), a prestigious academy of elite lawyers and judges, published the *Restatement of Torts*, a model code of tort principles that was not binding on any state but proved to be highly influential. The committee that prepared the *Restatement* was chaired by University of Pennsylvania law professor Francis Bohlen, a long-time critic of privity, and the *Restatement* reflected his and Cardozo's views. It provided that a manufacturer of products "which, unless carefully made, he should recognize as involving an unreasonable risk of causing substantial bodily

---

72. Mayer, *Consumer Movement*, 10–22; Kyle Graham, "Diffusion of Doctrinal Innovations," 86–87.

73. For example, *Collette v. Page*, 114 A. 136 (R.I. 1921) is frequently cited as an example of an early case adopting *MacPherson*, but in fact the court, while endorsing Cardozo's holding in strong terms, did not squarely adopt it: the case involved a garage owner's liability for a defective auto, not manufacturer liability. Scholars who have traced the evolution of products liability have generally assumed, not without reason, that a judicial dictum strongly approving of *MacPherson* was sufficient to establish the *MacPherson* rule as a practical matter. See, *e.g.*, Graham, "Diffusion of Doctrinal Innovations," 170–71.

74. See, *e.g.*, *Clement v. Rommeck*, 113 N.W. 286 (Mich. 1907); *Hasbrouck v. Armour & Co.*, 121 N.W. 157 (Wis. 1909); *Stone v. Van Noy R. News Co.*, 154 S.W. 1092 (Ky. 1913).

75. See, *e.g.*, *Coakley v. Prentiss-Wabers Stove Co.*, 195 N.W. 388 (Wis. 1923); *Miller v. A.B. Kirschbaum Co.*, 148 A. 851 (Pa. 1930); Dix W. Noel, "Manufacturer's Negligence of Design or Directions for Use of a Product," 71 Yale L.J. 816 (1962).

76. See, *e.g.*, *Ellis v. Lindmark*, 225 N.W. 395 (Minn. 1929); *Marsh Wood Prods. Co. v. Babcock & Wilcox Co.*, 240 N.W. 392 (Wis. 1932).

harm," would be liable to anyone who used the product "lawfully...for a purpose for which it is manufactured" and also to injured bystanders. The ALI explicitly stated that the rule was not limited to food, drugs or other products traditionally deemed inherently dangerous, and it gave an example of the rule's application that was based directly on *MacPherson*.[77]

Courts continued to attack privity steadily but incrementally. Some were reluctant to abolish privity in cases that involved only property damage; no court abolished privity for all types of defective-product cases and injuries until Massachusetts's highest court did so in *Carter v. Yardley & Co.* (1946), and other courts were slow to follow its lead. Nevertheless, by 1960 thirty states had abolished privity to some extent and two states, Michigan and Wisconsin, had joined Massachusetts in abolishing it completely.[78] After 1960, abolition forces rapidly broke down remaining resistance and completed their conquest of the privity citadel. Some states left limited areas of privity intact, for example, in cases involving claims for breach of warranty;[79] others followed *Yardley* and adopted complete abolition.[80] South Dakota, the last state to adopt the *MacPherson* rule for products that caused personal injury, did so in 1973.[81] These campaigns were less dramatic than they might seem because they were overtaken by another movement: a campaign to enact laws divorcing product liability from fault altogether.

---

77. ALI, *Restatement of the Law of Torts* (1934), § 395 and Comment b, Illustration 1; see also *Restatement* §§ 388, 394; Francis H. Bohlen, "Fifty Years of Torts," 50 *Harv. L. Rev.* 1225 (1937).

78. *Carter*, 64 N.E.2d 693 (Mass. 1946); *Spence v. Three Rivs. Builders and Masonry Supply*, 90 N.W.2d 876 (Mich. 1958); *Smith v. Atco Co.*, 94 N.W.2d 697 (Wis. 1959); Graham, "Diffusion of Doctrinal Innovations," 170–71. As late as the mid-1950s, some courts still clung to the analytical framework of inherently dangerous products and shied away from an open embrace of *MacPherson*. See, e.g., *Stout v. Madden*, 300 P.2d 461 (Or. 1956).

79. See, e.g., Daniel F. Thomas, "Implied Warranty Extending To Persons Not In Privity of Contract With Seller...," 21 *Md. L. Rev.* 247 (1961), 248 n. 6 and authorities there cited ; R.D. Hursh, "Privity of Contract as Essential to Recovery in Action Based on Theory Other Than Negligence...," 75 A.L.R.2d 39 (1961, updated 2021), §§ 3–4 and authorities there cited; see also notes 98–99 below.

80. See *American Reciprocal Insurers v. Bessonette*, 384 P.2d 223 (Or. 1963); *Suvada v. White Motor Co.*, 210 N.E.2d 182 (Ill. 1965); *Corprew v. Geigy Chemical Corp.*, 157 N.E.2d 98 (N.C. 1967); *Steinberg v. Coda Roberson Const. Co.*, 440 P.2d 798 (N.M. 1968); *Carolina Home Builders, Inc. v. Armstrong Furnace Co.*, 191 S.E.2d 774 (S.C. 1972); and *Temple Sinai—Suburban Reform Temple v. Richmond*, 308 A.2d 508 (R.I. 1973).

81. *Engberg v. Ford Motor Co.*, 205 N.W.2d 104 (S.D. 1973). For a useful compendium of first cases adopting the *MacPherson* rule in whole or in part, on which Figure 4.4 is based, see Graham, "Diffusion of Doctrinal Innovations," 170–71.

FIGURE 4.4
Stated Reducing or Abolishing Privity, 1892–1973[82]

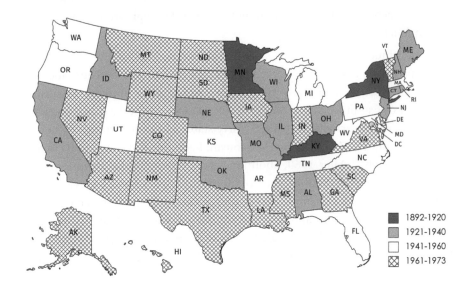

(Map generated from a template provided by courtesy of mapchart.net)

The Strict-Liability Campaign

Abolition of privity eliminated an important defense that manufacturers had long enjoyed and made it easier for those injured by defective products to socialize the cost of their accidents, but it did not attack the innermost fastness of the product-liability citadel: the principle that liability for a product must be accompanied by some negligence on the manufacturer's part. The campaign to impose strict liability on manufacturers of unreasonably dangerous products regardless of negligence, one that was led by Prosser and took inspiration from earlier no-fault movements as well as the privity abolition campaign, made that attack.

Prosser became the leader of the strict-liability campaign by a circuitous path. He was born in 1898 in Indiana; his father spent most of his life as a teacher and school administrator with a brief foray into the practice of law, and Prosser too would divide his life between those fields. Prosser was restless and independent-minded, viewing himself as a "wry observer of life." He tried several fields of work before completing law school at the age of thirty, and though he would become an academic star, he had

---

82. The map is derived from Graham, "Diffusion of Doctrinal Innovations," 159–60, 170–71, Appendix B. It includes states that abolished privity for products causing personal injury, property damage, or both. Cases in which a state supreme court approved of *MacPherson* in dictum are counted as effectively abolishing privity

a lifelong discomfort with pure intellectualism and an abiding affection for the "lot of low-browed individuals...shaking their fists under each other's noses down in the District Court." After a short period of practicing law in Minneapolis, he joined the University of Minnesota law faculty in 1930.[83]

Prosser's first encounter with legal reform came at the beginning of the Depression, a time when thousands of farmers and homeowners in Minnesota and millions across the nation were facing foreclosure and eviction due to inability to pay their loans. When a state legislator asked for help in preparing a foreclosure moratorium law, Prosser gave it. He advised that in order to survive constitutional challenge, the law should only delay, not prohibit foreclosure proceedings; should provide assurance that the mortgage holder would receive at least minimal payments during the moratorium period; and should be of limited duration. The legislature took his advice; the Minnesota law provided a model for other states, and the U.S. Supreme Court largely agreed with Prosser's constitutional analysis when it upheld the law in 1933.[84] Prosser did not turn his attention to tort law until the mid-1930s, but by then his academic reputation was such that a leading law publisher asked him to write a treatise on tort law. Prosser completed his self-education in tort law as he wrote the treatise, and during the process he developed novel theories and perspectives that would ultimately transform the field. After brief stints with the Office of Price Administration during World War II and at Harvard Law School after the war, Prosser became dean of the University of California Law School; the school's age limits forced him to retire in 1963 at the height of his fame, and he completed his career at the nearby Hastings College of the Law.[85]

Prosser's strict-liability campaign began in earnest in 1941 when he published his *Handbook of the Law of Torts*, which would become arguably the most influential tort law treatise of the twentieth century. Prosser viewed the *Handbook* as a vehicle for advancing, not merely stating the law. He argued that workers compensation and the privity-abolition movement were part of a "strong and growing tendency where there is blame on neither side, to ask, in view of the exigencies of social justice, who can best bear the loss." Fault, he argued, was a slippery concept that changed along with social mores. It generated so much legal confusion in the context of defective products that "it seems better not to make use of it at all, and refer instead to strict liability." Prosser noted that some states, beginning with Mississippi in 1927, had already fashioned a limited no-fault system for product-related injuries. Their courts had blended tort and contract law, holding that under the common law, processors of food implicitly warranted that their products were safe and by so doing assumed absolute liability to

---

83. Christopher J. Robinette, "The Prosser Letters: 1917–1918," 101 *Iowa L. Rev.* 1143, 1147–74 (2016); Kenneth S. Abraham and G. Edward White, "Prosser and His Influence," 6 *J. Tort L.* 27, 30–31 (2013).

84. William L. Prosser, "The Minnesota Mortgage Moratorium," 7 *S. Cal. L. Rev.* 353 (1934); see *Home Bldg. & Loan Assn. v. Blaisdell*, 290 U.S. 398 (1934).

85. Robinette, "The Prosser Notebook: Classroom as Biography and Intellectual History," 2010 *U. Ill. L. Rev.* 577, 582–86 (2010); Abraham and White, "Prosser and His Influence," 31–40.

buyers for products gone bad regardless of fault. Even though most courts had limited the implied-warranty rule to food and other products deemed inherently dangerous, Prosser saw an opportunity to expand the scope of implied warranties in tandem with the abolition of privity—and, conversely, for tort law to imitate warranty law by creating its own version of strict liability.[86]

Prosser realized that his campaign might be a long one. He was patient, and gradually events turned his way. In *Escola v. Coca-Cola Bottling Co. of Fresno* (1944), a defective-bottle case, California justice Roger Traynor, a friend of Prosser's, became the first American judge to squarely advocate strict liability. Traynor's concurring opinion suggested an analogy between products liability and workers compensation. "However intermittently injuries may occur and however haphazardly they may strike," he said, "the risk of their occurrence is a constant risk and a general one. Against such a risk there should be a general and constant protection and the manufacturer is best situated to afford such protection."[87] Traynor's colleagues preferred to rely in *Escola* on prior cases placing bottles within the framework of inherently dangerous products, but Traynor's opinion attracted notice. During the 1950s, other tort scholars including Yale law professor Fleming James, who co-authored a tort law treatise second only to Prosser's in influence, began to promote strict liability as a means of accident cost socialization.[88] In the late 1940s and early 1950s, the National Conference of Commissioners of Uniform State Laws (NCCUSL) prepared a Uniform Commercial Code (UCC) that created implied warranties of quality (expressed in terms of "merchantability") and fitness for expected use for nearly all products sold in commerce, and it extended those warranties to both direct purchasers and ultimate consumers. The UCC would not be widely adopted by states until the 1960s, but it gave Prosser a tool that was doubly useful to him: in the second edition of his treatise (1955), he cited the UCC's warranty provisions as evidence of the trend against privity, and in a later article he argued that warranties did not go far enough. They were a "freak hybrid born of the illicit intercourse of tort and contract," an evasion of the ultimate goal to eliminate manufacturer privity absolutely and for all products.[89]

During the late 1950s and early 1960s, Prosser advanced his campaign by writing two law review articles that arguably marked the height of his influence. In the first

---

86. Prosser, *Handbook* (1st ed. 1941), §§ 56, 59, 61; *Coca-Cola Bottling Works v. Lyons*, 111 So. 305 (Miss. 1927); White, *Tort Law in America*, 170–73, 180–84, 198–210.

87. *Escola*, 150 P.2d 436, 440–43 (Cal. 1944). One scholar has described Traynor as Prosser's "very best general." Denis W. Stearns, "Prosser's Bait-and-Switch: How Food Safety Was Sacrificed in the Battle for Tort's Empire," 15 *Nev. L.J.* 106, 131 (2014).

88. Priest, "Invention of Enterprise Liability," 465–77; *see also* David G. Owen, "The Intellectual Development of Modern Products Liability Law: A Comment on Priest's View of the Cathedral's Foundations," 14 *J. Leg. Stud.* 529, 531–33 (1985); Harper and James, *Law of Torts*, §§ 18.5, 28.11, 28.16, 28.27.

89. NCCUSL, *Uniform Commercial Code* (1958), § 2-318; *see also ibid.* § 2-314; Prosser, *Handbook* (2d ed. 1955), § 83; Prosser, "Assault Upon the Citadel," 1124–28; *see also* Kyle Graham, "Strict Products Liability at 50: Four Histories," 98 *Marq. L. Rev.* 555, 569–80 (2014).

article, entitled "The Assault Upon the Citadel" (1960), he portrayed *MacPherson* as the beginning of the end for both privity and fault in the area of products liability. He made full use of his military metaphor, describing the abolition movement as an unstoppable army; he also portrayed product-warranty law, in his view a clear forerunner of strict liability, as a lesser but still formidable force that had extended its reach from food to soap and other personal-care products and was continuing to advance. Prosser pointed to several recent and "spectacular" court decisions that, in his view, showed that traditional manufacturer liability limitations would soon be "thrown onto the ash pile" of history.[90]

Prosser then made his case for the complete elimination of fault. Negligence and breach-of-warranty theories provided a measure of justice, he said, but they often used convoluted and tortured legal reasoning to achieve their desired result, and they also raised serious obstacles to complete justice. Injured consumers could not always prove conclusively how product defects came about, and the process of sorting out the ultimate allocation of costs between manufacturers, distributors and sellers was inefficient and time-consuming.[91] Prosser endorsed Traynor's *Escola* opinion and hoped that "we are not nowadays disposed to flee shrieking in terror from the prospect of a spot of socialism in our law when the public interest demands it."[92] Scholars later criticized Prosser for exaggerating the strict-liability tilt of the cases he cited in his *Assault* article, but the article had tremendous influence among judges and scholars alike.[93]

In 1959, the ALI appointed Prosser as the reporter for a revised *Restatement of Torts*, thus giving him a new platform for advancing his cause. In 1961, the ALI committee tasked with preparing products-liability provisions drafted a new section, 402A, which endorsed strict liability but limited it to food manufacturers. Prosser lobbied committee members to broaden the section, and eventually his efforts paid off: in 1962 the committee expanded the section to include products for intimate bodily use and in 1964 it was expanded to apply to all products, with limited exceptions.[94] During the drafting process, Prosser received crucial outside assistance from two courts. In *Henningsen v. Bloomfield Motors* (1960), New Jersey's supreme court held that manufacturers and distributors alike could be held liable to consumers for product defects under an implied breach-of-warranty theory regardless of fault, and in *Greenman v. Yuba Power Products*, Inc. (1963) Justice Traynor, now speaking for a unanimous California supreme court, established absolute manufacturer lia-

---

90. Prosser, "Assault Upon the Citadel," 1099–1113, 1112 ("ash pile" quotation).
91. *Ibid.*, 1114–34.
92. *Ibid.*, 1120.
93. Articles critical of Prosser's techniques include Jay M. Smyser, "Products Liability and the American Law Institute: A Petition for Rehearing," 42 *U. Det. L.J.* 343 (1965) and Stearns, "Prosser's Bait-and-Switch." *See generally* Abraham, "Prosser's Fall." For a more appreciative analysis see White, *Tort Law in America*, 161–62.
94. *Restatement 2d*, § 402A (Tentative Draft No. 6, 1962); *ibid.* (Tentative Draft No. 7, 1962); *ibid.* (Tentative Draft No. 10, 1964); Stearns, "Prosser's Bait-and-Switch," 108–13.

bility for product defects regardless of warranty law. Other state courts fell in line with astonishing speed: nineteen states adopted strict liability during the 1960s and twenty-five more followed suit during the 1970s. The process was perhaps accelerated by Prosser's second article, "The Fall of the Citadel," which appeared in 1966. In that article, Prosser triumphantly reviewed recent developments and predicted that states that had not yet adopted strict liability would soon do so. He warned against the use of breach-of-warranty theories as a substitute for strict liability, repeating many of the criticisms made in the *Assault* article.[95]

But important questions remained. Would contributory negligence continue to be a defense in strict-liability cases? Would damages recoverable in strict-liability cases include economic losses, such as a commercial customer's loss of business because a manufacturer had provided defective components that the customer used in its own products, or would damages be limited to personal injuries and physical property loss? Neither question gave Prosser any serious concern. As to contributory negligence, he believed it was easy to draw a line: consumers could not be charged with negligence for failing to examine products for defects, but if they became aware of a dangerous defect and used the product nevertheless, it was fair to hold them partly responsible. The ALI added an official comment to section 402A that generally reflected Prosser's view: it pronounced that "voluntarily and unreasonably proceeding to encounter a known danger [which] commonly passes under the name of assumption of risk" could be treated as contributory or comparative negligence.[96]

Prosser took a conservative approach to economic loss. He argued that such damages would usually be suffered by commercial buyers, who could protect themselves through negotiation of terms of sale where individual consumers could not; thus, economic damages should be sought through breach-of-contract claims, not tort claims.[97] Many judges and jurists agreed with Prosser on this issue, thus revealing that at least one pocket of conservatism was holding out as the armies of reform swept through the citadel. Other pockets held out as well. Some courts eliminated all privity requirements for product-based tort claims but continued to require privity for warranty claims; like Prosser, they reasoned that elimination of privity was a better fit for tort claims (which usually arose from consumer transactions) than for warranty claims (which often arose from commercial transactions in which the parties could more

---

95. *Henningsen*, 161 A.2d 69 (N.J. 1960); *Greenman*, 377 P.2d 897 (Cal. 1963); Graham, "Diffusion of Doctrinal Innovations," 159–60; William L. Prosser, "The Fall of the Citadel (Strict Liability to the Consumer)," 50 *Minn. L. Rev.* 791, 791–803 (1966).

96. *Restatement 2d*, § 402A, comment n.

97. Prosser, "Fall of the Citadel," 822–25.

easily negotiate loss allocation).[98] Other courts, however, made no distinction and eliminated privity requirements for both types of claims.[99]

Defining the intersection between contributory negligence and strict product liability proved challenging for American courts. Supreme courts that addressed this issue during the first years after section 402A was published accepted Prosser's and the ALI's view that manufacturers should be allowed to assert product misuse and use of products with knowledge of their defects as defenses to liability, but that left a large grey zone of product-related behavior that Prosser and the ALI had not addressed. For example, could plaintiffs be held negligent who had not followed assembly instructions or who inadvertently put fingers or arms into machine openings that were unguarded but whose hazards were arguably clear? Here the courts took divergent paths, presaging the confusion and conflict that would characterize the effort to fully delineate strict liability during the decades to come. New Jersey's supreme court stated in broad terms that contributory negligence applied to all strict liability claims; Arizona's supreme court held that only assumption of risk, not negligence, could serve as a defense, but both courts viewed their holdings as consistent with the defenses approved by Prosser and the ALI. Wisconsin's supreme court suggested a broader field of defense by analogizing strict liability to safe-place-statute violations: existence of a product defect would be enough to establish that the manufacturer was negligent, and plaintiffs would not be required to prove how the defect came about, but it would be up to juries in every case to apportion fault between manufacturer and consumer.[100] By the end of the 1960s, it was clear that strict liability had advanced the socialization of American accident costs substantially, but the exact parameters of consumer responsibility remained to be decided.

The Erosion of Civil Immunities

Family Immunities

At the turn of the twentieth century, nearly all states held that certain relationships were so essential to the social fabric that persons within those relationships would not be allowed to make tort claims against each other for fear of disrupting that fabric. The leading example was that of family: husbands and wives, parents and children were immune from liability for injuring each other.

---

98. *See, e.g., Canton Provision Co. v. Gauder,* 196 N.E. 634 (Ohio 1935); *Crystal Coca-Cola Bottling Co. v. Cathey,* 317 P.2d 1094 (Ariz. 1957); *Atco,* 94 N.W.2d 697 (Wis. 1959).

99. *See, e.g., Borucki v. MacKenzie Bros. Co.,* 3 A.2d 224 (Conn. 1938); *Spence,* 90 N.W.2d 873 (Mich. 1958).

100. *Maiorino v. Weco Products Co.,* 214 A.2d 18 (N.J. 1965); *Dippel v. Sciano,* 155 N.W.2d 55, 59 (Wis. 1967); *O. S. Stapley Co. v. Miller (1968),* 447 P.2d 248 (Ariz. 1968).

Spousal immunity had arisen out of the common-law marital unity doctrine, which stated that a woman's separate legal identity disappeared at marriage and merged into that of her husband, "under whose wing, protection, and cover, she performs every thing."[101] The doctrine had originated in feudal England, a society in which marriage turned as much on acquiring and protecting property and security as on love; but beginning in the 1830s, as women came to play an increasingly important role in America's industrial revolution and the American frontier's advance, state legislatures engaged in a slow process of restoring to married women various property and civil rights they had enjoyed before marriage, including the right to control their own property and wages, to make contracts and to protect their separate interests in court. Nevertheless, spousal immunity held firm, bolstered by a strongly patriarchal and sentimental view of husbands as breadwinners and wives as preservers of the family, a view that remained in place well into the twentieth century.[102]

The first efforts to socialize accident costs among family members by eliminating immunities appeared during the Progressive era. Late-nineteenth-century efforts to persuade judges that the new married women's laws should be interpreted to allow interspousal lawsuits were uniformly rejected, but in *Thompson v. Thompson* (1910) three U.S. Supreme Court justices, all of whom had some progressive leanings, supported those efforts in a dissenting opinion. In 1914, Connecticut's supreme court became the first to abolish interspousal immunity, and during the next decade several other state courts followed suit, based largely on a new-found willingness to interpret married women's statutes liberally, on the increasing availability of liability insurance and on a general sense that women's expanding role in economic and political matters called for correspondingly expanded rights.[103] Other courts continued to defend immunity out of loyalty to traditional views of family and fears that eliminating immunity would lead to deeper social dislocations. In the 1941 edition of his treatise, Prosser criticized spousal immunity as the relic of "a social order which has been dead for more than a century," but mid-twentieth-century jurists paid relatively little attention to spousal immunity reform. The pace of abolition was slow throughout

---

101. William Blackstone, *Commentaries on the Law of England* (1765–69), 1:430; Marylynn Salmon, *Women and the Law of Property in Early America* (1986), 88–97, 100–19; Carl Tobias, "Interspousal Tort Immunity in America," 23 *Ga. L. Rev.* 359, 361–82 (1989).

102. Joan Hoff, *Law, Gender and Injustice: A Legal History of U.S. Women* (1991), 120–28; Norma Basch, *In the Eyes of the Law: Women, Marriage, and Property in Nineteenth-Century New York* (1982), 74–81; Richard H. Chused, "Married Women's Property Law: 1800–1850," 71 *Geo. L.J.* 1359, 1397–1404 (1983).

103. *Thompson*, 218 U.S. 611, 619 (1910) (Justice John Marshall Harlan dissenting, joined by Justices Charles Evans Hughes and Oliver Wendell Holmes); *Brown v. Brown*, 88 A. 889 (Conn. 1914); *Fiedler v. Fiedler*, 140 P. 1022 (Okla. 1914); *Johnson v. Johnson*, 77 So. 335 (Ala. 1917); *Crowell v. Crowell*, 105 SE 206 (N.C. 1920). The women's suffrage movement contributed to abolition in at least one state. Samantha Langbaum, "The Paradox of Aspiration and the Making of a Law: The Wisconsin Equal Rights Act of 1921" (M.A. thesis, Univ. of Wis., 1992), 1–45; 1921 Wis. Laws, ch. 529; *Wait v. Pierce*, 209 N.W. 475 (1926).

the mid-twentieth century. Like comparative negligence and several other tort-law reforms, it would not accelerate until the 1960s.[104]

Immunity from suit between parents and children was a much newer doctrine than spousal immunity. Despite the value that English common law placed on parental authority over children, it conferred certain rights on children including the right to financial support and protection and allowed them to sue their parents in limited circumstances. No American court barred such suits until Mississippi's supreme court did so in 1891, fashioning the new immunity from whole cloth in order to promote a "sound public policy, designed to subserve the repose of families and the best interests of society." Other courts soon followed Mississippi's lead, seeking to maintain "harmonious and proper family relations" as "conducive to good citizenship" and "the welfare of the state" and arguing that it would be difficult to draw a line between situations where immunity was appropriate and inappropriate.[105] Prosser argued that parent-child immunity from suit should end for the same reasons as spousal immunity, and between 1930 and 1960 courts in a handful of states abolished that immunity; but as with spousal immunity, abolition would not go forward in earnest until the 1960s.[106]

Governmental and Charitable Immunities

The doctrine of sovereign immunity, holding that the state could not be sued without its consent, was well established in the common law. After American independence, most states enshrined the doctrine in their constitutions, usually through clauses flatly prohibiting suits against the state in its own courts or providing that the state could set the terms on which it would consent to be sued.[107] Other states achieved the same result through judicial decisions.[108] But the immunities conferred on local governments and charitable organizations were more tenuous. English courts did not

---

104. Prosser, *Handbook* (1st ed. 1941), § 99; Tobias, "Interspousal Tort Immunity," 435–41.

105. Blackstone, *Commentaries*, 1:435–40; *Hewlett v. George*, 9 So. 885, 887 (Miss. 1891); *see also McKelvey v. McKelvey*, 77 S.W. 664 (Tenn. 1903); *Roller v. Roller*, 79 P. 788 (Wash. 1905); Gail D. Hollister, "Parent-Child Immunity: A Doctrine in Search of Justification," 50 *Fordham L. Rev.* 489, 493–94 (1982). Between 1891 and 1940, at least twenty states including Mississippi (1891), Illinois (1895), Tennessee (1903), Washington (1905), North Carolina (1923), Minnesota (1924), Pennsylvania and Rhode Island (1925), Michigan (1926), Wisconsin (1927), New York (1928), Connecticut (1929), Maryland and South Carolina (1930), California and West Virginia (1931), Virginia (1934), Alabama (1937), and Arkansas and Massachusetts (1938) adopted parent-child immunity. Hollister, "Parent-Child Immunity," at 494–95, n.40.

106. Prosser, *Handbook* (1st ed. 1941), § 99; Prosser, *Handbook* (2d ed. 1955), § 101; Tobias, "Interspousal Tort Immunity," 435–41.

107. See Ala. Const. (1902), art. I, § 14; Ark. Const. (1874), art. V, § 20; Ill Const. (1870), art. IV, § 26; W.Va. Const. (1862), art. IV, § 35; Cal. Const. (1879), art. XX, § 6; Fla. Const. (1887), art. III, § 22; Ky. Const. (1851), art. II, § 31; Nev. Const. (1864), art. IV, § 22; Ohio Const. (1912), art. I, § 16; Tenn. Const. (1870), art. I, § 17; Wis. Const. (1848), art. IV, § 27. Robert A. Leflar and Benjamin E. Kantrowitz, "Tort Liability of the States," 29 *NYU L. Rev.* 1363, 1367–1407 (1954).

108. Leflar and Kantrowitz, "Tort Liability of the States," 1367–1407.

fashion a common-law rule of municipal immunity until 1788, and during the nineteenth century most American state courts drew a line between "governmental" acts for which municipal immunity would be granted and "proprietary" acts for which it would not. The reasoning behind the distinction was that local governments' power to act for public purposes benefitting all citizens should not be hampered by litigation, but if a local government engaged in an enterprise that was purely for revenue or did not serve a basic governmental purpose, it should be held to account for any harm that the enterprise caused, just as a private company would be.[109]

The line between "governmental" and "proprietary" acts proved to be a tangled one. In 1873 Judge John F. Dillon, the preeminent authority of his day on American municipal law, admitted that he found it "impossible to state.... [a]ny rule so exact as to be of much practical value which will precisely embrace the torts for which a private action will lie against a municipal corporation." State courts divided as to whether accidents caused by defective highways, bridges and sidewalks belonged in the governmental or proprietary category. In an age when many Americans believed that government's powers should be limited to protecting health and public order, most state courts viewed such accidents as involving proprietary functions. The Five-State Survey indicates that such accidents generated a significant part of courts' tort caseloads during the nineteenth century, and a reduced but still noticeable part of their caseloads during the early twentieth century.[110]

In the 1920s, Yale law professor Edwin Borchard attracted national notice with a series of law review articles criticizing municipal immunity as outmoded. The need to compensate victims of public injury was paramount, he argued, and municipalities were much better able to bear the cost of accidents directly or through insurance than they had been in the nineteenth century. Prosser agreed with Borchard, but he concluded that the governmental-proprietary dichotomy was so entrenched in the law and so complicated that courts could not fix it: change could come only from state legislatures. Few legislatures responded to his invitation, and during the next three decades American courts continued to muddle along under the governmental-proprietary dichotomy.[111]

---

109. *Russell v. Men of Devon*, 100 Eng. Rep. 359 (1788); Prosser, *Handbook* (1st ed. 1941), 1066–75; John F. Dillon, *Law of Municipal Corporations* (2d ed. 1873), §§ 752–53; *see also, e.g., Wilson v. Mayor of City of N.Y.*, 1 Denio 595 (N.Y. 1845); *Goodrich v. City of Chi.*, 20 Ill. 445 (1858); *Hayes v. City of Oshkosh*, 33 Wis. 314, 318 (1873) (holding that immunity extends to "a public service...from which [the municipality] derives no special benefit or advantage in its corporate capacity").

110. Dillon, *Municipal Corporations*, § 753. Suits against municipalities for accidents, mostly resulting from defective bridges, streets, sidewalks and highways, composed a negligible portion of all Five-State Survey tort cases during the 1800–1850 period, 7 percent during the 1860–1900 period, and 3 percent during the 1910–1930 period. The calculations are described in Appendix 3.

111. Edwin Borchard, "Government Liability in Tort," 34 *Yale L.J.* 1, 129, 229 (1924); Borchard, "Governmental Responsibility in Tort—VI," 36 *Yale L.J.* 1 (1926); Borchard, "Governmental Responsibility in Tort—VII," 28 *Colum. L. Rev.* 577 (1928); Prosser, *Handbook* (1st ed. 1941), 774–80;

Charitable immunity was unknown to the common law until Great Britain's House of Lords, acting as an appeals court, created it in 1846. Government social welfare programs and public hospitals were virtually nonexistent in Britain and the United States at that time; private hospitals and benevolent organizations filled the gap, and the Lords felt that a grant of immunity was essential to encourage their growth. Other English courts questioned the Lords' decision and eventually rejected it, but Massachusetts's highest court endorsed the concept of charitable immunity in 1876 and other American courts soon followed suit.[112]

The doctrine had an uneasy life from its earliest days. Some courts created exceptions to immunity in cases involving injury to charitable institutions' employees, paying clients and visitors, and some took a narrow view of which institutions qualified as charitable.[113] The call for a general retreat from charitable immunity began in 1920, when Minnesota's supreme court became the first to explicitly repudiate the doctrine, and jurists soon joined in. In 1928, law professor Lester Feezer argued that modern charities did not need special legal protection: they no longer "[did] charity in the manner of the good Samaritan of old," but were "thing[s] of steel and stone and electricity... of boards and committees, of card indices and filing systems, and of rules and regulations." Feezer explicitly attacked charitable immunity as contrary to the era's ideal of "shifting... the loss, at least, partially, from the unfortunate victim of the injury to society."[114] During the early 1940s, Prosser and U.S. Supreme Court justice Wiley Rutledge also criticized charitable immunity, and a few state courts joined Minnesota in rejecting it. They argued that it amounted to a forced contribution from victims of charitable negligence, that charities could redistribute injury-related losses through insurance, and that the public's interest in proper care outweighed any negative effect that abolition of immunity would have on charitable donations.[115] But a majority of American courts continued to uphold immunity in some form, albeit with decreasing enthusiasm.

Symposium, "Governmental Tort Liability," 9 *Law & Contemp. Probs.* 179 (1942); Leslie Anderson, "Claims Against States," 7 *Vand. L. Rev.* 234 (1954).

112. *Feoffees of Heriot's Hospital v. Ross*, 12 C. & F. 507 (H. Lords 1846); *Mersey Docks Trustees v. Gibbs*, 11 H.L. Cas. 686 (H.L. 1866); *McDonald v Mass. Gen. Hosp.*, 120 Mass. 432 (1876); *Perry v. House of Refuge*, 63 Md. 20 (1884); see also Note, "'The Quality of Mercy': Charitable Trusts and Their Continuing Immunity," 100 *Harv. L. Rev.* 1382 (1987).

113. See Comment, "Charitable Immunity: A Diminishing Doctrine," 23 *Wash. & Lee L. Rev.* 109, 110–12 and n.4 (1966); Carl Zollman, "Damage Liability of Charitable Institutions," 19 *Mich. L. Rev.* 395 (1921).

114. *Mulliner v. Evangelischer Diakonniessenverein*, 175 N.W. 699 (Minn. 1920); Lester W. Feezer, "The Tort Liability of Charities," 77 *U. Pa. L. Rev.* 191, 195–96 (1928); *see also* Zollman, "Damage Liability of Charitable Institutions."

115. Prosser, *Handbook* (3d ed. 1964), 1023–24, notes 62–82; Prosser, *Handbook* (4th ed. 1971), 996, notes 68–69; *Geo. Coll. v. Hughes*, 130 F.2d 810 (D.C. Cir. 1942) (Rutledge); Bradley C. Canon and Dean Jaros, "The Impact of Changes in Judicial Doctrine: The Abrogation of Charitable Immunity," 13 *L. & Soc. Rev.* 969, 969–74 (1979); *see also,, e.g., St. Mary's Acad. v. Solomon*, 238 P. 22 (Colo. 1925); *Gable v. Salvation Army*, 100 P.2d 244 (Okla. 1940) (abolishing charitable immunity).

The Decline and Fall of Immunities, 1950–1970

By the early 1950s, as American receptivity to socialization of accident costs moved toward its peak, many state courts were ready to cut back or abolish family, governmental and charitable immunities. Judges were increasingly receptive to arguments that family members and charitable institutions should be held accountable for their wrongs, that doing so would not damage the fabric of American society, and that insurance would cushion them against the loss of immunity.[116] Between 1960 and 1980, seventeen states abolished spousal immunity, more than doubling the total number of abolition states. Judges were hesitant to abolish parental immunity altogether: despite increased acceptance of cost socialization and a recent decline in the proportion of Americans living in nuclear and extended families, there was still nearly universal agreement that parental control of children was essential to a stable society. Wisconsin's supreme court was the first to devise a solution: in *Goller v. White* (1963), it abolished parental immunity but carved out exceptions for disputes involving the exercise of parental authority and parental decisions about food, housing, schooling and other basic aspects of child care. *Goller*, in Prosser's view, "set off something of a long-overdue landslide," and by 1970 at least ten states had followed Wisconsin's lead.[117] Despite the drumbeat of academic and judicial criticism of charitable immunity that had existed since the 1920s, abolition did not gain momentum until the end of World War II, but then it moved rapidly: thirty-one states joined the charitable-immunity abolition movement during the 1950s and 1960s.[118]

---

116. See Prosser, *Handbook* (2d ed. 1955), § 116 (intra-family immunities), § 127 (charitable immunity), § 109 (governmental immunity); Leflar and, Kantrowitz, "Tort Liability of the States"; Harper and James, *Law of Torts*, §§ 29.3, 29.6, 29.16–17.

117. *Goller v. Goller*, 122 N.W.2d 193 (Wis. 1963); Prosser, *Handbook* (4th ed. 1971), § 122.

118. Canon and Jaros, "Abrogation of Charitable Immunity," 973; Comment, "Charitable Immunity: A Diminishing Doctrine," 23 *Wash. & Lee L. Rev.* 109 (1966); Janet Fairchild, "Tort Immunity of Nongovernmental Charities—Modern Status," 25 A.L.R. 4th 517 (1983, rev. 2021); *see also* Pew Research Center, "Social and Demographic Trends: The American Family Today" (2015), at https://www.pewsocialtrends.org/2015/12/17/1-the-american-family-today; Brigitte Berger, *The Family in the Modern Age* (2002); Arlene S. Skolnick and Jerome H. Skolnick, eds., *Family in Transition* (12th ed. 2003).

FIGURE 4.5
The Acceleration of Change in Tort Law, 1950–1970[119]

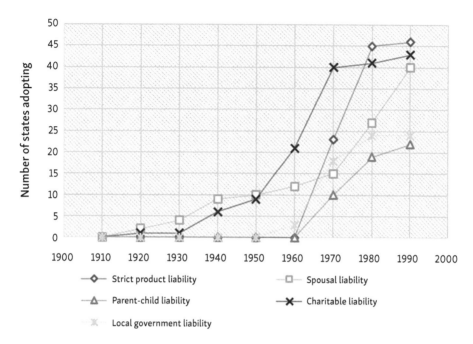

Some courts delayed abolition of family and charitable immunity out of deference to their legislatures, believing that it would be best to let the people's elected representatives have the first opportunity to act. New York provided an example: in *Badigian v. Badigian* (1961) the state's highest court rejected a call to abolish parental immunity, noting that exceptions had been made to the rule but indicating that further change should come from the legislature. New York legislators did not take the hint, and eight years later, the court stated in *Gelbman v. Gelbman* (1969) that it would wait no longer. Immunity, said Justice Adrian Burke, "was a court-created rule and, as such, the courts can revoke it. The inactivity of the Legislature... illustrates the fact that the rule will be changed, if at all, by a decision of this court"; and so it was changed.[120]

State courts were less assertive about abolishing municipal immunity, partly because that would touch the core of state power: states created municipalities and ultimately

---

119. Figure 4.5 is derived from the following sources: Graham, "Diffusion of Doctrinal Innovations," 159–60, 171–72 (strict liability and spousal and parent-child immunity); Canon and Jaros, "Abrogation of Charitable Immunity," 973, and Fairchild, "Tort Immunity of Nongovernmental Charities" (charitable liability); Leflar and Kantrowitz, "Tort Liability of the States," 1367–1407 (local government liability).

120. *Badigian*, 174 N.E.2d 218 (N.Y. 1961); *Gelbman*, 245 N.E.2d 192, 193 (N.Y. 1969). *See also, e.g., Schwenkhoff v. Farmers Mut. Ins. Co.*, 93 N.W, 867 (Wis. 1958) (upholding but criticizing parental immunity and suggesting legislative change); *Goller*, 122 N.W.2d at 198 (abolishing parental immunity).

were responsible for them. The courts may also have been mindful of Prosser's warning that judicial abolition would require disentangling the snarl of decisions that the proprietary-versus-governmental-function distinction had created. Prior to the 1950s, courts that wished to expand municipal liability did so by broadening the definition of proprietary functions, but as American sentiment for cost socialization reached high tide, direct attacks on immunity began to appear.[121] Florida's and Illinois' supreme courts took the first steps toward abolition of municipal immunity in 1957 and 1959 respectively. Illinois justice Ray Klingbeil identified several reasons for abolition that other courts echoed during this era: he noted that his state's legislature had already carved out several exceptions to immunity and he observed that although municipal governments equaled or exceeded large corporations in their scale of operation, they were "operating on a [liability] blueprint prepared a hundred, if not a thousand years ago."[122]

Roughly fifteen other state courts joined the municipal-immunity abolition movement during the 1960s and 1970s. Most took a cautious approach and preserved such immunity for acts that were legislative or judicial in nature; even so, their decisions were enough to arouse many state legislatures from slumber. Legislatures in Florida, Illinois and other states reacted by enacting laws that imposed notice-filing requirements and claim deadlines and capped the amount of damages municipalities would be liable to pay; indeed, some courts that abolished municipal immunity anticipated that their decisions would elicit such responses.[123] This call-and-response pattern suggested that efforts to limit municipal immunity would elicit continuing legislative resistance, and that replacing the proprietary-governmental dichotomy with a legislative-judicial dichotomy might lead to nothing more than one snarl of decisions replacing another. That would prove to be the case in the coming decades.

Continuing Confusion Over Causation

The principle that there could be no liability without causation, that wrongdoing had no significance unless it caused injury, had long been a fundamental part of tort law. Where to set the boundaries of legal duty that would define wrongdoing and

---

121. *See, e.g.,* Leon Green, "Freedom of Litigation (III): Municipal Liability for Torts," 38 *Ill. L. Rev.* 355 (1943); Allan F. Smith, "Municipal Tort Liability," 48 *Mich. L. Rev.* 41 (1950); Prosser, *Handbook* (2d ed. 1955), § 109.

122. *Hargrove v. Town of Cocoa Beach*, 96 So.2d 130 (Fla. 1957); *Molitor v. Kaneland Comm. Unit Dist. No. 302*, 163 N.E.2d 89, 96 (Ill. 1959).

123. For examples of the call-and-response pattern in other states, *see, e.g.,* **Wisconsin:** *Britten v. Eau Claire*, 51 N.W.2d 30 (Wis. 1952) (warning to legislature); *Holytz v. Milw.*, 115 N.W.2d 618 (Wis. 1962) (abolishing immunity after legislative inaction); 1963 Wis. Laws, ch. 198; 1975 Wis. Laws, ch. 333, § 182c (imposing notice requirements and payment limits). **Pennsylvania:** *Morris v. Mt. Lebanon Twp. School Dist.*, 144 A.2d 737 (Pa. 1958) (warning); *Ayala v. Phila. Bd. of Pub. Educ.*, 305 A.2d 877 (Pa. 1973) (abolishing immunity); 1978 Pa. Laws, ch. 53; 1980 Pa. Laws, ch. 142 (reestablishing limited immunity); **New Hampshire:** *Gossler v. City of Manchester*, 221 A.2d 242 (N.H. 1966); *Merrill v. City of Manchester,* 332 A.2d 378 (N.H. 1974); 1977 N.H. Laws, ch. 595.

Four The Golden Age of Tort Socialization, 1920–1970 143

the boundaries of causation that would define liability bedeviled American jurists from the beginning. During the mid-nineteenth century, American tort law had moved away from the pre-industrial concept of duty as a limited set of obligations tied to basic social relationships such as those between masters and servants, family members and citizens and the state, toward a broader concept that every individual owed a general duty of care to the world at large. This did not mean that the costs of wrongdoing would be fully socialized, but it opened up the question of how far socialization should go.[124]

During the nineteenth century, the debate over that question was framed in terms of both duty and causation. As a result, causation became one of the most contentious and confusing areas of tort law, and it remained so in the twentieth century, not least because it was intertwined with the equally contentious debate over the proper allocation of power between judges and juries. When injury resulted from a chain of acts by different persons, or when a minor act of carelessness ultimately led to a major disaster (for example, the fire that spread from a lantern kicked over by a cow and destroyed much of Chicago in 1871), where would the limits of causation and liability be drawn? In 1870, the jurist Nicholas St. John Green argued that adherence to concepts of physical and temporal proximity of cause too easily allowed judges to impose their own views of duty, wrongdoing and liability and to override juries under the guise of objectivity. The same year, perhaps partly in response to such criticism, Wisconsin chief justice Luther Dixon held that foreseeability must be considered as well, a factor that might not check judicial bias completely but would make its exercise more apparent.[125] But the melding of physical and temporal proximity and foreseeability brought only confusion. During the late nineteenth century, American courts addressed the problem by experimenting with causation standards expressed in terms of "natural" and "probable" cause and related terms, but their experiments were not successful.[126]

The debate over causation continued without cease as the twentieth century dawned. Beginning about 1890, a group of jurists, loosely known as legal realists, echoed Green's theme that causation was closely linked to the concept of legal duty and that both concepts were really tools for judicial policymaking. They also echoed Oliver Wendell Holmes's theme that concepts of duty should be adjusted to the "felt necessities of the times," and they launched a renewed search for improved causation rules. In 1912, Harvard law professor Jeremiah Smith proposed the concept of "sub-

---

124. White, *Tort Law in America*, 94–102; Morton Horwitz, *The Transformation of American Law, 1870–1960* (1992), 52–63; Patrick J. Kelley, "Proximate Cause in Negligence Law: History, Theory and the Present Darkness," 69 *Wash U. L.Q.* 49, 64–70 (1991); Nicholas St. John Green, "Proximate and Remote Cause," 4 *Am. L. Rev.* 201, 211–16 (1870); Oliver Wendell Holmes, *The Common Law* (1881), 79–81.

125. Green, "Proximate and Remote Cause," 213–16; Kelley, "Proximate Cause," 64–70; *Kellogg v. Chi. & Nw. R. Co.*, 26 Wis. 223 (1870).

126. See Chapter 2, notes 31–40 and accompanying text.

stantial cause" as a replacement for "natural," "probable" and "proximate" cause. The new term, Smith argued, would give juries greater freedom to determine holistically whether a wrongdoer's act was sufficiently important and sufficiently culpable to warrant imposing liability for the victim's injuries.[127] Smith's proposed rule gained some favor and was adopted by several state courts, beginning with Minnesota in 1920; but the debate over defining duty and causation continued, most famously in the New York case of *Palsgraf v. Long Island Railroad Co.* (1928).

Palsgraf involved an odd chain of events. A man dropped a package as railway guards helped push him through the closing doors of a commuter train. The package contained fireworks, which went off and caused a weighing scale at the other end of the platform to fall down and strike Helen Palsgraf; she then sued the railroad for her injuries. Justice Cardozo, speaking for the majority of a closely divided court, held that the railroad was not liable. He maintained that duty and causation should be viewed holistically, and chiefly in terms of foreseeability:

> The risk reasonably to be perceived defines the duty to be obeyed, and risk imports relation; it is risk to another or to others within the range of apprehension.... [A] distinction is to be drawn according to the diversity of interests invaded by the act, as where conduct negligent in that it threatens an insignificant invasion of an interest in property results in an unforeseeable invasion of an interest of another order.[128]

Cardozo's colleague William Andrews, speaking for the dissenters, defended the traditional views that duty and causation should be analyzed separately and that causation should be viewed primarily in terms of the physical and temporal proximity of a defendant's acts to the plaintiff's injury:

> Where there is the unreasonable act, and some right that may be affected there is negligence whether damage does or does not result. What we do mean by the word 'proximate' is that, because of convenience, of public policy, of a rough sense of justice, the law arbitrarily declines to trace a series of events beyond a certain point. This is not logic. It is practical politics.... We draw an uncertain and wavering line, but draw it we must as best we can.[129]

---

127. Holmes, *The Common Law*, 3; Jeremiah Smith, "Legal Cause in Actions of Tort," 25 *Harv. L. Rev.* 103, 223, 303 (1912); *Anderson v. Mpls., St. Paul & S.S.M. R. Co.*, 179 N.W. 45 (Minn. 1920); see also Roscoe Pound, "Causation," 67 *Yale L.J.* 1 (1957). Other important works that promoted this aspect of the legal-realist movement include Roscoe Pound, "Mechanical Jurisprudence," 8 *Colum. L. Rev.* 605 (1908) and Leon Green, *Rationale of Proximate Cause* (1927).

128. *Palsgraf*, 162 N.E. 99, 100–01 (N.Y. 1928).

129. *Ibid.* at 103–04 (Andrews dissent).

Benjamin Cardozo. Courtesy Library of Congress.

The most striking and important feature of *Palsgraf* was that both Cardozo and Andrews, despite their differing perspectives on causation, viewed it as a policymaking tool. Foreseeability for Cardozo, and proximate cause for Andrews, were inherently flexible concepts that could be tailored to achieve appropriate results in close cases. This view echoed the legal realists' arguments, and Cardozo's and Andrews' prestige in judicial circles gave other judges an opening to acknowledge their policymaking role in tort cases. When Prosser attempted to lay down a rule for causation in the first edition of his treatise in 1941, he leaned toward Cardozo's holistic view but stated bluntly that tort liability was based on "boundar[ies]...set...upon the basis of some social idea of justice or policy."[130]

---

130. Henry M. Edgerton, "Legal Cause," 72 *U. Pa. L. Rev.* 211, 211 (1924) (stating that tort liability depends "upon a balancing of conflicting interests, individual and social"); Prosser, *Handbook* (1st ed. 1941), § 45, p. 312.

Most courts that reconsidered duty and causation in the wake of *Palsgraf* sided with Cardozo's holistic view over Andrews' dual focus on duty and causation, but they were cautious about open acknowledgment of the relationship between duty, causation and social policy. Judges' credibility and authority depended on preserving a strong image as dispassionate interpreters, not makers of law, and a too-open acknowledgment of their policymaking role would do real damage to that image.[131] But jurists such as Prosser and Roscoe Pound continued to argue that the distinction between duty and causation was becoming artificial in an age of legal socialization, and by the 1960s, younger jurists such as Harvard law professor Robert Keeton were arguing that judges' reluctance to fully acknowledge their policymaking role, even though they were transforming tort law in many areas, was becoming counterproductive.[132]

Most courts eventually moved to a middle position: they retained duty and causation as an analytical framework but developed holistic lists of factors, many policy-oriented, that would serve as tests of whether duties had been breached and whether such breaches would be deemed a legal cause of injury. In *Biakanja v. Irving* (1958), California's supreme court developed one of the most influential lists: in determining whether a duty had been breached it would examine "the extent to which the transaction was intended to affect the plaintiff, the foreseeability of harm to him, the degree of certainty that the plaintiff suffered injury, the closeness of the connection between the defendant's conduct and the injury suffered, the moral blame attached to the defendant's conduct, and the policy of preventing future harm." Most states developed their own lists of factors, many of which were similar to the *Biakanja* list.[133]

---

131. A rare exception came in Wisconsin, whose supreme court endorsed with an unprecedented degree of frankness the connection between causation and judicial policymaking. Chief Justice Marvin Rosenberry leaned toward Andrews' view that courts must give causation equal attention with duty, but he felt that neither foreseeability nor terms such as "natural" and "probable" cause provided a useful rule of causation. In the end, said Rosenberry, "the conscience of society" must play a role in setting the limits of causation and those limits must "rest in the sound discretion of the court." *Osborne v. Montgomery*, 234 N.W. 372, 376 (Wis. 1931).

132. *See* Prosser, *Handbook* (2d ed. 1955); Harper and James, *Law of Torts*; Pound, "Causation," Leon Green, "Duties, Risks, Causation Doctrines," 42 *Tex. L. Rev.* 42 (1962); Keeton, "Judicial Law Reform—A Perspective on the Performance of Appellate Courts," 44 *Tex. L. Rev.* 1254 (1966).

133. *Biakanja*, 320 P.2d 16, 19 (Cal. 1958); *see also, e.g., Colla v. Mandella*, 85 N.W.2d 345, 348 (Wis. 1957) (a pre-*Biakanja* case that adopted a shorter list of factors). *See also* W. Jonathan Cardi, "The Hidden Legacy of *Palsgraf*: Modern Duty Law in Microcosm," 91 *B.U. L. Rev.* 1873,1878–84 (2011) (surveying the factors including in state lists); William L. Prosser, "Palsgraf Revisited," 51 *Mich. L. Rev.* 1, 12 (1953) (concluding that "[t]he state of the law...is one of troubled waters, in which anyone may fish"); Joseph W. Little, "Palsgraf Revisited (Again)," 6 *Pierce L. Rev.* 75 (2007); White, *Tort Law in America*, 96–101; William E. Nelson, "Palsgraf v, Long Island R.R.: Its Historical Context," 34 *Touro L. Rev.* 281 (2018); Kelley, "Proximate Cause," 73–80, 97–99.

Judges and Juries: An Old Struggle Takes New Forms

The fire that marked the Progressive-era debate over the proper balance of power between judges and juries died down after 1920, but it did not go out. Instead, it went down a new path: judicialists and jury defenders did not focus directly on allocation of power but considered whether American courts should adopt a comparatively new procedural device, summary judgment. Unlike nonsuits and judgments notwithstanding the verdict (JNOVs), which judges could employ only after allowing plaintiffs to present their case to the jury, summary judgment allowed judges to dispose of a case on its merits before a jury was ever impaneled. A litigant who asked for summary judgment was required to show that all facts on which the case's outcome turned were undisputed and were in its favor; the other side was then required to present evidence which, if believed by the jury, would support a decision in its favor. Unlike demurrers and nonsuits, litigants against whom a summary judgment was issued were given no opportunity to reformulate their case and try again.[134]

Because summary judgment had the potential to shift dramatically the balance of power between judges and juries, lawmakers initially approached it with great caution. When summary judgment first appeared in Great Britain in 1855, it was limited to suits for collection of amounts due on bills and promissory notes. Debtors frequently responded to such suits by denying liability even when their liability was clear, a practice that allowed them to delay and sometimes avoid payment altogether at the creditor's expense. British jurists viewed summary judgment as an innovative tool for preventing such abuses and allowing creditors to obtain quicker justice. In the 1870s, the new device was modestly expanded to include all lawsuits where the amount of plaintiff's damages was easily determined and was not truly subject to debate, and it appeared for the first time in the United States where it was adopted for limited use by Illinois (1872) and New Jersey (1873).[135]

For forty years thereafter, American lawmakers were reluctant to consider further expansion of summary judgment, perhaps because they feared that doing so would only aggravate the already contentious debate between judicialists and jury defenders. But two strains of early-twentieth century thought provided important intellectual and political underpinnings for expansion. First, Progressives believed strongly that social policies should be set by the people through their legislative representatives, but that policy details should be filled in and administered by experts. Many Progressive-era jurists, most notably Roscoe Pound, viewed tort law in similar fashion. In their view, tort cases were not so much individual exercises in justice as

---

134. *See* Robert W. Millar, *Civil Procedure of the Trial Court in Historical Perspective* (1952), 239–44, 298–99.

135. Charles E. Clark and Charles U. Samenow, "The Summary Judgment," 38 *Yale L.J.* 423, 424–25 (1929); Louis C. Ritter and Evert H. Magnuson, "The Motion for Summary Judgment and Its Extension to All Classes of Actions," 21 *Marq. L. Rev.* 33, 34–35 (1936); 18 & 19 Vict. ch. 67 (1855); *see* 1871 Ill. Laws, p. 338, §§ 36–37.

components of an ever-increasing caseload, many of which presented recurring fact situations and legal issues. Real justice could only be achieved through efficiency, and efficiency required that judges, who unlike jurors possessed legal and administrative expertise, be allowed to use their expertise to maximum effect. Summary judgment rules, if properly designed, would enable judges to dispose of unmeritorious cases swiftly and would avoid the delays and inefficiencies of jury trials. That theme was bolstered by the rising idea that causation and other parts of the tort law framework must inevitably reflect social policy choices and that judges should be allowed to state that view openly.[136]

As a result, the summary judgment movement began a new march forward during the later years of the Progressive era. New Jersey expanded its summary judgment law in 1912; Michigan and Virginia enacted omnibus summary judgment laws applying to nearly all types of lawsuits in 1915 and 1919 respectively; and in 1921, New York's highest court incorporated a summary judgment procedure more modest in scope into its rules.[137] Opponents challenged these laws, arguing that they were a judicial infringement of legislative power and of the right to trial by jury, but courts upheld the laws[138] and during the 1920s and 1930s, eleven more states adopted summary judgment rules of varying scope.[139] Summary judgment supporters, who recognized that the device was still controversial, continued to portray it as a means of reducing court congestion and downplayed its potential for shifting power to judges. Yale law professor Charles Clark, who led successful campaigns for use of summary judgment in Connecticut in the late 1920s and in the federal trial courts in the late 1930s, followed this strategy. He also argued that summary judgment would benefit plaintiffs by speeding up the justice process and that even if requests for summary judgment were denied, they would help clarify the issues to be decided at trial.[140] State courts and legislatures heeded Clark's call: by 1960, twenty states had adopted summary judgment for use in virtually all civil lawsuits, and by the 1970s it had spread throughout the nation.[141]

---

136. Stephen N. Subrin, "How Equity Conquered Common Law: The Federal Rules of Civil Procedure in Historical Perspective," 135 *U. Pa. L. Rev.* 909, 947–51 (1987); Holmes, *The Common Law*, 3, 94–95, 111–12, 122–27; Herbert Croly, *Progressive Democracy* (1914), 397.

137. 1912 N.J. Laws, ch. 380, Rules 57–60; 1915 Mich. Compiled Laws, § 12581; 1919 Va. Code Annotated, xii–xiii, c. 251, § 6046; New York Convention on Civil Practice, Rules 113–114 (1921); Clark and Samenow, "Summary Judgment," 442–48, 463–64; Ritter and Magnuson, "Motion for Summary Judgment," 34–36.

138. *Gen. Inv. Co. v. Int. R.T. Co.*, 139 N.E. 216 (N.Y. 1923); *Hanna v. Mitchell*, 139 N.E. 724 (N.Y. 1923); *Wittemann v. Giebe*, 123 A. 716 (N.J. 1924); *see also People's Wayne County Bank v. Wolverine Box Co.*, 230 N.W. 170 (Mich. 1930) (analogizing summary judgment to a directed verdict).

139. *See* Ritter and Magnuson, "Summary Judgment Motion," 38–39; Note, "Factors Affecting the Grant or Denial of Summary Judgment," 48 *Colum. L. Rev.* 780, 780 (1948).

140. Clark and Samenow, "Summary Judgment," 469–71; *see also* Subrin, "How Equity Conquered Common Law," 972–74.

141. Note, "Factors Affecting Summary Judgment," 780. During the 1940s, at least seven states enacted broad summary judgment provisions, most of which were modeled on the federal summary

Summary judgment did not immediately kill off the more traditional tools for judicial disposition of cases. A steady stream of nonsuits, directed verdicts and JNOVs continued to issue from American courts, but by 1970 their use had begun to shrink. Demurrers continued in use, but they seldom served as a case disposition tool: often, they merely forced plaintiffs to add more factual detail or revise their legal theories of recover before re-filing their lawsuits. Parties who believed their cases were so strong that the jury should not have a say were less willing to wait until trial for directed verdicts or JNOVs. They realized the value of a device that allowed for conclusive disposition of cases before trial based on a streamlined presentation of evidence, and increasingly they turned to it. Summary judgment gained ground at different paces in different states,[142] depending partly on when a state's legislature or supreme court decided to adopt the broad summary-judgment model suggested by Clark and partly on whether a state's justices encouraged or discouraged summary disposition of cases;[143] but by 1980, summary judgment was the dominant mode of case disposition short of trial.

---

judgment rule that Clark had sponsored. During the 1950s, at least thirteen states followed suit; at least eleven more followed in the 1960s and four more in the 1970s. *See* Appendix 3; *see also, e.g.*, Charles Clark, "The Federal Rules in State Practice," 23 *Rocky Mt. L. Rev.* 520 (1951) and note 143.

142. For example, the first Five-State Survey cases decided in trial courts by summary judgment appeared in Wisconsin in 1950 and in California, New York, North Carolina and Texas in 1980. *See* Appendix 2.

143. The Survey states provide an example. Wisconsin was the first to adopt a broad summary judgment statute (1940), followed by Texas (1949), New York (1963) and North Carolina (1967). Wis. Court Rules, 232 Wis. vi (1940) and 236 Wis. vi (1941); Note, "Factors Affecting Summary Judgment," 48 *Colum. L. Rev.* 780 (1948); Roy W. McDonald, "Summary Judgments," 30 *Tex. L. Rev.* 285, 285–86 (1951); Patrick M. Connors, "CPLR 3212(a)'s Timing Requirement for Summary Judgment Motions," 71 *Bklyn. L. Rev.* 1529, 1532–33, 1533 n.3 (2006); 1967 N.C. Laws, ch. 954. California adopted limited summary judgment rules in the 1920s, but its courts were more hostile to summary disposition of cases than courts of other states, and that culture did not change until the legislature adopted broader summary judgment rules in the early 1990s. *See Aguilar v. Atlantic Richfield Co.*, 24 P.3d 493 (Cal. 2001).

FIGURE 4.6
Five State Survey: Trial Court Use of Early Case Disposal Procedures, 1920–1980[144]

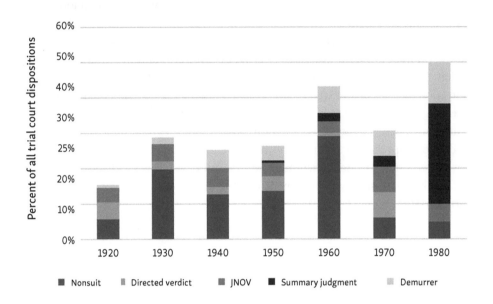

The gradual shift in preferred modes of summary disposition was not accompanied by a decrease in judicial deference to juries. During the golden age of tort socialization, trial courts and supreme courts took roughly half of all tort cases away from juries, either by summary disposition or by overturning verdicts based on procedural errors during trial—rates comparable to those of the late nineteenth century.[145] Curiously, the mild preference that nineteenth-century state supreme courts had given to defendants over plaintiffs in overturning jury and trial-court tort decisions now changed: it moved slowly but steadily toward plaintiffs from 1920 to 1960, when reversals for the first time favored plaintiffs overall, and the mild pro-plaintiff tilt continued during the next two decades.[146] The reasons for the change are not clear. The Depres-

---

144. The cases on which Figure 4.6 is based are described in Appendix 2; the calculations are described in Appendix 3.

145. Roughly 50% of all tort cases included in the Five-State Survey for 1920 were effectively taken away from the jury either by the trial court or the supreme court, either through summary disposition on the merits or granting a new trial based on procedural error. Figures for subsequent Survey years were 46 percent (1930), 50 percent (1940), 51 percent (1950), 62 percent (1960), and 53 percent (1970). The calculations are described in Appendix 3; *see also* Figure 5.3.

146. The average values for the Survey courts on the "shift" scale described in Chapter 2, ranging from –2 (strong propensity to reverse pro-plaintiff trial court decisions in favor of defendants) to +2 (strong propensity to reverse pro-defendant trial court decisions in favor of plaintiffs), were: –.402 in 1920, –.138 in 1930, –.226 in 1940 and –.123 in 1950. In 1960, the courts in the survey tilted slightly

sion may well have created some innate if unstated judicial sympathy for victims of misfortune, a sympathy which could have inclined some judges to give tort plaintiffs the benefit of the doubt more liberally than they had before. The trend may also have been influenced by the era's increasing social support for collective action to solve social problems.

By 1970, the tide of socialization in American tort law had been rising steadily for a half century. The product liability revolution was nearly complete, traditional immunities were in full retreat, and contributory negligence, although hardier, was also retreating. Many jurists and lawmakers anticipated final victory for the forces of socialization in the near future. The possibility of a no-fault auto accident system was again being raised, and a handful of scholars now spoke of a new vision in which a thoroughly socialized system of tort law would cover nearly all types of disputes involving personal injuries and property damage, including commercial transactions traditionally governed by contract law.

But resistance remained. Traditionalists complained that socialization had gone too far, and they warned of the need to preserve an element of fault and other limits and boundaries in tort law. The postwar prosperity that had made broader socialization of accident costs possible was flagging. Poverty and other social problems that had appeared ripe for solution through collective action at the end of World War II had proven more stubborn than expected, and enthusiasm for collective solutions was fraying. These forces would drive the debate between collectivists and traditionalists that has shaped tort law from 1970 to the present.

---

in favor of plaintiffs for the first time (+.114), and the pro-plaintiff tilt continued to grow steadily thereafter (+.212 in 1970 and +.217 in 1980). The exact degrees of shift varied among the Survey states, but all states except Texas followed a pro-plaintiff trend. The calculations supporting these statements are described in Appendix 3.

FIVE

Through a Glass Darkly
Tort Law in the Age of Individualism, 1970–Present

> [O]ne at least would hope that the government, through the legal system, would not actively undermine the fundamental sense of individual responsibility that is the necessary precondition for a civilized legal order.
>
> —Steven G. Calabresi and Gary Lawson (1992) [1]

At the dawn of the 1970s, as supporters of full socialization of accident costs looked to the future, they saw a glow on the legal horizon that might be the dawn of final victory. States were steadily replacing contributory negligence with comparative negligence and traditional privity defenses with strict products liability. The no-fault auto accident movement, dormant since the 1930s, had recently revived and was beginning to gain acceptance among state legislators. Yale law professor Grant Gilmore, a drafter of the Uniform Commercial Code and one of the nation's leading contract scholars, ventured that as tort law became fully socialized it would swallow contract law and traditional contract principles of individual obligation.[2] But the glow turned out to be the flames of continued fighting and stalemate, flames that have illuminated modern tort law's path.

The tragedies of three Oregonians illustrate the path's nature. One day in 1990, John Lakin of Portland used a nail gun designed to fire one nail at a time. Instead, it fired three; the second nail caused the gun to turn on Lakin and the third nail penetrated his brain, causing permanent paralysis and mental disability. How much were Lakin's non-economic damages, that is, his pain and suffering, worth? A jury awarded him $2

---

1. Calabresi and Lawson, "Symposium: Foreword: The Constitution of Responsibility," 77 *Cornell L. Rev.* 955, 957–58 (1992). Calabresi was one of the founders of the Federalist Society, discussed below.
2. Grant Gilmore, *The Death of Contract* (1974), 3, 87–88, 92–96.

million, but he now faced an obstacle. Beginning in the mid-1970s, insurers, product manufacturers and physicians had complained of skyrocketing claims and jury awards which, they argued, were jeopardizing access to vital products and services to the point of crisis.[3] Consumer groups and the plaintiffs' bar had argued that such claims were overblown, but state legislators throughout the nation had paid heed, and in 1987 Oregon's legislature had imposed a $500,000 statutory cap on non-economic damages. Lakin challenged the 1987 cap law, arguing that it deprived him of his constitutional right to have a jury decide his claim and determine his damages. Oregon's supreme court unanimously agreed. The legislature, said Justice George Van Hoomissen, had the right to create and alter torts and remedies that were not part of the common law when Oregon became a state, but it could neither limit the basic common-law right to recover damages for personal injuries nor interfere with the jury's right to determine the amount of damages in such cases.[4]

Division resurfaced twenty-five years later, when doctors at Oregon's state medical school inadvertently cut blood vessels of Lori and Steve Horton's six-month old son while removing a cancerous tumor. Because of the mistake, the Hortons' son had to undergo numerous additional surgeries and he would face special health risks for the rest of his life. A jury found the doctors negligent and awarded the boy $6 million in non-economic damages. Oregon's Tort Claims Act allowed lawsuits against state employees, but it limited non-economic damages awards to $3 million. Like Lakin, the Hortons argued that the limit violated their son's constitutional jury-trial rights. The supreme court now changed course and overruled its *Lakin* decision, even though *Lakin* had involved a different statute: the justices concluded that common-law rights, including the right to a remedy, "evolve to meet changing needs." Remedies could be altered as long as a "substantial" remedy remained, said Justice Rives Kistler, and that was the case here: the Tort Claims Act set a cap higher than those of many other states, and the disadvantage that Oregon's cap imposed on victims was offset by the assurance that they could recover from the state regardless of whether the erring state employee was solvent. Two justices dissented sharply. The majority, said Justice Martha Lee Walters, had "bargain[ed] away and belittle[d] ... constitutional provisions designed to guarantee justice for all."[5]

---

3. This chapter refers to the medical and insurance "crises" of the modern tort era. There was (and is) deep division among lawyers, jurists and judges as to whether such crises really existed, and the evidence on that point is conflicting. Using the word "crisis" with quotation marks would suggest that no true crisis existed; omitting quotation marks might suggest that it did exist. Quotation marks are omitted in this chapter for the sake of easier reading and because tort reformers were largely successful in persuading the American public that crises did exist, but the omission does not represent a conclusion that they did exist.

4. *Lakin v. Senco Prods., Inc.*, 987 P.2d 463, 467, 472–75 (Or. 1999); 1987 Or. Laws, ch. 774, § 6; Or. Const. (1857), art. I, § 17.

5. *Horton v. Or. Health and Sci. Univ.*, 376 P.3d 998 (Or. 2016), 1007, 1015–16, 1028–44 (majority), 1064, 1070 (Walters, J., dissenting); Or. Rev. Stats. § 30.271.

Four years later, Scott Busch of Portland lost his leg and was disabled for life when he was run over by a garbage truck. A jury awarded him $10.5 million in non-economic damages, but the trial judge then applied the 1987 cap law (which Oregon's legislature had never modified despite thirty-five years of inflation) and reduced the award to $500,000. This time, the reduction did not stand. Busch challenged it not as a violation of his right to a jury trial, but as violative of the remedy clause of Oregon's constitution, which provided that "every man shall have remedy by due course of law for injury done him in his person, property, or reputation."[6] Walters, now speaking for a majority of the court, agreed. The legislature might have the right to set caps, and she did not doubt that the 1987 legislature believed the cap law would make insurance more available and affordable, but under the remedy clause it could do so only if it gave accident victims something in return. Unlike the Tort Claims Act, the general cap law did not guarantee that victims would receive payment from the state, and the increased insurance availability and affordability that it supposedly provided was a benefit given to all Oregonians, not just Busch. Justice Jack Landau, who had sided with the majority in *Horton*, now openly regretted his vote to overturn *Lakin*. In his view, Oregon's law of remedies was "a mess" that produced inconsistent results for similarly situated plaintiffs, and he called for comprehensive legislative reform.[7]

The themes that run through Oregon's debate over caps and remedies—judicial division and changes of course as to the constitutionality of reform measures, debate as to the proper boundary between legislative and judicial authority, repeated legislative tinkering with the details of reform, and conflicting evidence of whether reforms limiting socialization of accident costs are effective or even desirable—have recurred throughout the modern era of American tort law. These themes have been shaped by larger social and economic forces. Many of the currents that encouraged socialization of tort law during the mid-twentieth century changed course after 1970. The dominant position that America enjoyed in the world economy after World War II, a position that enabled it to fund socialization of accident costs, slowly eroded as Europe, China, Japan and the Middle Eastern oil states regained economic strength. Many of the social welfare programs enacted under presidents Lyndon Johnson (1963–69) and Richard Nixon (1969–74) were slow to produce results and came to be viewed by many as expensive failures, and Americans' trust in government and collective action as a means of solving social problems also eroded.[8]

These currents became intertwined with a resurgence of free-labor sentiment, emphasizing the importance of individual responsibility, that had long played a central role in tort law, and with a broader social struggle between advocates of "expressive

---

6. *Busch v. McInnis Waste Sys., Inc.*, 468 P.3d 319 (Or. 2020); Or. Const. (1857), art. I, § 10.
7. *Busch*, 468 P.3d at 434 (concurring opinion).
8. *See* James T. Patterson, *Restless Giant: The United States from Watergate to Bush v. Gore* (2005), 47–52, 69–75, 81–83, 167–70; Kyle Formbry, ed., *The War on Poverty: A Retrospective* (2014), xi-xxi; Anneliese Orlock and Lisa Gayle Hazirjian, *The War On Poverty: A New Grassroots History 1964-1980* (2011), 437–56.

individualism"—an expanded notion of liberty as freedom to express one's individuality nearly without limit, one which first took deep hold in American culture in the 1960s—and their opponents, who adhered to a more traditional view of liberty as freedom to act and debate within a broad but finite universe of shared social norms.[9] Since the 1970s, several movements have arisen with the shared goal of restoring individual responsibility to a more powerful role in tort law and moderating cost socialization, including movements to modify comparative negligence by limiting defendants' joint and several liability to accident victims; to limit liability for medical malpractice and damages awards; and to limit the scope of strict products liability. These movements have been collectively, and loosely, referred to as "tort reform."[10] The resurrection of free-labor principles and the struggle between expressive individualism and traditionalism have produced a modest trimming of socialization in tort law and a firm refusal to extend it further.

Another, less-recognized current is the changing nature of tort litigation in the modern era. Early American tort law coincided with the rise of railroads and was heavily shaped by railroad accident cases; the ensuing era coincided with the maturing of America's industrial revolution and was shaped by workplace accident cases and the debate over transition to workers compensation systems. America entered the auto age as workers compensation took workplace injuries out of the tort system, and automobile-accident cases made up the largest share of tort cases during the mid-twentieth century.[11] Auto use and auto accidents continued to increase after 1970, but auto cases lost their dominant place in tort law for several reasons. First, auto insurance coverage became increasingly common after World War II. By the late 1970s, most states required auto owners to carry accident insurance and the vast majority of accident claims were settled without litigation.[12] Second, after 1960 many states created intermediate appellate courts in order to ease the burden that the ever-expanding number

---

9. *See, e.g.,* Daniel T. Rodgers, *The Age of Fracture* (2011); Lawrence M. Friedman, *Crime and Punishment in American History* (1993), 12–13; Naomi Cahn and June Carbone, *Red Families v. Blue Families: Legal Polarization and the Creation of Culture* (2010), 66–68. The struggle over expressive individualism has shaped the law in areas as diverse as the movement to expand gay Americans' civil rights, the battle over abortion and reproductive choice and the movement to for government funding of private schools. Joseph A. Ranney, *Wisconsin and the Shaping of American Law* (2017), 194–212.

10. *See* Thomas F. Burke, *Lawyers, Lawsuits and Legal Rights: The Battle Over Litigation in American Society* (2002), 2–3, 27–32; F. Patrick Hubbard, "The Nature and Impact of the Tort Reform Movement," 35 *Hofstra L. Rev.* 437, 438–45, 475–80 (2006); Sandra F. Gavin, "Stealth Tort Reform," 42 *Valparaiso U. L. Rev.* 431 (2008).

11. *See* Chapter 2, Figure 2.1; Chapter 4, Figure 4.1; and the text accompanying each figure.

12. Nora Freeman Engstrom, "An Alternative Explanation for No-Fault's 'Demise,'" 61 *DePaul L. Rev.* 303, 365–67 (2012). In 1925, Massachusetts became the first state to enact a compulsory insurance law; after several decades of inactivity, New York followed suit in 1956, and a wave of compulsory-insurance laws followed in the 1960s and 1970s. *See, e.g.,* 1925 Mass. Laws, ch. 346; *Bookbinder v. Hults,* 192 N.Y.S. 331 (N.Y. S.Ct. 1959); 1957 N.C. Laws, ch. 1393.

of appeals imposed on their supreme courts.[13] Supreme courts were now allowed to choose the cases they would hear, and most have exercised that power fully. They have limited themselves to a select mix of tort cases presenting novel and important issues, a mix in which professional malpractice, product liability and disputes over recovery of economic losses have featured prominently.[14]

FIGURE 5.1
Five-State Survey: Types of Tort Cases, 1970–2010[15]

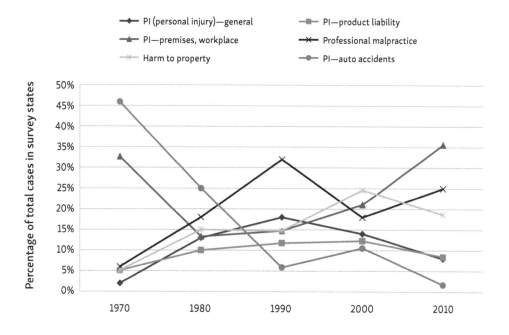

The Big Four of Tort Reform

Advocacy organizations have become a prominent feature of the modern tort-law landscape, but the actual extent of their influence on tort law's evolution is not clear. Prior to 1970, American businesses generally confined their lobbying efforts

---

13. A few states created intermediate courts in the nineteenth and early twentieth centuries, but most were created in the late twentieth century. At least twenty-two states created such courts between 1963 and 1996. John P. Doerner and Christine A. Markman, *The Role of State Intermediate Appellate Courts: Principles for Adapting to Change* (2012), 2–4.

14. For example, the Five-State Survey courts decided an average of 67 tort cases per court in 1940, 58 in 1950, 43 in 1960, 19 in 1970, 12 in 1980, 7 in 1990, 10 in 2000 and 11 in 2010. *See* Appendix 2. Three of the Survey states created intermediate courts before the 1960s: Texas (1892), New York (1895) and California (1905), but their supreme courts also reduced their caseloads after 1960. North Carolina and Wisconsin created their intermediate courts in 1967 and 1977 respectively.

15. The cases on which Figure 5.1 is based are described in Appendix 2; the calculations are described in Appendix 3.

to government contracts and other matters that directly affected their interests. After 1970 they began to focus on broader social and economic legislation as well, partly in reaction to the rising tide of cost socialization and expressive individualism that had marked the 1960s.[16] Four organizations, collectively referred to as the "Big Four" in this book, have been particularly influential in tort-reform debates: the American Legislative Exchange Council (ALEC), the American Tort Reform Association (ATRA), the U.S. Chamber of Commerce, and the Federalist Society.

ALEC was formed in 1973 to develop and promote business-friendly state laws. From the beginning it was highly successful, gaining numerous corporate sponsors and eventually attracting nearly one-quarter of all state legislators to its membership. Beginning in the 1990s, ALEC drafted a series of model laws to limit socialization of accident costs.[17] ATRA was formed in 1984, at the height of the mid-1980s insurance crisis, and has focused almost exclusively on tort reform. ATRA has done little law-drafting, but it has actively promoted laws limiting socialization of accident costs. It has encouraged sympathetic lawyers and academics to promote such laws through litigation and favorable articles and books, and it has systematically identified and praised legislatures and courts that have helped its campaign and has denounced those that have not.[18]

The Federalist Society was founded in 1982, primarily by conservative law students and academics who believed that expressive individualism posed a serious threat to liberty and property rights and feared that it would eventually dominate American law. The Society has consistently disclaimed any role as an advocacy group and has not engaged in law-drafting, but it has helped its members promote a variety of reforms ranging from restriction of government's ability to take private property for public use to limitation of administrative agencies' regulatory power, of abortion rights and of racial affirmative action. The Society has also been active in promoting tort reform, most notably by providing support for President George W. Bush's unsuccessful effort to enact federal limits on medical-malpractice damage awards.[19] In 1998, the U.S. Chamber of Commerce entered the tort-reform arena when it formed the Institute for Legal Reform (ILR). Like ATRA, the Chamber has not engaged in law-drafting but it has heavily publicized the need for tort reform, consistently sounding the theme that a

---

16. Burke, *Lawyers, Lawsuit and Legal Rights*, 23–24; Hubbard, "Tort Reform Movement," 438–40; see also Tim Cullen, *Ringside Seat: Wisconsin Politics: The 1970s to Scott Walker* (2015), 212–13 (describing business's increasing involvement in Wisconsin politics).

17. See ALEC's website, at www.alec.org/model-policy/; Jay M. Feinman, *Un-Making Law: The Conservative Campaign to Roll Back the Common Law* (2004), 177–80.

18. Burke, *Lawyers, Lawsuit and Legal Rights,* 29–30; Feinman, *Un-Making Law*, 35, 175–76; Hubbard, "Tort Reform Movement," 472–80, 513–15; see also ATRA's website, www.atra.org/about.

19. Michael Avery and Danielle McLaughlin, *The Federalist Society: How Conservatives Took the Law Back from Liberals* (2013), 1–9, 17–37, 47–50, 71–89; Steven M. Teles, *The Rise of the Conservative Legal Movement: The Battle for Control of the Law* (2008); Feinman, *Un-Making Law*, 183–86; Calabresi and Lawson, "Constitution of Responsibility," 956–58.

tort system overly friendly to plaintiffs is harmful to America's economy. The Chamber has advanced this theme primarily through symposia and publications designed to reach lawmakers and local business leaders. It regularly identifies states with tort law systems deemed friendly and hostile to business, praising the former and denouncing the latter.[20]

In recent years, the Big Four have received substantial publicity, not all of it positive. In 2011, Wisconsin enacted a law dramatically reducing public-employee unions' collective bargaining rights, a law that encountered fierce opposition, polarized the state and triggered national controversy. Opponents of the law believed its drafters had used ALEC model laws as a resource; they examined ALEC's array of model laws and the extent to which American state legislatures had enacted such laws, and ultimately portrayed ALEC as a behind-the-scenes orchestrator of state laws. In 2012, ALEC drew unfavorable attention for promoting a "stand your ground" law that a Florida gun owner successfully invoked to gain acquittal after he shot Trayvon Martin, an unarmed black teenager. ALEC responded by cutting back its involvement with social issues, but its tort reform efforts continued.[21] The Federalist Society's role in federal government during Republican administrations, particularly its role as an incubator of conservative lawmakers and its influence over Department of Justice policies and selection of federal judges, attracted substantial attention during George W. Bush's and Donald Trump's presidencies. As a result, the Society has increasingly been perceived as a political organization despite its protestations to the contrary.[22]

The Big Four have emphasized free-labor individual responsibility, economic efficiency, and traditionalism as cornerstones of their philosophy. They have argued that tort reform promotes individual freedom and autonomy; that broad socialization of accident costs impedes economic growth; and that lawmakers should resist

---

20. Feinman, *Un-Making Law*, 35, 175–76; *see also* ILR's website, www.instituteforlegalreform.com/about.

21. Jason Stein and Patrick Marley, *More Than They Bargained For: Scott Walker, Unions and the Fight for Wisconsin* (2013), 35–39; Cullen, *Ringside Seat, passim;* as to investigation of ALEC, *see, e.g.,* John Nichols, "ALEC Exposed," *Nation,* July 12, 2011; Lisa M. Graves, "ALEC Exposed: The Koch Connection," *Nation,* July 12, 2011; Nancy Schola, "Exposing ALEC: How Conservative-Backed State Laws Are All Connected," *The Atlantic,* April 14, 2012; Brendan Fischer, "Koch-Funded Mackinac Center Brings Wisconsin Act 10 Provisions to ALEC," Center for Media and Democracy, PR Watch (May 1, 2012); Center for Media and Democracy, "ALEC Exposed," viewable at www.alecexposed.org; Molly Jackman, "ALEC's Influence Over Lawmaking in State Legislatures," Brookings Inst. (Dec. 6, 2013), viewable at www.brookings.edu/articles/alecs-influence-over-lawmaking-in-state-legislatures/; Eric Lichtblau, "Martin Death Spurs Group to Readjust Policy Focus," *N.Y. Times,* April 17, 2012.

22. Avery and McLaughlin, *Federalist Society,* 31–38. Other organizations have played important but less enduring roles in the tort-reform movement. For example, in the 1980s and 1990s the Manhattan Institute supported academic work of Peter Huber and Walter Olson who published, respectively, *Liability: The Legal Revolution and Its Consequences* (1988) and *The Litigation Explosion* (1991). The authors and their books received wide attention and played an influential role in state and federal tort-reform efforts in the mid-1990s. See Burke, *Lawyers, Lawsuits and Legal Rights,* 45.

"newfangled" concepts of liability, such as efforts to expand property owners' legal responsibilities to persons coming on their property without permission. Their traditionalist allies have argued that the "headlong pursuit of safety," litigation and socialization of accident costs are "killing off...the "simple pleasures of life" and replacing them with a law of "ad hoc plebiscite, applied retrospectively on whatever theory anyone cares to invent...changeable from jury to jury." In response to socialization advocates' focus on full compensation of accident victims, ALEC has urged the public to redirect its empathy toward those who are asked to pay, arguing that they too are victims when asked to pay more than their fair share.[23]

New Battles Over Comparative Negligence: Joint and Several Liability

By 1970, state legislatures and courts were steadily shifting from contributory negligence to comparative negligence. Five states had done so during the 1960s, and an additional thirty-three would follow during the 1970s and early 1980s. Contributory negligence's core principle, that persons who contributed in any way to their own injury should bear the entire responsibility, was being decisively rejected; but comparative negligence was not a conclusive victory for accident cost socialization. All agreed that *some* element of personal responsibility should be preserved: at a minimum, a victim's recovery should be reduced in proportion to her own fault, and among the states that adopted comparative negligence, nearly two-thirds enacted diluted systems reflecting a belief that victims who were primarily or equally at fault with others in causing an accident should recover nothing.[24]

Adoption of comparative negligence raised several collateral questions, including aggregation: in cases involving multiple defendants, should the plaintiff's negligence should be compared to each defendant's individual negligence or to their negligence lumped together, which would increase plaintiffs' chances of recovery in diluted systems? As described in the previous chapter, Wisconsin, the first state to adopt a diluted system, rejected aggregation in 1934 but three decades later Arkansas, another early

---

23. *See, e.g.*, Philip K. Howard, *The Collapse of the Common Good: How America's Lawsuit Culture Undermines Our Freedom* (2001), 4, 31; Amy Kjose Anderson, *The State Legislator's Guide: Tort Reform Boot Camp* (2011), 13–14; Amy Kjose Anderson, *Lawsuit Reform for Competitive State Economies* (2013). Anderson is an ALEC official. See also ALEC's and ATRA's websites, www.alec.org/about and www.atra.org.issues.

24. See Figure 4.3 and accompanying text. Four states (Alabama, Maryland, North Carolina and Virginia) retained contributory negligence; two (Nebraska and South Dakota) retained contributory negligence except in cases where a defendant was grossly negligent. Arthur Best, "Impediments to Reasonable Tort Reform: Lessons from the Adoption of Comparative Negligence," 40 *Ind. L. Rev.* 1, 18–22 (2007).

adopter, endorsed it.[25] Courts that have ruled on the issue during the modern era have generally favored aggregation, as have legislatures that have spoken on the subject.[26]

In the early 1980s, debate arose over an issue closely related to aggregation: the doctrine of joint and several liability (JSL), which held that any defendant found liable for damages was responsible for the shares of liability and damages of all other defendants found liable. JSL had become well entrenched during the age of contributory negligence precisely because contributory negligence rejected socialization of accident costs: if a plaintiff was at fault in any way, no defendant was responsible for his loss, but if he was not at fault, each defendant who was at fault in any way should be held responsible for the full loss. The JSL doctrine was seldom challenged during the nineteenth and early twentieth centuries. In situations where more than one person contributed to a victim's injury, most states required the victim to file separate lawsuits against each defendant; thus, trial judges were seldom forced to consider whether liability should be apportioned among them. If a plaintiff prevailed against multiple defendants in separate lawsuits, the defendants could work out allocation of the cost among themselves, although American courts were slow to create a legal right of contribution among defendants. But even after states began to revise their rules in the 1920s to allow multi-defendant lawsuits, courts reflexively clung to JSL because it reflected still-prevalent contributory negligence principles.[27]

The rise of comparative negligence called for jurists and lawmakers to reconsider JSL, but reconsideration came slowly. Mississippi and Wisconsin did not feel a need to change JSL when they first instituted comparative negligence: both states' supreme courts declined to use their common-law powers to that end.[28] Critics argued that JSL was inconsistent with comparative negligence's embrace of proportional liability, but defenders pointed out that eliminating JSL could produce unjust results—for example, in cases where defendants who were found primarily liable enjoyed statutory immunity or were insolvent, which effectively shifted their portion of the loss back to

---

25. *Walker v. Kroger Groc. & Baking Co.*, 252 N.W. 721 (Wis. 1934); *Walton v. Tull*, 356 S.W.2d 20 (Ark. 1962). Some states that rejected aggregation as a general rule eventually allowed it in limited circumstances, most notably where two or more defendants had acted in concert (that is, had coordinated their harmful acts) or where the law made one defendant automatically liable for the acts of another (for example, by imposing vicarious liability on employers for their workers' employment-related acts). *See, e.g., Reber v. Hanson*, 51 N.W.2d 505 (Wis. 1952); *see also Miss. Riv. Fuel Corp. v. Senn*, 43 S.W.2d 255 (Ark. 1931) (a pre-*Walton* case).

26. *See* J. Evans and A.M Swarthout, "Comparative Negligence Rule Where Misconduct of Three or More Persons Is Involved," 8 A.L.R.3d 722 (1966, rev. 2021) and authorities there cited; *Mt. Mobile Mix, Inc. v. Gifford*, 660 P.2d 882, 886–87 (Colo. 1983) (adopting aggregation rule and collecting cases and statutes on both sides).

27. Robert S. Peck, "The Development of the Law of Joint and Several Liability," 55 *Fed. Def. and Corp. Counsel Q.* 469, 470–73 (Summer 2005); NCCUSL, Draft, *Uniform Apportionment of Tort Responsibility Act* (2002), 2–3; Larry Pressler and Kevin V. Schieffer, "Joint and Several Liability: A Case for Reform," 64 *Denv. U. L. Rev.* 651, 655–56 (1988).

28. *Nelson v. Ill. Cent. R. Co.*, 53 So. 619 (Miss.1910); *Walker*, 252 N.W. at 728.

the victim.[29] As comparative negligence took hold, a new source of support for change emerged. Insurance companies experienced temporary downturns in profits during the mid-1970s and mid-1980s and raised their premiums sharply in order to rebalance their books; they characterized these downturns as a crisis caused in part by the burden that JSL imposed on defendants whose fault was minor but who had insurance and, thus, ended up paying insolvent co-defendants' portion of liability.[30]

Jurists and legislators took heed. In 1978, Kansas became the first state to abolish traditional JSL in favor of a limited-JSL rule, under which defendants would be liable for each other's negligence only if they acted in concert. During the 1980s, thirty other states abolished or modified JSL, most during 1986 and 1987 when Congressional hearings prompted by the insurers' cries of crisis attracted nationwide publicity.[31] A smaller wave of change followed during a new insurance crisis in 1994–95, as nine states either addressed JSL for the first time or adjusted earlier reform laws.[32] But the move away from JSL was a cautious one: most states preserved fragments of JSL rather than abandon it altogether. Four main fragments survived: "threshold" JSL, typically allowing application of joint and several liability to defendants found more than fifty percent at fault; "types of harm" JSL, applicable to defendants who improperly disposed of hazardous waste; "moral limits" JSL, applicable to defendants who acted maliciously or recklessly; and continuing application of JSL to defendants who acted in concert.[33] Since 1990, JSL reforms have occasionally faced constitutional challenges, but nearly all of the challenges have failed: courts have generally deferred to legisla-

---

29. *See, e.g., Am. Motorcycle Assn. v. Sup. Ct.*, 578 P.2d 899, 906 (Cal. 1978) (stating that "abandonment of the joint and several liability rule would work a serious and unwarranted deleterious effect on the practical ability of negligently injured persons to receive adequate compensation for their injuries"); *Rosevink v. Faris*, 342 N.W.2d 845 (Iowa 1983) (same); Richard Wright, "Allocating Liability Among Multiple Responsible Causes: A Principled Defense of Joint and Several Liability for Actual Harm and Risk Exposure," 21 *U.C. Davis L. Rev.* 1141 (1988); Aaron D. Twerski, "The Joint Tortfeasor Legislative Revolt: A Rational Response to the Critics," 22 *U.C. Davis L. Rev.* 1125, 1127–39 (1989).

30. Pressler and Schieffer, "A Case for Reform," 654–55; Twerski, "Joint Tortfeasor Legislative Revolt," 1127–39; Jonathan Cardi, "Apportioning Responsibility to Immune Nonparties: An Argument Based on Comparative Responsibility and the Proposed Restatement (Third) of Torts," 82 *Iowa L. Rev.* 1293, 1300–04 (1997). One United States senator (Larry Pressler, a South Dakota Republican), concluded after participating in Congressional hearings on tort reform in the mid-1980s that there was "insufficient evidence" to support any of the competing theories as to whether a genuine crisis existed, but that "at the very least it appears that the [insurance] industry is taking advantage of the 'crisis' in its push for reform and using it to deflect criticisms of its own contribution to the problem." Pressler and Schieffer, "A Case for Reform," 654 n. 12.

31. *Brown v. Keill*, 580 P.2d 867 (Kan. 1978); Pressler and Schieffer, "Case for Reform," 656–59; *Restatement (Third) of Torts: Apportionment of Liability* (2000), § 17, pp. 147–58.

32. *Restatement (Third) of Torts: Apportionment of Liability*, § 17, pp. 147–59.

33. Ibid.; Peck, "Development of the Law," 474–75; Cardi, "Apportioning Responsibility," 1302–06.

tures' broad power to create and modify tort law, and have concluded that limiting JSL is reasonable and does not violate constitutional equal-protection guarantees.[34]

The Big Four have played a meaningful but ultimately not a decisive role in shaping comparative-negligence and JSL reform. In 1995, ALEC prepared model laws accepting comparative negligence in its most diluted form, the 49-percent model; limiting JSL to defendants who acted in concert; and requiring juries to apportion negligence among all persons involved in an accident whether or not they were impleaded as parties.[35] ALEC's model comparative-negligence law is conservative but is not an outlier: several states had adopted a 49-percent model before ALEC proposed it,[36] and in 2002 the National Conference of Commissioners on Uniform State Laws (NCCUSL), an influential nonpartisan group, endorsed a model JSL act similar to ALEC's in some respects.[37] Most states have preserved more of JSL than the single fragment advocated by ALEC, and the wide variation in state JSL laws shows that none of the Big Four has been able to orchestrate anything approaching lockstep among state lawmakers. It appears that legislators have listened to both the Big Four and JSL supporters but have created customized laws based on local politics and economics.[38] The Big Four's efforts to change JSL continue, and perhaps will produce additional fruit in the future.

Medical Malpractice: An Unlikely Flash Point

Medical malpractice claims have played a role in tort reform debates far out of proportion to their economic importance and their modest share of space on modern-era court dockets. Malpractice suits were rare in the nineteenth century, a time when malpractice insurance was not available, medicine was an uncertain science and physicians had closer personal relationships with patients than they do today. Those constraints on litigation began to erode in the 1920s as malpractice insurance

---

34. Decisions upholding JSL reforms include *Church v. Rawson Drug & Sundry Co.*, 842 P.2d 1355 (Ariz. App. 1992) and *Unzicker v. Kraft Foods Corp.*, 783 N.E.2d 1024 (Ill. 2002). In 2006 Pennsylvania's supreme struck down a JSL reform law on the technical ground that it had been improperly combined into one bill with legislation on another subject, but the legislature subsequently enacted a new law which cured the defect. *Deweese v. Weaver*, 880 A.2d 54 (Pa. Cmwlth. 2005), *aff'd without opinion*, 906 A.2d 1193 (Pa. 2006); 2011 Pa. Laws, ch. 17.

35. Anderson, *Tort Reform Boot Camp*, 4–5. The model laws are posted on ALEC's website: see www.alec.org/model-policy/comparative-fault-act and www.alec.org/model-policy/joint-and-several-liability-act. ATRA has not published a model act but it advocates abolition of joint and several liability on its website. See www.atra.org/issue/joint-several-liability.

36. *See, e.g.*, 1931 Wis,. Laws, ch. 242; 1971 Idaho Laws, ch. 186; 1974 Kan. Laws, ch. 239; 1992 Neb. Laws, ch. 262.

37. The NCCUSL model law limits apportionment of negligence to those persons whom a plaintiff sued or settled with and preserves JSL by requiring that negligence of insolvent defendants be reallocated to solvent defendants. NCCUSL, *Uniform Apportionment of Tort Responsibility Act* (2002), §§ 5–6; *see also* NCCUSL, *Uniform Comparative Fault Act* (1977), § 2.

38. *See* notes 31–34 above and accompanying text; *see also* Twerski, "Joint Tortfeasor Legislative Revolt," 1127–28, 1131–32.

became widely available, physician-patient contacts became less personal as a result of specialization and increased health-care demand, and advances in public health and medicine raised patient expectations. Insurers' power over medical payments and treatment decisions grew steadily, aided by the American Medical Association's decision to oppose a nationalized health-care system in the late 1940s, by the postwar proliferation of employer-sponsored health insurance, and by the advent of managed-care programs.[39]

Malpractice insurance premiums were volatile from the beginning. Insurers depended on premiums and investment income to pay administrative expenses and malpractice claims. Some states and trade organizations required insurers to invest the bulk of their assets in high-grade bonds, and fluctuations in the bond market regularly produced dramatic, if temporary, reductions in income which in turn required premium increases that physicians could not always pass on to patients. Malpractice litigation grew during the 1960s, and many physicians and insurers increasingly perceived litigation as part of the problem. In 1973, as premiums spiked, the federal Department of Health, Education and Welfare warned that future bond-market downturns could limit the availability of health care and suggested that imposing legal limits on claims might be a partial solution.[40] Insurers and physicians labeled the mid-1970s premium spike a crisis; that label resonated with lawmakers and other Americans worried about health-care availability, and it prompted a wave of laws cabining medical malpractice claims. The wave subsided in the late 1970s but returned with new bond-market downturns in the mid-1980s, mid-1990s and mid-2000s.[41]

The crisis-driven laws took a variety of forms, including general caps on damages awards; caps limited to non-economic damages; elimination of the collateral-source rule, which prohibited reduction of damages awards by amounts that insurers and others paid on the victim's behalf; shortened deadlines for filing malpractice claims; heightened proof requirements for plaintiffs; and limits on the amount of contingent fees plaintiffs' lawyers could collect. The Big Four played an active role in advocating these measures: ALEC prepared several model laws incorporating the reforms, and it and ATRA promoted the reforms heavily on their websites and in educational efforts.[42]

---

39. Kenneth S. Abraham, *The Liability Century: Insurance and Tort Law from the Progressive Era to 9/11* (2008), 104–121.

40. Abraham, *Liability Century*, 108–22.

41. Kevin J. Gfell, "The Constitutional and Economic Implications of a National Cap on Non-Economic Damages in Medical Malpractice Actions," 37 *Ind. L. Rev.* 773, 776–77 (2004); Abraham, *Liability Century*, 121–22, 136–37; Joseph Sanders and Craig Joyce, "Off to the Races: The 1980s Tort Crisis and the Law Reform Process," 27 *Hous. L. Rev.* 437, 211–23 (1990); Ronen Avraham, *Database of State Tort Law Reforms (Version 6.1)*, available at https://law.utexas.edu/faculty/ravraham/dstlr.php.

42. Sanders and Joyce, "Off to the Races," 217–23, 259–63; Hubbard, "Tort Reform Movement," 475-79; *see also* Avraham, *Database*. For statements regarding these reforms and ALEC model acts, *see, e.g.*, www.atra.org/issues; www.alec.org/issue; www.alec.org/model-policy/joint-and-several-

Nearly all of the malpractice reforms were controversial, but caps on non-economic damages attracted the most attention. The malpractice insurance crisis was effectively a fight over socialization of accident costs, and caps were a direct blow against socialization. Because the value of pain and suffering could not be objectively measured, the debate over non-economic damage caps was based as much on emotion as reason. Traditionalists took the view that suffering was an inevitable part of life and should be borne individually, that Americans were becoming too litigious, and that juries were taking advantage of non-economic damages' subjectivity to compensate plaintiffs excessively and punish wealthy defendants. ATRA, the insurance industry and the Reagan-era U.S. Department of Justice gave high priority to capping non-economic damages in both medical-malpractice and other tort cases.[43] The first cap laws were enacted in 1975, and the ensuing waves of proclaimed crisis in the mid-1980s, mid-1990s and mid-2000s produced additional cap laws. Approximately thirty-five states enacted non-economic damage caps,[44] but a significant number of states never did, often because their constitutions effectively prohibited caps. At least one state, Texas, amended its constitution to allow caps on damages.[45]

As experience with litigation under the cap laws accumulated, academics and think tanks made empirical studies of whether caps and other liability-limiting laws were effective in controlling health-care costs and ensuring an adequate supply of physicians. Collectively, the studies were inconclusive. Several, including an influential RAND Institute study and a survey of Texas personal-injury lawyers, indicated that caps and laws abolishing the collateral-source rule were somewhat effective in reducing malpractice-related awards,[46] but other studies, including a 2006 Congressional

---

liability act; www.alec.org/model-policy/legal-consumer-bill-of-rights-act; www.alec.org/model-policy/ten-year-statute-of-repose-act; Anderson, *Tort Reform Boot Camp*, 8–14, 30–37.

43. Hubbard, "Tort Reform Movement," 475–79; Avery and McLaughlin, *Federalist Society*, 8–9.

44. Caps first appeared in California (1975 Cal. Laws, 2d Ex. Sess., ch. 2); South Dakota (1976 S.D. Laws, ch. 154); and Ohio (1976 Ohio Laws, p. 3843). Sixteen other states enacted caps between 1985 and 1988 (Alabama, Missouri, West Virginia, Alaska, Colorado, Florida, Hawaii, Kansas, Massachusetts, Maryland, Minnesota, New Hampshire, Idaho, Oregon, Utah and Wisconsin); six states enacted caps between 1995–97 (Illinois, Maine, Montana, North Dakota and Michigan); and six states enacted caps between 2003 and 2006 (Mississippi, Nevada, Oklahoma, Texas, Georgia and South Carolina). See Avraham, *Database*.

45. *See, e.g.,* New York Const. (1894), art. I, § 16 (prohibiting enactment of laws limiting personal-injury damages); Wyoming Const. (1890), art. X, § 4 (same); Utah Const. (1896), art. XVI, § 5 (same, but limited to wrongful-death lawsuits); Ariz. Const. (1912), art. II, § 31 (same). *See also Lucas v. U.S.*, 757 S.W.2d 687 (Tex. 1988) (striking down 1986 cap as violative of provision guaranteeing remedy for wrongs); Tex. Const. (2003), art. III, § 66 (2003 amendment authorizing enactment of damages caps); 2003 Tex. Laws, ch. 204 (enacting new cap); Robert S. Peck and Hartley Hampton, "A Challenge Too Early: The Lawsuit to Invalidate Texas Damages Caps Ten Years Ago and Its Likely Future Vindication," 51 *Tex. Tech L. Rev.* 667 (2019).

46. *See, e.g.,* Nicholas M. Pace et al., RAND Institute for Civil Justice, "Capping Non-Economic Awards in Medical Malpractice Trials: California Jury Verdicts Under MICRA" (2004); Stephen Daniels and Joanne Martin, "The Strange Success of Tort Reform," 53 *Emory L.J.* 1225 (2004); Daniels and Martin, "Where Have All the Cases Gone: The Strange Success of Tort Reform Revisited,"

Budget Office study, cast doubt on that conclusion. Nearly all studies concluded that other types of limiting laws had little effect.[47]

Caps frequently elicited constitutional challenges, and they proved controversial among judges. Challengers most commonly argued that caps violated constitutional rights to trial by jury and due process of law because they effectively nullified jury awards that exceeded the cap; that they violated the right to equal protection of the law by discriminating against badly-injured plaintiffs whose damages exceeded the cap; and that they were an impermissible legislative incursion on judges' common-law power to review damage awards. Cap defenders replied that legislatures had long had broad power to create and modify tort law; that the cap laws fell within legislatures' police power to promote public safety and welfare; that caps were a reasonable means of meeting the malpractice insurance crisis, which was genuine, and ensuring an adequate supply of physicians; and that the inherently uncertain value of pain and suffering blunted any concern that non-economic damage caps would work an injustice to plaintiffs.

The first challenges to caps on non-economic damages appeared in Indiana and California in the early 1980s. They failed: both states' supreme courts deferred to their legislatures' judgments that a crisis existed and that caps were a reasonable if not a proven antidote.[48] But during 1988–89, five state supreme courts struck down cap laws.[49] Five more courts, including Oregon's, followed suit during the early 1990s,[50] although other challenges during that decade failed.[51]

Successful challenges elicited varying reactions from lawmakers and voters. Some legislatures enacted new caps, adjusted to meet their courts' concerns. Some of the

---

65 *Emory L.J.* 1445 (2016). Studies in the field are listed and discussed in detail in Scott DeVito and Andrew W. Jurs, "Doubling Down for Defendants: The Pernicious Effects of Tort Reform," 118 *Penn St. L. Rev.* 543, 546–48, 555–67 (2014).

47. *See, e.g.,* Catherine M. Sharkey, "Unintended Consequences of Medical Malpractice Damages Caps," 80 *NYU L. Rev.* 391 (2005); Congressional Budget Office Publication No. 2668, *Medical Malpractice Tort Limits and Health Care Spending* (2006); RAND Institute, "Capping Non-Economic Awards"; DeVito and Jurs, "Doubling Down," 555–67.

48. *Johnson v. St. Vincent Hosp., Inc.,* 404 N.E.2d 585 (Ind. 1980); *Fein v. Permanente Med. Group,* 695 P.2d 665 (Cal. 1985).

49. *Kan. Malpractice Victims Coalition v. Bell,* 757 P.2d 251 (Kan. 1988); *Richardson v. Carnegie Lib. Rest.,* 763 P.2d 1153 (N.M. 1988); *Lucas v. U.S.,* 757 S.W.2d 687 (Tex. 1988); *Condemarin v. Univ. Hosp.,* 775 P.2d 348 (Utah 1989); *Sofie v. Fibreboard Corp.,* 771 P.2d 711 (Wash. 1989).

50. *Brannigan v. Usitaio,* 587 A.2d 1232 (N.H. 1991); *Morris v. Savoy,* 576 N.E.2d 765 (Ohio 1991); *Smith v. Dept. of Ins.,* 507 So.2d 1080 (Fla. 1993); *Lakin,* 987 P.2d 463 (Or. 1993); *Smith v. Schulte,* 671 So.2d 1334 (Ala. 1995). Courts have continued to strike down caps in recent years. See, e.g., *Atlanta Oculoplastic Surg., P.C. v. Nestlehutt,* 691 S.E.2d 218 (Ga. 2010); *Watts v. Lester E. Cox Med. Centers,* 376 S.W.3d 633 (Mo. 2012); *Kalitan,* 219 So.3d 49 (Fla. 2017).

51. *Wright v. Colleton County Sch. Dist.,* 391 S.E.2d 564 (S.C. 1990); *Butler v. Flint Goodrich Hosp.,* 607 So.2d 517 (La. 1992); *Scholz v. Metro. Pathologists, P.C.,* 851 P.2d 901 (Colo. 1993); *Adams v. Children's Mercy Hosp.,* 832 S.W.2d 898 (Mo. 1993).

new caps survived renewed constitutional challenges,[52] some did not.[53] A few courts struck down caps but later changed their minds, upholding similar subsequently-enacted caps and overturning their initial decisions.[54] Several courts drew a distinction between caps on damages in wrongful-death lawsuits (in which a deceased victim's heirs or estate made claims on her behalf) and damages in other types of lawsuits. They reasoned that wrongful-death claims did not exist in the common law but were created by the legislature, which therefore could impose any restrictions it wanted, but that the common law had long recognized other types of negligence claims, which in their eyes was a bar to further legislative tinkering with such claims.[55]

Courts that have struck down caps have done so based on conclusions that caps violate constitutional rights to trial by jury, equal-protection guarantees and separation of judicial and legislative powers. A few courts have relied on distinctive state constitutional provisions, for example, Illinois's constitutional prohibition of special legislation and other states' constitutional guarantees of remedies for wrongs.[56] Judges who have voted to uphold caps have typically relied heavily on traditional rules of deference to legislative judgment; judges who have voted to strike down caps have taken a very different view. For example, in a series of cases in which Florida's supreme court struck down caps on non-economic damages in medical malpractice cases, one faction of the court argued that to "simply rubber stamp the Legislature's asserted jus-

---

52. *See Kan. Malpractice Victims Coalition*, 757 P.2d 251 (Kan. 1988) (striking down 1986 law imposing overall cap on medical-malpractice damages awards); 1986 Kan. Laws, ch. 229, 1987 Kan. Laws, ch. 176, 1988 Kan. Laws, ch. 216 (enacting non-economic damages cap); *Samsel v. Wheeler Transp. Services, Inc.*, 789 P.2d 541 (Kan. 1990) (upholding 1987 cap and stating that 1986 cap was still valid as to wrongful-death cases); *Miller v. Johnson*, 289 P.3d 1098 (Kan. 2012) (rejecting new arguments against cap).

53. Examples include **New Hampshire**: *see* 1977 N.H. Laws, ch. 417 ($250,000 non-economic damages cap); *Carson v. Maurer*, 424 A.2d 825 (1980) (striking down 1977 cap); 1986 N.H. Laws, ch. 227 ($850,000 non-economic damages cap); *Brannigan*, 587 A.2d 1232 (N.H. 1991) (striking down 1986 cap); **Florida**: *see* 1986 Fla. Laws, ch. 160 (non-economic damages cap); *Smith*, 507 So.2d 1080 (Fla. 1993) (striking down cap); 2003 Fla. Laws, ch. 416, 2011 Fla. Laws, ch. 135 (new caps); *McCall*, 134 So.3d 894 (Fla. 2014) (holding $500,000 aggregate cap on damages invalid except as to wrongful-death cases); *Kalitan*, 219 So.3d 49 (Fla. 2017) (striking down slightly modified cap); **Illinois**: 1989 Ill. Laws, ch. 7 ($500,000 non-economic damages cap); *Best v. Taylor Mach. Works*, 689 N.E.2d 1057 (Ill. 1997) (striking down 1989 cap); 1994 Ill. Laws, ch. 677 ($500,000 cap for physicians, $1 million cap for hospitals); *Lebron v. Gottlieb Mem. Hosp.*, 930 N.E.2d 895 (Ill. 2010) (striking down 1994 cap).

54. *See Ferdon v. Wis. Patients Comp. Fund*, 701 N.W.2d 440 (Wis. 2005); *Mayo v. Wis. Injured Patients & Families Comp. Fund*, 914 N.W.2d 678 (Wis. 2018) (overruling *Ferdon*); *Lakin*, 987 P.2d 463 (Or. 1993); *Horton*, 376 P.2d 998 (Or. 2016) (overruling *Lakin*).

55. *See, e.g., Samsel*, 789 P.2d 541 (Kan. 1990); *McCall*, 134 So.3d 894 (Fla. 2014); *Rose*, 801 S.W.2d 841 (Tex. 1990); *Lakin*, 987 P.2d 463 (Or. 1993); *Griest v. Phillips*, 906 P.2d 789 (Or. 1995).

56. Gfell, "Constitutional and Economic Implications of a National Cap," 783–98; *see, e.g., Best*, 689 N.E.2d 1057 (striking down cap as violative of provision prohibiting special legislation); *Lucas*, 757 S.W.2d 687 (Tex. 1988) (cap violative of provision guaranteeing remedy for wrongs); *Lebron*, 930 N.E.2d 895 (Ill. 2010) (same); *Nestlehutt*, 691 S.E.2d 218 (Ga. 2010) (same); *Watts*, 376 S.W.3d 633 (Mo. 2012) (same); *Kalitan*, 219 So.3d 49 (Fla. 2017) (same).

tification" would be to "abandon" its judicial obligations. Those justices then analyzed the evidence on which the legislature had relied and assembled other evidence; they concluded that taken as a whole, the evidence did not support the "alleged medical malpractice crisis" that the legislature had invoked in support of the caps. Another faction of the court objected that such scrutiny was "inappropriate and unprecedented," but then assembled its own evidence that supported the existence of a crisis and justified the caps.[57] These divisions indicate that American judges' views of tort law in the modern era, like the public's, have been heavily shaped by perception and emotion as well as rational analysis.

Product Liability: Holding Back the Sea of Tort

New Problems: Comparative Negligence and the Consumer-Expectations Standard

Section 402A of the *Restatement (Second) of Torts*, which provided that sellers would be liable for products sold "in a defective condition unreasonably dangerous to the user or consumer" even if they had exercised "all possible care" in making or distributing the product, was a major victory for supporters of accident cost socialization. Many hoped that section 402A would lead, either through legislative expansion or liberal court interpretation, to a thoroughgoing no-fault system in which manufacturers bore near-absolute liability for product-related injuries. But some states made clear from the beginning that they would not eliminate concepts of fault from strict liability altogether. In their view, sale of a defective product meant only that the seller was deemed legally negligent; the consumer still had to prove that the product defect caused her injury, and the seller could try to reduce its liability by showing that the consumer too was negligent.[58] Some courts believed that application of compar-

---

57. *McCall*, 134 So.3d at 905–15 (justices supporting independent evaluation of evidence), 921 (other justices supporting deferential standard), 931–32 (same); *see also Kalitan*, 219 So.3d at 56–58 (dissenters supporting independent evaluation), 60–61 (supporting deferential standard). In other states, judges supporting a deferential standard have also presented evidence supporting the existence of a medical malpractice crisis and supporting caps in response to colleagues who have presented their own evidence as a basis for striking down caps. See, e.g., *Ferdon*, 701 N.W.2d at 499–512 (Prosser, J., speaking for cap supporters), 466–74, 477–89 (Abrahamson, C.J., speaking for opponents).

58. Early state adopters of comparative negligence for strict-liability claims included Wisconsin, *Dippel v. Sciano*, 155 N.W.2d 55 (Wis. 1967); New Hampshire, *Thibault v. Sears, Roebuck & Co.*, 395 A.2d 843 (N.H. 1978); and West Virginia, *Morningstar v. Black & Decker Mfg. Co.*, 253 S.E.2d 666 (W. Va. 1979). Legislatures in at least six states (Mississippi, New Jersey, Ohio, Oregon, Utah and Wyoming) enacted statutes extending comparative negligence to strict-liability cases. See Bexis, "What's Up With The Third Restatement?" (2010) at www.druganddevicelawblog.com/2010/09/whats-up-with-the-third-restatement; *see also* James A. Henderson, Jr. and Theodore Eisenberg, "The Quiet Revolution in Products Liability: An Empirical Study of Legal Change," 37 *UCLA L. Rev.* 479, 487 (1990).

ative negligence was necessary to achieve proper socialization of costs. Section 402A allowed manufacturers to invoke customer misuse of a product as a defense and in such cases, Vermont justice John Dooley explained, without comparative negligence "we are left with the harsh 'all-or-nothing' approach of negligence actions prior to the adoption of our comparative negligence statute."[59] Other state supreme courts refused to allow sellers to invoke comparative negligence. They reasoned that doing so would defeat strict liability's central purpose of allocating risk to manufacturers, who were best positioned to socialize that risk by purchasing insurance and passing the cost on to the consuming public.[60]

Despite the trend toward incorporation of comparative negligence into strict liability, it appeared for a time that strict liability might expand in other ways. Strict liability had been enacted mainly to address manufacturing defects, but state courts soon made clear that it also applied to claims of defective design[61] and failure to warn consumers of a product's inherent dangers.[62] Some courts hinted at creating absolute manufacturer liability for products that were inherently dangerous, such as pharmaceuticals and tobacco products, regardless of whether they were defective in manufacture or design.[63]

But those currents met with strong reaction beginning in the late 1970s. Manufacturers and insurers raised the specter of unlimited liability and economic ruin if strict liability were further expanded; they also stressed their need for clear liability rules and boundaries in order to manage their businesses efficiently, a theme that ALEC and ATRA also emphasized.[64] Application of strict liability to defective-design

---

59. *Webb v. Navistar Int'l Transp. Corp.*, 692 A.2d 343, 347 (Vt. 1996). Jurists began making this point soon after courts began to adopt § 402A strict liability. See Dix W. Noel, "Defective Products: Abnormal Use, Contributory Negligence, and Assumption of Risk," 25 *Vand. L. Rev.* 93, 129 (1972).

60. *See, e.g., Smith v. Smith*, 278 N.W.2d 155 (S.Dak. 1979); *Seay v. Chrysler Corp.*, 609 P.2d 1382 (Wash. 1980); Romualdo P. Eclavea, "Applicability of Comparative Negligence Doctrine to Actions Based on Strict Liability in Tort," 9 A.L.R. 4th 633 (1981, updated 2021).

61. *See, e.g., Arbet v. Gussarson*, 225 N.W.2d 431 (Wis. 1975); *Thibault*, 395 A.2d 843 (N.H. 1978); *Turner v. Gen. Motors Corp.*, 584 S.W.2d 844 (Tex. 1979).

62. *See, e.g., Greenman v. Yuba Power Prods., Inc.*, 377 P.2d 897 (Cal. 1963); *Anderson v. Klix Chem. Co., Inc.*, 472 P.2d 806 (Or. 1970); *Garrett v. Nissen Corp.*, 498 P.2d 1292 (N.M. 1972); Henderson and Eisenberg, "Quiet Revolution," 484; Robert C. Severson, "Strict Products Liability in Wisconsin," 1977 *Wis. L. Rev.* 227 (1977).

63. *See Restatement (Second) of Torts* § 402A, comment k (1965) (stating that strict liability does not apply to "unavoidably unsafe" products); *Finn v. G.D. Searle & Co.*, 677 P.2d 1147, 1166 (Cal. 1984) (Bird, J., dissenting); Henderson and Eisenberg, "Quiet Revolution," 485–87; Robert L. Rabin, "A Sociolegal History of the Tobacco Tort Litigation," 44 *Stan. L. Rev.* 853, 866–67 (1992); Charlotte Smith Siggins, "Strict Liability for Prescription Drugs: Which Shall Govern—Comment k or Strict Liability Applicable to Ordinary Products?", 16 *Golden Gate Univ. L. Rev.* 309 (1986).

64. Henderson and Eisenberg, "Quiet Revolution," 487. *See also, e.g.,* a model legislative resolution prepared by ALEC, at www.alec.org/model-product-liability-resolution (stating that "product liability law has created a situation where product sellers have little or no predictability with respect to their obligations in designing a warning about products") and ATRA's position statement at www.atra.org/issue/product-liability ("Product liability laws in some states fail to send clear signals to

and failure-to-warn claims also created unexpected problems. Furthermore, section 402A did not explicitly define what "defects" and "unreasonable dangers" would trigger strict liability. Initially, most courts looked for guidance to an official comment by section 402A's drafters that a product must be dangerous "to an extent beyond that which would be contemplated by the ordinary consumer." But some commentators argued that the consumer-expectations standard was hopelessly subjective and that it effectively restored an element of negligence to strict liability, something that William Prosser and his colleagues had been at pains to eliminate. Some courts, most notably California's, also criticized the standard.[65]

The Rise of the Risk-Utility Standard

In 1973 John Wade, a Vanderbilt University law professor, proposed an alternative "risk-utility" standard for determining when products would be deemed defective and unreasonably dangerous. The risk-utility standard would gauge all aspects of product defectiveness and danger by weighing factors such as a product's usefulness and customer demand; how hazardous the product was, how obvious its hazards would be to consumers, and whether cost-effective safety improvements existed; the availability of substitute products; and how easy it would be for the manufacturer to socialize accident costs by passing them on to consumers.[66] The risk-utility standard was a modest step back from socialization in that it shifted the decisional focus from social expectations about product performance to an analysis best performed by technocrats. In 1978, California's supreme court held that injured consumers could recover if they established that a product was defective under either the consumer-expectations or the risk-utility standard; in 1979 the federal Department of Commerce, responding to pleas from business groups for a national standard, published a model act that adopted the risk-utility standard and required plaintiffs in design-defect cases to identify a practical alternative design that would have prevented their injury.[67] The Department's

---

manufacturers about how to avoid liability, and hold manufacturers liable for failure to adopt certain designs when the manufacturers neither knew, nor could have anticipated, the risk").

65. Compare *Vincer v. Esther Williams All-Alum. Swim. Pool Co.*, 230 N.W.2d 794 (Wis. 1975) (endorsing consumer-expectations standard) and *Cronin v. J.B.E. Olson Corp.*, 501 P.2d 1153 (1973) (criticizing standard and suggesting that a broader standard should apply); see also Douglas A. Kysar, "The Expectations of Consumers," 103 *Colum. L. Rev.* 1700, 1702-06, 1709-18 (2003); Bexis, "What's Up With The Third Restatement?" (surveying the status of the consumer-expectation and risk-utility standards and the reasonable-alternative-design requirement in each state); Mike McWilliams and Margaret Smith, "An Overview of the Legal Standard Regarding Product Liability Design Defect Claims and a Fifty State Survey on the Applicable Law in Each Jurisdiction," 82 *Def. Counsel J.* 80 (January 2015) (same).

66. John W. Wade, "On the Nature of Strict Tort Liability for Products," 44 *Miss. L.J.* 825, 837–38 (1973).

67. *Barker v. Lull Eng'ring Co.*, 576 P.2d 443 (Cal. 1978); 44 Federal Register 62,714 (1979); Connie Kemp Jobe, "The Model Uniform Product Liability Act—Basic Standards of Responsibility for Manufacturers," 46 *J. Air Law and Comm.* 389 (1981).

model act was not binding and was adopted by only a handful of states, but during the 1980s, discontent with the consumer-expectations standard continued to rise.[68]

The American Law Institute took notice, and in the mid-1990s it commissioned a new *Restatement* devoted exclusively to products liability. Prosser had died in 1972, and the ALI appointed law professors James Henderson and Aaron Twerski, two of the leading critics of existing standards, to supervise the project. Henderson and Twerski consulted with business representatives as well as jurists, a first for ALI; and when the products-liability *Restatement* was published in 1998, it included section 2(b) which, like the Department of Commerce's model act, adopted Wade's risk-utility standard and included an alternative-design requirement. The section 2(b) standard proved popular, but it also attracted criticism and was never universally accepted.[69] Ten states adopted the risk-utility standard and an alternative-design requirement before section 2(b) was published;[70] seven formally endorsed section 2(b) after it was published,[71] and other state courts made increased use of risk-utility criteria without fully embracing section 2(b).[72] Section 2(b)'s rejection of a consumer-oriented liability standard

---

68. *See, e.g., Miller v. Lee Apparel Co.*, 881 P.2d 576 (Kan. App. 1994) and *Timberline Air Svcs., Inc. v. Bell Helicopter-Textron, Inc.*, 884 P.2d 920 (Wash. 1994) (looking to the Department's act for guidance). ALEC has never supported either standard. In 1995 it published a model Product Liability Act that omitted the concept of defectiveness and would make manufacturers liable for products "unreasonably dangerous...in design." In 2012, ALEC amended its model Act to advocate return to a negligence standard: the Act would require plaintiffs to prove that the manufacturer "knew or, in light of then-existing scientific and technical knowledge, reasonably should have known of the danger that caused the claimant's harm." 1995 Act § 4(A)(1)(c); 2012 Act § 4(B).

69. *See* Joseph W. Little, "The Place of Consumer Expectations in Product Strict Liability Actions for Defectively Designed Products," 61 *Tenn. L. Rev.* 1189 (1994) (criticizing changes proposed in the draft *Restatement (Third)*); Donald Patterson, "The Citadel Reburied: Restatement of the Law (Third) Torts: Products Liability," 63 *Def. Counsel J.* 191 (1996) (explaining proposed changes); Victor E. Schwartz, "The Restatement (Third) of Torts: Products Liability—The American Law Institute's Process of Democracy and Deliberation," 26 *Hofstra L. Rev.* 743, 753 (1998) (defending the *Restatement's* provisions as a reasonable compromise between consumers and manufacturers); James A. Henderson, Jr., "Restatement (Third) Torts: Products Liability: What Hath the ALI Wrought?", 64 *Def. Counsel J.* 501 (1997) (same); Elizabeth Laposata, Richard Barnes and Stanton Glantz, "Tobacco Industry Influence on the American Law Institute's Restatements of Torts and Implications for Its Conflict of Interest Policies," 98 *Iowa L. Rev.* 1 (2012); *Restatement (Third) of Torts—Products Liability* (1998), § 2(b).

70. Missouri (1986), Nevada and Idaho (1987), Maine and Louisiana (1988), West Virginia (1989) and Colorado and Mississippi (1993). *See* Bexis, "What's Up With The Third Restatement?" and authorities cited therein; McWilliams and Smith, "Overview and Fifty State Survey."

71. States that adopted § 2(b) after the *Restatement (Third)* was published include Massachusetts (1998), Texas (1999), Nebraska (2000), Georgia (2001), Illinois (2007) and Iowa (2009). New Mexico adopted a published draft version of § 2(b) in 1995. *See* Bexis, "What's Up With The Third Restatement?"; McWilliams and Smith, "Overview and Fifty State Survey."

72. *See* Bexis, "What's Up With The Third Restatement?"; McWilliams and Smith, "Overview and Fifty State Survey"; *see also, e.g., Potter v. Chi. Pneumatic Tool Co.*, 694 A.2d 1319 (Conn. 1997); *Vautour v. Body Masters Sports Inds., Inc.*, 784 A.2d 1178 (N.H. 2001); *Tincher v. Omega Flex, Inc.*, 104 A.3d 328 (Pa. 2014). Two state legislatures adopted § 402A by statute, thus foreclosing their courts from adopting § 2(b), and to date their legislatures have not amended the statutes to adopt

and its raising of the burden for plaintiffs in design-defect cases were setbacks to those who hoped for a full socialization of accident costs, but judicial caution and division continue to surround strict liability more than a half century after its birth. Debate over the extent to which strict liability should move back toward traditional negligence standards or serve as a pathway to absolute liability surely will continue during the decades to come.[73]

Attack of the Contract Blob: The Economic Loss Doctrine

The post-1970 debates over the parameters of strict liability focused on the acts for which manufacturers and suppliers should be held liable. Another debate simultaneously unfolded over the types of harm for which they should be held liable: specifically, whether consumers should be allowed to make tort claims for indirect as well as direct loss flowing from a defective product. For example, if a commercial customer bought defective components, incorporated them into its own products and then lost business because its products were defective, should the component manufacturer be liable to the buyer in tort for that loss of business? The answer would require consideration not only of how far accident cost socialization should go, but of how far the scope of tort law itself should extend.

Beginning in the mid-1960s, many courts adopted the economic loss doctrine which held that generally, buyers could use tort law only to recover direct damages, namely the replacement value of a defective product and the value of personal injuries directly caused by the product. If they wanted to recover indirect damages such as business loss, they would have to rely either on their contract with the seller or on warranties created by statute and contract law. As a practical matter that ended many buyers' ability to recover indirect damages, thus representing another step backward for socialization of costs.[74] Manufacturers often disclaimed liability for indirect damages to the maximum extent possible under the Uniform Commercial Code, and as the twentieth century drew to a close, they increasingly inserted clauses in their

---

§ 2(b). 1979 Or. Laws, ch. 866; 1987 Mo. Laws, p. 808. At least one state legislature effectively adopted § 2(b) by statute. 2011 Wis. Act 2.

73. ALEC advocates a pared-back version of the risk-utility test. In 2012 it introduced a revised Model Product Liability Act that would confine design liability to designs that were dangerous "in light of then-existing scientific and technical knowledge" and for which a practical alternative design was available. The revised Model Act essentially advocates abandonment of strict liability and a return to a pre-§ 402A negligence standard for manufacturing defects and deficient warnings. Model Act, § 4; www.alec.org/model-policy/product-liability-act.

74. Catherine M. Sharkey, "The Remains of the Citadel (Economic Loss Rule in Products Cases)," 100 *Minn. L. Rev.* 1845, 1847–49 (2016); Jeffrey L. Goodman, Daniel R. Peacock and Kevin J. Rutan, "A Guide to Understanding the Economic Loss Doctrine," 67 *Drake L. Rev.* 1, 2–9, 12–14 (2019).

sales contracts requiring buyers to seek relief through arbitration, an expensive and time-consuming process that discouraged claims.[75]

Curiously, California justice Roger Traynor, who in the 1944 *Escola* case had become the first American judge to advocate strict liability, also became the first judge to espouse the ELD, in *Seely v. White Motor Co.* (1965). At first blush, Traynor's positions in *Escola* and *Seely* seemed inconsistent, but in *Seely* he argued that they were not. In his view, the long struggle to move away from privity in the context of personal injuries caused by defective products, and the difficulties courts had encountered when they had tried to reshape warranty law to cover such injuries, had made clear that contract law was not a good means of compensating injured consumers. But, said Traynor, business-related losses were well within contract's traditional domain: manufacturers and commercial buyers could easily use contracts to allocate such risks between them. The unpredictability of personal injuries made it appropriate to socialize their cost, but in Traynor's view, that "in no way justifie[d] requiring the consuming public to pay more for their products so that a manufacturer can insure against the possibility that some of his products will not meet the business needs of some of his customers."[76] Other courts took issue with Traynor, most notably New Jersey's supreme court in *Santor v. A. & M. Karagheusian, Inc.* (1965). Unlike Traynor, New Jersey's justices viewed the earlier movement to apply warranty law to personal injuries not as an exercise in futility but as confirmation that strict liability should extend to all types of injury, thus helping to seed the ground for Professor Gilmore's later prediction that tort law would ultimately swallow contract law.[77]

---

75. Sharkey, "Remains of the Citadel," 1876–78; *see Uniform Commercial Code*, §§ 2–316; Shelley McGill, "Consumer Arbitration Clause Enforcement: A Balanced Legislative Response," 47 *Am. Bus. L.J.* 361 (2010); *AT&T Mobility LLC v. Concepcion*, 563 U.S. 333 (2011) (holding that federal law preempts state law regarding unconscionability of arbitration clauses); *Am. Exp. Co. v. Italian Colors Rest.*, 570 U.S. 228 (2013) (upholding a clause waiving buyers' rights to participate in class actions); Peter B. Rutledge and Christopher B. Drahozal, "'Sticky' Arbitration Clauses? The Use of Arbitration Clauses after Concepcion and Amex," 67 *Vand. L. Rev.* (2014) (suggesting that sellers have only modestly increased their use of arbitration clauses since the *Concepcion* and *American Express* decisions).

76. *Seely*, 403 P.2d 145, 151 (Cal. 1965); *Escola v. Coca-Cola Bottling Co. of Fresno*, 150 P.2d 436 (Cal. 1944).

77. *Seely*, 403 P.2d 145, 151 (Cal. 1965); *Santor*, 207 A.2d 305 (N.J. 1965).

Roger Traynor. Courtesy of the Honorable Roger J. Traynor Collection at the UC Hastings Law Library.

The issue attracted little attention at first: only two other state courts addressed the economic loss doctrine between 1965 and 1980.[78] But during the 1980s, fifteen additional state courts, perhaps influenced by rising concerns that tort law was becoming too socialized and encouraged by the U.S. Supreme Court's endorsement of the ELD in 1986 and its warning that contract law should not be allowed to "drown in a sea of tort," adopted the ELD in some form.[79] Ten more states have followed suit since the 1990s, although the pace has slowed greatly since 2000.[80] But many judges shared Wisconsin justice Ann Walsh Bradley's feeling that if the ELD were not cabined, it could come to resemble "the ever-expanding, all-consuming alien life form portrayed in

---

78. *Melody Home Mfg. Co. v. Morrison*, 455 S.W.2d 825 (Tex. Civ. App. 1970) (adopting the ELD); *Crowell Corp. v. Topkis Const. Co.*, 280 A.2d 730 (Del. 1971) (same).

79. *East Riv. Steamship Corp. v. Transamerica Delaval, Inc.*, 476 U.S. 858, 866 (1986). Early-adopting states included Nevada (1982); Nebraska, Pennsylvania (both 1983); North Dakota (1984); New Jersey (1985); Missouri (1986); Florida, Idaho, Indiana (all 1987); North Carolina (1988); Alabama, New Mexico, Ohio, South Carolina, Wisconsin and Wyoming (all 1989). See Goodman et al., "Guide," 17–18.

80. Oklahoma (1990); South Dakota (1994); New York, Tennessee (both 1995); Hawaii (1996); Vermont (1998); Mississippi (1999); Minnesota (2000, by statute); Kentucky (2011); and Maine (2014). See Goodman et al., "Guide," 17–18.

the 1958 B-movie classic *The Blob*...the more it eats, the more it grows."[81] In the end, most state courts did not believe the transition required a binary choice between *Seely* and *Santor*: they carved out a variety of exceptions to the ELD, and nearly all states, including California and New Jersey, adopted diluted forms of the ELD recognizing one or more of the exceptions.[82]

The central thread running through the ELD and its exceptions is the desire to draw a line between risks that can be anticipated and allocated through seller-buyer negotiation and those that cannot. The "dangerous defect" exception allows tort claims where a product creates a safety hazard;[83] the "disappointed expectations" exception allows tort claims for unusual types of property damage that could not have been foreseen and addressed during the parties' negotiations.[84] The "independent duty" exception allows tort claims where the product defect is related to violation of a legal duty outside the parties' agreement, for example, a manufacturer's concealment of the fact that its product did not comply with government regulations related to quality or safety; and the "fraud-in-the-inducement" exception allows consumers to make in some cases tort claims against manufacturers who made intentional misrepresentations in order to procure a sale.[85]

It proved difficult to draw clear definitional lines for ELD exceptions, precisely because they were woven into the central theme of ability to negotiate. Judicial concepts of what could be addressed through contract negotiations necessarily contained an element of subjectivity, and as a result, judges who applied the exceptions were regularly accused of charting an inconsistent course and imposing their personal preferences on the law. The problem surfaced most prominently in the debate over whether an "integrated system" exception should be added to the ELD: should makers of components intended to be incorporated into larger products, such as buildings

---

81. *1325 N. Van Buren, LLC v. T-3 Group, Ltd.*, 716 N.W.2d 822 (Wis. 2006), 841 (Bradley dissent).

82. Goodman et al., "Guide," 27–29; *see Jimenez v. Sup. Ct.*, 58 P.2d 450 (Cal. 2002); *Spring Motors Dists., Inc. v. Ford Motor Co.*, 489 A.2d 660 (N.J. 1985); *Alloway v. Gen. Marine Inds., Inc.*, 695 A.2d 264 (N.J. 1997).

83. Goodman et al., "Guide," 29–31.

84. *Ibid.*, 31–32.

85. Goodman et al., "Guide," 31–32; *see, e.g., Robinson Helicopter Co., Inc. v. Dana Corp.*, 102 P.3d 268 (Cal. 2004). Courts further divided as to the fraud-in-the-inducement exception: some limited the exception to misrepresentations unrelated to the product itself, reasoning that protection against misrepresentations about the product could be negotiated into the contract or, alternatively, the buyer could rely on the Uniform Commercial Code's implied-warranty provisions and rules against misrepresentation. *See Uniform Commercial Code*, §§ 2-314 and 2-315; *see also, e.g., Huron Tool & Engr. Co. v. Precision Consulting Svcs., Inc.*, 532 N.W.2d 541 (Mich. App. 1995); *Grynberg v. Questar Pipeline Co.*, 70 P.3d 1 (Utah 2003) (construing Wyoming law); R. Joseph Barton, Note, "Drowning in A Sea of Contract: Application of the Economic Loss Doctrine to Fraud and Negligent Misrepresentation Claims," 41 *Wm. & Mary L. Rev.* 1789 (2000). Other courts concluded it was better policy to make an exception for all cases of fraud. *See, e.g., Robinson Helicopter*, 102 P.3d 268 (Cal. 2004); *Formosa Plastics Corp. USA v. Presidio Eng'rs & Contractors, Inc.*, 960 S.W.2d 41 (Tex. 1998).

and computers, be liable in tort for the entire physical loss when their components' defects caused the building or the computer to fail? Most courts have rejected such an exception, reasoning that when sellers and buyers know that a product will be used in a larger system, they can allocate the risk of system failure in their contract. But the line between components that dominate and effectively constitute the larger system and secondary "add-on" features is not always clear, and it has engendered much controversy as courts have tried to draw it.[86]

The ELD has also come under attack from another quarter: consumer advocates have argued that the doctrine creates serious injustice in an age when many products that prove defective are sold on a take-it-or-leave-it basis to unsophisticated buyers, who are presented with manufacturer-drafted, manufacturer-friendly terms hidden in sales contracts' fine print or in links on a computer screen. During the modern tort era, American courts have generally left it to Congress and state legislatures to address this problem through consumer-protection statutes. In the absence of protective statutes, most courts have applied the ELD in its exception-diluted form to consumer transactions, although a few courts have flatly refused to do so. But the ELD's erratic evolution and courts' continuing division over its exceptions likely reflects real, if unstated, concerns among many judges about fairness to consumers.[87]

Immunities Redux

In 1970, supporters of tort socialization could look with satisfaction at recent progress in eliminating traditional immunities that had insulated key social institutions from much of the cost that their negligence imposed on others. Forty states had already abolished charitable immunity, and very few jurists now defended the concept. Eighteen states had cut back or abolished local governmental immunity during the 1960s, and hopes of universal abolition were bright.[88] Progress had also been made

---

86. Goodman et al., "Guide," 34–49; *see* Andrew Gray, Note, "Drowning in a Sea of Confusion: Applying the Economic Loss Doctrine to Component Parts, Service Contracts, and Fraud," 84 *Wash. U. L. Rev.* 1513 (2006); Ralph C. Anzivino, "The Economic Loss Doctrine: Distinguishing Economic from Non-Economic Loss," 91 *Marq. L. Rev.* 1081 (2008).

87. Goodman et al., "Guide," 49–55; *see, e.g., Franklin Grove Corp. v. Drexel*, 936 A.2d 1272 (R.I. 2007) (declining to apply ELD to consumers) and *State Farm Mut. Ins. Co. v. Ford Motor Co.*, 592 N.W.2d 201, 205 (Wis. 1999) (declining to distinguish between commercial and consumer transactions for ELD purposes).

88. *See* Chapter 4, notes 107–15 and accompanying text. Three states abolished charitable immunity between 1970 and 1990, bringing the total to forty-three. *See Garlington v. Kingsley*, 289 So.2d 88 (La. 1974); *Fitzer v. Greater Greenville YMCA*, 282 S.E.2d 239 (S.C. 1981); 1987 S. Dak. Laws, ch. 344 (providing that municipalities who purchased liability insurance would be deemed to have waived immunity).

in limiting family members' immunity for harm to each other, including immunity for injuries to children[89] and spouses.[90]

But the reactive forces that slowed or stopped other socializing reforms after 1970 also made their presence felt here. Abolition of charitable and spousal immunity eventually became nearly universal, but the movement to abolish municipal immunity slowed to a near-halt. Legislatures in most abolition states restored limited municipal immunity and some courts preserved pockets of immunity and construed them so broadly that municipal immunity nearly regained its pre-reform status. In so doing, lawmakers again sounded a central theme of post-1970 tort law: they had become cautious about further socialization and would not hesitate to check it when they saw fit.

The Fluid Borders of Municipal Immunity

Courts that abolished municipal immunity in the 1950s and 1960s were reluctant to hold officials to account for good-faith policy decisions that turned out to be mistaken, and they left immunity in place for such acts. They used multiple labels for the acts, ranging from "quasi-legislative or quasi-judicial" to "discretionary," a term that first appeared in in the Federal Tort Claims Act (FTCA) in 1946.[91] Abolitionist courts also made clear that their legislatures could reinstate immunity if they chose, and most legislatures did so to a limited extent: they typically incorporated immunity provisions for policy decisions into their statutes, together with strict claim deadlines and detailed claim-filing procedures that were designed to make the claims process difficult and thus reduce local governments' liability exposure.[92]

---

89. Ten states had abolished or limited parental immunity by 1970. Twelve more states did so during the 1980s, but only three additional states joined the movement thereafter. William L. Prosser, *Handbook of the Law of Torts* (4th ed. 1971), § 122; Romualdo P. Eclavea, "Liability of Parent for Injury to Unemancipated Child Caused By Parent's Negligence—Modern Cases (1981, updated 2021); *Ard v. Ard*, 414 So.2d 1066 (Fla. 1982); *Kirchner v. Crystal*, 474 N.E.2d 275 (Ohio 1982); *Hartman v. Hartman*, 821 S.W.2d 852 (Mo. 1991). *See generally* Chapter 4, notes 105–106 and accompanying text.

90. Twenty-nine states had abolished spousal immunity by 1970, the number grew to thirty-seven by 1980 and forty-seven by 1990. *See* Wayne F. Foster, "Modern Status of Interspousal Tort Immunity in Personal Injury and Wrongful Death Actions," 92 A.L.R.3d 901 (1979, updated to 2021). *See generally* Chapter 4, notes 103–104 and accompanying text.

91. *See, e.g., Holytz v. City of Milw.*, 115 N.W.2d 618 (Wis. 1962) (quasi-legislative, quasi-judicial); 60 U.S. Stat. 812 (1946); John W. Bagby and Gary L. Gittings, "The Elusive Discretionary Function Exception from Government Tort Liability: The Narrowing Scope of Federal Liability," 30 *Am. Bus. L.J.* 223, 223–30 (1992); *see also Dunbar v. United Steelworkers of Am.*, 602 P.2d 21 (Idaho 1979) (discussing origins and interpretation of the federal discretionary/nondiscretionary distinction).

92. *See, e.g.*, 1963 Cal. Laws, ch. 1681; 1963 Wis. Laws, ch. 198; Joe R. Greenhill and Thomas V. Murto, "Observation—Governmental Immunity," 49 *Tex. L. Rev.* 462 (1970) (discussing Texas's enactment of a tort claims law in 1969). For examples of court decisions in other states leaving the door open to legislative reenactment of immunity and legislative responses thereto, see Chapter 4, note 122.

Drawing a clear line between discretionary and non-discretionary acts for immunity purposes proved difficult. Some state courts defined discretionary functions to include everything except officials' clear failure to follow explicit rules or directives issued by their superiors.[93] The discretionary/non-discretionary standard became less workable as both federal and state government activities expanded in order to serve an increasingly complex society. It also began to draw criticism from jurists and lawyers sympathetic to accident victims' interests; a substantial number of judges shared their concerns, but change proved difficult.[94] In *Dalehite v. United States* (1953), the U.S. Supreme Court suggested that courts applying the FTCA's discretion standard should look at whether a given act involved "planning" or was merely "operational," and during the 1950s and 1960s many courts found the distinction a workable one for FTCA purposes. In 1977, Massachusetts became the first state to formally adopt the *Dalehite* standard for all cases,[95] and the standard slowly but steadily gained favor among state courts. Nine states adopted it during the 1980s,[96] six during the 1990s,[97] and at least six more have followed suit since 2000.[98] But the planning-operational distinction has not proved to be a panacea. After *Dalehite* was decided, some courts construing the FTCA folded negligent implementation of government policies and activities into the "planning" category, and in 1984 the federal high Court had to make clear that no immunity attached to such activities. States that have experimented with *Dalehite*'s planning-operational standard have struggled with it in other ways as well.[99]

---

93. *See, e.g., Lister v. Bd. of Regents*, 240 N.W.2d 610 (Wis. 1976); *McLean v. City of N.Y.*, 905 N.E.2d 1167 (N.Y. 2009).

94. *See, e.g.,* Roy K. Snell, "A Plea for a Comprehensive Governmental Liability Statute," 74 *Ky. L.J.* 521 (1986); Gail Ann McCarthy, "The Varying Standards of Governmental Immunity: A Proposal to Make Such Statutes Easier to Apply," 24 *N. Eng. L. Rev.* 991 (1990); Bagby and Gittings, "Elusive Discretionary Function Exception"; *see also, e.g., Whitney v. City of Worcester*, 366 N.E.2d 1210 (Mass. 1977).

95. *Dalehite v. United States*, 346 U.S. 15, 32 (1953); *Whitney*, 366 N.E.2d 1210 (Mass. 1977); Bagby and Gittings, "Elusive Discretionary Function Exception," 226–27, 246–49. Colorado adopted the distinction two years later. *Cooper v. Hollis*, 600 P.2d 109 (Colo. App. 1979).

96. New Jersey (1980), Florida and Hawaii (1982), Alaska and Ohio (1983), Michigan (1984), Idaho (1986), Indiana (1988) and Louisiana (1989). *See* cases compiled at Bullard, "Pushing the Reset Button," 826 n. 213.

97. Oklahoma and Pennsylvania (1990), Tennessee (1992), New Hampshire (1993), Nebraska (1994) and Wyoming (1996). *See ibid.*

98. Minnesota (2000), Arkansas (2001), Utah (2006), Texas (2007), Maine (2009) and California and Washington (2012). *See ibid.*

99. *U.S. v. Varig Airlines*, 467 U.S. 797 (1984); Bagby and Gittings, "Elusive Discretionary Function Exception," 227, 251–52, 259–61. As to state-court struggles, *see, e.g., Dunbar*, 602 P.2d 21 (Idaho 1973) (adopting a distinction between "governing conduct" and conduct with a parallel in the private sector); *Chandler Supply Co., Inc. v. City of Boise*, 660 P.2d 1323, 1329 (Idaho 1983) (adding immunity for "planning and operational decision-making necessary to the performance of traditional governmental functions"); *Sterling v. Bloom*, 723 P.2d 755 (Idaho 1986) (adopting a detailed version of the planning-operational distinction); Brian H. Hess, Comment, "The Planning/Operational Dichotomy: A Specious Approach to the Discretionary Function Exception in the Federal Tort Claims Act," 40 *Idaho L. Rev.* 223 (2003). *See also, e.g., Trianon Park Condo. v. City of Hialeah*,

Efforts to redraw the line between protected and non-protected governmental acts likely will continue.

The Growth of Customized Immunities

As old immunities eroded, others, less expansive but more numerous, arrived to take their place. The first of the new immunities appeared in the form of "Good Samaritan" statutes shielding physicians who provided care during emergencies they encountered while off duty. California enacted the first such law in 1959, apparently in response to a widely reported incident in which several doctors had refused to help a ski accident victim for fear of liability if their ministrations failed. Subsequent studies indicated that most doctors would help in an emergency regardless of legal risk and that emergency patients were more grateful and less likely to sue than regular patients, but the good-Samaritan image struck a chord with the public. By 1965, thirty states had enacted similar laws, and eventually all other states followed suit.[100] The laws varied in scope: some were limited to physicians, some applied to a wide spectrum of health care personnel, and a few applied to all persons who helped injury victims.

The Good Samaritan laws were so popular that they largely escaped constitutional challenge,[101] and other new immunity laws followed. Many of the new laws reflected a reaction against legislative and judicial expansion of landowners' liability during the first part of the twentieth century through such innovations as safe-place statutes and the attractive nuisance doctrine[102] and courts' subsequent extension of owners' duty of ordinary care to licensees (customers and others permitted but not

---

468 So.2d 912 (Fla. 1985) (attempting to create detailed lists of government construction-related activities as to which immunity does and does not exist); *Kimps v. Hill*, 546 N.W.2d 151 (Wis. 1996) (recognizing need for change but questioning whether the planning-operational distinction would work).

100. Frank B. Mapel and Charles J. Weigel, "Good Samaritan Laws: Who Needs Them: The Current State of Good Samaritan Protection in the United States," 21 *S. Tex. L.J.* 327, 330 (1980); Eric A. Brandt, "Good Samaritan Laws—The Legal Placebo: A Current Analysis," 17 *Akron L. Rev.* 303, 305–06 (1983).

101. Georgia's supreme court summarily rejected an argument that its state's law violated equal protection guarantees by giving Samaritans special protection. *Anderson v. Little & Davenport Funeral Home, Inc.*, 251 S.E.2d 250 (Ga. 1978).

102. See Chapter 2, notes 56–60; Chapter 4, notes 10–16 and accompanying text.

directly invited to enter the owner's property)[103] and even to trespassers.[104] Michigan enacted the first customized landowner immunity statute in 1953, protecting owners who allowed others to use their land for hunting, water sports and other recreational activities. Other states soon followed suit; in 1965 the NCCUSL developed a model recreational-use act which proved popular, and by the early 1990s every state had a recreational-use statute.[105]

The turn of the twenty-first century witnessed a proliferation of customized immunity statutes not related to land ownership. Some were adopted only in a single state or a handful of states and reflected no central theme, other than showing what groups were interested in protection and had sufficient political influence to obtain it.[106] Other statutes, including statutes that immunized from liability those who donated food to charities and firefighting equipment to fire departments, were adopted in numerous states.[107] Two categories of immunity statutes responded to events that figured prominently in the American social landscape at the end of the twentieth century: the explosion of youth sports and clerical sexual exploitation of church youth. A 1965 federal civil rights law requiring parity for women in school sports greatly increased

---

103. Under the old common law, owners were not liable to licensees unless the condition causing injury (such as a floor opening, a slippery spot or a hidden fence) was concealed from the invitee. See W. Page Keeton et al., eds., *Prosser and Keeton on the Law of Torts* (5th ed. 1984), §§ 60–62. At least seventeen states extended such duty to licensees but not trespassers, including Minnesota (1972), Florida and Massachusetts (1973), Wisconsin (1975), North Dakota (1977), Maine (1979), New Jersey (1982), Tennessee (1984), Illinois (1985), New Mexico (1994), Iowa and North Carolina (1998), West Virginia (1999), Nebraska (2002), Kansas (2005), Wyoming (2011) and Kentucky (2017). See Kyle Graham, "The Diffusion of Doctrinal Innovations in Tort Law," 99 *Marq. L. Rev.* 75, 168–69 (2015); Victor M. Gulbis, "Modern Status of States Conditioning Landowner's Liability Upon Status of Injured Party as Invitee, Licensee or Trespasser," 22 A.L.R. 4th 294 (1983, updated 2019).

104. Under the old common law, owners were not liable to trespassers unless they had deliberately or recklessly created the hazard at issue. See Keeton et al., *Law of Torts* (5th ed. 1984), §§ 60–62. California was the first state to extend owners' general duty of care to trespassers. *Rowland v. Christian*, 443 P.2d 561 (Cal. 1968). At least ten states have followed suit including Hawaii (1969), Colorado (1971), New Hampshire, Louisiana and New York (1976), Missouri and Montana (1985), Nebraska (1996) and Kansas and Minnesota (2009). Graham, "Diffusion of Doctrinal Innovations," 168–69; Gulbis, "Modern Status of Landowner's Liability."

105. 1953 Mich. Laws, ch. 201 (immunizing landowners for all conduct except willful and reckless conduct); Terrance J. Centner, "Tort Liability for Sports and Recreational Activities: Expanding Statutory Immunity for Protected Classes and Activities," 26 *J. Legis.* 1, 12, 17–19 (2000); Comment, "Private Lands and Public Recreation," 1991 *Wis. L. Rev.* 491 (1991).

106. Examples include 1986 Wyo. Laws, ch. 48 (granting immunity to volunteers at rodeo events; 1993 Wis. Laws, ch. 455 (agricultural-equipment dealers who made emergency replacement parts for farm customers); 2011 Tex. Laws, ch. 530 (volunteers caring for stray animals); 2016 N.C. Laws, ch. 88 (caregivers participating in needle-exchange anti-addiction programs).

107. See, e.g., as to food donors: 1981 Wis. Laws, ch. 219; 1981 Pa. Laws, ch. 234, No. 76; 1981 Mont. Laws, ch. 259; 1981 Nev. Laws, ch. 694; 1982 Iowa Laws, ch. 1168; 1994 Minn. Laws, ch. 623; as to firefighting equipment donors: 2004 Pa. Laws, ch. 1747, No. 225; Ariz. Rev. Stats § 12-715. Laws granting immunity to farmers who engaged in agritourism to supplement their income were also popular. See, e.g.,, 2013 Wis. Laws, ch. 269; 2015 Mont. Stats, ch. 44.

overall student participation, and youth soccer, hockey, football, basketball and other sports programs in and outside of school became a way of life for millions of families. Injuries were an inevitable part of sports, and the specter of liability hovered over volunteer coaches and assistants. Legislators in many states believed protection was necessary to preserve this new way of life, and they enacted immunity statutes for persons involved in school sports activities.[108]

Reports first surfaced in the 1980s of incidents in which clerics had sexually abused children in connection with church activities. As the reports continued to appear, they attracted public attention and eventually created a national scandal. Lawsuits and class actions against offending clerics and their churches followed, and instances of abuse turned out to be so numerous and widespread that some churches were forced into bankruptcy.[109] Churches asserted three principal defenses: that they were not vicariously liable for abusive acts of their clergy because those acts were not a part of a cleric's employment; that constitutional provisions against state involvement with religion meant that churches could not be sued; and that the claims, many of which were advanced by adults who had been abused decades earlier, were made too late. State supreme courts divided over the issue of vicarious liability;[110] they also divided as to whether constitutional guarantees of religious liberty and separation of church and state immunized churches from liability for clerics' abusive acts.[111]

---

108. *See* Centner, "Tort Liability for Sports and Recreational Activities," 8–11, 14–17; Title IX of the Education Amendments of 1972, 86 Stat. 235 (1972); Vern D. Seefeldt and Martha E. Ewing, "Youth Sports in America: An Overview," President's Council on Physical Fitness and Sports, *Sports R'sch Dig.*, Series 2, No. 11 (September 1997), 1–3. The number of students participating in interscholastic sports rose from 3.9 million in 1971 to 5.8 million in 1995. *Ibid.; see also, e.g.*, Hilary Levey Friedman, "When Did Competitive Sports Take Over American Childhood?", *Atlantic Magazine* (September 20, 2013). For examples of school-sports immunity statutes, see 1986 Pa. Laws, ch. 1324; 1994 Minn. Laws, ch. 623; 2011 Wis. Act 162.

109. *See* Marie Rohde, "Winners and Losers in the Milwaukee Archdiocese's Bankruptcy Settlement," *New Catholic Rptr.* (November 10, 2015); *see also* Frank Bruni, *A Gospel of Shame: Children, Sexual Abuse, and The Catholic Church* (2002).

110. *See, e.g., Fearing v. Bucher*, 977 P.2d 1163 (Or. 1999) (holding that church could be held vicariously liable for clerical child abuse); *Byrd v. Faber*, 565 N.E.2d 584 (Ohio 1991) (holding that church could not be held vicariously liable); *Gibson v. Brewer*, 952 S.W.2d 239 (Mo. 1997) (same); Joseph B. Conden, "Liability of Church or Religious Society for Sexual Misconduct of Clergy," 5 A.L.R. 5th 530 (1992, updated 2021).

111. *See, e.g., Moses v. Diocese of Denver*, 863 P.2d 310 (Colo. 1993) (holding that the constitutional guarantees in question did not immunize the Catholic Church from a claim that it negligently hired a priest who later committed sexual abuse); *Malicki v. Doe*, 814 So.2d 347 (Fla. 2002) (same); *Roman Catholic Diocese of Jackson v. Morrison*, 905 So.2d 1213 (Miss. 2005) (same); *compare Swanson v. Roman Catholic Bishop of Portland*, 692 A.2d 441 (Me. 1997) (holding that such constitutional guarantees create civil immunity); *Gibson*, 952 S.W.2d 239 (Mo. 1997) (same); *L.L.N. v. Clauder*, 563 N.W.2d 434 (Wis. 1997) (same). *See also, e.g.*, Victor E. Schwartz and Christopher E. Appel, "The Church Autonomy Doctrine: Where Tort Law Should Step Aside," 80 *U. Cinn. L. Rev.* 431 (2012); Ira C. Lupu and Robert W. Tuttle, "Sexual Misconduct and Ecclesiastical Immunity," 2004 *BYU L. Rev.* 1789 (2004); Mark E. Chopko, "Continuing the Lord's Work and Healing the People: A Reply to Professors Lupu and Tuttle," 2004 *BYU L. Rev.* 1897 (2004).

The timeliness issue was particularly sensitive. Many claimants contended that as children, they had coped with their abuse by burying their memories so deep that the memories had not resurfaced until well into adulthood; they argued that the time for filing claims should be extended to accommodate that reality. Churches replied that extension of existing time limits would lead to their financial ruin and would unfairly penalize congregants who had had no part in events of long ago. Time limits on tort claims are generally set by statute, and American legislatures divided over the proper response. Some extended and even eliminated time limits for abuse claims.[112] Others, concerned that claims might continue to surface for decades and would irreparably damage churches, replaced existing laws that gave litigants a period of time to sue after they discovered (or reasonably should have discovered) that they had a claim, with statutes of repose that imposed deadlines based on when the abuse had occurred and made no allowance for a possible delay in discovery. The statutes of repose effectively operated as limited-immunity laws.[113]

The first Good Samaritan statutes, arising as the tort socialization movement reached its peak in the 1950s and 1960s, appeared to be an isolated effort to help one set of particularly sympathetic defendants, but in tort law's modern era, customized immunity statues have become an important part of the movement away from socialization of tort costs. Despite their seemingly ad hoc nature they, like the struggle to preserve and define a limited municipal immunity, underscore modern-era lawmakers' continuing willingness to cabin socialization of accident costs by protecting from liability institutions and activities deemed particularly important to society.

The Resurrection and Reburial of No-Fault Auto Insurance

In the 1910s, workers compensation established a no-fault, absolute-liability beachhead in one area formerly occupied by tort law. A movement to extend that beachhead to automobile accidents arose in the 1920s and early 1930s but guttered out after New

---

112. *See, e.g.*, 2007 Del. Laws, ch. 102; *see generally* National Conference of State Legislatures, "State Civil Statutes of Limitation in Sexual Abuse Cases," accessible at www.ncsl.org/research/human-services/state-civil-statutes-of-limitations-in-child-sexual.aspx.

113. *See, e.g.*, 2003 Md. Laws, ch. 360 (setting absolute 20-year time limit on abuse claims); 2006 Ohio Laws, p. 1108 (requiring that abuse victims make claims by the age of 24); 2013 Minn. Laws, ch. 89 (same); see also 2003 Wis. Laws, ch. 279 (exempting church officials from liability unless at the time of abuse they had known of prior incidents involving the cleric in question and had failed to take action to prevent a recurrence). Statutes of repose imposing absolute time limits on various types of tort claims were popular among tort-reform advocates. For example, ALEC published a model products-liability statute of repose providing that all product-liability claims must be brought within ten years after the product was first purchased for use or consumption. ALEC, Ten-Year Statute of Repose Act § 2(A)(5)(b), at www.alec.org/model-policy/ten-year-statute-of-repose-act.

York's legislature refused to adopt the Columbia Plan in 1938.[114] Twenty years later, the auto no-fault movement rose again, fueled partly by the general increase in support for socialization of accident costs and partly by changes in America's car culture. During the early twentieth century, Americans had viewed driver carelessness as the root cause of auto accidents; they had subsequently shifted their focus to inadequate driver education and traffic engineering but had paid little attention to the relationship between vehicle design and safety. Power and speed were essential to the American vision of autos as a key to freedom and mobility; safety was not.[115] After World War II, cars became more powerful; injury and death tolls rose—annual auto fatalities increased from 34,763 in 1950 to 54,633 in 1970—and concerns about auto safety design rose correspondingly. Design-improvement studies began in the 1940s. During the mid-1960s, widely-publicized exposes of deceptive trade practices by auto dealers and efforts by Ralph Nader, *Consumer Reports* magazine and other consumer advocates to publicize the shaky state of auto safety commanded the public's full attention, and in 1966 Congress enacted the National Traffic and Motor Safety Act which mandated installation of seatbelts and other basic safety devices in all cars.[116]

Safety concerns went hand in hand with concerns that auto accident victims have assurances of adequate compensation. In 1965, law professors Robert Keeton of Harvard and Jeffrey O'Connell of the University of Illinois published an influential book, *Basic Protection for the Traffic Victim,* and in so doing they resurrected the no-fault auto-accident movement. Keeton and O'Connell proposed that auto owners be required to purchase liability insurance, which would automatically cover an accident victim's medical expenses and a portion of her lost wages up to a cap of $10,000 ($83,000 in 2020 dollars). Claims for non-economic damages would be prohibited unless the victim's injuries were serious enough that her compensable no-fault costs exceeded the cap, but property-damage claims could be made in the courts without restriction. In 1970 Michael Dukakis, a former Keeton student (and future governor and presidential candidate), persuaded his fellow Massachusetts legislators to adopt the Keeton-O'Connell plan. During the early 1970s, Congress seriously considered enacting a national plan, and by the late 1970s nearly half the states had adopted some form of no-fault auto legislation.[117]

---

114. Engstrom, "No-Fault's Demise," 314–17; see also Chapter 4.

115. James J. Flink, *The Automobile Age* (1990), 383–84; John A. Heitmann, *The Automobile and American Life* (2009), 19–47; David Blanke, *Hell on Wheels: The Promise and Peril of America's Car Culture, 1900–1940* (2007), 1–4, 17–24, 27–30, 38–42, 52–55, 91–94, 112–18; Edward C. Fisher, *Vehicle Traffic Law* (1973 rev. ed.), 2–4.

116. 80 U.S. Stats. 718 (1966); U.S. Census Bureau, *Historical Statistics of the United States: Colonial Times to 1970* (1975), 718; Heitmann, *Automobile and American Life,* 135–36, 144–47, 171–74; Blanke, *Hell on Wheels,* 195–99; Fisher, *Vehicle Traffic Law,* 25; Engstrom, "No-Fault's 'Demise," 312–13, 348–53.

117. Keeton and O'Connell, *Basic Protection for the Traffic Victim,* 6–10, 299–339; Engstrom, "No-Fault's Demise," 320–22, 350–52; Patrick F. Maroney, "No-Fault Automobile Insurance: A Suc-

Supporters of auto no-fault frequently analogized it to workers compensation and hoped it would advance the cause of socialization in similar fashion,[118] but the weaknesses that had contributed to auto no-fault's failure in the 1930s remained in place in the 1960s. Conditions that contributed to workplace accidents were in the control of a single, easily identifiable group: employers, who could pass on the cost of these accidents to the consuming public; but auto accidents were caused by individual drivers who could not pass on costs except in limited fashion by buying insurance. Private insurance had played only a limited role in workplace accidents prior to workers compensation; it was not entrenched, and that made the transition to a new, employer-based insurance system comparatively easy. But by the 1960s, auto insurance was a widespread, well-established institution and insurers had had decades of experience insuring large numbers of individual drivers. Neither insurers nor drivers felt an urgent need to change to a more universalized, government-supervised system. Insurers gave guarded support to no-fault in some states, particularly during the first insurance crisis of the mid-1970s when no-fault damages caps seemed to offer a way to reduce claim payments and improve their balance sheets, but their support waned as the crisis passed.[119]

No-fault supporters also had difficulty determining what benefit system would work best. No state enacted a "pure" no-fault system that would have precluded accident victims from litigating altogether. Most enacting states followed the Keeton-O'Connell model but struggled to formulate workable damages caps and litigation restrictions. Caps on medical and wage expenses in early no-fault statutes ranged from $2,000 to $10,000; some state legislatures limited the right to sue for non-economic damages to "serious" cases, a term which they defined with varying degrees of precision, and others defined the right to sue in terms of whether medical expenses exceeded a prescribed amount.[120] Florida provided an example of the struggle. Its original law (1972) prohibited lawsuits for non-economic damages unless a victim's medical expenses exceeded $1,000; in 1976 it eliminated the cap but allowed lawsuits only in cases of death, permanent injury or nonpermanent injury lasting at least ninety days. When that formula too proved unsatisfactory, the

---

cess or Failure After Eleven Years?", 51 *Ins. Counsel J.* 75, 75–76 (1984); Jack Davies, "A No-Fault History," 24 *Wm. Mitchell L. Rev.* 839 (1998).

118. Engstrom, "No-Fault's Demise," 339.

119. See Davies, "A No-Fault History," 844–46; Abraham, *Liability Century*, 69–74, 92–98; Engstrom, "No-Fault's Demise," 347–79. Supporters asserted as one of their chief selling points that no-fault insurance would reduce auto owners' premium costs, and some insurers feared that no-fault caps would reduce the premiums they could charge. Engstrom, "No-Fault's Demise," 334–37, 339.

120. States that followed the Keeton-O'Connell model included Massachusetts (1971); Florida (1972); Connecticut, Hawaii, Michigan, New Hampshire, New Jersey and Nevada (1973); Colorado, Kansas, New York and Utah (1974); Georgia, Kentucky, Minnesota, and Pennsylvania (1975); and North Dakota (1976). *See* Engstrom, "No-Fault's Demise," 306 n. 17; Maroney, "No-Fault Automobile Insurance," 75–76, notes 6, 14 (1984) and statutes there cited; American Bar Association, *No-Fault Insurance: A Study by the Special Committee on Automobile Insurance Legislation* (1978), 22–23.

legislature eliminated lawsuits for all nonpermanent injuries.[121] A few states placed no limits at all on lawsuits, hoping that injuries in most accidents would be minor enough to fall within the limits of no-fault coverage.

No-fault laws also encountered constitutional challenges, and they did not fare as well as workers compensation laws had in the 1910s. Limits on lawsuits and non-economic damages claims based on the amount of a victim's medical expenses were regularly challenged: because the cost of treating an injury did not always correlate with a victim's pain and suffering, said opponents, the limits discriminated against accident victims with low medical expenses and violated their rights to due process. Challenges were also made under state constitutional provisions guaranteeing access to the courts. American courts again divided: such challenges were rejected in Massachusetts but upheld in Florida and Illinois.[122] In some cases, flawed provisions could be, and were, corrected to overcome constitutional objections.[123] In several states, no-fault laws were challenged on the broader ground that they improperly singled out citizens involved in auto accidents for special treatment, but those challenges were also rejected. No-fault insurance, the courts said, was a good-faith effort to rationalize and reduce accident costs and, thus, was a legitimate use of the police power.[124]

The auto no-fault movement flagged in the late 1970s and soon returned to dormancy. No-fault advocates, like their workers compensation predecessors, had relied heavily on arguments that the new system would reduce litigation costs, thus ensuring that more premium dollars would go to accident victims and fewer to lawyers; but studies of auto no-fault laws in action indicated that many accident victims opted for liberal medical treatment so that they could exceed statutory caps and obtain the right to sue for non-economic damages, and that in many states, promised cost savings and lowered premiums had not materialized.[125]

No-fault also declined because many groups with an interest in the subject had been skeptical from the beginning. Many attorneys who specialized in representing

---

121. 1971 Fla. Laws, ch. 252; 1976 Fla. Laws, ch. 266; 1978 Fla. Laws, ch. 374; Maroney, "No-Fault Automobile Insurance," 79.

122. *Pinnick v. Cleary*, 271 N.E.2d 592 (Mass. 1971); *Kluger v. White*, 281 So.2d 1 (Fla. 1973); *Lasky v. State Farm Ins. Co.*, 296 So.2d 9 (Fla. 1974) (striking down a statutory revision enacted in response to *Kluger*); *Grace v. Howlett*, 283 N.E.2d 474 (Ill. 1972) (holding that certain statutory limits on recovery violated state constitutional prohibition of special legislation and that compulsory-arbitration provision violated constitutional right to trial by jury).

123. *Dillon v. Chapman*, 415 So.2d 12 (Fla. 1982) (upholding a statutory revision enacted in response to *Lasky*); see also 1972 Mich. Laws, ch. 294 (no-fault act); *Shavers v. Kelly*, 267 N.W.2d 72, 88–93 (Mich. 1978) (striking down provisions of act pertaining to insurance ratemaking structures); 1980 Mich. Laws, ch. 444 (revising structures in response to *Shavers*).

124. *Pinnick*, 271 N.E.2d 592, 602–03 (Mass. 1971); *Opinion of the Justices*, 304 A.2d 881 (N.H. 1973).

125. Engstrom, "No-Fault's Demise," 332–36, 341–46; see also Davies, "No-Fault History," 845–46.

accident victims were hostile to no-fault, and insurers' support was mild at best.[126] In 1978, the American Bar Association issued an influential no-fault study reported by University of Chicago law professor Richard Posner, a devout believer in law as a servant of economic efficiency who would soon go on to a long and influential career as a federal appellate judge. Posner believed that a no-fault system limited to minor accidents might be cost effective, but he doubted that any wide-ranging system would work. He also criticized limits on non-economic damages as unfair and defended existing fault-based systems, undergirded by private insurance, as "a positive feature in a society which values individual freedom of choice."[127] Several states repealed their no-fault laws in the early 1980s. Other no-fault laws remained in place but were not expanded, and no new laws were enacted after 1976.[128]

Judges and Juries in the Modern Era: Summary Judgment Triumphant

The mid-twentieth century had produced a steady increase in the socialization of tort law but a stasis in the balance of power between judges and juries in tort cases. Summary judgment, a uniquely powerful tool that allowed judges to analyze evidence and make a final disposition of cases without any jury involvement, was widely adopted during the era of peak socialization, but at first summary judgment motions were rarely filed and rarely granted. In an era of steadily-expanding court caseloads, many judges were unenthusiastic about the additional work that evaluating summary judgment motions would require, and some were fearful of being labeled as jury usurpers.[129] But during the 1970s, as court filings increased sharply and tort reformers decried the "litigation explosion" and cited it as a key reason for reform, jurists took a

---

126. Engstrom, "No-Fault's Demise," 322–27; *see Citizens Study Committee, Summary Transcript of Hearings on No-Fault Automobile Accident Reparation* (1972), A1–2, A6, at Wisconsin State Law Library, Madison (statement of insurance industry official explaining his organization's skepticism as to no-fault).

127. Am. Bar Ass'n, *Automobile No-Fault Insurance* (1978), 10, 60–64.

128. Repealing states included Nevada (1980), Pennsylvania (1984), New Jersey (1989), Georgia (1991), Connecticut (1994) and Colorado (2003). See Engstrom, "No-Fault's Demise," 306–07 and 306 notes 17–18; *see also, e.g.*, L.C. Folzon, "Michigan No-Fault: The Rise and Fall of Socialized Negligence," 56 *U. Det. J. Urban L.* 99 (1979).

129. *See, e.g.*, Mark W. Bennett, "Essay: From the 'No Spittin', No Cussin' and No Summary Judgment' Days of Employment Discrimination Litigation to the 'Defendant's Summary Judgment Affirmed Without Comment' Days: One Judge's Four-Decade Perspective," 57 *N.Y. L. Sch. L. Rev.* 685, 688–89 (2012); Philip A. Trautman, "Motions for Summary Judgment: Their Use and Effect in Washington," 45 *Wash. L. Rev.* 1, 3–4 (1970). As a young lawyer during the late 1970s and 1980s, the author saw several Wisconsin state trial judges state in open court that they were uncomfortable with summary judgment and preferred to leave the merits of cases to the jury. At one summary judgment hearing where both sides had moved for summary judgment and had filed reams of supporting documents, the judge entered the courtroom holding one side's stack of papers under one arm and the other side's stack under his other arm. He put the stacks down, smiled wryly, stated that given

new look at summary judgment as a possible solution to these problems and judicial wariness of summary judgment began to soften.[130]

In 1986, the U.S. Supreme Court issued three decisions, known as the "*Celotex* trilogy," that lowered the hurdles litigants were required to clear in order to obtain summary judgment in their favor. Prior to the trilogy, most courts required defendants to present conclusive evidence of non-liability in order to win a summary judgment motion and would deny the motion if the plaintiff presented any contrary evidence, no matter how thin; but now the high Court shifted the burden to opponents to produce more substantial evidence if they wished to avoid having summary judgment entered against them.[131] The *Celotex* trilogy elicited widespread criticism from jurists and judges who viewed it as an inappropriate encroachment on juries' fact-deciding powers,[132] but it proved popular at the state level. Six state supreme courts indicated during the late 1980s that they would follow the *Celotex* standard and that their trial courts should do the same;[133] seventeen states followed suit during the 1990s,[134] and

---

the volume of paper there was surely a dispute of material fact somewhere, and then denied both motions without further explanation.

130. *See, e.g.,* Walter Olson, *Liability: The Legal Revolution and Its Consequences* (1988); Olson, *The Litigation Explosion* (1991); Burke, *Lawyers, Lawsuits and Legal Rights*, 45; William W. Schwarzer, "Summary Judgment Under the Federal Rules: Defining Genuine Issues of Material Fact," 99 F.R.D. 465, 466 (1984); Stuart R. Pollak, "Liberalizing Summary Adjudication: A Proposal," 36 *Hastings L.J.* 419 (1985). More recent literature examining these events includes Marc A. Galanter, "An Oil Strike in Hell: Contemporary Legends About the Civil Justice System," 40 *Ariz. L. Rev.* 717, 717–18, 726 (1998); Deborah L. Rhode, "Frivolous Litigation and Civil Justice Reform: Miscasting the Problem, Recasting the Solution," 54 *Duke L.J.* 447 (2004); Stephen N. Subrin and Thomas O. Main, "The Fourth Era of American Civil Procedure," 162 *U. Pa. L. Rev.* 1839, 1840–41, 1845–46, 1861–63 (2014); and Zachary D. Clopton, "Procedural Retrenchment and the States," 106 *Cal. L. Rev.* 411, 417–18 (2018).

131. *Celotex Corp. v. Catrett*, 477 U.S. 317 (1986); *Anderson v. Liberty Lobby, Inc.*, 477 U.S. 242 (1986); *Matsushita Elec. Indus. Co. Ltd. v. Zenith Radio Corp.*, 475 U.S. 574 (1986). In 2007 the Supreme Court went a step further, instructing trial judges to grant summary judgment motions even when plaintiffs produced substantive evidence in opposition if, in the judge's view, that evidence "blatantly contradict[ed] the record." *Scott v. Harris*, 550 U.S. 372, 380 (2007).

132. Subrin and Main, "Fourth Era," 1840–41; *see also, e.g.,* Arthur R. Miller, "The Pretrial Rush to Judgment: Are the 'Litigation Explosion,' 'Liability Crisis,' and Efficiency Cliches Eroding Our Day in Court and Jury Trial Commitments?", 78 *NYU L. Rev.* 982 (2003); Miller, "Are the Federal Courthouse Doors Closing? What Happened to the Federal Rules of Civil Procedure?", 43 *Tex. Tech L. Rev.* 587 (2011); Bennett, "'No Spittin', No Cussin' and No Summary Judgment'"; Patricia M. Wald, "Summary Judgment at Sixty," 76 *Tex. L. Rev.* 1897 (1998).

133. Colorado, Maryland, Mississippi, West Virginia (all 1987); Vermont and Washington (1989). Cases in which these states indicated adherence to the *Celotex* standard are compiled at Clopton, "Procedural Retrenchment," 476–80.

134. Arizona (1990); Delaware, Massachusetts, Michigan, Ohio, South Carolina (all 1991); Nebraska (1992); Wisconsin (1993); Iowa (1994); New Jersey (1995); Pennsylvania (1996); Minnesota (1997); Arkansas (1998); and Alabama, Louisiana, Maine and Wyoming (all 1999). Clopton, "Procedural Retrenchment," 476–80. A decade after the *Celotex* trilogy was handed down, a leading federal judge concluded that summary judgment, "[i]ts flame lit by [the trilogy], and fueled by

an additional fourteen states have followed suit since 2000.[135] Thirteen states have declined to follow the trilogy and have adhered to the traditional, more jury-friendly summary judgment standard:[136] in the words of one New Mexico justice, their courts believe that "[p]ermitting trial courts a license to quantify or analyze the evidence in a given case...would...infringe on the jury's function as the trier of fact and the true arbiter of the credibility of witnesses."[137]

The *Celotex* trilogy was influential, but there is evidence that trial courts had increased their use of summary judgment even before the trilogy appeared. In 1960, federal courts disposed of only two-and-a-half percent of their cases by summary judgment; a subsequent study indicated that the rate increased in the 1970s and early 1980s to about fifteen percent, although the increase may have been due primarily to a sharp rise in civil-rights cases, which elicit summary judgment motions more frequently than other types of cases. Federal courts' use of summary judgment grew only modestly after the *Celotex* trilogy appeared.[138] No comparably broad studies exist for state courts, but the Five-State Survey suggests a similar pattern. Trial-court use of summary judgment in Five-State Survey tort cases increased sharply between 1970 and 1980, before *Celotex*, and, as in the federal courts, there was no noticeable uptick in this trend after the *Celotex* trilogy was decided. Nonetheless, by 1990 summary judgment had become the dominant case-disposition tool: nonsuits and other alternative forms of early case disposition (other than demurrers, which, as previously explained, generally did not function as true case-disposition tools)[139] had virtually disappeared in the Five-State Survey courts, and they have not returned since.

---

overloaded dockets...has spread swiftly through the underbrush of undesirable cases, taking down some healthy trees as it goes." Wald, "Summary Judgment at Sixty," 1941.

135. Illinois (2000); California (2001); North Dakota, South Dakota (both 2003); New Hampshire (2004); Nevada (2005); Alaska, Rhode Island (both 2007); Idaho; Kansas (both 2009); Montana (2010); North Carolina (2011); Hawaii (2013); and Tennessee (2015). *See* Clopton, "Procedural Retrenchment," 476–80.

136. Connecticut, Florida, Georgia, Indiana, Kentucky, Missouri, New Mexico, New York, Oklahoma, Oregon, Texas, Utah and Virginia. *See* Clopton, "Procedural Retrenchment," 476–80.

137. *Romero v. Philip Morris Inc.*, 242 P.2d 280, 288 (N.M. 2010) (citations omitted); *see also Powel v. Chaminade Coll. Prep., Inc.*, 197 S.W.3d 576, 591 note 7 (Mo. 2006) (criticizing federal courts for "overly aggressive" use of summary judgment); *Yun Tung Chow v. Reckitt & Colman, Inc.*, 950 N.E.2d 113 (N.Y. 2011) (Smith, J., concurring).

138. Joe S. Cecil et al., "A Quarter-Century of Summary Judgment Practice in Six Federal District Courts," 4 *J. Emp. Leg. Stud.* 861, 875–76, 882–87 (2007); Stephen P. Burbank, "Vanishing Civil Trials and Summary Judgments in Federal Civil Cases: Drifting Toward Bethlehem or Gomorrah," 1 *J. Emp. Leg. Stud.* 591, 608 (2004). The same study indicated that federal courts have consistently granted about 40–45 percent of summary judgment motions since the 1970s. Cecil et al., 887.

139. *See* Chapter 3, note 125 and accompanying text.

FIGURE 5.2
Five-State Survey: Trial Court Use of Early Case Disposal Procedures, 1960–2010[140]

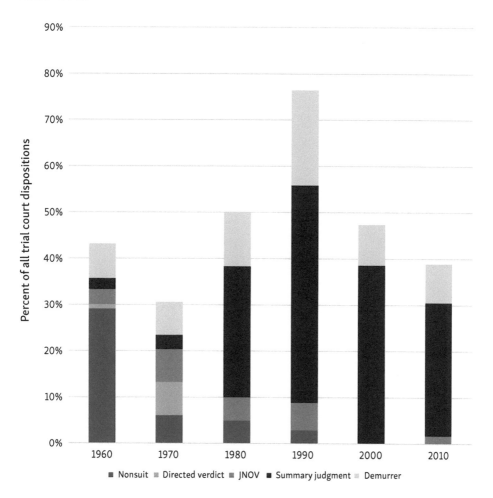

■ Nonsuit ■ Directed verdict ■ JNOV ■ Summary judgment ■ Demurrer

But the Five-State Survey also suggests that increased use of summary judgment may not have resulted in an overall shift of power from juries to judges, at least in the Survey states. The proportions of Survey cases in which the trial court took the case away from the jury or prevented it from going to the jury, or in which the supreme court overturned a jury verdict upheld by the trial court, remained remarkably stable throughout the Second Industrial Era, the Progressive era and the era of peak socialization, consistently between fifty and sixty percent of all cases. In 1980 and 1990 the

---

140. The cases on which Figure 5.2 is based are described in Appendix 2; the calculations are described in Appendix 3.

proportion rose, but since 2000 the proportion of cases taken away from juries has moved back toward pre-1980 levels.[141]

FIGURE 5.3
Five-State Survey: Judicial Deference to Juries, 1930–2010

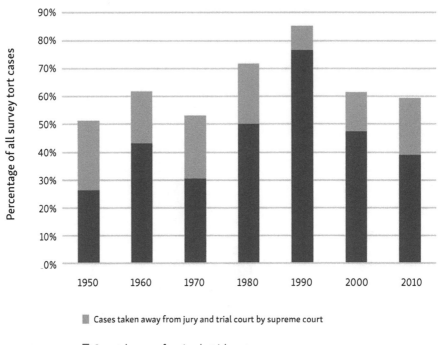

■ Cases taken away from jury and trial court by supreme court

■ Cases taken away from jury by trial court

One should not read too much into the Survey figures. They do not show whether trial courts used summary judgment liberally or conservatively in tort cases that did not reach state supreme courts. It is unknown whether other states would produce similar results; and the reasons for the 1980–1990 rise and the subsequent move back toward historical levels are not clear. These are matters worthy of future study. Nevertheless, the Survey confirms that if the debate over the proper balance of power between judges and juries continues, as it surely will, the virtues and pitfalls of summary judgment will be a central part of that debate.

The vision of complete socialization of the cost of accidents, so tantalizingly close in 1970, has proven to be a mirage, but the path away from that vision has been anything but direct. Such indirection allows only a glimpse through dark glass of what tort law's future may hold. Courts and legislatures have decisively checked efforts at complete accident cost socialization and have affirmed individual responsibility's con-

---

141. *See* Figure 5.3; *see also* Chapter 3, Figure 3.2; Chapter 4, Figure 4.6, and the notes and text accompanying all figures. The cases on which Figure 5.3 is based are described in Appendix 2; the calculations are described in Appendix 3.

tinuing importance as a core element of tort law. Reduction of a victim's recovery in proportion to his own fault has become an integral part of comparative negligence and, increasingly, of strict product liability. The economic loss doctrine has halted tort law's incursion into contract law, thus protecting contract law's core principles of individual freedom to set the terms of one's relationship with others and responsibility for honoring those terms. The decline of immunities during the era of peak socialization led not to death but to transformation during the modern era: new forms of immunity have proliferated, most notably damages caps and customized laws that shield from liability a wide variety of groups and activities deemed socially desirable. The hope that auto accidents would provide a showcase for socialization of accident costs, just as workplace accidents had done at the turn of the twentieth century, was dashed for a second time: the auto no-fault experiment demonstrated socialization's limits more than its promise.

But socialization has not retreated on all fronts: it too has proved hardy at its core. Though comparative negligence and strict liability have been cabined, their basic socializing elements have become deeply embedded in tort law. Since 1970, contributory negligence has gone from being a minority rule to a near relic. Modern-era lawmakers have provided new defenses to manufacturers of defective products, but there has been no thought of reverting to privity or to a requirement that consumers injured by defective products prove manufacturer negligence. It is also important to remember that not all states have fully joined the modern movement away from socialization. Some have preserved full joint and several liability for defendants; some have refused to allow manufacturers to soften strict liability through comparative negligence; some have rejected the economic loss doctrine or have weakened it through adoption of numerous exceptions; and some have declined to adopt damages caps or other laws designed to lessen the burden of damages for socially-preferred defendants, either because of continuing judicial hostility to such changes or because their constitutions prevent them from doing so.

It remains to be seen whether, in the coming decades, the resistance to increased socialization and resurgence of free-labor principles of individual responsibility that have marked the modern era will advance further or will halt or reverse course. It also remains to be seen whether the future will produce a reactive movement, similar to that which arose during the Progressive era, to reduce the role of summary judgment in tort cases and shift the balance of power in the courtroom back toward juries. The complexity and conflicts of the modern era provide no sure clues. American tort law has consistently reflected the larger social and economic movements and debates that have shaped the nation's history, and all one can say with assurance is that that is likely to continue.

APPENDIX ONE

Survey of State Court Cross-Citations, 1800–1860

Figure 1.1 and the accompanying text are based on a sample survey of all American state supreme court decisions for the years 1800, 1820, 1840 and 1860. The sample was obtained by selecting approximately 20 decisions for each state for each of these years. Separate samples were taken of New York (1820–1840) and New Jersey (1820–1860) law and equity decisions which were reported separately in the years just identified. Rhode Island (1800–1840), Ohio (1820) and Michigan (1840) are not included for the years just identified because they did not publish case reports for those years.

The sample for each state in a particular year was obtained by selecting the earliest decision for that year and then selecting decisions appearing at intervals equal to the quotient of the total number of pages occupied by cases for that year divided by 20. For example, if all decisions for a state for 1820 were contained in one volume of 400 pages, the decisions which appear at pages 1, 20, 40, and so on up to page 400 would be selected. The citations in each sampled decision to English decisions, to decisions of other state courts and to the court's own decisions, including citations in concurring and dissenting opinions, were then tabulated.

Where the total number of initially sampled decisions for a given state and year was substantially less than 20 (as was the case for several states in 1800), decisions were added from other years. In such cases, the years are identified in the table in italics. When a selected decision was long and covered several interval page numbers, cases were added to reach a total count of approximately 20 cases.

The table below identifies the volumes of case reports and the page numbers at which sampled decisions appeared. "n" means the total number of decisions sampled for each state and year. Bracketed page numbers, e.g. "(20,40, 60)," denote a long decision comprising all of the listed interval numbers. Ellipses indicate a regular sequence of page numbers sampled: for example, "90, 105,...225" means that all decisions appearing at 15-page intervals between pages 105 and 225 were sampled. In some cases, it was necessary to deviate from a regular page interval in order to obtain an adequate sample.

Appendix One Survey of State Court Cross-Citations, 1800–1860

1800	n	
Connecticut	20	**1 Day** 1, 15, 30, (45, 60, 75); 90, 105,…315. *(1802–04)*
Massachusetts	16	**1 Mass.** 1; 12, 24,…96; 101; 212, 224,…272. *(1804)*
Vermont	20	**1 Vt.** 12, 24,…72; (84, 96); 112, 124,…184; 212, 224,…272. *(1800–01)*
New Hampshire	20	**Smith** 1, 39, 45, 49, 52, 53, 60, 63, 74, 80, 87, 91, 100, 104, 109, 113, 115, 117, 122, 127. *(1798–1805)*
New York	19	**Johns.** 1; 11,…121; **Coleman & Caines** 91, 101…141.
New Jersey	22	**2 Pennington** 1; 15, 30,…, 315. *(1806–07)*
Pennsylvania	22	**2 Yeates** 529, 530, 540; (550, 570); 580; **3 Yeates** 1; 10, 15,…45; 50, 60,…100; (110–120).
Maryland	21	**1 Harr. & J.** 10, 20,…(70, 80, 90); 100, 110,…230. *(1800–01)*
Delaware	21	**1 Boorstin** 170, 180,…310; 460, 470; **2 Boorstin** 130, 140, 150, 160.
Virginia	23	**2 Call** 180, 190,…270; (280, 290); 300, 310, 320, (330, 340); 350, 360, 370; (380, 400); 412, 420, 430.
North Carolina	21	**Taylor** 145, 159, 161, 165, 170, 172, 176, 196, 201, 204, 207, 210, 214, 216, 223, 225, 227, 231, 237, 240, 243.
South Carolina	22	**2 Bay** 240, 270,…540; **Brevard** 30, 60,…330.
Georgia	20	**T. Charlton** 15, 30; (45, 60); 75, 90,…315.
Kentucky	23	**Sneed** 15, 30,…345.
Tennessee	21	**1 Tenn.** 25, 50,…525. *(1791–1815)*

1820	n	
Connecticut	23	**3 Conn.** (230–240); 250, 260,…320; (330–340); 350, 360,…470.
Massachusetts	23	**16 Mass.** 274; 290, 305,…335; 350, 365; 385, 400,…520; 522; **17 Mass.** (1, 15, 30); 32; 45, 60,…90.
Vermont	22	**1 D. Chipman** 362, 372,…452; **2 D. Chipman** 9, 19,…69; (79, 89); 91; 99, 109, 119.
New Hampshire	25	**2 N.H.** 166, 169, 174, 184, 190, 197, 202, 212, 216, 223, 227, 236, 242, 2251, 263, 282, 284, 289, 203, 296, 300, 303, 306, 310, 317.
Maine	19	**1 Me.** 1, 7, 15, 22; (30, 57); 60, 67, 75, 82, 90, 97, 105, 112, 120, 127, 135, 142, 150, 152.

Appendix One Survey of State Court Cross-Citations, 1800–1860

New York (law)	20	**17 Johns.** 440, 470,…530, (560, 590); **18 Johns.** 1; 30, 60,…420.
New York (equity)	18	**4 Johns. Ch.** (228, 250); 275, 300,…675.
New Jersey	25	**5 N.J.** 845, 862, 863, 872, 878, 885, 896, 904, 906, 911, 914, 917, 924, 928, 936, 953, 955, 957, 961, 964, 967, 970, 976, 988.
Pennsylvania	22	**5 Serg. & Rawle** 450, 470,…530; **6 Serg. & Rawle** 1; 20, 40,…320.
Maryland	33	**5 Harr. & J.** 1, 10, 23, 27, 36, 45, 51, 59, 50, 51, 63, 64, 68, 69, 78, 82, 86, 100, 111, 113, 115, 117, 120, 122, 125, 127, 130, 135, 139, 147, 150, 155.
Delaware	26	**2 Boorstin** 459, 468, 471, 473, 478, 489, 505, 515, 517, 520, 523, 524, 532, 535, 537, 539, 542, 546, 550, 555, 557, 571, 572, 576, 578, 587.
Virginia	20	**20 Va.** 460, 475, 490, 501; 520, 535,…580; **21 Va.** 15, 30; (45, 60, 75, 90); 105, 123; 135, 150,…210.
North Carolina	19	**2 Hawks** 10, 20,…90; (100, 110, 120, 130); (140, 150, 160); (170, 180); 190, 200, 210, 221, 225, 230, 240.
South Carolina	20	**Nott & McCord** 220, 240,…580, 596.
Georgia	24	**R.M. Charlton** 40, 50,…140; (150, 160, 170); 180, 190,…240; 244; 250, 260, 270, 280.
Indiana	21	**1 Blackford** 53, 56, 58, 60, 63, 66, 69; 71, 74,…110.
Illinois	12	**Breese** 23, 24,…28; 30, 31, 32, 34, 35, 36.
Kentucky	22	**9 Ky.** 200, 230,…620; **10 Ky.** 30, 60,…210.
Tennessee	20	**4 Tenn.** 1; 25, 50,…450. *(1816–17)*
Missouri	21	**1 Houck** 20, 25,…60; 66; 70, 75,…120.
Alabama	24	**Minor** (all cases).
Mississippi	20	**1 Miss.** 1, 7, 24, 30, 36, 43, 49, 54, 64, 66, 67, 69, 72, 74, 75, 80, 83, 86, 87, 91. *(1818–21)*
Louisiana	20	**7 Martin** (O.S.) 375, 435,…675; **8 Martin** (O.S.) 60, 120,…480; (540, 600); 660, 720; **9 Martin** (O.S.) 60, 120, 180.

1840	n	
Connecticut	23	**13 Conn.** 375, 390,…570; **14 Conn.** 1; 15, 30,…135.
Massachusetts	16	**42 Mass.** 210, 245,…560; **43 Mass.** 35, 70,…175.
Vermont	21	**12 Vt.** 9; 35, 70,…700.

Appendix One Survey of State Court Cross-Citations, 1800–1860

New Hampshire	22	10 N.H. 500, 525, 550, 575; 11 N.H. 25, 50,...450.
Maine	24	16 Me. 425, 450, 475; 17 Me. 9; 25, 50,...450; 18 Me. 9, 25.
New York (law)	23	23 Wend. 9; 80, 160,...640; 24 Wend. 9; 80, 160,...640; 25 Wend. 9; 80, 160, 240, 320.
New York (equity)	20	8 Paige 74; 100, 125,...525; 527.
New Jersey (law)	23	17 N.J.L. 360, 375; (390–405); 420, 435,...495; 18 N.J.L. 1; 15, 30, 46; 60, 75,...195.
New Jersey (equity)	20	4 N.J. Eq. 42, 52, 62, 73; (82–92); (102–112); 122, 132,...182; (192, 202); 212, 222,...262.
Pennsylvania	21	5 Wharton 426; 450, 475,...575; 6 Wharton 9; 25, 250,...325.
Maryland	23	11 Md. 110, 120,...180; (190, 200); 212; (220, 230, 240); 250, 260; (270, 280); 283; 290, 300, 310, 320; (330, 340); 342, 350, 360.
Delaware	20	3 Harr. 60, 70,...120; 136, 140, (150, 160,...240); 241, 266, 267, 271, 280, 283, 290, 300, 312.
Virginia	16	37 Va. 560, 590,...710; 38 Va. (1, 30); 60, 90,...450.
North Carolina		23 N.C. 1; 15, 30,...285.
South Carolina	19	McMull. 15, 30, 45; Cheves 60, 75,...285.
Georgia	20	1 Dec. Sup. Ct. Ga. (10, 20); 34, 40; (50, 60); 70, (80, 90); 91, 100, (110, 120); 130, 140,...170 (1841–42); 2 Dec. Sup. Ct. Ga. (1, 10); (20, 30); 33, 40, 50, 60.
Ohio	18	10 Ohio St. 1; 20, 40,...340.
Indiana	23	5 Blackford 260, 270,...480.
Illinois	19	3 Ill. 208, 219, 236, 257, 280, 297, 319, 340, 357, 377, 410, 438, 460, 480, 499, 516, 539, 559, 575.
Arkansas	19	2 Ark. 300, 310,...430; 3 Ark. 440, 450,...480. (1837–40)
Kentucky	21	39 Ky. 275, 300,...600; 40 Ky. 25, 50,...175.
Tennessee	20	20 Tenn. 459, 480, 500, 520, 540; 21 Tenn. 13; 20, 40,...280.
Missouri	21	6 Houck 25, 40,...325.
Alabama	22	1 Ala. 9; 35, 70,...735.
Mississippi	19	5 Miss. 260, 300,...540; (580, 620); 660, 690; 6 Miss. 14; 40, 80, 120, 160; (200, 240); 242, 280, (320, 360).

Appendix One   Survey of State Court Cross-Citations, 1800–1860   197

Louisiana	21	**14 La.** 250, 320,...530; **15 La.** 70, 140,...560; **16 La.** 70, 140,...560.
Texas	19	**Dallam** 360, 375,...630. (*1840–44*)

1860	n	
Connecticut	21	**29 Conn.** 1; 20, 40,...280; (300, 320); 340, 360,...400.
Rhode Island	20	**6 R.I.** 380, (390, 400); 404; 410, 420,...470; (480, 490); 491; 500, 510; (520, 530); 534; 543; 550, 560, 570.
Massachusetts	22	**80 Mass.** 365, 435, 505, 575; **81 Mass.** 1; 70, 140,...560; **82 Mass.** 1; 70, 140,...560.
Vermont	21	**33 Vt.** 30, 60,...330; (360, 390); 420, 450,...630; 659.
New Hampshire	24	**40 N.H.** 120, 180,...540; **41 N.H.** 9; 60, 120,...540; **42 N.H.** 9; 60, 120, 180, 240.
Maine	21	**47 Me.** 90, 120, 330, 360, 390, 480; **48 Me.** 40, 250, 275, 380, 400, 440, 500; **49 Me.** 30, 225, 300, 340, 416, 500, 530; **50 Me.** 180.
New York	24	**20 N.Y.** 531, 590; **21 N.Y.** 9; 60, 120,...600; **22 N.Y.** 9; 60, 120,...540.
New Jersey (law)	20	**28 N.J.L.** 180, 205, 219, 230, 255; (280–478); 480; 487; 505, 530, 555, 560, 580; **29 N.J.L.** 15, 40, 44, 65, 90, 96, 115.
New Jersey (equity)	21	**13 N.J. Eq.** 13, 23,...73; (83, 93); 103, 113,...223.
Pennsylvania	23	**36 Pa.** 150, 200,...500; 546; **37 Pa.** 9; 50, 100,...500; **38 Pa.** 9, 50, 100.
Maryland	24	**16 Md.** 90, 120,...480; 502, 540, 570; **17 Md.** 1; 30, 60,...180.
Delaware	15	**7 Houst.** 206, 209, 223, 234, 242, 243, 246, 268, 277, 282, 286, 287, 300, 305, 311.
Virginia	19	**56 Va.** (460, 475); 490, 505, 520, 535; (551, 565); 580; (595, 610, 625); 640, 655, 671; **57 Va.** (1, 15); (30, 45); 60, 75,...120; 133.
North Carolina	22	**58 N.C.** 300, 315,...435; **59 N.C.** 1; 15, 30,...165.
South Carolina	20	**11 Rich. Eq.** 220, 260, 300,...480; (500, 520); 540; **12 Rich. L.** 420, 460,...700; **13 Rich. L.** 40, 80, 120.
Georgia	23	**29 Ga.** 600, 680, 760; **30 Ga.** 80, 160,...960; **31 Ga.** 80, 160,...640.

Florida	21	9 Fla. 10, 15; (30, 45); 60, 75, 90; (105, 120); 150, 156, 160, 180, 187, 210, 212, 240, 255, 256, 270, 278 285, 300.
Ohio	20	11 Ohio St. 1; 35, 70, … 665.
Indiana	23	14 Ind. 100, 150, …. 500; 542, 600; 15 Ind. 1; 50, 100, … 500; 16 Ind. 9.
Illinois	21	23 Ill. 237, 298, 348, 400, 450, 500, 531, 599; 24 Ill. 50, 100, 150, 200, 249, 299, 347, 387, 444, 500, 536, 598, 648; 25 Ill. 49, 100.
Michigan	19	8 Mich. 33, 67, 100, 133, 167, (200, 233); 267, 300, 333, … 533; 9 Mich. 33, 67, 100, 133.
Wisconsin	22	10 Wis. 200, 300, 400, 500; 11 Wis. 1; 100, 200, … 500; 12 Wis. 1; 100, 200, … 700; 13 Wis. 1; 100, 200, 300.
Minnesota	25	4 Minn. 25, 50, … 425; 5 Minn. 25, 50, … 200.
Iowa	21	10 Iowa 300, 335, 370, … 580; 11 Iowa 1; 35, 70, … 385.
Arkansas	23	21 Ark. 9; 50, 100, … 600; 22 Ark. 1; 50, 100, … 450.
Kentucky	20	60 Ky. 20, 40, … 400.
Tennessee	21	41 Tenn. 30, 60, … 600; 630.
Missouri	20	29 Mo. 250, 310, … 550; 30 Mo. 60, 120, … 600; 31 Mo. 60, 120, 180, 240..
Alabama	21	36 Ala. 351; 375, 400, … 725; 37 Ala. 17; 25, 50, 75, 100
Mississippi	20	38 Miss. 350, 400, … 650; (700, 750); 39 Miss. 50, 100, 150, 200, (250, 300); 350, 400, … 650.
Louisiana	21	15 La. Ann. 35, 70, … 715.
Texas	21	24 Tex. 606, 670; 25 Tex. 65, 130, … 800; 25 Tex. Supp. 15, 80, … 405.
California	22	15 Cal. 60, 120, … 300; 362; 420, 480; (540, 600); 16 Cal. 60, 120, … 600; 17 Cal. 60, 120, 180.
Oregon	22	1 Or. 220, 230, … 330; 2 Or. 20; (30, 40); 50, 60 … 120; (130, 140); (150, 160).

APPENDIX TWO

The Five-State Survey

Five-State Survey methodology. The five Survey states, New York, North Carolina, Wisconsin, Texas and California, were chosen in order to provide geographical diversity. The Survey includes the decisions of each state's highest court at ten-year intervals beginning in 1810 and ending in 2010. For each Survey year, all tort cases reported in volumes covering all or part of the year in question were examined. For example, if a court's 1820 decisions were reported in a volume that also included decisions from 1819 and 1821, the 1819 and 1821 cases for that volume were included in the survey; 1819 and 1821 cases reported in other volumes not containing 1820 decisions were not included. Some state courts produced no decisions or only a few decisions for 1800, 1810 and 1820. In those instances, cases in the nearest years were included in the survey.

Tort cases were classified as follows ("PI" means personal injury):

- *PI—railroad accidents (PIR),* not including injuries to railroad workers.
- *PI—accidents causing injuries to railroad workers (PIRW).*
- *PI—workplace accidents (PIW),* not including injuries to railroad workers.
- *PI—personal injury on business premises (PIPM).* Injuries to store customers and other visitors to business premises.
- *PI—products liability (PIPD).* Injuries and loss resulting from defective products.
- *PI—professional malpractice (PIML).*
- *Personal injury-general (PI).* All personal injury cases other than those in the above categories.
- *Debt (D).* This includes suits against creditors and sheriffs for improper debt-collection practices.
- *Property harm (HP).* This includes business torts and harm to land.
- *Automobile accidents (A).*
- *Other (O).* This includes all tort cases not classifiable in the above categories.

Appendix Two The Five-State Survey

Table. The Survey included the following cases:

1810	
NC	5 N.C. 39 (PI); 6 N.C. 61 (PIW).
NY	6 Johns. 5 (PIW), 9 (PIW), 62 (D), 121 (D), 168 (HP), 195 (D), 270 (D), 277 (D); 7 Johns. 1 (HP), 137 (D), 165 2(D), 168 (D), 174 (D), 189 (D), 254 (HP), 477 (D), 535 (HP).

1820	
NC	6 N.C. 389 (HP).
NY	17 Johns. 63 (D), 92 (HP), 306 (HP), 439 (HP); 18 Johns. 48 (D), 52 (D), 257 (PI), 390 (D).

1830	
NC	13 N.C. 370 (PI), 388 (HP).
NY	5 Wend. 170 (D), 231 (D), 237 (D), 240 (D), 298 (D), 506 (HP); 6 Wend. 367 (D), 382 (HP), 418 (PI).

1840	
NC	23 N.C. 56 (HP), 143 (PI), 163 (HP), 240 (PI), 265 (HP).
NY	20 Wend. 51 (PI), 79 (PI), 172 (HP), 188 (PI), 210 (PI), 223 (HP), 236 (D), 281 (PI), 394 (D), 615 (PI); 23 Wend. 354 (HP), 425 (PIR), 462 (D), 480 (D); 24 Wend. 31 (D), 188 (HP), 379 (HP), 381 (D), 418 (PI), 429 (PI).
TX	Dallam 496 (PI), 518 (D), 561 (PI).

1850	
NC	No reported tort cases.
NY	2 Comstock 115 (HP), 126 (D),159 (HP), 163 (HP), 165 (PI), 293 (HP),517 (D); 25 Wend. 371 (PI), 462 (HP); 3 Comstock 463 (HP), 489 (HP), 506 (HP); 4 Comstock 38 (PI), 173 (D), 195 (HP), 349 (HP).
TX	None.
WI	None.
CA	1 Cal. 160 (D), 365 (PI), 459 (PI).

1860	
NC	52 N.C. 4 (D), 64 (PI), 169 (D), 182 (PI), 225 (HP), 272 (HP), 439 (PI), 468 (HP); 58 N.C. 57 (HP).
NY	6 Smith 65 (PI), 492 (PIR); 7 Smith 103 (HP), 111 (HP), 241 (HP), 386 (HP), 481 (D); 8 Smith 191 (PIR), 209 (HP).
TX	24 Tex. 655 (O); 25 Tex. 172 (HP), 345 (HP); 25 Tex. Supp. 188 (HP), 205 (HP).
WI	11 Wis. 68 (PI), 167 (PIR), 248 (O).

CA	14 Cal. 387 (HP), 553 (HP); 15 Cal. 66 (D), 853(HP), 319 3(HP); 17 Cal. 87 (D), 97 (HP), 308 (HP), 436 (D), 487 (PI), 613 (HP).

1870	
NC	64 N.C. 44 (HP), 235 (HP), 382 (O), 399 (PI), 479 (D), 688 (HP), 780 (PI).
NY	2 Hand 42 (HP), 113 (PI), 296 (PIR), 464 (D), 498 (PI), 502 (PIR), 525 (PIR), 544 (HP); 3 Hand 44 (D), 47 (PI), 132 (D), 140 (HP), 212 (HP), 258 (HP), 351 (O), 459 (PI), 468 (PIR); 4 Hand 75 (PI), 152 (PI), 202 (PIR), 514 (D), 527 (PIR), 539 (HP), 566 (PI).
TX	32 Tex. 195 (HP), 208 (HP), 355 1 (PI).
WI	25 Wis. 654 (HP); 26 Wis. 56 (HP), 145 (HP), 223 (HP), 537 (HP); 27 Wis. 158 (PIR), 191 (HP).
CA	39 Cal. 315 (PI), 412 (HP), 485 (PI), 587 (PIR), 700 (D); 40 Cal. 14 (HP), 121 (HP), 188 (PI), 396 (HP), 428 (HP), 532 (HP), 578 (PI), 657 (HP).

1880	
NC	83 N.C. 80 (HP), 128 (HP), 159 (PI), 575 (HP).
NY	34 N.Y. 19 (HP), 72 (PIR), 240 (PIW), 464 (PIR), 470 (HP); 35 N.Y. 46 (PIW), 82 (HP), 100 (HP), 162 (HP), 212 (PIR), 236 (PIR), 239 (HP), 353 (HP), 390 (HP), 408 (HP) ,458 (PIW), 579 (HP), 614 (HP), 622 (PI); 36 N.Y. 21 (PI), 26 (HP), 52 (PI), 86 (HP), 206 (PIW), 285 (HP), 373 (PIW), 428 (PI), 516 (PIW); 37 N.Y. 278 (HP), 308 (HP), 327 (HP), 370 (PIW), 424 (PIR); 38 N.Y. 7 (PIW), 121 (PIR), 178 (PI), 201 (HP), 231 (HP), 358 (PI), 514 (HP), 572 (PIR), 595 (PIR), 620 (PIR).
TX	52 Tex. 19 (PIR), 112 (PIR), 178 (PIR), 534 (PI), 587 (PI), 638 (HP); 53 Tex. 46 (PIR), 139 (PIR), 206 (PIW), 289 (PIR), 318 (PIW), 364 (PIR); 54 Tex. 45 (PI), 233 (PIR), 556 (PIW), 563 (HP), 578 (HP), 615 (PIR), 641 (HP).
WI	49 Wis. 254 (HP), 358 (PIR), 529 (PIR), 605 (HP), 609 (PIW), 669 (PI); 50 Wis. 231 (PIR), 292 (PI), 375 (PI), 381 (PIW), 419 (PIW), 462 (PIW), 494 (PI).
CA	54 Cal. 339 (HP), 418 (PI), 491 PI); 55 Cal. 570 (PIR), 593 (PIR); 56 Cal. 136 (HP), 388 (PIR), 513 (PIR); 57 Cal. 15 (PIR), 462 (HP).

1890	
NC	105 N.C. 63 (PIR), 100 (PIR), 168 (PIR), 272 (PIR), 279 (PIR), 301 (PIR), 381 (HP), 404 (PIR), 537 (PIW), 549 (HP), 567 (HP); 106 N.C. 1 (PIW), 178 (PIR), 327 (PIR), 370 (HP), 415 (D), 449 (HP), 576 (PIR), 686 (PIR), 721 (HP), 731 (PIW), 748 (PIR).

NY	117 N.Y. 118 (PIW), 285 (PI), 293 (PIR), 505 (PIR), 542 (PIW), 638 (PIW); 118 N.Y. 55 (HP), 77 (PIR), 118 (HP), 156 (PI), 199 (PI), 224 (PIW), 244 (HP), 304 (PIR), 314 (PIR), 99 (PI), 89 (PIW), 497 (PIR), 527 (PIW), 533 (PIR), 556 (PIR), 571 (PIW), 575 (PI), 666 (HP); 119 N.Y. 147 (PIR), 188 (PIW), 221 (PIW), 241 (PI), 263 (HP), 316 (HP), 380 (HP), 468 (PIW), 540 (HP), 603 (HP); 120 N.Y. 98 (PI), 117 (PIR), 164 (HP), 170 (PIR), 178 (HP), 223 (PI), 228 (HP), 290 (PIR), 315 (PI), 323 (PIW), 332 (HP), 337 (PI), 427 (HP), 433 (PIW), 467 (PIR), 506 (PI), 526 (PIW), 571 (PIR); 121 N.Y. 22 (HP), 119 (HP), 126 (PIR), 147 (PI), 207 (PIW), 415 (HP); 122 N.Y. 1 (HP), 18 (HP), 91 (PIR), 118 (HP), 153 (HP), 222 (HP), 371 (PIW), 423 (HP), 539 (PIW), 557 (PIW), 618 (PIW), 646 (PI); 123 N.Y. 1 (PIW), 52 (HP), 236 (HP), 280 (PIW), 363 (HP), 391 (PIR), 405 (PI), 641 (PIW), 645 (PIR); 125 N.Y. 15 (PIW), 50 (PIW), 118 (HP), 155 (HP), 164 (HP), 299 (PI), 353 (HP), 407 (PIR), 422 (PIR), 526 (PIR), 641 (HP), 715 (PIR), 737 (PIW), 760 (PIR), 774 (PIW).
TX	75 Tex. 1 (HP), 4 (PIW), 18 (HP), 19 (PIR), 26 (HP), 41 (PIR), 56 (PIW), 61 (PIW), 77 (PIR), 151 (PIW), 155 (PIR), 158 (PIR), 220 (PIW), 256 (HP), 270 (PI), 300 (HP), 310 (PIW), 334 (HP), 531 (HP), 537 (HP), 557 (PIR), 583 (PIR), 634 (HP), 667 (PIW); 76 Tex. 66 (HP), 73 (PIR), 90 (PIR), 121 (HP), 141 (PI), 168 (PIR), 210 (PI), 217 (HP), 219 (PIW), 235 (PIW), 262 (PIW), 310 (D), 350 (PIW), 353 (PI), 409 (HP), 421 (PIW), 437 (PIW), 473 (PIW), 499 (PIW), 502 (PIR), 611 (PIW), 630 (PIW), 642 (HP); 77 Tex. 83 (HP), 73 (HP), 179 (HP), 232 (PIR), 245 (HP), 291 (PI), 310 (PI), 356 (PIW), 494 (PIR), 560 (PIR), 583 (PI); 78 Tex. 211 (HP), 279 (HP), 294 (PIW), 298 (PIR), 300 (PIR), 307 (PIR), 314 (PIR), 333 (HP), 353 (D), 369 (PIR), 372 (HP), 397 (PIR), 421 (PIR), 439 (PIW), 486 (PIW), 536 (PIW), 621 (PIR), 657 (PIW), 661 (PIR); 79 Tex. 13 (PIW), 26 (HP), 65 (HP), 78 (PIR), 85 (PIR), 104 (PIW), 130 (PIW), 224 (HP), 341 (PIR), 371 (PIR), 427 (HP), 444 (HP), 448 (HP), 457 (PIR), 468 (PIR), 531 (PIW), 540 (PIW), 584 (PIR), 604 (HP), 608 (PIR), 619 (PIW), 642 (PIR), 649 (HP), 675 (PIW), 678 (PIW); 80 Tex. 56 (HP), 59 (PIW), 69 (PI), 71 (HP), 73 (PIR), 85 (PIW), 117 (PIW), 146 (HP), 152 (PIW), 178 (PIW), 202 (PIR), 270 (HP), 289 (HP), 308 (HP), 356 (HP), 406 (HP), 420 (HP), 572 (PIR), 602 (HP), 608 (PI), 652 (PIW).
WI	75 Wis. 1 (PI), 18 (PI), 24 (PI), 62 (PI), 77 (PI), 121 (PIR), 130 (HP), 381 (PIR), 444 (PIR), 517 (PIR), 532 (PIR), 579 (PIW), 642 (PI), 654 (PIR); 76 Wis. 43 (PIR), 120 (PIW), 136 (PIW), 242 (O), 335 (PI), 344 (PIW), 399 (PIR), 422 (PIR), 499 (PI), 542 (PIR); 77 Wis. 9 (PIW), 14 (PIW), 51 (PIW), 152 (PI), 174 (O), 218 (PIR), 228 (PIR), 247 (PIR), 349 (PIR), 371 (PIR), 505 (PIR), 523 (PI), 544 (PI), 585 (PIR), 621 (PIR); 78 Wis. 22 (PIW), 66 (PI), 89 (O), 98 (O), 120 (PIR), 127 (PIW), 251 (PI), 339 (HP), 382 (PIR), 396 (PIR).

CA	82 Cal. 77 (HP), 184 (HP), 595 (HP), 604 (D); 83 Cal. 18 (PIR), 96 (HP), 198 (HP), 636 (HP); 84 Cal. 12 (HP), 89 (PI), 219 (PIW), 311 (HP), 489 (PIW), 515 (PIW); 85 Cal. 63 (PIR), 291 (PIR), 329 (HP); 86 Cal. 374 (PIR), 445 (PIW), 633 (PI); 87 Cal. 62 (PIR), 134 (HP), 464 (PIW), 483 (HP), 545 (PI), 629 (PI).

1900	
NC	126 N.C. 88 (PIR), 103 (PIR), 200 (PIR), 304 (HP), 343 (PIR), 370 (PIR), 385 (PIPD), 431 (HP), 563 (PIR), 629 (PIR), 725 (PIR), 735 (PIR), 797 (PIR), 803 (PIPM), 811 (PI), 894 (PIR), 908 (PI); 127 N.C. 29 (PIW), 85 (PI), 146 (PI), 203 (PIPM), 255 (PIPM), 293 (PIPD), 304 (PIPD), 328 (PIPM), 349 (HP), 448 (HP).
NY	161 N.Y. 35 (PIW), 96 (PI), 222 (PIR), 290 (PIPM), 301 (PIPM), 317 (PIR), 565 PIPM); 162 N.Y. 21 (PIR), 52 (PIR), 193 (PIR), 255 (PI), 380 (PIR), 399 (PIW); 163 N.Y. 1 (PIPM), 108 (PIR), 391 (PIPM), 447 (PIR), 461 (PIW), 472 (PIW), 527 (PIW); 164 N.Y. 30 (PIPM), 121 (PIPM), 415 (HP), 491 (PIW), 553 (PIW); 165 N.Y. 139 (PIR), 146 (PIR), 222 (HP), 241 (PIR), 378 (PIW), 420 (PIW), 584 (PIW), 603 (PIR), 667 (PIR).
TX	93 Tex. 31 (PIR), 38 (PI), 62 (PIR), 64 (PIR), 74 (PIPM), 114 (HP), 239 (PIR), 262 (PIPM), 446 (PIR), 503 (PIW), 527 (PIR), 530 (HP), 604 (PI), 616 (PIPM), 625 (PIR), 632 (PIR); 94 Tex. 53 (PIPM), 100 (PIPM), 31 (PIR), 155 (HP), 196 (PIR), 242 (PIR), 255 (PIPM), 266 (HP), 84 (HP), 304 (HP), 313 (HP), 334 (PIR), 505 (PIR), 510 (PIR), 518 (PIR) .
WI	105 Wis. 69 (PIW), 138 (PI), 142 (PIW), 146 (PIPM), 311 (PIR), 340 (PIW), 480 PIR), 618 (PIR); 106 Wis. 67 (PIW), 87 (PI), 152 (PIW), 191 (PIW), 239 (PIR), 301 (PIR), 324 (O), 403 (PI), 434 (O), 460 (PIR), 577 (PI), 611 (PI), 618 (PI), 662 (PI); 107 Wis. 35 (PIR), 54 (PIPM), 88 (PI), 122 (PIW), 201 (PI), 216 (PIW), 260 (PIW), 305 (PIW), 436 (PI), 559 (PI), 620 (PI); 108 Wis. 1 (PIR), 57 (PIW), 122 (PIR), 255 (PIR), 319 (PIR), 329 (PIPM), 333 (PIR), 353 (PIW), 359 (HP), 530 (PIW), 580 (PIR), 593 (PIR).
CA	127 Cal. 61 (PI), 232 (PIW), 312 (PI), 438 (PIW), 608 (PIR); 128 Cal. 22 (PIPM), 31 (PI), 48 (PIW), 97 (PI), 141 (PI), 173 (PIR), 187 (PIW), 230 (HP), 493 (HP), 674 HP); 129 Cal. 114 (PIR), 123 (PIPM), 168 (PI); 130 Cal. 20 (PIR), 177 (PIR), 342 (HP), 374 (HP), 435 (PIR), 521 (PIW), 574 (PI), 657 (HP); 131 Cal. 96 (HP), 105 (PIPM), 125 (PIW), 333 (HP), 390 (PIR), 430 (PIW), 455 (PIW), 501 (HP), 521 (PIR), 582 (HP).

1910	
NC	152 N.C. 23 (PIPM), 35 (PIW), 42 (PIRW), 66 (PIR), 68 (PIW), 79 (PIR), 110 (PIRW), 123 (PIRW), 125 (HP), 157 (PI), 200 (HP), 211 (HP), 361 (PIRW), 397 (PIRW), 404 (PIW), 411 (PIRW), 439 (PIR), 441 (A), 469 (PIRW), 494 (PI), 505 (PIR), 524 (PIRW), 525 (PI), 531 (HP), 583 (PIPM), 603 (PIW), 648 (PIW), 669 (PIW), 682 (PIPM), 689 (PIRW), 702 (PIRW), 723 (PI), 745 (PIW), 760 (PIR), 762 (PIRW); 153 N.C. 1 (PI), 116 (PIR), 117 (PIR), 120 (PIW), 148 (HP), 153 (PI), 212 (PIRW), 239 (PIRW), 257 (HP), 262 (PIW), 296 (PIR), 322 (PIR, PIW), 331 (PI), 346 (HP), 351 (PIR), 384 (PIW), 394 (A), 396 (PI), 398 (HP), 413 (PI), 432 (HP), 437 (PI), 457 (PIRW), 488 (PI), 508 (PIPD), 513 (PIPM), 567 (PIR); 154 N.C. 24 (PIR), 34 (HP), 44 (PIW), 51 (PIRW), 71 (PIW), 91 (PIRW), 112 PI), 131 (PI), 140 (HP), 147 (PIW), 224 (PIPM), 237 (PIRW), 254 (PIW), 270 (PIPM), 323 (PIW), 328 (PIW), 384 (PIR), 389 (PIR), 394 (PIW), 399 (PIRW), 408 (PIRW), 474 (PIW), 485 (PIW), 523 (PIR), 569 (PIRW), 577 (PIRW), 586 (PIR), 607 (PIR).
NY	198 N.Y. 58 (PIRW), 71 (PIW), 98 (PIPM), 102 (PIW), 221 (PIRW), 312 (D), 324 (PIW), 344 (PIPM), 362 (PIW), 390 (PIW), 463 (PI); 199 N.Y. 79 (PI), 88 (PI), 178 (PI), 233 (PIW), 388 (PIPM), 466 (HP); 200 N.Y. 21 (PIW), 183 (PIR), 379 (PI), 393 (PI), 464 (PI), 478 (PIRW), 585 (PI).
TX	103 Tex. 4 (PIRW), 27 (HP), 31 (PIR), 54 (PIR), 59 (HP), 69 (PIRW), 72 (PIRW), 173 (PIW), 183 (PI), 187 (PIRW), 228 (PIRW), 253 (PIW), 256 (HP), 259 (PIRW), 320 (PIRW), 336 (PIRW), 349 (HP), 387 (PIR), 402 (PIR), 409 (HP), 422 (HP), 434 (PIR), 441 (PIR), 515 (PIR), 594 (PIRW), 601 (PI), 603 (PIPD); 104 Tex. 26 (PIR), 36 (PIRW), 62 (PI), 82 (PIR), 87 (PIW), 127 (PIR), 130 (PIPM), 142 (PIR), 171 (PI), 203 (PI), 230 (PIPM), 272 (PI), 320 (PIPM), 340 (PIRW), 483 (PIR), 493 (PIPM), 603 (HP), 632 (PIR).
WI	141 Wis. 185 (PIW), 191 (PIW), 244 (PIW), 294 (PIW), 298 (PIW), 321 (PIW), 329 (PIR), 411 (HP), 423 (HP), 453 (PIW), 457 (PI), 464 (HP), 515 (PIR); 142 Wis. 49 (A), 65 (HP), 87 (PIW), 128 (PIW), 167 (PIW), 207 (PIW), 215 (PIW), 219 (PIW), 238 (PI), 413 (PI), 486 (PIW), 517 (PIR), 546 (PIW), 570 (PIW), 624 (PIR), 631 (PIW); 143 Wis. 52 (HP), 60 (PIR), 179 (HP), 220 (PI), 415 (PIR), 442 (PIR), 446 (PIW), 454 (PIW), 462 (PIW), 477 (PIR), 557 (PI), 598 (PIW), 609 (PIW); 144 Wis. 106 (PIW), 140 (HP), 231 (PIW).
CA	157 Cal. 41 (PI), 168 (HP), 182 (PIW), 240 (PIR), 248 (PIPM), 333 (PI), 348 (PIPM), 591 (HP), 599 (PIR); 158 Cal. 284 (PIW), 359 (PIW), 412 (PIR), 499 (PIPM), 514 (PIR), 596 (A); 159 Cal. 89 (PIW), 270 (PIR), 368 (PIR), 494 (PIR), 651 (PIPM).

1920	
NC	179 N.C. 73 (PIPM), 83 (PIRW), 112 (PIW), 118 (HP), 123 (PIW), 137 (PIR), 142 (PIW), 216 (PIR), 279 (HP), 280 (PI), 293 (PIW), 389 (A), 433 (HP), 449 PIR), 467 (PIW), 489 (PIW), 508 (PIR), 529 (PIR), 540 (HP), 566 (PI), 619 (PIRW), 678 (HP), 686 (PIPM); 180 N.C. 24 (PIW), 34 (PIR), 37 (PIW), 42 (HP), 64 (PIW), 71 (HP), 130 (PIR), 223 (PIR), 240 (PIRW), 267 (A), 274 (PIR), 290 (PIR), 330 (PIR), 406 (PIR), 413 (PIR), 490 (PIRW), 511 (PIR), 543 (PIPM), 546 (PIPM), 561 (PIPM), 573 (PIW), 597 (PI), 612 (PIW), 622 (HP), 627 (PIW), 636 (PIW), 645 (PI).
NY	227 N.Y. 25 (HP), 34 (PIW), 39 (PIR), 58 (PIR), 74 (PIPM), 197 (PIR), 204 (PIPM), 208 (PI), 291 (A), 345 (PIPM), 361 (PIW), 448 (PIPM), 459 (HP), 465 (PI), 474 (PIR), 486 (A), 507 (PIRW), 531 (PIW), 559 (PIPM), 565 (PIW), 567 (PIW), 570 (PIR), 610 (A), 613 (PIPM), 618 (PIRW), 619 (PIR), 620 (PIRW), 622 (PIRW), 634 (PIPM), 638 (PIR), 647 (PIR), 649 (A), 650 (PIRW), 651 (PIR), 652 (PIR), 654 (PIW), 655 (PIW), 663 (PIRW), 665 (A), 666 (PIRW); 228 N.Y. 54 (PIRW), 73 (PI), 88 (PI), 94 (PIRW), 106 (PI), 113 (PI), 164 (A), 183 (A), 249 (PIRW), 269 (PI), 383 (PIR), 396 (PIPM), 398 (PI), 514 (PIR), 519 (A), 521 (PIPM), 532 (PIW), 537 (PIPM), 539 (PIPM), 546 (PIRW), 547 (PIR), 550 (A), 551 (A), 554 (PIW), 572 (PI), 579 (PIW), 588 (PIRW), 589 (PIPM), 592 (A), 594 (PIPM), 595 (PIRW), 603 (A), 605 (PIPM), 611 (PIW), 643 (PIRW); 229 N.Y. 10 (PIPM), 33 (HP), 120 (PIPM), 148 (A), 161 (HP), 537 (PI); 230 N.Y. 23 (A), 106 (A), 132 (PIW), 194 (PIR), 205 (PIW), 230 (PIRW), 351 (HP), 357 (PIW), 538 (PIR), 539 (PI), 548 (PIPM), 549 (PIR), 550 (PIR), 551 (PIRW), 561 (PIRW), 564 (PIW), 567 (PIPM), 568 (PIR), 570 (PIR), 571 (PIPM), 575 (PI), 576 PIPM), 582 (A), 583 (HP), 618 (PIW), 619 (PIW), 629 (HP).
TX	110 Tex. 104 (PIR), 106 (PIR), 190 (PIR), 213 (PIRW), 218 (PIW), 225 (PIW), 250 (PIRW), 262 (PIRW), 505 (PIW), 546 (HP), 577 (PIRW); 111 Tex. 1 (PI), 8 (PIRW), 268 (PI), 324 (PIR), 361 (PIR), 461 (PIPM), 477 (PIW).
WI	170 Wis. 454 (PIR), 487 (A), 519 (PIW), 579 (PIML), 582 (PIPM), 590 (A); 171 Wis. 7 (A), 11 (PIR), 25 (PI), 116 (PIW), 154 (PIR), 228 (A), 234 (PI), 242 (PI), 429 (HP), 464 (A), 508 (PIW), 614 (PIPM), 620 (A), 625 (PIML), 627 (A), 632 (A); 172 Wis. 1 (A), 6 (PIPM), 20 (A), 44 (A), 53 (A), 61 (A), 163 (PIML), 262 (PIR), 325 (PI), 377 (HP), 400 (A), 421 (PIML), 438 (PIR), 75 (A), 522 (PIPM), 537 (A); 173 Wis. 29 (PIPM), 53 (PIR), 65 (A), 84 (PIPD).
CA	182 Cal. 34 (A), 93 (PI), 108 (A), 130 (A), 140 (PIR), 168 (D), 369 (PIW), 515 (HP); 183 Cal. 24 (PI), 149 (PI), 264 (A), 326 (PIRW), 454 (A), 572 (PIPM), 548 (PIW), 720 (PIR), 777 (A), 801 (A); 184 Cal. 202 (PIR), 209 (A), 252 (PI), 295 (HP), 357 (PIRW), 401 (PIPM), 662 (PIR), 710 (PIR), 714 (HP), 764 (PIPM), 797 (A).

1930	
NC	198 N.C. 8 (A), 23 (PI), 27 (PIW), 43 (PIW), 75 (PIW), 98 (HP), 108 (A), 140 (A), 142 (PIR), 145 (PIW), 150 (PIW), 180 (PIPM), 193 (A), 207 (PIW), 227 (PIW), 247 (PIW), 267 (PIW), 380 (PIW), 448 (PIPD), 457 (PIW), 475 (PIW), 492 (HP), 541 (A), 559 (PIPM), 603 (PIW), 638 (A), 640 (A), 672 (A), 673 (A), 687 (PIW), 736 (PIW), 739 (A), 740 (A), 741 (A), 742 (PIW), 760 (PIR), 771 (A), 776 (PIW), 780 (A), 795 (PIPM); 199 N.C. 1 (PIR), 18 (A), 22 (PIW), 173 (PIPM), 224 (PIW), 246 (PIML), 314 (PIML), 343 (PIW), 379 (PIW), 389 (PIRW), 397 (PIRW), 409 (PIR), 413 (PIW), 431 (A), 452 (PIW), 496 (PIR), 504 (PI), 532 (A), 560 (A), 590 (PIR), 613 (PIRW), 630 (A), 631 (PIR), 651 (PIR), 652 (PIW), 682 (PIR), 695 (PIR), 753 (PIW), 767 (PIRW), 775 (PIW), 786 (PIR),794 (PIW), 798 (PIR); 200 N.C. 44 (A), 47 (PIW), 49 (PIR), 55 (PIPD), 82 (PIPM), 92 (A), 177 (PIR), 213 (PIW), 276 (PIPM), 293 (PI), 310 (PI), 312 PIW),324 (PIRW), 326 (PIW), 381 (PIPM), 398 (PIR), 483 (PIR), 519 (A), 527 (PIR), 543 (PIRW), 580 (PI), 589 (A), 612(PI), 619 (A), 680 (A), 690 (HP), 702 (HP), 731 (HP), 750 (A), 759 (A), 784 (PIR).
NY	252 N.Y. 97 (PIPM), 101 (A), 127 (PIR), 202 (PI), 325 (PIPM), 330 (A), 454 (PIPM), 483 (PIPM); 253 N.Y. 124 (A), 270 (HP), 300 (PIPM), 324 (PIW), 398 (PIR), 423 (A), 440 (PIPM), 486 (PIW), 491 (PIW); 254 N.Y. 64 (PIPM), 148 (PIR), 206 (PIR), 346 (PIW), 407 (HP), 468 (HP); 255 N.Y. 16 (A), 81 (PIW), 104 (A), 170 (HP), 226 (PIPM), 388 (PIPD), 442 (PIW).
TX	118 Tex. 303 (PIRW), 461 (PIW), 607 (PIR); 119 Tex. 377 (PIRW), 391 (PIPM); 120 Tex. 103 (HP), 232 (PIPM), 456 (HP), 586 (PIR).
WI	200 Wis. 26 (A), 80 (A), 87 (A), 110 (PIR), 205 (A), 261 (A), 292 (PIPM), 299 (A), 312 (A), 321 (A), 353 (A), 388 (A), 394 (A), 401 (PIR), 420 (A), 471 (PIW), 485 (A), 491 (PIR), 504 (A), 598 (A), 601 (A), 608 (A), 643 (A), 644 (A), 646(PI), 647 (A); 201 Wis. 57 (A), 111 (A), 113 (A), 141 (A), 170 (A), 190 (A), 193 (A), 214 (A), 259 (A), 269 (A), 285 (A), 401 (A), 533 (PIW), 565 (PI), 653 (A), 655 (A), 657 (A), 658 (A), 659 (PI); 202 Wis. 77 (PIW), 111 (PIPM), 251 (A), 277 (PIR), 289 (PIPM), 416 (A), 499 (PIPM), 517 (A), 563 (PIRW), 648 (A), 649 (A), 650 (PI), 651 (PI), 651 (A), 652 (A); 203 Wis. 223 (A), 61 (A), 479 (A), 598 (A), 532 (PIR), 554 (PIR), 665 (A), 666 (A), 667 (A), 668 (PI).
CA	208 Cal. 29 (HP), 74 (HP), 568 (PIR), 652 (PIR), 697 (HP), 749 (PIR), 770 (PIPM); 209 Cal. 303 (PIR), 383 (PIW), 412 (PIW), 418 (PIR), 429 (PIPM), 456 (A), 520 (A), 562 (A), 745 (A), 774 (HP); 210 Cal. 39 (PIML), 65 (A), 171 (HP), 200 (A), 206 (PIML), 229 (HP), 308 (HP), 330 (A), 450 (A), 524 (A), 526 (PIR), 569 (A), 636 (A), 644 (PIR), 211 Cal. 36 (PIPM), 192 (PIR), 202 (A), 336 (A), 370 (A), 383 (A), 404 (PIPM), 445 (PIPM), 497 (PIPM), 548 (HP), 556 (PIPM), 670 (HP), 771 (A).

1940	
NC	217 N.C. 1 (HP), 82 (A), 127 (PIR), 164 (A), 190 (A), 361 (PI), 437 (HP), 440 (A), 476 (A), 479 (A), 488 (HP), 516 (PIPD), 518 (PIPM), 534 (PIPM), 542 (PIPD), 552 (PIPD), 560 (A), 561 (PIPM), 568 (PI), 573 (A), 577 (PIPM), 586 (A), 610 (PIPM), 674 (PIPM), 684 (PIR), 686 (HP), 730 (PIPM), 737 (PIRW), 750 (A), 756 (A), 768 (PIPM); 218 N.C. 49 (PIR), 63 (PIR), 105 (A), 116 (HP), 122 (A), 129 (HP), 146 (D), 152 (A), 157 (PIPD), 166 (PIPM), 204 (A), 217 (PIPD), 266 (A), 277 (HP), 283 (A), 287 (HP), 292 (PIR), 305 (A), 308 (A), 320 (A), 390 (A), 392 (A), 457 (PIR), 464 (A), 515 (A), 525 (PIW), 560 (HP), 564 (A), 574 (HP), 582 (A), 642 (PIR), 667 (A), 680 (A), 697 (PIW), 732 (PIPM), 740 (HP), 758 (PIPM), 779 (PIPD); 219 N.C. 25 (A), 35 (A), 134 (A), 163 (PI), 178 (PIML), 185 (PI), 191 (A), 205 (PIR), 254 (HP), 273 (PIR), 279 (HP), 324 (A), 416 (PIPM), 457 (A), 476 (PIPM), 479 (A), 528 (PIR), 535 (A), 607 (HP), 628 (PIML), 629 (A), 652 (A), 689 (PIRW), 717 (A), 727 (A), 743 (A), 772 (A), 822 (PIML), 823 (A), 850 (HP).
NY	282 N.Y. 17 (A), 88 (HP), 217 (PIPM), 348 (PIPM), 442 (PIPM), 522 (PIPM), 535 (A), 540 (A), 549 (PIML), 556 (PIPM), 563 (A), 575 (PIPM), 579 (A), 580 (PIR), 607 (PI), 626 (PIPM), 627 (A), 636 (PI), 642 (A), 645 (A), 651 (PI), 652 (HP), 664 (PIR), 670 (PIPM), 673 (PIPM), 685 (PIW), 694 (A), 711 (PI), 730 (PIPM), 735 (A), 752 (A), 754 (A), 755 (PIPM), 760 (PI), 769 (A), 773 (PIR), 774 (PIPM), 793 (PIPM), 795 (A); 283 N.Y. 130 (PIPM), 393 (A), 454 (PIR), 467 (PIPM), 497 (PIPM), 505 (PIPM), 554 (PIW), 574 (PIPM), 581 (PIW), 585 (PIML), 591 (PIR), 595 (PIPM), 600 (PIPM), 610 (PIW), 612 (HP), 619 (PIR), 620 (PIW), 626 (A), 628 (PIPD), 648 (PIR), 660 (HP), 692 (PIPD), 696 (A), 708 (PI), 709 (A), 714 (PIR), 721 (PIR), 722 (A), 723 (PIPM), 732 (PIW), 735 (PIPM), 737 (A), 739 (A), 741 (PIPM); 284 N.Y. 176 (PIML), 279 (PIML), 350 (A), 397 (PIPM), 535 (PIR), 647 (PIPM), 648 (PIPM), 653 (A), 662 (PIPM), 665 (A), 706 (PIPM), 709 (PIPD), 723 (PIPM), 741 (A), 743 (A), 754 (PIR), 755 (A), 761 (PIR), 765 (PIPM), 774(A), 782 (PIR), 797 (PIPM), 798(A), 804 (PIW), 807 (PIPD), 809 (A).
TX	134 Tex. 46 (A), 55 (A), 156 (HP), 215 (A), 308 (A), 318 (PIW), 490 (A), 496 (A), 529 (PI); 135 Tex. 7 (PIR), 67 (A), 314 (PIR), 353 (A), 520 (A), 532 (A), 538 (A).

WI	233 Wis. 39 (A), 66 (A), 69 (A), 86 (A), 100 (HP), 118 (A), 130 (A), 155 (PIPM), 246 (A), 329 (A), 335 (PIR), 349 (A), 381 (A), 391 (PIR), 416 (A), 420 (A), 489 (PIPM), 540 (A), 565 (A), 572 (A), 595 (PIPM), 606 (PIPM), 661 (A), 677 (PI), 678 (A), 678 (PI), 679 (PIPM), 680 (A); 234 Wis. 19 (A), 123 (PI), 149 (A), 188 (PIPM), 201 (HP), 231 (PIPM), 332 (A), 343 (A), 348 (A), 385 (A), 407 (A), 517 (A), 568 (PIPM), 593 (A), 681 (A), 682 (A), 682 (PIR), 682 (A), 683 (A); 235 Wis. 55 (A), 100 (PIW), 198 (A), 220 (A), 259 (PIPD), 391 (PIPD), 398 (A), 403 (PIPM), 411 (A), 579 (A), 645 (A), 680 (A), 681 (PIR), 681 (A), 682 (A), 683 (A); 236 Wis. 21 (A), 87 (A), 116 (A), 138 (PIPM), 205 (PIPM), 226 (A), 292 (A), 419 (A), 444 (PIR), 500 (A), 539 (PI), 597 (A), 642 (A), 662 (PI), 662 (A), 664 (A), 665 (PI), 666 (A), 667 (A), 668 (PIML).
CA	15 Cal.2d 89 (A), 195 (PIPM), 380 (A), 486 (A), 502 (PIPM), 554 (A), 562 (PIPM); 16 Cal.2d 80 (PIPM), 238 (A), 285 (A), 460 (PIRW), 500 (A), 668 (A), 696 (HP).

1950	
NC	231 N.C. 47 (HP), 71 (A), 108 (A), 157 (HP), 181 (PI), 190 (PIR), 203 (A), 208 (A), 270 (PIPD), 285 (PIPM), 318 (A), 336 (A), 373 (A), 400 (PI), 404 (A), 416 (PIPM), 427 (A), 472 (PIPM), 494 (A), 499 (PIRW), 533 (A), 546 (PIPM), 566 (A), 629 (PI), 680 (PIPM), 692 (A), 701 (A); 232 N.C. 42 (A), 144 (HP), 149 (A), 158 (A), 171 (A), 183 (PIR), 192 (PIR), 267 (PIW), 281 (A), 295 (A), 327 (A), 328 (A), 355 (A), 362 (PIML), 367 (A), 457 (HP), 472 (PIR), 478 (A), 487 (PIRW), 497 (PI), 523 (PIR), 542 (A), 609 (A), 611 (A), 623 (PIR), 698 (PI), 699 (A), 744 (HP), 745 (A); 233 N.C. 38 (A), 42 (A), 65 (A), 74 (HP), 81 (PIPM), 99 (A), 109 (HP), 126 (HP), 160 (A), 167 (A), 180 (A), 195 (A), 212 (PIR), 215 (PIR), 221 (A), 272 (PI), 283 (PIPD), 354 (A), 377 (A), 415 (A), 456 (A), 463 (A), 472 (PIPM), 480 (A), 484 (A), 519 (A), 555 (A), 560 (PIPM), 564 (A), 591 (PIR), 607 (PIPM), 627 (PIPM), 637 (A), 661 (PIR), 673 (A).
NY	300 N.Y. 48 (PIPM), 294 (A), 306 (PIPM), 473 (PI), 484 (A), 486 (PIPM), 501 (PI), 507 (PI), 512 (PIPM), 533 (A), 537 (A), 540 (PIPM), 547 (A), 567 (A), 572 (PIPM), 574 (A), 603 (PIPM), 632 (PI), 638 (PIR), 640 (PIR), 660 (PIW), 665 (PIW), 665 (PIPM), 680 (PIPM), 683 (A), 700 (PIPM), 701 (PIW), 711 (PIR), 720 (PI); 301 N.Y. 103 (PIR), 153 (PIPM), 176 (A), 182 (PIW), 202 (PIPM), 206 (PI), 233 (PIPM), 265 (PIPD), 450 (PIR), 468 (PIPD), 508 (A), 511 (A), 521 (PIW), 593 (PIPM), 599 (PIPM), 631 (PIPM), 634 (PI), 641 (PIR), 646 (PI), 660 (PIPM), 698 (PIPM), 703 (PIPM), 735 (PIPM), 736 (HP), 739 (PIPM), 741 (A), 755 (PIR), 768 (A), 770 (PI), 780 (A); 302 N.Y. 367 (A), 413 (PIPM), 563 (O), 579 (PIPM), 582 (A), 598 (A), 609 (PI), 610 (PIR), 626 (PIPM), 633 (PIPM), 637 (PIPM), 639 (A), 653 (PI), 705 (PIPM), 717 (PIW), 722 (PIPM), 726 (PIPM), 747 (PIPD), 755 (PIPM), 759 (PIPM), 793 (A), 802 (A), 804 (PIPM), 827 (PIW), 864 (A), 870 (PIML), 871 (PI), 884 (PIPM).

Appendix Two   The Five-State Survey   209

TX	148 Tex. 1 (PIML), 126 (HP), 175 (A), 191 (HP), 242 (A), 456 (PIPM), 509 (HP), 521 (A), 565 (A), 584 (PIR), 677 (A); 149 Tex. 139 (PIPM), 181 (PIR), 189 (PIR), 217 (PIR), 224 (PIPM), 319 (PIPM), 343 (HP), 432 (PIPM), 445 (PIRW), 487 (HP), 507 (PIPM), 599 (PIW).
WI	256 Wis. 1 (A), 28 (A), 47 (A), 69 (PIR), 102 (A), 113 (A), 119 (A), 125 (A), 131 (PIR), 146 (PIR), 176 (PIPM), 192 (A), 217 (A), 222 (A), 252 (PI), 256 (PIR), 256 (A), 261 (A), 286 (PIPM), 304 (A), 314 (A), 370 (A), 388 (A), 417 (PIML); 257 Wis. 6 (A), 21 (PIR), 25 (PIML), 92 (A), 100 (A), 238 (A), 315 (PIR), 323 (PI), 365 (A), 462 (A), 469 (A), 485 (PIR), 532 (PIPM), 571 (A), 574 (A), 594 (A), 604 (A), 622 (A); 258 Wis. 128 (A), 133 (PIR), 154 (PIPM), 229 (A), 252 (A), 351 (A), 356 (PIPM), 408 (A), 413 (A), 437 (A), 448 (A), 496 (PIPM), 519 (PIPM), 526 (A), 592 (A), 610 (PIR).
CA	34 Cal.2d 176 (A), 209 (A), 226 (PIPM), 525 (PIML), 580 (HP), 589 (A), 806 (A); 35 Cal.2d 10 (A), 16 (A), 40 (PIR), 76 (A), 170 (HP), 263 (A), 338 (PIML), 343 (HP), 355 (PIW), 389 (A), 409 (PIPM), 474 (A); 36 Cal.2d 152 (PIPM), 272 (HP), 301 (PIML), 349 (A), 406 (A), 426 (A), 437 (A), 493 (PIPM), 553 (A), 582 (A), 654 (PIPM), 812 (PIW).

1960	
NC	252 N.C. 40 (HP), 54 (A), 90 (A), 118 (A), 123 (PIPD), 185 (PIPM), 190 (A), 214 (A), 220 (A), 224 (PIPM), 283 (A), 289 (A), 300 (A), 305 (HP), 316 (PI), 337 (PIPD), 346 (PIPM), 352 (A), 368 (A), 380 (A), 425 (HP), 434 (A), 446 (A), 459 (A), 463 (A), 471 (A), 474 (A), 476 (A), 477 (A), 479 (A), 488 (A), 506 (A), 520 (A), 574 (A), 699 (A), 706 (A), 731 (A), 769 (A), 787 (A), 803 (HP); 253 N.C. 31 (A), 60 (PIPD), 67 (A), 70 (A), 112 (HP), 176 (A), 185 (A), 214 (HP), 220 (A), 243 (PIPD), 252 (A), 271 (A), 278 (A), 288 (A), 291 (PI), 355 (PIPD), 370 (PIPM), 381 (A), 387 (A), 394 (A), 406 (A), 459 (HP), 482 (PI), 541 (A), 545 (A), 558 (A), 571 (A), 572 (PIR), 679 PIR), 687 (A), 695 (PIPM), 725 (A), 532 (A), 746 (PIR), 764 (PIPM), 807 (PIR); 254 N.C. 252 (A), 266 (A), 292 (A), 342 (PIW), 414 (A), 421 (A), 428 (A), 443 (A), 447 (A), 454 (A), 467 (A), 489 (A), 493 (PIR), 502 (A), 553 (PIPM), 568 (PI), 575 (A), 582 (D), 599 (A), 611 (A), 615 (A), 662 (A), 673 (A), 680 (PIPM), 697 (PI), 741 (PIPM), 756 (A), 775 (PIPM).
NY	7 N.Y.2d 65 (A); 8 N.Y.2d 878 (PIPM), 938 (A).
TX	160 Tex. 171 (PIPM), 628 (A), 32 (PIPM), 222 (A), 456 (HP), 525 (PIPM), 532 (PI).

WI	9 Wis.2d 12 (PI), 51 (PIPM), 153 (A), 177 (A), 211 (PIPM), 217 (PIPM), 245 (A), 307 (A), 369 (PIPM), 428 (A), 472 (PIPM), 530 (PIPM), 540 (A), 547 (PIPM), 631 (HP); 10 Wis.2d 70 (A), 107 (PI), 129 (PI), 163 (A), 185 (A), 197 (A), 224 (PIPM), 251 (A), 274 (PIPM), 293 (PIPM), 297 (PIPM), 308 (PIPM), 314 (A), 323 (PIPD), 398 (A), 491 (A), 500 (A), 515 (PIW), 555 (A), 610 (A); 11 Wis.2d 32 (A), 53 (PI), 155 (PIML), 170 (A), 177 (A), 185 (A), 192 (A), 207 (PI), 214 (A), 238 (PIPM), 371 (PIPD), 462 (A), 471 (A), 539 (PIPM), 554 (A), 594 (PIPM), 604 (PIR), 627 (A), 634 (A); 12 Wis.2d 1 (PIPM), 14 (A), 72 (A), 168 (PIPM), 176 (A), 203 (A), 252 (PIR), 267 (A), 284 (A), 311 (A), 319 (A), 326 (A), 367 (PIML), 405 (PIPM), 421 (A), 478 (A), 482 (PIW), 517 (A), 537 (A), 571 (PIPM), 574 (A).
CA	53 Cal.2d 49 (HP), 105 (A), 266 (PIPM), 340 (PIPM), 347 (PIW), 361 (PIW), 427 (A), 443 (PIPM), 544 (PIPM), 826 (PIR), 860 (PIPM); 54 Cal.2d 231 (A), 313 (A), 339 (PIPD), 469 (A), 632 (PIML), 841 (PIRW).

1970	
NC	276 N.C. 68 (PIPD), 134 (PIML), 172 (A), 178 (PIPM), 231 (HP), 329 (A), 398 (A), 475 (HP); 277 N.C. 94 (A), 179 (A), 337 (A), 447 (A); 278 N.C. 181 (HP), 438 (A).
NY	26 N.Y.2d 990 (PI), 103 (PIW), 762 (A).
TX	449 S.W.2d 452 (PIW); 450 S.W.2d 62 (A); 451 S.W.2d 752 (PIPM); 452 S.W.2d 437 (A), 691 (A); 453 S.W.2d 466 (PIPM), 812 (PIW); 455 S.W.2d 701 (PIW), 703 (PIML); 456 S.W.2d 901 (PIML); 457 S.W.2d 889 (PIR); 458 S.W.2d 180 (PIPD); 461 S.W.2d 119 (PIML), 591 (A).
WI	45 Wis.2d 111 (A), 135 (PIPM), 147 (PIPM), 155 (A), 271 (PIPM), 331 (PIPM), 340 (PIPM), 368 (A), 407 (A), 458 (A), 471 (PIPM), 536 (A), 657 (A), 698 (A); 46 Wis.2d 130 (A), 337 (PIPM), 374 (PIPM), 423 (A), 534 (PIPM), 605 (PIPM), 637 (PIPM), 677 (PIPM); 47 Wis.2d 76 (A), 120 (A), 220 (PIPM), 368 (PIPM), 617 (PIPM), 629 (PIPD); 48 Wis.2d 25 (A), 43 (PIPM), 82 (A), 190 (A), 251 (A), 305 (PIPM), 321 (PIR), 408 (PIPM), 429 (PIPM), 472 (A), 498 (PIML), 598 (A), 665 (PIPM), 679 (PIPM); 49 Wis.2d 1 (PIPM), 15 (A), 85 (A), 97 (HP), 150 (A), 415 (A), 463 (A), 491 (A), 695 (A).
CA	1 Cal.3d 253 (PIR), 460 (A), 518 (A), 586 (HP), 801 (HP); 2 Cal.3d 1 (A), 19 (A), 245 (PIPD), 465 (PIPD), 575 (PI), 741 (PIPM), 956 (A);3 Cal.3d 359 (PIW), 567 (A), 756 (PIPM), 780 (PIML), 914 (A).

1980	
NC	299 N.C. 42 (PI), 360 (A), 662 (A); 300 N.C. 247 (HP), 631 (HP), 669 (PIPD); 301 N.C. 68 (PIML), 108 (PIML), 677 (A); 302 N.C. 77 (HP), 437 (PI).

NY	49 N.Y.2d 882 (HP), 965 (PIML); 50 N.Y.2d 143 (A), 176 (A), 892 (A).
TX	596 S.W.2d 113 (A); 600 S.W.2d 257 (PIRW), 755 (A), 773 (A); 601 S.W.2d 931 (HP); 602 S.W.2d 517 (PI); 603 S.W.2d 777 (HP), 786 (PI), 805 (A), 814 (PIPM), 818 (A); 604 S.W.2d 73 (HP); 605 S.W.2d 544 (A); 608 S.W.2d 897 (PI), 901 (PIPM); 609 S.W.2d 534 (O), 743 (PIPD); 610 S.W.2d 144 (PIML), 456 (PIPD), 735 (HP), 736 (PIW), 740 (O); 612 S.W.2d 198 (PIPM).
WI	92 Wis.2d 210 (PIML); 93 Wis.2d 173 (PIML), 433 (PI); 94 Wis.2d 364 (A), 504 (PIML); 95 Wis.2d 461 (PIPM); 96 Wis.2d 314 (PIML), 607 (PIPD).
CA	26 Cal.3d 86 (HP), 131 (A), 486 (PIW), 588 (PIPD), 744 (A); 27 Cal.3d 285 (PIML), 465 (PIW), 661 (PIML), 741 (PI), 916 (PIML); 28 Cal.3d 480 (PI), 714 (PIPD).

1990	
NC	326 N.C. 24 (PIML), 231 (PI), 701 (PIPM); 327 N.C. 283 (PIML), 412 (PIPM), 491 (HP), 587 (PI).
NY	75 N.Y.2d 366 (PIML); 76 N.Y.2d 379 (PIW), 507 (PIML); 77 N.Y.2d 200 (HP).
TX	781 S.W.2d 504 (PIML); 785 S.W.2d 137 (PIML); 786 S.W.2d 263 (HP), 266 (PIML), 659 (PIRW); 787 S.W.2d 50 (PI), 348 (PIPD), 369 (A); 790 S.W.2d 559 (PIPD); 793 S.W.2d 948 (PIML); 794 S.W.2d 2 (PIW); 795 S.W.2d 741 (PIPM); 801 S.W.2d 841 (PIML).
WI	153 Wis.2d 59 (PIML), 538 (PIPD); 155 Wis.2d 1 (PIML), 674 (PIML); 156 Wis.2d 488 (PI).
CA	50 Cal.3d 189 (A), 718 (PI), 1118 (HP); 51 Cal.3d 120 (HP); 52 Cal.3d 502 (PI).

2000	
NC	351 N.C. 38 (PIPM), 40 (HP), 183 (PI), 184 (PIPM), 318 (HP), 331 (HP), 458 (HP), 462 (HP), 580 (PIML); 352 N.C. 343 (PIW); 353 N.C. 188 (HP), 252 (A), 647 (HP).
NY	94 N.Y.2d 183 (PIW), 218 (PI), 231 (PIML), 242 (HP), 839 (PIW); 95 N.Y.2d 275 (PIPD), 330 (HP).
TX	8 S.W.3d 326 (PIPD); 11 S.W.3d 153 (PIW), 157 (PIML); 18 S.W.3d 202 (PIW); 20 S.W.3d 692 (PIML); 22 S.W.3d 378 (HP), 411 (A), 425 (HP), 444 (PIPD); 23 S.W.3d 347 (PIW), 357 (PIPM), 362 (PIPD); 28 S.W.3d 15 (PIML); 34 S.W.3d 887 (PIML); 35 S.W.3d 12 (HP), 605 (PI), 608 (A); 38 S.W.3d 578 (PI).
WI	233 Wis.2d 371 (A); 235 Wis.2d 325 (PIPD), 678 (A), 700 (PIPM), 781 (PI); 236 Wis.2d 137 (A), 411 (PIML); 237 Wis.2d 150 (PI), 239 Wis.2d 595 (PI).

CA	22 Cal.4th 1 (PIML), 316 (PIPD), 471 (PIPD), 531 (PIML), 550 (PIPM), 568 (PI), 1127 (PIW); 23 Cal.4th 429 (HP); 24 Cal.4th 627 (HP), 676 (PIML).

2010	
NC	363 N.C. 140 (PIML), 334 (PI), 715 (PI); 364 N.C. 76 (PIML), 222 (HP).
NY	14 N.Y.3d 67 (PI), 83 (PIW), 192 (PIW), 392 (PIPM), 535 (PIPD), 877 (PIML); 15 N.Y.3d 50 (PIW), 264 (PIML), 297 (PI), 306 (PIML), 319 (PIW), 446 (PIML), 676 (PI), 797 (PIPM), 946 (PIPM); 16 N.Y.3d 74 (PIML).
TX	306 S.W.3d 230 (A); 307 S.W.3d 283 (PIML), 292 (PIML), 762 (PIPM); 308 S.W.3d 909 (HP); 310 S.W.3d 419 (O), 441 (PIPM); 313 S.W.3d 796 (PIPM); 314 S.W.3d 912 (PIPM), 913 (PIML); 315 S.W.3d 867 (HP); 318 S.W.3d 867 (HP), 882 (HP), 893 (PIPD); 319 S.W.3d 638 (PIPM), 658 (PIPM); 324 S.W.3d 539 (PIW), 544 (PIML); 328 S.W.3d 526 (PIML), 883 (HP); 329 S.W.3d 475 (PIPD); 330 S.W.3d 211 (PIW); 331 S.W.3d 419 (HP); 335 S.W.3d 126 (PIW), 192 (PIML).
WI	325 Wis.2d 56 (HP); 326 Wis.2d 155 (HP); 328 Wis.2d 320 (PIPD).
CA	47 Cal.4th 272 (PIW), 686 (PIW), 1327 (HP); 48 Cal.4th 68 (PIW), 788 (PIPD); 49 Cal.4th 518 (PIW); 50 Cal.4th 68 (PIPM), 372 (PIML), 638 (PIML).

APPENDIX THREE

Explanatory Notes

CHAPTER ONE

Figure 1.1 (patterns of judicial influence, 1800–60). The figures calculated from the cases in Appendix 1 are:

Cases cited:	1800	1820	1840	1860
English	519 (83%)	1,091 (65%)	1,495 (24%)	1,111 (24%)
Other states	66 (11%)	259 (15%)	857 (24%)	1,487 (32%)
Home state	39 (6%)	341 (20%)	1,290 (35%)	2,031 (44%)
TOTAL	624	1,691	3,642	4,629

Figure 1.2 and accompanying text (types of tort cases in Five-State Survey courts, 1810–70). The number of cases in each category, used to calculate the percentages shown in the figures, are:

Figure 1.2		1810	1820	1830	1840	1850	1860	1870
PI—general	PI	1	1	2	12	5	6	14
PI—railroad accidents	PIR, PIRW	0	0	0	1	0	2	8
PI workplace accidents	PIW	1	0	0	0	0	2	2
Property harm	HP	5	4	3	8	10	20	24
Debt	D	12	4	6	7	4	6	6
Total cases		19	9	11	28	19	36	54

Note 36 and accompanying text (plaintiffs' success rates in railroad cases, 1810–1870). The success-rate figures are as follows:

	1810	1820	1830	1840	1850	1860	1870	Total
Total cases	-	-	-	1	2	6	15	24
Verdict for plaintiff at trial	-	-	-	1		5	12	18
Supreme court—plaintiff verdict reversed, judgment to defendant	-	-	-	-	-	-	1	1
Supreme court—case remanded for new trial	-	-	-	1	-	1	5	7

Note 93 and accompanying text (effect of Field Code on summary case dispositions). All Wisconsin tort cases between 1848 and 1870 were examined, namely 7 Wis. 200, 425, 527; **9** Wis. 182; **11** Wis. 68, 167, 248; **13** Wis. 713; **15** Wis. 662; **17** Wis. 441, 503; **18** Wis. 33, 80, 185, 347; **19** Wis. 150, 158, 515, 637; **20** Wis. 267, 362; **21** Wis. 39, 74, 78, 81, 258, 375, 377, 236, 603, 612, 643; **23** Wis. 152, 186, 287, 437; **24** Wis. 139, 270, 342, 383, 578, 618; **25** Wis. 654; **26** Wis. 56, 145, 223, 537; **27** Wis. 158, 191. The results were:

	In trial court	In supreme court
Total cases involving jury trial	47	
Trial court entered judgment on jury verdict	39	
• Supreme court affirmed judgment		17
• Supreme court reversed judgment		6
• Supreme court sent case back for new trial		16
Trial court dismissed case prior to verdict:	6	
• Supreme court upheld decision	2	
• Supreme court overturned decision		3
Trial court denied motion to dismiss:		3
• Supreme court upheld decision		1
• Supreme court overturned decision		1

CHAPTER TWO

Figure 2.1 and accompanying text (*types of tort cases in Five-State Survey courts, 1870–1920*). The number of cases in each category, used to calculate the percentages shown in the figure, is:

		1870	1880	1890	1900	1910	1920
PI—general	PI	14	17	46	39	55	46
PI—RR accidents	PIR, PIRW	8	25	93	62	46	37
PI—workplace accidents	PIW	2	16	70	46	99	44
Auto	A	0	0	0	0	4	35
Property harm	HP	24	31	89	25	27	21
Debt	D	6	0	4	0	1	1
Total		54	89	302	172	232	184

Figure 2.2 and accompanying text (*comparison of railroad and other workplace accidents*). The number of cases in each category, used to calculate the percentages shown in the figure, is:

	1860	1870	1880	1890	1900	1910	1920
Railroad non-employee accidents	2	8	25	93	62	46	37
Railroad employee accidents	0	0	11	45	13	39	16
Workplace accidents	2	2	5	25	33	60	28

Note 110 and accompanying text (*cases involving procedural issues, 1870–1920*). The figures are:

	1870	1880	1890	1900	1910	1920
Total cases	54	90	306	174	233	184
Verdicts overturned by trial court due to procedural errors	6 (11%)	15 (17%)	38 (12%)	37 (22%)	44 (19%)	32 (17%)
Cases remanded by supreme court for procedural error	18 (34%)	25 (28%)	94 (31%)	68 (39%)	87 (37%)	56 (31%)

Figure 2.4, note 111 and accompanying text (judicial "shift" scale). The "shift" scale can be summarized thus:

Degree of shift	Value	Types of Cases Included	
		Outcome in Trial Court	Outcome in Supreme Court
Strong for defendant	−2	Decision on merits for plaintiff	Decision on merits for defendant
Intermediate for defendant	−1	Decision on merits for plaintiff	Reversed for procedural error; new trial ordered
		Defendant's motion for demurrer, nonsuit or directed verdict denied	Reversed
Neutral	0	Trial-court procedural or merits decision upheld in supreme court	Neutral
Intermediate for plaintiff	+1	Decision on merits for defendant	Reversed for erroneous admission of evidence, jury instructions or verdict form; new trial ordered
		Defendant's motion for demurrer, nonsuit or directed verdict granted	Reversed, new trial ordered
Strong for plaintiff	+2	Decision on merits for defendant	Decision on merits for plaintiff

Shifts were calculated for all of the Five-State Survey decisions in each Survey year from 1870 to 1920. The distribution of shifts for each year was as follows:

Shift value	1870	1880	1890	1900	1910	1920
−2	4	9	17	14	26	25
−1	17	24	93	44	58	43
0	26	43	171	92	125	100
1	6	9	23	23	24	13
2	2	3	2	0	1	3
Total	55	88	306	173	234	184

Note 112 (overall shifts by state). An overall shift is the average shift over all tort cases for a particular state or a particular year. For example, the overall shift for 1870 in the table above would be calculated as follows: $((4*-2) + (17*-1) + (26*0) + (6*1) + (2*2)) / 55 = -.0273$. Overall shifts were calculated for individual states based on the Survey data for each state and each Survey year from 1870 to 1920. The results were:

	1870	1880	1890	1900	1910	1920	State average, 1870–1920
New York	−0.625	−0.326	−0.304	−0.088	−0.367	−0.756	*−0.411*
North Carolina	−0.286	0.250	−0.356	−0.111	−0.312	−0.240	*−0.176*
Wisconsin	0.143	−0.461	−0.300	−0.673	−0.156	−0.238	*−0.281*
Texas	0.333	−0.474	−0.363	−0.387	−0.696	−0.500	*−0.348*
California	−0.154	−0.100	−0.440	−0.056	−0.250	−0.310	*−0.218*

CHAPTER THREE

Note 98 and accompanying text (construction cases as percentage of workplace-accident cases). The number of cases in each category is:

	1870	1880	1890	1900	1910	1920
Total cases	54	90	306	174	233	184
Total workplace accident cases	2	5	27	33	61	39
Total cases involving construction work	-	-	3	6	11	6

Figure 3.2 and accompanying text (cases taken away from jury by trial courts and supreme courts, 1860–1920). The number of cases in each category, used to calculate the percentages shown in the figure, is:

	1860	1870	1880	1890	1900	1910	1920
Total cases	37	54	90	306	174	233	184
Cases taken away from jury by trial court	3	6	15	37	37	45	32
Cases taken away from jury and trial court by supreme court	13	26	36	117	67	90	72

CHAPTER FOUR

Figure 4.1 and accompanying text (types of tort cases in Five-State Survey courts, 1920–70). The number of cases in each category, used to calculate the percentages shown in the figures, are:

		1920	1930	1940	1950	1960	1970
PI—general	PI, PIPM	56	41	81	80	45	29
PI—product liability	PIPD	1	3	12	5	8	5
PI—railroad accidents	PIR	50	37	30	33	8	3
PI—workplace accidents	PIW, PIRW	67	52	14	13	6	5
PI—auto accidents	A		44	105	166	132	128	45
Harm to property	HP	22	20	25	20	10	5
Total		246	263	337	292	213	98

Note 64 and accompanying text (appeals of cases finding plaintiff 50 percent negligent in a diluted comparative-negligence state). The Wisconsin cases referenced in the text are:

Jury found parties equally negligent	225 Wis. 547; 226 Wis. 602; 238 Wis. 598; 242 Wis. 516; 251 Wis. 558; 252 Wis. 585; 262 Wis. 174; 267 Wis. 265; 268 Wis. 394; 269 Wis. 50; 2 Wis.2d 102; 3 Wis.2d 544; 4 Wis.2d 194; 10 Wis.2d 163; 10 Wis.2d 185, 500; 11 Wis.2d 32; 12 Wis.2d 517; 24 Wis.2d 420; 41 Wis.2d 448; 42 Wis.2d 170; 48 Wis.2d 408.
Trial court found plaintiff at least 50% negligent	232 Wis. 97; 246 Wis. 647; 255 Wis. 637; 264 Wis. 358; 265 Wis. 19; 266 Wis. 378; 2 Wis.2d 540; 21 Wis.2d 467; 22 Wis.2d 56.

Note 110 and accompanying text (suits against municipalities for accidents). The figures are:

	1800–1850	1860–1900	1910–1930
Total cases	99	674	744
Municipal accident cases	4 (4%)	64 (9%)	30 (4%)

Note 141 and accompanying text (states adopting broad summary judgment procedures). Notes to state summary judgment statutes and contemporaneous law review articles indicate that the following states adopted broad summary judgment procedures similar to and/or modeled on the federal summary judgment rule in the following decades:

1940s	Arizona (1940); Colorado, Wisconsin (1941); New Mexico (1942); Iowa (1943); Maryland (1947); New Jersey (1948).
1950s	Texas (1950); Delaware, Minnesota, Nebraska (1951); Kentucky (1953); Florida (1954); New Hampshire, Washington (1955); North Dakota, Wyoming (1957); Alaska, Maine, Nevada (1959).
1960s	Louisiana, Missouri (1960); Montana (1962); Indiana, Kansas, New York (1963); Pennsylvania, Rhode Island, South Dakota (1966); North Carolina (1967); Hawaii (1968).
1970s	Alabama, Massachusetts (1973); Oregon (1975); Arkansas (1978).

Appendix Three   Explanatory Notes   219

Figure 4.6 and accompanying text (methods of case disposal other than jury verdict, 1920–1980). The number of cases in each category, used to calculate the percentages shown in the figure, is:

	1920	1930	1940	1950	1960	1970	1980
Demurrer	2	5	17	12	16	7	7
Nonsuit	14	52	43	40	62	6	3
Directed verdict	12	6	7	12	2	7	0
JNOV	10	13	18	11	7	7	3
Summary judgment	0	0	0	2	5	3	17
Total cases	246	263	337	292	213	98	60

Note 145 and accompanying text (taking cases away from juries, 1920–80). The figures are:

	1920	1930	1940	1950	1960	1970	1980
Verdict overturned by trial court	38	76	85	77	92	30	30
Verdict overturned by supreme court	87	46	83	73	40	22	13
Total cases	246	263	337	292	213	98	60

Note 146 and accompanying text ("shift index" showing tilt in favor of plaintiffs or defendants, 1920–1980). The overall figures by year are:

Number of cases in shift category	1920	1930	1940	1950	1960	1970	1980
−2	24	28	48	31	7	3	2
−1	43	21	37	39	21	8	7
0	100	177	210	169	127	57	29
1	13	29	27	43	53	27	20
2	3	6	15	11	3	4	3
Total cases	184	261	337	293	211	99	61
Overall shift	−0.402	−0.138	−0.226	−0.123	+0.114	+0.212	+0.217

The overall shift figures for each of the Survey states by year are:

	1920	1930	1940	1950	1960	1970
N.Y.	−0.756	−0.600	−0.337	−0.276	+0.667	−0.333
N.C.	−0.240	−0.010	−0.178	+0.011	+0.100	+0.571
Wis.	−0.238	−0.230	−0.210	−0.172	+0.108	+0.059
Tex.	−0.500	−0.222	−0.500	−0.304	−0.429	0.000
Cal.	−0.310	+0.045	+0.428	+0.129	+0.352	+0.647

CHAPTER FIVE

Figure 5.1 and accompanying text (types of tort cases in Five-State Survey courts, 1970–2010). The number of cases in each category, used to calculate the percentages shown in the figure, is:

		1970	1980	1990	2000	2010
PI—premises, general	PI, PIPM	2	8	6	8	5
PI—product liability	PIPD	5	6	4	7	5
PI—workplace, premises accidents	PIR, PIW, PIRW, PIPR	32	9	6	12	21
PI—malpractice	PIML	6	11	11	10	15
Harm to property	HP	5	9	5	14	11
PI—auto accidents	A	45	15	2	6	1
Total		98	60	34	57	59

Figure 5.2 and accompanying text (methods of case disposal other than jury verdict, 1960–2010). The figures are:

	1960	1970	1980	1990	2000	2010
Nonsuit	62	6	3	1	0	0
Directed verdict	2	7	0	0	0	0
JNOV	7	7	3	2	0	1
Summary judgment	5	3	17	16	22	17
Total cases	213	98	60	34	57	59

Figure 5.3 and accompanying text (taking cases away from juries, 1950–2010). The figures are:

	1950	1960	1970	1980	1990	2000	2010
Verdict overturned by trial court	77	92	30	30	26	27	23
Verdict overturned by supreme court	73	40	22	13	3	8	12
Total cases	292	213	98	60	34	57	59

Selected Bibliography

Books

Abraham, Kenneth S. *The Liability Century: Insurance and Tort Law from the Progressive Era to 9/11.* Cambridge, MA: Harvard University Press, 2008.

Aronson, Amy. *Crystal Eastman: A Revolutionary Life.* New York: Oxford University Press, 2019.

Avery, Michael and McLaughlin, Danielle. *The Federalist Society: How Conservatives Took the Law Back from Liberals.* Nashville, TN: Vanderbilt University Press, 2013.

Bergstrom, Randolph E. *Courting Danger: Injury and Law in New York City, 1870–1910.* Ithaca, NY: Cornell University Press, 1992.

Blanke, David. *Hell on Wheels: The Promise and Peril of America's Car Culture, 1900–1940.* Lawrence, KS: University Press of Kansas, 2007.

Burke, Thomas F. *Lawyers, Lawsuits and Legal Rights: The Battle Over Litigation in American Society.* Berkeley, CA: University of California Press, 2002.

Cook, Charles M. *The American Codification Movement: A Study of Antebellum Legal Reform.* Westport, CT: Greenwood Press, 1981.

Commons, John R., ed. *History of Labour in the United States 1896–1932.* New York: Macmillan, 1935.

Cornish, W.R. and Clark, G. de N. *Law and Society In England: 1750–1950.* London: Sweet & Maxwell, 1989.

Eastman, Crystal. *Work Accidents and the Law.* New York: Charities Publication Committee, 1910.

Ely, Jr., James W. *Railroads and American Law.* Lawrence, KS: University Press of Kansas, 2001.

Fass, Paula S. and Mason, Mary Ann, eds. *Childhood in America.* New York: New York University Press, 2000.

Feinman, Jay M. *Un-Making Law: The Conservative Campaign to Roll Back the Common Law.* New York: Random House, 2004.

Friedman, Lawrence J. and McGarvie, Mark D. eds. *Charity, Philanthropy and Civility in American History.* New York: Cambridge University Press, 2003.

Friedman, Lawrence M. *A History of American Law.* New York: Simon and Schuster, 1973.

Glickman, Lawrence B., ed. *Consumer Society in American History: A Reader.* Ithaca, NY: Cornell University Press, 1999.

Green, Leon. *Rationale of Proximate Cause.* Kansas City, MO: Vernon Law Book Co., 1927.

Gregory, Charles O. *Legislative Loss Distribution in Negligence Actions.* Chicago: University of Chicago Press, 1936.

Heitmann, John A. *The Automobile and American Life.* Jefferson, NC: McFarland & Co., 2009.

Hindman, Hugh D. *Child Labor: An American History.* Armonk, NY: M.E. Sharpe, 2002.

Hoff, Joan. *Law, Gender and Injustice: A Legal History of U.S. Women.* New York: New York University Press, 1991.

Holdsworth, William. *A History of English Law* (7th ed.). London: Methuen, Sweet & Maxwell, 1956.

Holmes, Oliver Wendell. *The Common Law.* Boston: Little, Brown, 1881.

Horwitz, Morton J. *The Transformation of American Law 1780–1860.* Cambridge, MA: Harvard University Press, 1977.

Horwitz, Morton. *The Transformation of American Law, 1870–1960.* New York: Oxford University Press, 1992.

Hurst, J. Willard. *Law and the Conditions of Freedom in the Nineteenth-Century United States.* Madison, WI: University of Wisconsin Press, 1956.

Karsten, Peter. *Heart Versus Head: Judge-Made Law in Nineteenth-Century America.* Chapel Hill, NC: University of North Carolina Press, 1997.

Keeton, Robert and O'Connell, Jeffrey. *Basic Protection for the Traffic Victim: A Blueprint for Reforming Automobile Insurance.* Boston: Little, Brown, 1965.

Leiby, James. *Carroll Wright and Labor Reform: The Origin of Labor Statistics.* Cambridge, MA: Harvard University Press, 1960.

Mayer, Robert N. *The Consumer Movement: Guardians of the Marketplace.* Boston: Twayne Publishers, 1989.

Millar, Robert W. *Civil Procedure of the Trial Court in Historical Perspective.* New York: Law Center of New York University, 1952.

Pollock, Frederic and Maitland, Frederic W. *The History of English Law Before the Time of Edward I* (2d ed.). Washington: Lawyers Literary Club, 1959.

Puskar, Jason R. *Accident Society: Fiction, Collectivity and the Production of Chance.* Stanford, CA: Stanford University Press, 1999.

Rabin, Robert L. and Sugarman, Stephen D., eds. *Torts Stories.* New York: Foundation Press, 2003.

Rosenberg, Norman. *Protecting the Best Men: An Interpretive History of the Law of Libel.* Chapel Hill, NC: University of North Carolina Press, 1986.

Teles, Steven M. *The Rise of the Conservative Legal Movement: The Battle for Control of the Law.* Princeton, NJ: Princeton University Press, 2008.

White, G. Edward. *Tort Law in America: An Intellectual History.* New York: Oxford University Press, 1980.

Willoughby, William. *Workingmen's Insurance.* New York: T.Y. Crowell & Co., 1898.

Witt, John Fabian. *The Accidental Republic: Crippled Workingmen, Destitute Widows, and the Remaking of American Law.* Cambridge, MA: Harvard University Press, 2004.

Codes, Reports, Treatises and Dissertations

American Bar Association. *No-Fault Insurance: A Study by the Special Committee on Automobile Insurance Legislation.* Chicago: American Bar Association, 1978.

American Law Institute. *Restatement of the Law of Torts.* Philadelphia: American Law Institute, 1923–.

American Law Institute. *Restatement (Second) of Torts.* Philadelphia: American Law Institute, 1956–.

American Law Institute. *Restatement (Third) of Torts—Products Liability.* Philadelphia: American Law Institute, 1992–.

Asher, Robert. "Workmen's Compensation in the United States, 1880–1935." Ph.D. thesis, University of Minnesota, 1971.

Beach, Charles F., Jr. *A Treatise on the Law of Contributory Negligence, or Negligence as a Defense* (2d ed.). New York: Baker, Voorhis & Co., 1892.

Berry, C.P. *The Law of Automobiles* (7th ed.). Chicago: Callaghan & Co., 2d ed. 1916; 3d ed. 1921; 4th ed. 1924; 5th ed. 1926; 7th ed. 1935.

Bevan, Thomas. *Negligence in Law* (3d ed.). London: Stevens and Haynes, 1908.

Brooks, John Graham. *Fourth Special Report of the Commissioner of Labor: Compulsory Insurance in Germany.* Washington, DC: Government Printing Office, 1893.

Clark, Lindley D. and Frincke, Jr., Martin C. *Workmen's Compensation Legislation of the United States and Canada.* Washington, DC: Government Printing Office, 1921.

Cooley, Thomas M. *Treatise on the Law of Torts or the Wrongs Which Arise Independent of Contract.* Chicago: Callaghan & Co., 1880.

Field, David D. et al. *The Code of Civil Procedure of the State of New York, Reported Complete by the Commissioners on Practice and Pleadings*. Albany, NY: Weed, Parsons & Co., 1850.

Fisher, Edward C. *Vehicle Traffic Law* (2d ed.) Evanston, IL: Northwestern University Traffic Institute, 1973.

French, Patterson H. *The Automobile Compensation Plan: A Solution for Some Problems of Court Congestion and Accident Litigation in New York State*. New York: Columbia University Studies in History, Economics and Public Law, No. 393, 1933.

Harper, Fowler and James, Jr., Fleming. *The Law of Torts*. Boston: Little, Brown, 1956.

Hilliard, Francis. *The Law of Torts or Private Wrongs* (4th ed.). Boston: Little, Brown, 1874.

Legislature of the State of Wisconsin. *Report of the Special Committee on Industrial Insurance, 1909–1910*. Madison, WI: State of Wisconsin, 1910.

Massachusetts Bureau of Statistics of Labor. *Thirty-First Annual Report, Part II* (1901). Boston: Commonwealth of Massachusetts, 1901.

Minnesota Bureau of Labor, Industries and Commerce. *Twelfth Biennial Report 1909–10* (1909). St. Paul, MN: State of Minnesota, 1909.

National Conference of Commissioners on Uniform State Laws. *Uniform Apportionment of Tort Responsibility Act*. Chicago: National Conference of Commissioners on Uniform State Laws, 2002.

New York Bureau of Labor Statistics. *Seventeenth Annual Report...for the Year 1899* (1899). Albany, NY: State of New York, 1899.

New York Commission to Enquire Into the Question of Employers' Liability. *First Report* (1910). Albany, NY: State of New York, 1910.

Owen, David G. and Davis, Mary J. *Owen and Davis on Products Liability*. Eagan, MN: Thomson Reuters, 2014.

Prosser, William L. *Handbook of the Law of Torts*. St. Paul, MN: West Publishing Co., 1st ed. 1941, 2d ed. 1955, 3d ed. 1964, 4th ed. 1971.

Redfield, Isaac. *A Practical Treatise Upon the Law of Railways*. Boston: Little, Brown, 1858.

Reno, Conrad. *A Treatise on the Law of Employers' Liability Acts*. Boston: Houghton Mifflin, 1896.

Schwartz, Victor E. *Comparative Negligence* (2d ed.) Indianapolis, IN: Allen Smith Co., 1986.

Shearman, Thomas and Amasa Redfield. *A Treatise on the Law of Negligence*. New York: Baker, Voorhis & Co., 1st ed. 1869; 2d ed. 1870, 3d ed. 1874, 4th ed. 1888, 5th ed. 1898, 6th ed. 1913.

Thayer, James B. *A Preliminary Treatise on Evidence At the Common Law*. Boston: Little, Brown, 1898.

U.S. Department of Labor, *Workmen's Compensation Laws of the United States and Foreign Countries,* Bulletin No. 203. Washington, DC: Government Printing Office, 1917.

Westervelt, James. *American Pure Food and Drug Laws.* Kansas City, MO: Vernon Law Book Co., 1912.

Wharton, Francis. *A Treatise on the Law of Negligence.* Philadelphia: Kay and Brother, 1st ed. 1874, 2d ed. 1878.

Wisconsin Bureau of Labor and Industrial Statistics. *1907–08 Report.* Madison, WI: State of Wisconsin, 1908.

Wright, Carroll D. *Tenth Special Report of the Commissioner of Labor: Labor Laws of the United States, With Decisions of Courts Relating Thereto.* Washington, DC: Government Printing Office, 1904.

Articles

Abraham, Kenneth S. and White, G. Edward. "Prosser and His Influence." 6 *Journal of Tort Law* 27 (2013).

Abraham, Kenneth. "Prosser's *The Fall of the Citadel*." 100 *Minnesota Law Review* 1823 (2016).

Anderson, Leslie. "Claims Against States." 7 *Vanderbilt Law Review* 234 (1954).

Anonymous. "Automobiles—Statutory Liability of Owners for the Negligence of Persons Operating Automobiles With The Owner's Consent." 21 *Minnesota Law Review* 823 (1937).

Anonymous. "Charitable Immunity: A Diminishing Doctrine." 23 *Washington and Lee Law Review* 109 (1966).

Anonymous. "Comparative Negligence in Pennsylvania." 17 *Temple Law Quarterly* 276 (1943).

Anonymous. "Construction of Child Labor Statutes." 23 *Yale Law Journal* 175 (1913).

Anonymous. "Contributory Negligence As Defense to Actions Based on Statutes." 25 *Harvard Law Review* 163 (1912).

Anonymous. "Contributory Negligence on the Part of an Infant." 4 *American Law Review* 405 (1870).

Anonymous. "The Doctrine of Negligence." 8 *American Law Register (O.S.)* 385 (1860).

Anonymous. "The Doctrine of Negligence." 9 *American Law Register (O.S.)* 129 (1860).

Anonymous. "Drowning in a Sea of Confusion: Applying the Economic Loss Doctrine to Component Parts, Service Contracts, and Fraud." 84 *Washington University Law Review* 1513 (2006).

Anonymous. "Factors Affecting the Grant or Denial of Summary Judgment." 48 *Columbia Law Review* 780 (1948).

Anonymous. "The Family Purpose Doctrine in Virginia." 24 *Virginia Law Review* 931 (1938).

Anonymous. "Financial Responsibility of Owners and Operators of Motor Vehicles." 30 *Columbia Law Review* 109 (1930).

Anonymous. "Negligence—Liability of Manufacturers to Third Parties—Nature of the Goods as Test—MacPherson v. Buick Motor Co.." 25 *Yale Law Journal* 679 (1916).

Anonymous. "'The Quality of Mercy': Charitable Trusts and Their Continuing Immunity." 100 *Harvard Law Review* 1382 (1987).

Anonymous. "The Recall of the Ives Decision." 4 *Bench & Bar (New Series)* 1 (1913).

Anonymous. "The Responsibility of Vehicle Owners: An Exception to the Law of Agency." 38 *Harvard Law Review* 513 (1925).

Anonymous. "Tort—Comparative Negligence Statute." 18 *Vanderbilt Law Review* 327 (1964).

Anonymous. "Tort Liability of Contractor or Vendor to Parties Not Privy to the Contract." 19 *Harvard Law Review* 372 (1906).

Anonymous. "Torts—Negligence—Liability of Contractor to Third Party." 27 *Yale Law Journal* 961 (1917).

Anonymous. "Torts—Negligence—Liability of a Manufacturer." 32 *Harvard Law Review* 89 (1918).

Anonymous. "Validity of Contract Providing that Acceptance of Benefits from Relief Association Shall Bar Action Against Employer." 12 *American Law Reports* 477 (1921).

Anzivino, Ralph C. "The Economic Loss Doctrine: Distinguishing Economic from Non-Economic Loss." 91 *Marquette Law Review* 1081 (2008).

Asher, Robert. "The 1911 Wisconsin Workmen's Compensation Law: A Study in Conservative Labor Reform." 57 *Wisconsin Magazine of History* 123 (Winter 1973-74).

Bagby, John W. and Gittings, Gary L. "The Elusive Discretionary Function Exception from Government Tort Liability: The Narrowing Scope of Federal Liability." 30 *American Business Law Journal* 223, 223-30 (1992).

Barton, R. Joseph. "Drowning in A Sea of Contract: Application of the Economic Loss Doctrine to Fraud and Negligent Misrepresentation Claims." 41 *William & Mary Law Review* 1789 (2000).

Bennett, Mark W. "Essay: From the 'No Spittin', No Cussin' and No Summary Judgment' Days of Employment Discrimination Litigation to the 'Defendant's Summary Judgment Affirmed Without Comment' Days: One Judge's Four-Decade Perspective." 57 *New York Law School Law Review* 685 (2012).

Benson, Frederick S. "Comparative Negligence—Boon or Bane." 23 *Insurance Counsel Journal* 204, (April 1956).

Berthrong, Donald J. "Employer's Liability Legislation in Wisconsin, 1874–1893." 34 *Southwestern Social Science Quarterly* 57 (1953).

Best, Arthur. "Impediments to Reasonable Tort Reform: Lessons from the Adoption of Comparative Negligence." 40 *Indiana Law Review* 1 (2007).

Blakemore, Arthur W. "Is the Law Fair to the Motor Vehicle?." 65 *U.S. Law Review* 20 (1931).

Blymyer, William H. "The Jury System in Civil Cases the Greatest Drag in Delaying Justice." 26 *Green Bag* 203 (1914).

Bohlen, Francis H. "Liability of Manufacturers to Persons Other Than Their Immediate Vendees." 45 *Law Quarterly Review* 343 (1929).

Bohlen, Francis H. "Voluntary Assumption of Risk: II." 20 *Harvard Law Review* 91 (1906).

Borchard, Edwin. "Government Liability in Tort." 34 *Yale Law Journal* 1 (1924).

Borchard, Edwin. "Governmental Responsibility in Tort—VI." 36 *Yale Law Journal* 1 (1926).

Borchard, Edwin. "Governmental Responsibility in Tort—VII." 28 *Columbia Law Review* 577 (1928).

Brandt, Eric A. "Good Samaritan Laws—The Legal Placebo: A Current Analysis." 17 *Akron Law Review* 303 (1983).

Brown, Henry Billings. "The Administration of the Jury System." 17 *Green Bag* 623 (1905).

Bruce, Andrew W. "Employers' Liability in the United States." 32 *Forum* 48 (1902).

Bruce, Andrew W. "The New York Employers' Liability Act." 9 *Michigan Law Review* 684 (1910).

Burnet, James R. "Critical Opinions Upon Recent Employers' Liability Legislation in the United States." 50 *Journal of Social Science* 53 (1902).

Calabresi, Steven G. and Lawson, Gary. "Symposium: Foreword: The Constitution of Responsibility." 77 *Cornell Law Review* 955 (1992).

Caldwell, Henry C. "Trial by Judge and Jury." 33 *American Law Review* 321 (1899).

Canon, Bradley C. and Jaros, Dean. "The Impact of Changes in Judicial Doctrine: The Abrogation of Charitable Immunity." 13 *Law & Society Review* 969 (1979).

Cardi, W. Jonathan. "Apportioning Responsibility to Immune Nonparties: An Argument Based on Comparative Responsibility and the Proposed Restatement (Third) of Torts." 82 *Iowa Law Review* 1293 (1997).

Cardi, W. Jonathan. "The Hidden Legacy of *Palsgraf*: Modern Duty Law in Microcosm." 91 *Boston University Law Review* 1873 (2011).

Carman, Ernest C. "Is A Motor Vehicle Accident Compensation Act Advisable." 4 *Minnesota Law Review* 1 (1919).

Centner, Terrance J. "Tort Liability for Sports and Recreational Activities: Expanding Statutory Immunity for Protected Classes and Activities." 26 *Journal of Legislation* 1 (2000).

Chamberlain, J.P. "Compulsory Insurance of Automobiles." 12 *American Bar Association Journal* 49 (1926).

Chopko, Mark E. "Continuing the Lord's Work and Healing the People: A Reply to Professors Lupu and Tuttle." 2004 *Brigham Young University Law Review* 1897 (2004).

Clark, Charles E. and Samenow, Charles U. "The Summary Judgment." 38 *Yale Law Journal* 423 (1929).

Clopton, Zachary D. "Procedural Retrenchment and the States." 106 *California Law Review* 411 (2018).

Crane, R. Newton. "Injury Actions and Workmen's Compensation in England." 18 *Green Bag* 216 (1906).

Daniels, Stephen and Martin, Joanne. "The Strange Success of Tort Reform." 53 *Emory Law Journal* 1225 (2004).

Daniels, Stephen and Martin, Joanne. "Where Have All the Cases Gone: The Strange Success of Tort Reform Revisited." 65 *Emory Law Journal* 1445 (2016).

DeVito, Scott and Jurs, Andrew W. "Doubling Down for Defendants: The Pernicious Effects of Tort Reform." 118 *Penn State Law Review* 543 (2014).

Edgerton, Henry M. "Legal Cause." 72 *University of Pennsylvania Law Review* 211 (1924).

Engstrom, Nora Freeman. "An Alternative Explanation for No-Fault's 'Demise." 61 *DePaul Law Review* 303 (2012).

Fairchild, Fred R. "The Factory Legislation of the State of New York." *Publications of the American Economic Association*, 3d series, Vol. 6 (November 1905).

Farley, R.J. "Instructions to Juries—Their Role in the Judicial Process." 42 *Yale Law Journal* 194 (1932).

Feezer, Lester W. "The Tort Liability of Charities." 77 *University of Pennsylvania Law Review* 191 (1928).

Finkelman, Paul. "Slaves as Fellow Servants: Ideology, Law, and Industrialization." 31 *American Journal of Legal History* 269 (1987).

Folzon, L.C. "Michigan No-Fault: The Rise and Fall of Socialized Negligence." 56 *University of Detroit Journal of Urban Law* 99 (1979).

Foran, M.A. "The Scintilla Rule and Its Relations to Trial By Jury." 4 *Western Reserve Law Journal* 143, 144 (Nov. 1898).

Forbath, William E. "The Ambiguities of Free Labor: Labor and the Law in the Gilded Age." 1985 *Wisconsin Law Review* 767 (1985).

Freund, Ernest. "Constitutional Aspects of Employers Liability Legislation." 19 *Green Bag* 80 (1907).

Friedman, Lawrence M. "Civil Wrongs: Personal Injury Law in the Late 19th Century." 1987 *American Bar Foundation Research Journal* 351 (1987).

Friedman, Lawrence M. and Russell, Thomas D. "More Civil Wrongs: Personal Injury Litigation, 1901–1910." 34 *American Journal of Legal History* 295 (1990).

Galanter, Marc A. "An Oil Strike in Hell: Contemporary Legends About the Civil Justice System." 40 *Arizona Law Review* 717 (1998).

Gavin, Sandra F. "Stealth Tort Reform." 42 *Valparaiso University Law Review* 431 (2008).

Gfell, Kevin J. "The Constitutional and Economic Implications of a National Cap on Non-Economic Damages in Medical Malpractice Actions." 37 *Indiana Law Review* 773 (2004).

Gitterman, John M. "The Cruelties of Our Courts." 35 *McClure's Magazine* 151 (June 1910).

Gold, David M. "Redfield, Railroads and the Roots of 'Laissez-Faire Constitutionalism.'" 27 *American Journal of Legal History* 254 (1983).

Goodman, Jeffrey L., Peacock, Daniel R. and Rutan, Kevin J. "A Guide to Understanding the Economic Loss Doctrine." 67 *Drake Law Review* 1 (2019).

Graham, Kyle. "The Diffusion of Doctrinal Innovations in Tort Law." 99 *Marquette Law Review* 75 (2015).

Graham, Kyle. "Strict Products Liability at 50: Four Histories." 98 *Marquette Law Review* 555 (2014).

Graham, Samuel C. "Directing Verdicts." 16 *Virginia Law Register* 401 (October 1910).

Green, Leon. "Duties, Risks, Causation Doctrines." 42 *Texas Law Review* 42 (1962).

Green, Leon. "Freedom of Litigation (III): Municipal Liability for Torts." 38 *Illinois Law Review* 355 (1943).

Green, Leon. "Illinois Negligence Law." 39 *Illinois Law Review* 36 (1944).

Green, Nicholas St. John. "Proximate and Remote Cause." 4 *American Law Review* 201 (1870).

Hall, James Parker. "The New York Workmen's Compensation Act Decision." 19 *Journal of Political Economy* 694 (1911).

Hart, James L. "Private Law and Public Policy: Negligence Law and Political Change in Nineteenth-Century North Carolina." 66 *North Carolina Law Review* 421 (1988).

Haugh, John J. "Comparative Negligence: A Reform Long Overdue." 49 *Oregon Law Review* 38 (1969).

Hayes, Gerald P. "Rule of Comparative Negligence and Its Operation in Wisconsin." 23 *Ohio State Bar Association Reports* 233 (1950).

Heidemann, Craig R. "Fencing Laws in Missouri: Confusion, Conflict, and a Need for Change." 63 *Missouri Law Review* 537 (1998).

Henderson, Charles R. "Workingmen's Insurance in Illinois." *Proceedings of the First Annual Meeting, American Association for Labor Legislation* (1907).

Henderson, James A., Jr. and Eisenberg, Theodore. "The Quiet Revolution in Products Liability: An Empirical Study of Legal Change." 37 *UCLA Law Review* 479 (1990).

Henderson, James A., Jr. "Restatement (Third) Torts: Products Liability: What Hath the ALI Wrought?" 64 *Defense Counsel Journal* 501 (1997).

Hess, Brian H. "The Planning/Operational Dichotomy: A Specious Approach to the Discretionary Function Exception in the Federal Tort Claims Act." 40 *Idaho Law Review* 223 (2003).

Hilkey, Charles. "Comparative Negligence in Georgia." 8 *Georgia Bar Journal* 51 (1945).

Hobbs, Marland C. "Statutory Changes in Employers' Liability." 2 *Harvard Law Review* 212 (1888).

Hofstadter, Samuel H. "A Proposed Automobile Accident Compensation Plan." 328 *Annals of the American Academy of Political and Social Science* 53 (1960).

Honson, Nathan. "Iowa Tort History, 1839–1869: Subsidization of Enterprise or Equitable Allocation of Liability?" 81 *Iowa Law Review* 811 (1996).

Horwitz, Morton J. "The Rise of Legal Formalism." 19 *American Journal of Legal History* 251 (1975).

Hubbard, F. Patrick. "The Nature and Impact of the Tort Reform Movement." 35 *Hofstra Law Review* 437 (2006).

Irwell, Lawrence. "The Case Against Jury Trials in Civil Actions." 54 *Central Law Journal* 243 (1902).

Jacobsohn, Gary J. "The Right to Disagree: Judges, Juries, and the Administration of Criminal Justice in Maryland." 1976 *Washington University Law Quarterly* 571 (1976).

James, Jr., Fleming. "Contributory Negligence." 62 *Yale Law Journal* 691 (1953).

Jobe, Connie Kemp. "The Model Uniform Product Liability Act—Basic Standards of Responsibility for Manufacturers." 46 *Journal of Air Law and Commerce* 389 (1981).

Kaczorowski, Robert J. "The Common-Law Background of Nineteenth-Century Tort Law." 51 *Ohio State Law Journal* 1127 (1990).

Kaczorowski, Robert J. "From Petitions for Gratuities to Claims for Damages: Personal Injuries and Railroads During the Industrialization of the United States." 57 *American Journal of Legal History* 261 (2017).

Kantor, Shawn E. and Fishback, Price V. "How Minnesota Adopted Workers' Compensation." 2 *Independent Review* 557 (1998).

Kantor, Shawn E. and Kousser, J. Morgan. "Common Sense or Commonwealth? The Fence Law and Institutional Change in the Postbellum South." 59 *Journal of Southern History* 201 (1993).

Kawashima, Yasuhide. "Farmers, Ranchers, and the Railroad: The Evolution of Fence Law in the Great Plains, 1865–1900." 30 *Great Plains Quarterly* 21 (Winter 2010).

Keeton, Robert. "Judicial Law Reform—A Perspective on the Performance of Appellate Courts." 44 *Texas Law Review* 1254 (1966).

Kelley, Patrick J. "Proximate Cause in Negligence Law: History, Theory and the Present Darkness." 69 *Washington University Law Quarterly* 49 (1991).

Kent, Andrew. "The Jury and Empire: The Insular Cases and the Anti-Jury Movement in the Gilded Age and Progressive Era." 91 *Southern California Law Review* 375 (2018).

Konefsky, Alfred. "'As Best to Subserve Their Own Interests': Lemuel Shaw, Labor Conspiracy and Fellow Servants." 7 *Law & History Review* 219 (1989).

Kysar, Douglas A. "The Expectations of Consumers." 103 *Columbia Law Review* 1700 (2003).

Laposata, Elizabeth, Barnes, Richard and Glantz, Stanton. "Tobacco Industry Influence on the American Law Institute's Restatements of Torts and Implications for Its Conflict of Interest Policies." 98 *Iowa Law Review* 1 (2012).

Lattin, Norman D. "Vicarious Liability and the Family Automobile." 26 *Michigan Law Review* 846 (1928).

Leflar, Robert A. "The Declining Defense of Contributory Negligence." 1 *Arkansas Law Review* 1 (1947).

Leflar, Robert A. and Kantrowitz, Benjamin E. "Tort Liability of the States." 29 *NYU Law Review* 1363 (1954).

Lerner, Renee Lettow. "The Rise of the Directed Verdict: Jury Power in Civil Cases Before the Federal Rules of 1938." 81 *George Washington Law Review* 448 (2013).

Lettow, Renee B. "New Trial for Verdict Against Law: Judge-Jury Relations in Early Nineteenth-Century America." 71 *Notre Dame Law Review* 505 (1996).

Little, Joseph W. "Palsgraf Revisited (Again)." 6 *Pierce Law Review* 75 (2007).

Little, Joseph W. "The Place of Consumer Expectations in Product Strict Liability Actions for Defectively Designed Products." 61 *Tennessee Law Review* 1189 (1994).

Loring, Charles. "Liability of a Manufacturer or a Vendor to Persons With Whom He Has No Contractual Relations for Negligence in the Construction or Sale of Chattels." 58 *Central Law Journal* 365 (1904).

Lupu, Ira C. and Tuttle, Robert W. "Sexual Misconduct and Ecclesiastical Immunity." 2004 *Brigham Young University Law Review* 1789 (2004).

Malone, Wex S. "The Formative Era of Contributory Negligence." 41 *Illinois Law Review* 151 (1946).

Maloney, Frank E. "From Contributory to Comparative Negligence: A Needed Law Reform." 11 *University of Florida Law Review* 135 (1958).

Mapel, Frank B. and Weigel, Charles J. "Good Samaritan Laws: Who Needs Them: The Current State of Good Samaritan Protection in the United States." 21 *South Texas Law Journal* 327 (1980).

Maroney, Patrick F. "No-Fault Automobile Insurance: A Success or Failure After Eleven Years?" 51 *Insurance Counsel Journal* 75 (1984).

Marston, Jerrilyn. "Creation of a Common Law Rule: The Fellow Servant Rule, 1837–1860." 132 *University of Pennsylvania Law Review* 579 (1984).

McCarthy, Gail Ann. "The Varying Standards of Governmental Immunity: A Proposal to Make Such Statutes Easier to Apply." 24 *New England Law Review* 991 (1990).

McEvoy, Arthur F. "The Triangle Shirtwaist Factory Fire of 1911: Social Change, Industrial Accidents, and the Evolution of Common-Sense Causality." Chicago: American Bar Foundation, 1993.

McWilliams, Mike and Smith, Margaret. "An Overview of the Legal Standard Regarding Product Liability Design Defect Claims and a Fifty State Survey on the Applicable Law in Each Jurisdiction." 82 *Defense Counsel Journal* 80 (January 2015).

Miller, Arthur R. "The Pretrial Rush to Judgment: Are the 'Litigation Explosion,' 'Liability Crisis,' and Efficiency Cliches Eroding Our Day in Court and Jury Trial Commitments?" 78 *NYU Law Review* 982 (2003).

Mitchell, John. "Automatic Compensation—The Injured Workman's Right." 17 *American Federationist* 971 (1910).

Mole, A. Chalmers and Wilson, Lyman P. "A Study of Comparative Negligence: Part II." 17 *Cornell Law Quarterly* 604 (1932).

Munger, Frank W. "Social Change and Tort Litigation: Industrialization, Accidents, and Trial Courts in Southern West Virginia, 1872–1910." 36 *Buffalo Law Review* 75 (1987).

Nelson, William E. "Palsgraf v, Long Island R.R.: Its Historical Context." 34 *Touro Law Review* 281 (2018).

Nelson, William E. "The Province of the Judiciary." 37 *John Marshall Law Review* 325 (2004).

Noel, Dix W. "Defective Products: Abnormal Use, Contributory Negligence, and Assumption of Risk." 25 *Vanderbilt Law Review* 93 (1972).

Owen, David G. "The Intellectual Development of Modern Products Liability Law: A Comment on Priest's View of the Cathedral's Foundations." 14 *Journal of Legal Studies* 529 (1985).

Padway, Joseph A. "Comparative Negligence." 16 *Marquette Law Review* 3 (1931).

Patterson, Donald. "The Citadel Reburied: Restatement of the Law (Third) Torts: Products Liability." 63 *Defense Counsel Journal* 191 (1996).

Peck, Epaphroditus. "The Massachusetts Proposition for an Employers' Compensation Act." 14 *Yale Law Journal* 18 (1904).

Peck, Robert S. "The Development of the Law of Joint and Several Liability." 55 *Federation of Defense and Corporate Counsel Quarterly* 469 (Summer 2005).

Philbrick, Francis S. "Loss Apportionment in Negligence Cases: Part II." 99 *University of Pennsylvania Law Review* 766 (1951).

Phillips, John B. "Modifications of the Jury System." 16 *Green Bag* 514 (1904).

Pollak, Stuart R. "Liberalizing Summary Adjudication: A Proposal." 36 *Hastings Law Journal* 419 (1985).

Pound, Roscoe. "Causation." 67 *Yale Law Journal* 1 (1957).

Pound, Roscoe. "Mechanical Jurisprudence." 8 *Columbia Law Review* 605 (1908).

Powell, Jr., Lewis F. "Contributory Negligence: A Necessary Check on the American Jury." 43 *American Bar Association Journal* 1005 (1957).

Pressler, Larry and Schieffer, Kevin V. "Joint and Several Liability: A Case for Reform." 64 *Denver University Law Review* 651 (1988).

Priest, George H. "The Invention of Enterprise Liability: A Critical History of the Intellectual Foundations of Modern Tort Law." 14 *Journal of Legal Studies* 461 (1985).

Prosser, William L. "The Assault Upon the Citadel (Strict Liability to the Consumer)." 69 *Yale Law Journal* 1099 (1960).

Prosser, William L. "Comparative Negligence." 51 *Michigan Law Review* 465 (1953).

Prosser, William L. "The Fall of the Citadel (Strict Liability to the Consumer)." 50 *Minnesota Law Review* 791 (1966).

Prosser, William L. "Palsgraf Revisited." 51 *Michigan Law Review* 1 (1953)

Prosser, William L. "Trespassing Children." 47 *California Law Review* 427 (1959).

Rabin, Robert L. "A Sociolegal History of the Tobacco Tort Litigation." 44 *Stanford Law Review* 853 (1992).

Regier, C.C. "The Struggle for Federal Food and Drugs Legislation." 1 *Law and Contemporary Problems* 3 (1933).

Rhode, Deborah L. "Frivolous Litigation and Civil Justice Reform: Miscasting the Problem, Recasting the Solution." 54 *Duke Law Journal* 447 (2004).

Rhodes, J.E. "Inception of Workmen's Compensation in the United States." 11 *Maine Law Review* 35 (1917).

Ritter, Louis C. and Magnuson, Evert H. "The Motion for Summary Judgment and Its Extension to All Classes of Actions." 21 *Marquette Law Review* 33 (1936).

Rogers, Donald W. "From Common Law to Factory Laws: The Transformation of Workplace Safety Law in Wisconsin Before Progressivism." 39 *American Journal of Legal History* 177 (1995).

Rucker, Robert D. "The Right to Ignore the Law: Constitutional Entitlement Versus Judicial Interpretation." 33 *Valparaiso Law Review* 449 (1999).

Rutledge, Peter B. and Drahozal, Christopher B. "'Sticky' Arbitration Clauses? The Use of Arbitration Clauses after Concepcion and Amex." 67 *Vanderbilt Law Review* 255 (2014).

Sanders, Joseph and Joyce, Craig. "Off to the Races: The 1980s Tort Crisis and the Law Reform Process." 27 *Houston Law Review* 437 (1990).

Schwartz, Gary T. "The Character of Early American Tort Law." 36 *U.C.L.A. Law Review* 651 (1989).

Schwartz, Gary T. "Tort Law and the Economy in Nineteenth-Century America: A Reinterpretation." 90 *Yale Law Journal* 1717 (1981).

Schwartz, Victor E. "The Restatement (Third) of Torts: Products Liability—The American Law Institute's Process of Democracy and Deliberation." 26 *Hofstra Law Review* 743 (1998).

Schwartz, Victor E. and Appel, Christopher E. "The Church Autonomy Doctrine: Where Tort Law Should Step Aside." 80 *University of Cincinnati Law Review* 431 (2012).

Schwarzer, William W. "Summary Judgment Under the Federal Rules: Defining Genuine Issues of Material Fact." 99 *Federal Rules Digest* 465 (1984).

Seavey, Warren A. "Mr. Justice Cardozo and the Law of Torts." 52 *Harvard Law Review* 372 (1939).

Sharkey, Catherine M. "The Remains of the Citadel (Economic Loss Rule in Products Cases)." 100 *Minnesota Law Review* 1845 (2016).

Sharkey, Catherine M. "Unintended Consequences of Medical Malpractice Damages Caps." 80 *NYU Law Review* 391 (2005).

Sherman, P. Tecumseh. "Can the German Workmen's Insurance Law Be Adapted to American Conditions?" 61 *University of Pennsylvania Law Review* 67 (1912).

Siggins, Charlotte Smith. "Strict Liability for Prescription Drugs: Which Shall Govern—Comment k or Strict Liability Applicable to Ordinary Products?" 16 *Golden Gate University Law Review* 309 (1986).

Smith, Allan F. "Municipal Tort Liability." 48 *Michigan Law Review* 41 (1950).

Smith, Douglas G. "The Historical and Constitutional Contexts of Jury Reform." 25 *Hofstra Law Review* 377 (1996).

Smith, Jeremiah. "Legal Cause in Actions of Tort." 25 *Harvard Law Review* 103 (1912).

Smith, Jeremiah. "Liability of Landowners to Children Entering Without Permission." 11 *Harvard Law Review* 349 (1898).

Smyser, Jay M. "Products Liability and the American Law Institute: A Petition for Rehearing." 42 *University of Detroit Law Journal* 343 (1965).

Snell, Roy K. "A Plea for a Comprehensive Governmental Liability Statute." 74 *Kentucky Law Journal* 521 (1986).

Stearns, Denis W. "Prosser's Bait-and-Switch: How Food Safety Was Sacrificed in the Battle for Tort's Empire." 15 *Nevada Law Journal* 106 (2014).

Subrin, Stephen N. "David Dudley Field and the Field Code: A Historical Analysis of an Earlier Procedural Vision." 6 *Law and History Review* 311 (1988).

Subrin, Stephen N. and Main, Thomas O. "The Fourth Era of American Civil Procedure." 162 *University of Pennsylvania Law Review* 1839 (2014).

Subrin, Stephen N. "How Equity Conquered Common Law: The Federal Rules of Civil Procedure in Historical Perspective." 135 *University of Pennsylvania Law Review* 909 (1987).

Sunderland, Edson R. "The Problem of Trying Issues." 5 *Texas Law Review* 18 (1926).

Symposium, "Governmental Tort Liability." 9 *Law and Contemporary Problems* 179 (1942).

Tamanaha, Brian Z. "The Mounting Evidence Against the 'Formalist Age.'" 92 *Texas Law Review* 1667 (2014).

Tobias, Carl. "Interspousal Tort Immunity in America." 23 *Georgia Law Review* 359 (1989).

Troup, James. "Should the Scintilla Rule Be Abolished?" 4 *Western Reserve Law Journal* 117 (October 1898).

Turk, E.A. "Comparative Negligence on the March—Part II." 28 *Chicago-Kent Law Review* 304 (1950).

Twerski, Aaron D. "The Joint Tortfeasor Legislative Revolt: A Rational Response to the Critics." 22 *U.C. Davis Law Review* 1125 (1989).

Wade, John W. "On the Nature of Strict Tort Liability for Products." 44 *Mississippi Law Journal* 825 (1973).

Wald, Patricia M. "Summary Judgment at Sixty." 76 *Texas Law Review* 1897 (1998).

Weinstein, James. "Big Business and the Origins of Workers Compensation." 8 *Labor History* 156 (1967).

Wertheim, Frederick. "Slavery and the Fellow-Servant Rule: An Antebellum Dilemma." 61 *NYU Law Review* 1112 (1986).

White, G. Edward. "The Chancellor's Ghost." 74 *Chicago-Kent Law Review* 229 (1998).

Witt, John Fabian. "The Long History of State Constitutions and American Tort Law." 36 *Rutgers Law Journal* 1159 (2005).

Wright, Richard. "Allocating Liability Among Multiple Responsible Causes: A Principled Defense of Joint and Several Liability for Actual Harm and Risk Exposure." 21 *U.C. Davis Law Review* 1141 (1988).

Zollman, Carl. "Damage Liability of Charitable Institutions." 19 *Michigan Law Review* 395 (1921).

Index

A

Abinger, Lord, 17, 41
Achtenhagen v. City of Watertown (Wis. 1864), 33
Adams, Charles F., Jr., 51–52
Aggregation of negligence, 160
Agnew, David, 44
Alabama
   adopts 1880 British Employers Liability Act, 54
American Association for Labor Legislation (AALL), 73–74, 81–82
American Bar Association (ABA), 121, 186
American Law Institute (ALI),
   and products liability, 128–29
   and *Restatement (Second) of Torts* § 402A, 133, 135
   and *Restatement (Third) of Product Liability*, 171
American Legislative Exchange Council (ALEC)
   and joint and several liability, 163
   and limitation of strict product liability, 169–70, 172 n73
   and medical malpractice reform, 164
   origins, 158–59
American Medical Association, 163–64
American Tort Reform Association (ATRA)
   and medical malpractice reform, 164
   and strict product liability, 169–70
   origins, 158
Anderson, William, 108
Andrews, William, 143–44
Arizona
   and workers compensation, 86
Arizona Copper Co. v. Hammer (U.S. 1919), 86
Arkansas
   and aggregation of negligence, 126
Asquith, Herbert, 72
Attainder. *See* Juries
Attractive-nuisance doctrine, 49–51
Automobiles
   construction of highways, 114
   early safety laws, 114, 114 n19
   early safety measures, 115
   origins, 113–14
   safety measures in 1930s, 115–16
   safety measures during late 20th century, 183
Automobile accidents
   and driver liability to passenger, 118–19
   and effect on court dockets, 112–13
   and family-purpose doctrine, 118–19
   early increase in, 114–15
   popular reaction to, 115
   socialization of costs, 118

B

Bacon, Augustus O., 89
Badigian v. Badigian (N.Y. 1961), 141
Balance of power. *See* Judge-jury balance of power
Barstow v. City of Berlin (Wis. 1874), 34
Bartlett, Willard, 97–98
Berry, C.P., 119
Biakanja v. Irving (Cal. 1958), 146
Bismarck, Otto von, 71
Blackford, Isaac, 27

Blackstone, Sir William
   on immunities, 135 n101, 137 n105
   on property rights, 8 n10
Bohlen, Francis, 128
Borchard, Edwin, 138
Borgnis v. Falk Co. (Wis. 1911), 81
Bradley, Ann Walsh, 174–75
Breese, Sidney, 22, 42, 88
Brett, William, 95
Brown v. Kendall (Mass. 1850), 9–10
Bruce, Andrew, 62–63
Burden of proof. *See* Contributory negligence
Busch v. McInnis Waste Systems, Inc. (Or. 2020), 155
Bush v. Brainard (N.Y. 1823), 9
Bushell's Case (1670), 24–25
Butterfield v. Forrester (K.B. 1809), 10–11

C

Caldwell, Henry Clay, 99
Caldwell, William, 19–20
California
   and early product liability decisions, 133
   and economic loss doctrine, 173
   and evolution of product liability standards, 170
   and workers compensation, 83
Cardozo, Benjamin
   and duty and proximate cause, 143–44
   and product liability, 97
Carter v. Yardley & Co. (Mass. 1946), 129
Causation
   and judicial policymaking, 145–46, 146 n131
   and multi-factor analysis, 146
   and proximity analysis, 143
   and William Prosser, 145
   developments in early 20th century, 143–46
   developments in early- and mid-19th century, 11–12, 142–43
   developments in late 19th century, 43–45, 142–43
   Palsgraf case, 143–44
Celotex trilogy (U.S. 1986), 187–88
Chamberlain, Joseph, 72
Charitable immunity. *See* Immunity, charitable
Children
   and 19th century attitudes toward, 45–46
   and imputation of parental negligence, 48
   and standards of negligence, 46–47
   and streetcars, 50–51,
   and workplace accidents, 49
Clark, Charles, 148
Clark, Walter, 100–01
Clerical immunity. *See* Immunity, clerical
Codification movement, 28
Cole, Orsamus, 34
Collectivism
   and automobiles, 108–09
   and Cold War, 110
   and comparative negligence, 110
   and consumerism, 108–09
   and Great Depression, 109
   and incremental effect on tort law, 110
   and late 20th century social culture, 110
   and product liability, 110–11
   and radio and television, 108–10
   and socialization of auto accident costs, 110
   and tort immunities, 111
   and World War II, 109–10
   reaches height in 1970s, 153–55
Colorado
   adopts British Employers Liability Act, 54
Columbia Plan, 116–17
Commons, John, 75–76, 111
Commonwealth v. Anthes (Mass. 1856), 28
Comparative negligence
   adoption in 1960s and 1970s, 122–24, 160
   and contributory negligence, 86
   and pure model, 123–25
   and socialization of accident costs, 120
   and strict product liability, 135, 168–69
   diluted model, 120, 125, 125 n64, 169, 123–24
   growth during mid-20th century, 92, 172
   growth during Progressive Era, 70–71
   in Florida, 88
   in Georgia, 87, 89
   in Illinois, 88
   in Mississippi, 92
   in Wisconsin, 90, 121
Connecticut
   and auto safety laws, 114
   and spousal immunity, 136
Consumerism
   and product liability, 96
   and tort law, 109
   changing safety attitudes, 127–28

Index

during early 20th century, 127
during late 19th century, 96
Consumer Reports, 127–28, 183
Contractual waiver clauses
    American judicial attitudes toward, 58
    and burden of proof, 20
    benefit clauses, 58
    British judicial attitudes toward, 57–58
    Contributory negligence: role in tort law, 20–21
    persistence during early- and mid-20th century, 120
Cooley, Thomas, 39, 52, 63, 114
Corwin v. New York & Erie R. Co. (Ohio 1851), 24
Courtroom procedures
    demurrers, 29–30
    judges' instructions to juries, 30
    nonsuits, 29–30
    orders for new trials, 28–29
    role in tort law, 27–31
    special verdicts, 29
Cowen, Esek, 9, 10–11, 46–48, 87
Croly, Herbert, 70
Crumpacker, Edgar, 89

D

Dalehite v. United States (U.S. 1953), 178
Demurrers, 29–30
Denman, Lord, 49
Devlin v. Smith (N.Y. 1882), 94
Dickinson, Daniel, 95
Dillon, John F., 138
Distraction rule, 39–40
Dixon, Luther S., 4, 20, 22, 34, 43, 52, 87, 143
Dukakis, Michael, 183

E

Earl, Robert, 67
Eastman, Crystal, xii, 68–69, 69 n5, 73–74, 77–78
Economic loss doctrine
    applicability to integrated systems, 175–76
    debate over, 175–76
    exceptions to, 175, 175 n85
    origins, 172, 174–75
Emergency rule, 40
Employer liability laws
    British act (1880), 54
    constitutional challenges, 56–57
    judicial reaction to, 57
    origins, 51, 54–55
Employers
    duty of care in hiring, 41–42
    duty to child workers, 49
    safe place duty, 41
Employers Liability Act of 1880 (Great Britain), 54
English law
    role in American tort law, 5–6
Escola v. Coca-Cola Bottling Co. of Fresno (Cal. 1944), 132
Expressive individualism, 155–56, 156 n9

F

Family purpose doctrine. *See* Automobile accidents
Farwell v. Boston & Worcester R. Corp. (Mass. 1842), 17–18
Food and Drug Act, 96
Federal Employers Liability Act (FELA)
    and U.S. Supreme Court, 90
    first act (1906), 89–90
    origins, 70–71
    second act (1908), 90
    state adoption of "little FELAs," 92, 120–21
Federal Tort Claims Act, 177
Federalist Society, 158–59
Feezer, Lester, 139
Fellow-servant rule
    in Ohio, 19
    in Indiana, 20
    in Southern states, 17–19
    in Wisconsin, 20
    origins, 17–18
Fencing laws, 23, 60
Field Code, 30–31
Field, David D., 30, 61–62
Fires
    role in early tort law, 21
Five-State Survey, xv, Appendices 2–3
    and case disposition techniques, 63, 188–89
    and summary judgment, 189–90, Fig. 5.3
    case disposal procedures during mid-20th century, 149–50, Fig. 4.6
    shift in outcomes for accident victims and defendants, 63–66, Fig. 2.4
    tort cases during early 19th century, 14–16, Fig. 1.2

tort cases during late 19th century, 35–37, Figs. 2.1, 2.2
tort cases during late 20th and early 21st centuries, 156–57, Fig. 5.1
tort cases during mid-20th century, 12–13, Fig. 4.1
Flanders v. Meath (Ga. 1859), 87
Florida
and comparative negligence, 88
Flower v. Adam (C.P. 1810), 10–11
Flower, Frank, 59–60
Free-labor doctrine
and workers compensation, 70
early opposition to, 37–39
resurgence since 1970, 155–56
role in tort law, 37–38
Fullerton, Mark, 80–81

G

Galena & Chicago Union R. Co. v. Jacobs (Ill. 1858), 88
Gelbman v. Gelbman (N.Y. 1969), 141
Georgia
and comparative negligence, 11, 87, 89
and fellow-servant rule, 53 n70
and product liability, 96
and role of juries in tort cases, 26
Gillenwater v. Madison & Indianapolis R. Co. (Ind. 1856), 20
Gilmore, Grant, 153
Goller v. Goller (Wis. 1963), 140
Good Samaritan laws, 179
Grace-period rule. See Safe-place duty
Granger laws, 51–52
Green, Nicholas St. John, 143
Greenman v. Yuba Power Products Co. (Cal. 1963), 133

H

Haight, Albert, 44–45, 61
Hart v. Western Rail Road Corp. (Mass. 1847), 22
Hartfield v. Roper (N.Y. 1839), 10–11, 13, 46–58, 87
Hawkins v. Bleakly (U.S. 1917), 85–86
Heaven v. Pender (Eng. Ct. App. 1883), 95
Henderson, James, 171
Henningsen v. Bloomfield Motors (N.J. 1960), 133
Hilliard, Francis, 39
Hiscock, Charles, 97
Hitchcock, Peter, 19–20
Holman, Jesse, 27
Holmes, Oliver Wendell, 143–44
Hooker, Frank, 49–50
Horton v. Oregon Health & Science Univ. (Or. 2016), 154
Horwitz, Morton, 16
Houg v. Girard Lumber Co. (Wis. 1910), 77
Hunt, Ward, 22, 49
Hurst, James Willard, 16
Hyzer, Edward, 90

I

Illinois
and comparative negligence, 11, 88
and judge-jury balance of power, 28 n78
and summary judgment, 147
and workers compensation, 75–76
Immunities
during late 19th and early 20th centuries, 138–39
during late 20th century, 179–80, 182
roles of courts and legislatures, 141. *See also* headings for specific types of immunities
Immunity, charitable, 138–40
Immunity, clerical, 181–82
Immunity, landowner, 179–80, 180 n103, 180 n104
Immunity, municipal, 138–42, 177–78
Immunity, parent-child, 135–37, 139–40
Immunity, recreational, 180
Immunity, spousal, 135–36, 139–40, 177
Immunity, youth sports, 180–81
Indiana
adopts British Employers Liability Act, 54
and fellow-servant doctrine, 20, and judge-jury allocation of power, 27
Ingersoll, Charles J., 5–6
In re Opinion of Justices (Mass. 1911), 80, 80 n42
Institute for Legal Reform, 158–59
Instrumentalism, 16
Insurance, rise of compulsory, 117–18
Iowa
and employer liability law, 53
and workers compensation, 85
Ives v. South Buffalo R. Co. (N.Y. 1911), 79–82

J

James, Fleming, Jr., 132
Joint and several liability
   and concerted-action application, 162–63
   and contributory and comparative negligence, 161
   and moral- limits application, 162–63
   and threshold application, 162
   and types-of-harm application, 162
   during 19th century, 161
   during late 20th century, 161–62
   role of tort reform organizations in modifying, 163
Judges
   judicial reaction to Progressive criticisms, 100–02. *See also* Courtroom procedures, Judge-jury balance of power
   Progressive reaction against, 99–101
Judge-jury balance of power; *See also* Judicial instruction; Juries; Proper-verdict rule; Scintilla rule
   attitudes toward jurors during late 19th century and Progressive era, 62–63, 100–01
   case disposition procedures during late 20th and early 21st centuries, 188–90, Figs. 5.2, 5.3
   case disposition procedures during same, 104–05, Fig. 3.2, 149–50, Fig. 4.6
   case disposition procedures during same, comparative negligence and, 92
   debate during late 19th century, 103–04
   debates during Progressive era, 71, 99, 100–01, 106
   directed verdicts and, 102
   elimination of unanimous-verdict requirements and, 106
   evidentiary burden and, 103
   trends during late 20th and early 21st centuries, 150
Judicial instruction
   debate during early 19th century, 30
   debate during late 19th century, 65–66
Judicial recall movement, 100–01
Juries
   and judicial instruction, 26
   and seditious libel law, 25
   attainder, 24–25
   origins of jury trial, 24–25
   perceptions of pro-plaintiff bias, 29 n83, 62–63, 62 n107
   role in 17th and 18th centuries, 24–25
   role of in early 19th century, 26–27

K

Kallet, Arthur, 127–38
Kansas
   and employer liability law, 53
   and joint and several liability, 162
Keeton, Robert, 146, 183
Kellogg v. Chicago & Northwestern R. Co. (Wis. 1870), 22, 43
Kent, James, 6–7, 26
Kentucky
   and fellow-servant rule, 19 n24
   and product liability, 98 n109
   and workers compensation, 83–84
Kerr, William, 75
Kiley v. Chicago, Milwaukee & St. Paul R. Co. (Wis. 1909), 91
Kistler, Rives, 154

L

Labor bureaus
   accident studies, 72
   in New York, 75
   in Wisconsin, 75–76
   origins, 59–60, 67–68
La Follette, Robert M., 100
Lakin v. Senco Products, Inc. (Or. 1999), 153–54
Landau, Jack, 155
Landowner immunity. See Immunity, landowner
Langhoff v. Milwaukee & Prairie du Chien R. Co. (Wis. 1866, 1868), 3–4
Libel law, jury's role in, 25
Lincoln, Abraham, 10
Little Miami R. Co. v. Stevens (Ohio 1851), 19–20
Lochner v. New York (U.S. 1904), 99–100
Lowrie, Walter, 37
Lumpkin, Joseph, 18–19, 87
Lynch v. Nurdin (Q.B. 1841), 49
Lyon, William P., 4, 48

M

Macon & Western R. Co. v. Winn (Ga. 1856), 87

MacPherson v. Buick Motor Co. (N.Y. 1916), 71, 97–98, 127
Manhattan Institute, 159 n22
Marital unity doctrine, 135–36
Marshall, Roujet D., 77, 81, 91
Marvin, Richard, 24
Maryland
    and employer liability law, 54, 55 n76
    and workers compensation, 73
Mason, Henry, 60–61
Massachusetts
    abolition of product-liability privity, 129
    adopts British Employers Liability Act, 54
    and charitable immunity, 138–19
    and municipal immunity, 178
    and no-fault insurance, 183
    and workers compensation, 68, 80–81
    influence on early American tort law, 6–7
    labor bureau, 59–60
    safe-place statutes, 112
McCarthy, Charles, 70
McCumber, Porter, 96
McWhorter, George, 89
Medical malpractice
    and liability caps, 165–68
    and tort reform movement, 163–64
    effect of crises on socialization of accident costs, 165
    expansion of liability in early 20th century, 163–64
    late-20th-century crises, 164
    response to crises, 164
    role of insurers in tort reform movement, 163–64
Merrick, Pliny, 48
Michigan
    and attractive-nuisance doctrine, 49–50
    and landowner immunity, 179–80
Middleton v. Texas Power & Light Co. (U.S. 1919), 86
Miller, Samuel, 104
Minneapolis & St. Louis R. Co. v. Herrick (U.S. 1888), 53, 56–67
Minnesota
    and charitable immunity, 139
    and product liability, 95
    and workers compensation, 76
Mississippi
    and comparative negligence, 92
    and fellow-servant doctrine, 56–57
    and parent-child immunity, 136–37

Missouri Pacific R. Co. v. Mackey (U.S. 1888), 53, 56–57
Mitchell, John, 76
Mondou v. New York, New Haven & Hartford R. Co. (U.S. 1912), 91
Montana
    and workers compensation, 83–84
Montgomery Ward & Co., 93
Montgomery, Robert, 49–50
Mountain Timber Co. v. Washington (U.S. 1917), 85–86
Municipal immunity. *See* Immunity, municipal

N

Nader, Ralph, 183
Natchez & Southern R. Co. v. Crawford (Miss. 1911), 107–08
National Association of Manufacturers (NAM), 73–74
National Conference of Commissioners on Uniform State Laws (NCCUSL)
    and implied product warranties, 132
    and landowner immunity, 163
    and strict product liability, 172 n73
National Civic Federation, 73–74
Negligence
    aggregation of, 160
    conceptual origins in United States, 8–11
    development of degree framework, 13–14, 87
    standards for child negligence, 46–47
    role in product liability, 130
Nevada
    and workers compensation, 79
New Jersey
    and economic loss doctrine, 173
    and product liability, 133
    and summary judgment, 147
New York
    adopts Field Code, 30
    and development of causation doctrine, 44–45
    and product liability, 96–98
    and safety statutes, 59
    and workers compensation, 72–73, 79–82
    influence on early American tort law, 6–7
    labor bureau, 75
New York Central R. Co. v. White (U.S. 1917), 85–86

No-fault auto insurance
    constitutional challenges to, 185
    movement in 1930s, 116–17, 182–83
    movement in 1960s and 1970s, 183–86
Nonsuits, 29–30

O

O'Connell, Jeffrey, 183
Ohio
    and fellow-servant rule, 19–20
    and judicial recall movement, 100

P

Padway, Joseph, 121
Paine, Byron, 20
Palsgraf v. Long Island R. Co. (N.Y. 1928), 143–45
Parent-child immunity. *See* Immunity, parent-child
Paxson, Edward, 47
Peckham, Rufus, 60
Pitney, Mahlon, 85
Pittsburgh Survey, 68–69
Pleasants v. Fant (U.S. 1874), 104
Posner, Richard, 186
Pound, Roscoe, 146
Powell, Lewis, 123
Priestly v. Fowler (Exch. 1837), 17
Privity
    and *Restatement of Torts*, 128–29
    erosion in early 20th century, 94–98
    erosion in late 19th century, 92–95
    erosion in mid- and late 20th century, 127–29. *See also* Product liability
    imminent- and inherent-danger exception, 94
    origins, 92–94
Product liability
Product safety laws, 93 n93, 96
    evolution during early 20th century 96
    evolution during late 19th century
    evolution during late 20th and early 21st centuries, 168–72. *See also* Strict liability
    origins of privity rule, 92–93
    role of *MacPherson* case, 97–98
    rise of strict liability, 130–34
    William Prosser's role in evolution, 130–34
Progressive movement
    and comparative negligence, 89–92
    and workers compensation, 71–79
    hostility toward judiciary, 99–101
    influence on tort law, 70–71
    judicial reaction to, 100–01
Proper-verdict rule, 103–04
Prosser, William
    "Assault on the Citadel" article, 132–33
    campaign for abolition of privity in product liability, 127
    campaign for strict liability, 130–34
    early life, 130–31
    "Fall of the Citadel" article, 134
    Handbook of the Law of Torts, 122 n54, 131
    influence on evolution of causation concepts, 145
    influence on mortgage-moratorium law during Great Depression, 131
    influence on socialization of accident costs, 131–32
    influence on warranty law, 132
    late career, 131
    on comparative negligence, 122–23
    on economic loss doctrine, 134
    on role of negligence in strict product liability, 134
    on spousal immunity, 136
    work with American Law Institute, 133
Proximate cause
    application in fire cases, 21
    conceptual origins, 11–12
    evolution during 19th century, 12–14, 43–45
    evolution during early and mid-20th century, 142–46

R

Railroads
    and employer liability laws, 53
    and fencing laws, 23–24
    and Granger laws, 52
    influence on early tort law, 51–52
RAND Institute, 165
Recreational immunity. *See* Immunity, recreational
Redfield, Amasa, 13–14, 39, 96–97
Redfield, Isaac, 11–12, 11 n19, 23, 46–48
Restatement of Torts, 128–29
Restatement (Second) of Torts, § 402A, 133, 135, 168–69
Robinson v. Cone (Vt. 1850), 46–48

Roosevelt, Theodore, 73–74, 81–82, 96, 100
Russell Sage Foundation, 68–69
Rust v. Low (Mass. 1809), 8–9
Ryan v. New York Central R. Co. (N.Y. 1866), 22, 44–45
Ryan, Edward, 3–4, 44–45, 53

S

Safe-place duty
  grace-period rule, 42–43
  origins, 41
Safe-place statutes, 111–12
Santor v. A. & M. Karagheusian, Inc. (N.J. 1965), 173
Savage, John, 9
Schlink, Frederick, 127–28
Schubert v. J.R. Clark Co. (Minn. 1892), 95
Scintilla rule, 103–04
Scudder v. Woodbridge (Ga. 1846), 18–19
Sears, Roebuck & Co., 93
Second Industrial Era
  origins, 35
  relationship to tort law, 35–36
  tort cases during, 36–37
Seely v. White Motor Co. (Cal. 1965), 173
Seven Bishops Case (1688), 26
Shaw, Lucien, 83
Shearman, Thomas, 13–14, 39, 96–97
Spousal immunity. *See* Immunity, spousal
State ex rel. Davis-Smith Co. v. Clausen (Wash. 1911), 80–81
Statler v. George A. Ray Manufacturing Co. (N.Y. 1909), 97
Strict liability
  evolution during late 20th and early 21st centuries, 168–72
  rise of, 130–34
  William Prosser's role in evolution, 130–34

T

Thomas v. Winchester (N.Y. 1852), 94
Torgesen v. Schultz (N.Y. 1908), 97
Tort law
  and legal instrumentalism, 16
  and property rights, 7–9
  during late 20th and early 21st centuries, xv, 160–86
  during mid-20th century, xiii–xiv, 111–36
  during Progressive era, xii–xiii, 71–98
  during Second Industrial Era, xiii, 34–61
  early law and railroads, 22–25
  eras of, xii–xv
  influence of English law on, 5
  origins and pre-industrial era, xii, 6–11
Tort reform movement
  and medical malpractice, xiv–xv, 163–68
Townsend v. Hale (Ind. 1828), 27
Traynor, Roger, 132, 173
Trespass, 8
Triangle Shirtwaist Factory fire, 80
Trow v. Vermont Central R. Co. (Vt. 1852), 11–12
Tullis v. Lake Erie & Western R. Co. (U.S. 1899), 56–57
Turntable doctrine. *See* Attractive-nuisance doctrine
Twain, Mark, 51–52
Twerski, Aaron, 171
Types of tort cases in courts
  early 19th century, 14–16, Fig. 1.2
  late 20th and early 21st centuries, 156–57, Fig. 5.1
  mid-20th century, 112–13, Fig. 4.1
  Second Industrial Era and Progressive Era, 35–37, Figs. 2.1, 2.2

U

U.S. Chamber of Commerce, 158–59
U.S. Department of Commerce, 170–71
U.S. Department of Justice, 165
U.S. Supreme Court
  and FELA, 91
  and judge-jury balance of power, 104
  and summary judgment, 187–88
  and workers compensation, 85

V

Van Hoomissen, George, 153–54
Vaughan, John, 24–25

W

Wainwright Commission, 77–78
Wainwright, Jonathan, 77–78
Waiver clauses. *See* Contractual waiver clauses
Walton v. Tull (Ark. 1962), 126
Walker v. Kroger Grocery & Baking Co. (Wis. 1934), 126
Washington
  and workers compensation, 80–81
Watson v. Augusta Brewing Co. (Ga. 1905), 97

Werner v. Erie R. Co. (N.Y. 1868), 41
Werner, William, 79–80
Winslow, John B., 44, 50, 100, 102
Winterbottom v. Wright (Exch. 1842), 93
Wisconsin
    and attractive-nuisance doctrine, 50 n 59
    and comparative negligence, 90–91
    and employer liability law, 53
    and fellow-servant rule, 20
    and workers compensation, 81
    and workplace safety laws, 59–60
    labor bureau, 75–76
Workplace safety laws
    and children, 61
    during late 19th century, 59
    effect on tort litigation, 60–61
    in New York, 58
    in Wisconsin, 59–60
Wright, Carroll, 67–69, 69 n5

Y
Young, George, 49
Youth sports. *See* Immunity, youth sports

Z
Zeratsky v. Chicago, Milwaukee & St. Paul R. Co. (Wis. 1909), 91